SACRED COW, MAD COW

Arts and Traditions of the Table

SACRED COW,

MAD COW

A History of Food Fears

MADELEINE FERRIÈRES

Translated by Jody Gladding

Columbia University Press   New York

Columbia University Press wishes to express its appreciation for assistance
given by the government of France through the Ministère de la Culture in
the preparation of this translation.

Columbia University Press

Publishers Since 1893

New York   Chichester, West Sussex

Histoire des peurs alimentaires: Du Moyen âge à l'aube du xxe Siècle © Éditions
du Seuil, 2002

Library of Congress Cataloging-in-Publication Data

Ferrières, Madeleine.

   [Histoire des peurs alimentaires English]

   Sacred cow, mad cow: a history of food fears/Madeleine Ferrières; translated
by Jody Gladding.

      p. cm. — (Arts and traditions of the table)

Includes bibliographical references and index.

ISBN 0–231–13192–5 (alk. paper)

   1. Nutritionally induced diseases—France—History. 2. Food habits—Psychological aspects.
3. Food—Safety measures—France—History. 4. Food—Toxicology—France—History.
5. Food adulteration and inspection—France—History. I. Title. II. Series.

   RC622.F47613   2005

   616. 3'9'00944—dc22   2005051796

⊗

Columbia University Press books are printed on
permanent and durable acid-free paper.

Printed in the United States of America

c 10 9 8 7 6 5 4 3 2 1

CONTENTS

SERIES EDITOR'S PREFACE

"Tell me what you do not eat, and I can tell you who you are!" This rephrasing of a much-quoted and revered culinary axiom could serve as epigraph to this splendidly detailed history of food phobias.

Exhuming the documentation of the lives of ordinary people has revitalized historical studies and informs Ferrières's methodology. Yet too often Annales historians hesitate to move beyond microhistory (menus of wedding feasts in fifteenth-century Limousin, say) to a macro-overview. Our author suffers from no such timid scruples.

In Ferrières's broader historical perspective (from the Middle Ages to the twentieth century) there lies a murky twilight zone between the rational (scientific) and the religious irrational (mythic and superstitious). She illuminates those shadows by her careful study of medieval, renaissance, and early modern primary documents.

Throughout much of the Middle Ages, Galen's theory of humors was accepted as incontrovertible science. Bodies were dominated by the phlegmatic, sanguine, bilious, or melancholic fluid. Galen offered with perfect clarity a complete physiognomy and psychology, and his imagery was inextricably linked to digestive processes: ingested foods became humors.

Disease was a disturbance of the humors. Phlegm was poorly cooked; bile and melancholy, overcooked; blood, perfectly cooked. So the medieval aversion to fish, denounced as the embodiment of phlegm itself, was attributed to its aqueous nature; similarly, the cucumber, a 1572 treatise held, was food "only for mules and asses." Yet in the folkloristic penumbra, the same author maintained, "a cucumber placed lengthwise near a feverish child relieves him of fever."

Of course, the importation of ingredients discovered after 1492 inspired ever more recondite phobias. As new foods arrived from the New World, they disrupted the accustomed nomenclature and mindsets so typical of the medieval and Renaissance tradition of herbaria. "The Caribbean Taino peoples have neither bread nor wine nor salt," a sailor reported. Each day, a Lyons doctor wrote in 1560, new diseases spread from hitherto unknown foods. For more than two centuries, for example, the potato remained suspect and surrounded by ominous folk myths linking the (to us) indispensable tuber to leprosy.

We moderns vaunt a delusional superiority: the Middle Ages, we think, were largely marked by famine and anarchy. In contradiction, Ferrières documents the prodigious consumption of meat prior to 1700 (100+ kilos of meat per capita per annum in fourteenth-century Germany!). Inevitably, this carnivorous diet led to irrational fears as well as to detailed, precise, scientifically based regulations.

Patissiers could not sell "pâtés," meat-filled pasties, for example. And pasties, legend tells us, were often stuffed with cat meat. Of course, at the time, cats were not considered household pets. Later, it was held, heretically, that animals had souls. A prolonged theological controversy ensued. Ferrières documents how the teachings and subsequent canonization of St.Francis of Assisi legitimized animal rights and vegetarianism; how English sentimentality toward animals as pets compromised the national diet; and how the development of the automobile legitimized the consumption of horsemeat in the working-class population.

But were not food regulations economically inspired by competing trade guilds, lobbying interests, and landowners' power rather than by hygienic principles?

For example, slaughterhouses were mostly in the city proper, so the *rève* tax could be collected at the city portals. Move the stockyards out of town? The city's budget would be compromised. Still, the entry of livestock into the city polluted the air with foul odors, noise, and ultimately diseases. There is a fascinating discussion on air pollution and efforts at pure air legislation dating back to the 1570's. To be sure, rivers could wash out waste (hence the frequent relocation of *abattoirs* onto islands). But then the water supply might be corrupted. A complex network of regulations was erected to ensure (often in vain as pandemics of the plague attest) the public weal, especially in the warmer climates.

Fascinating aspects of butcher/slaughterhouse regulatory agendas are narrated here thanks to the author's unearthing of long-lost decrees and broadsides. She uncovers a characteristically medieval confusion of the moral and the hygienic. Here superstition and science intersect in a disturbing way.

Impure, unwashed hands corrupted foods, as laws promulgated in medieval Burgundy attest. The hands of unbaptized Jews, lepers, and prostitutes in particular transmitted defilement.

Although meat regulators initially focused on the centuries-old disputes on the role of blood and blood sacrifice in the livestock slaughtering processes of the two well-documented religious traditions (Judaic and Christian), even more irrational folk mythology soon supervened.

Women were impure only on certain days (during which their mere presence even dried up and putrefied melons and squash). Thus, in the chain of being, animals by injunction could not be killed when in heat or just after having given birth. Else contagion would ensue.

Moreover, those pariahs of the medieval mindset (Jews, lepers, and prostitutes) were always impure: the mere touch of their hands, perhaps even their very presence, corrupted the foodstuffs regulators catalogued in lengthy detail. Ferrières refers to this as a contagion of the sacred, leading to a "pollution phobia."

As I look at my own kitchen lined with gleaming copper cookware, I return to the culinary history of this duplicitous metal offered here. In 1749 a learned professor had called copperware "a whited sepulcher and truly poisonous." Are lead or iron preferable? Was the rise of pottery guilds in Provence the result of a food phobia or merely thanks to the availability of clay-rich soil?

We live today in the age of "mad cow," "hoof and mouth," allergens, and a host of food-related afflictions, some real, some the result of collective food hysteria.

The story of the corruption of food by reality and by legend is narrated here with ample and intriguing documentation, and thankfully no recipes. It should fascinate food scholars, anthropologists, folklorists, cultural historians and chroniclers of medicine alike. I found it eminently readable, for the author has fully incorporated into narrative the amazing details unearthed in her researches (43,000+ bars in Paris in 1790, serving in lead pitchers!) and she writes pellucid prose.

We are dealing here both with history as it was and with history as it were. Madeleine Ferrières's patient deciphering of documents allows her to compose a narrative that speaks to our own culinary culture permeated as it is by our own collective food fears and follies.

Albert Sonnenfeld

PREFACE TO
THE AMERICAN EDITION

For several weeks, the rumor grew and circulated: had Yasser Arafat been fatally poisoned by some unknown substance? And what about Viktor Yushchenko? Was he the victim of an assassination attempt by poisoning as well? And that was how the rumors, escaping the Palestinian and Ukrainian borders, spread throughout the world. We do not know if they are credible or hoaxes; all we do know is that such allegations are as old as history. They usually seem to be linked to the great and powerful, to those who, fearing what the French called the "poudre de succession," made sure their private physicians tested the dishes served at their tables.

Is it possible that other eaters—the poor, the man on the street, the ordinary consumer—have been less sensitive to dangers, that they have fallen on any food offered with a voraciousness belying the least doubt or suspicion? That is the question this book attempts to answer. What I want to demonstrate here is that the fear of poisoning has never been reserved for the world's great and powerful. It is a collective fear, shared socially. Furthermore, we still experience it. In the last few years, it has been a question not only of food poisoning but also of fears fueled by repeated crises: dioxin, avian flu, *E. coli* outbreaks.

Fears sometimes vary from one country to another, and they do not always cross the Atlantic. Thus, while Americans serenely ate their steaks, Europeans were afraid of becoming as mad as the cows they consumed. And when Americans worried over consuming their daily bananas, Europeans continued to peel them without qualms. Today's food fears are sometimes specific, most often general, and they all contribute everywhere to widespread anxiety. Conditions are favorable for dramatization by the media and for the development of gloomy discourse: we no longer know what we eat; our food paradise is a thing of the past; we are courting disaster. That explains this fear in our bellies and our poor appetites, and nevertheless . . .

Nevertheless, we should not cultivate nostalgia or paint the past too rosily, in comparison to the present. Because "the good old days" for eating were just as filled with doubts, fears, and objections when it came to the contents of one's bowl or plate. Cro-Magnon man has told us nothing of his eating life, and yet he certainly must have had to try the products Mother Nature offered, often poisoning himself and dying so that one day we would know what is comestible and what is not. The Stone Age was the age of plenty, perhaps, but a food paradise? Assuredly not. As soon as man learned how to write, he left evidence of his fear of poisoning himself with toxic food. Such evidence became more abundant in the late Middle Ages, in the epoch when the need for safety shifted from the heavens to the earth and when the first insurance systems were invented, along with the first health and safety regulations for the city markets. What were they afraid of then? Sometimes, as with the powerful, it was deliberate poisoning, as administered by malevolent human hands. But, to tell the truth, the fear of being poisoned tormented our ancestors less than the fear of poisoning themselves with the contents of their own plates. During the Enlightenment, testimonies to this abounded. Consider that old grump, Matthew Bramble, listing for us all the risks of eating in London in the 1760s:

> The bread I eat in London, is a deleterious paste, mixed up with chalk, alum, and bone-ashes; insipid of taste, and destructive to the constitution. . . . The same monstrous depravity appears in their veal, which is bleached by repeated bleedings, and other villainous arts, till there is not a drop of juice left in the body, and the poor animal is paralytic before it dies; so void of all taste, nourishment, and savour, that a man might dine as comfortably on a white fricasee of kid-skin gloves, or chip hats from Leghorn.
>
> As they have discharged the natural colour from their bread, their butcher's-meat, and poultry, their cutlets, ragouts, fricasees, and sauces of all kind; so they insist upon having the complexion of their pot-herbs mended, even at the hazard of their lives. Perhaps, you will hardly believe they can be so mad as to boil their greens with brass half-pence, in order to improve their colour; and yet nothing is more true—Indeed, without this improvement in the colour, they have no personal merit. They are produced in an artificial soil, and taste of nothing but the dunghills, from whence they spring. My cabbage, cauliflower, and 'sparagus in the country, are as much superior in flavour to those that are sold in Coventgarden, as my heath-mutton is to that of St. James's market; which, in fact, is neither lamb nor

mutton, but something betwixt the two, gorged in the rank fens of Lincoln and Essex, pale, coarse, and frowzy—As for the pork, it is an abominable carnivorous animal, fed with horse-flesh and distillers' grains; and the poultry is all rotten, in consequence of a fever, occasioned by the infamous practice of sewing up the gut, that they may be the sooner fattened in coops, in consequence of this cruel retention.

> (Tobias Smollett, letter to Dr. Lewis,
> *The Expedition of Humphry Clinker*, vol. 2)

And so it was that, from the thirteenth century to 1900, from Mirepoix (southern France) to Chicago, one by one, all foods were called into question: Meat first of all, especially pork, though later beef. All perishable foods before refrigeration prolonged their shelf life and guaranteed their wholesomeness: fish, fruits, vegetables. New foods, like the potato, and even superfoods, like rye bread, wheat bread, beer, and, later, milk.

And so our memories are short. All human beings before us questioned the contents of their plates. Many of them experienced fear. We have forgotten that, as we have forgotten the threat of famine. And we are often too blinded by this amnesia to view our present food situation clearly. This amnesia is very convenient. It allows us to reinvent the past and construct a complaisant, retrospective mythology. Let us strive for lucidity, and let us look to the past for support.

SACRED COW, MAD COW

INTRODUCTION

The notion of food risk covers a wide and widely interdisciplinary field of inquiry. It falls into the domain of hard science: it involves calculations, scientific evaluation of risks, and recommendations for controlling them. It falls into the domain of law: it involves determining standards and establishing rules to guarantee maximum safety. It also falls into the domain of the historian.

What does history have to do with this? Nothing, if we consider the notion of risk in its strictest and most objective sense. Quite a lot, if we study not risk itself but the perception of risk. It is with this recent concept, created for the study of consumer behavior, that the historian can and must begin. Perceived risk "consists of the perception of uncertainty relative to potentially negative consequences associated with an alternative choice."[1] For historians, this theme applies instead to the history of emotions, as Lucien Febvre presents it, stressing that feelings are not constants, that they come into play in one period or another, that they are translations, various modes of expression. Thus the history of food risk could be charted from two sides, one positive (the need for safety), the other negative (the fear or fears of food).[2]

An initial epistemological obstacle must be removed: what is the use of such a study if we consider fear, the perception of risk, to be primarily an individual affair? And indeed it is just that: one cannot deny that fear and its double—the need for safety it engenders—vary from one individual to the next. One late March day in 1996, when the newspapers were running big headlines on what would become the mad cow crisis, —*Libération*'s read "England Sick from the Prion" and the *Figaro*'s "When Herbivores Become Cannibals"—I was having lunch with a colleague in a restaurant on Boulevard Raspail, across from the old Arts College. I had become a vegetarian as a precaution; he ate a thick, bloody steak. Was it English? (I mean the steak). He continued to eat with carnivorous gusto while I imagined with dismay the infectious prion attacking my colleague's brain, worming its way into each of his neurons, eventually making them burst and turning his brain into a sponge....

If the individual dimension of fear cannot be denied, neither can the collective dimension, so the mad cow crisis and listeriosis epidemics are at the heart of our eating preoccupations and behavior, thus becoming a social problem. And as soon as there is collective behavior, the historian has something to say. Moreover, current events provide fodder. England was sick from the prion, as *Libération* proclaimed, but it was the French consumer who was most afraid. A paradoxical attitude, if we consider that the French are known for their more emotional and hedonistic relationship with food. We would have expected a stronger reaction on the part of the Anglo-Saxons, who cultivate the link between food and health more vigorously. The standard analysis of the different psychological impact on the French and the English facing the prion problem, the hypersensitivity of the first group compared to the less obsessive fear of the second, relates back to the recent past: our mass psychogenic uneasiness might have been exacerbated by matters such as our contaminated blood banks. Having no similar experience, the English remained more confident in their safeguard systems. This analysis, which shows how collective behavior is inscribed in a given culture, constitutes a historical explanation.

In our understanding of people and things of the past, we possess an attitude that is often contradictory, even antinomic. Collective fears are a good example of this: we are ready to attribute to people of the past fears that, in fact, did not exist. For example, everyone is familiar with the theme repeated since the romantic period of the terrors of the year one thousand. What everyone does not know, however, is that historians have bent over backward to analyze this terror as a myth, the product of our own fears facing the approach of the year two thousand. "In the year one thousand, the fear of the world's end, the coming of the Antichrist, the Last Judgment. In the year 2000, for good measure, the famous computer 'bug,' ecological catastrophe, and who knows what new 'yellow peril,' the modern incarnation of Gog and Magog. This mirror game is amusing, but, for the historian, it has not the least scientific justification."[3] No doubt the apocalyptic fears of the year one thousand existed only in the imaginations of the romantic historians.

The famines, the wars, the epidemics were hardly taken as signs announcing the reign of the devil. Moreover, who knew that it was the year one thousand? Who, outside of the clergy and the chancery, measured time by applying the computation introduced by Dionysius Exiguus in the sixth century? Events were generally dated according to the years of a reign or a pontificate or even to when the parish priest took up his post.[4]

If fears are invented that never existed, there is also the opposite tendency to pass over in silence, or even to deny, very real terrors. That is the case with food risk fears. Most of us would wager that if the phenomenon exists today, or if it is developing on an unprecedented scale, it did not exist in the past. We begin with the following prejudice: we are informed, demanding, connoisseur consumers; they were simply eaters. We require a certain number of qualities in our food: balance, lightness, and especially safety. They required their food to be nourishing, substantial, and, above all, abundant. In short, the need for security was just as recognized, just as felt, but it resided elsewhere. Ours depends on quality; theirs depended on quantity. They lived under continual stress with regard to food, always in fear of shortages following a bad harvest or the ravages of war. Ours is a different kind of anxiety. We are afraid of eating the mad cow; they worried about keeping the wolf from the door. If we agree to these premises, then a single history can be written, the history of hunger. "The history of men has never been anything but the history of their hunger," noted the poet Jean Guéhenno. And that history is widely known.

It is hardly my intention, of course, to deny what is an obvious truth. The fear of shortage is at the heart of all past food behaviors. It marks cultures at the deepest level. It is the "Give us tomorrow's bread" in evening prayers. It is the mind-set of the submerged man, as Taine so aptly described it: "The people resemble a man walking into a pond, with water up to his neck: at the slightest depression in the ground, the least wave, he loses his footing, sinks and drowns."

Jean Delumeau recently compiled an impressive catalog of Western fears between the fourteenth and eighteenth centuries.[5] The fear of unsafe food does not appear there. It is all a question of knowing if, in this abundant warehouse of former fears, it is legitimate to add a new shelf.

Current events at the century's end are a call for reflection, an invitation, and, at the same time, they present two powerful objections to this historical inquiry. The first can be formulated in this way: since the fear of shortage is at the heart of past behaviors, since scarcity—

or, worse, famine—is the most serious food risk we can name, how can that possibly leave room for any other food fear? Our first impulse is to think that fears must exclude each other. But isn't that also a projection of our own experience? Since 1955 the French no longer live with the danger of hunger and rationing, and this reality is so well integrated that the fear of shortage no longer exists in our consumer societies. Through an almost compensatory phenomenon, the fear of scarcity has been replaced by the fear of unwholesome food. In our society, there is only room for one food fear, which becomes more and more invasive. Don't we assume that the same must be true for the past? One fear, fine, but not two, according to the current thinking.

And there is a second current trend that would discourage this historical inquiry. It is all the rage now to denounce bad food or eating horrors. But, in certain respects, this repeated theme could be seen as a version of the "good old days" myth. The green paradox now popular promotes a vision of the past nearly symmetrical to and the inverse of the old positivism that taught that, even if it followed circuitous routes, human history progressed in a single flow from the dark past to the bright future. Today's relentless pastorals say the same thing but reverse it: we are racing to the precipice; the paradise of food is behind us. To follow such a *petitio principii*, before or without examining the issue, would lead to the foregone conclusion: food fears and risks cannot have manifested themselves in the past.

We are between a rock and a hard place, for there is yet another temptation. This trap would lead the historian to ascribe to the past—a past with prophetic aspects—the crises and the anxieties of the present. It would simply consist of extricating, like a red thread running the length of the fabric, a continual, ever-present, ever-recurring health fear, without taking into account that this fear is rooted each time in the specific historical constellation. To assume that risk did not exist or that it always existed amounts to the same thing: in both cases, the historical perspective is denied.

I propose the thesis that the perception of food risk (according to the current meaning of the word: the fear of harmful food) existed in the past as well. Security—or safety, as it is called—had two sides to it. The first, the essential and known side—a south-facing slope well lit by historical research—involves the quantity and regularity of the food supply; the other—a north-facing slope—involves the healthiness of foods. These two perspectives on food can overlap, as the sources indicate. It is in regulations enacted to ensure regular food supply that health laws were introduced. There is a kind of symbiosis between legislation meant to guarantee regular and abundant food supplies (in quantitative terms) and legislation guaranteeing food's wholesomeness. The law built around the problem of quantity also contains the first rules regarding quality.

Societies have left little written testimony on the act of eating, an activity as essential as it is mundane. It is hard to glean directly from the archives anxieties and apprehensions regarding food. Anguish is mute and fears silent. But we know that they exist when regulations regarding food safety arise. Through refraction, the norm reveals the concern. Comprehensive food laws, on the national level, are a very contemporary creation. The earliest ones date back to the nineteenth century (Belgium, 1830; Germany, 1870; Great Britain, 1875). The famous Food and Drugs Act that governs the trade and distribution of food and medicine in the United States dates back to 1906. The law historians' vulgate, which considers only state laws or standardized codes, ignores or passes over the fact that those state laws were preceded by rules and regulations adopted by various authorities—cities, trades associations—that constitute a first corpus on food safety, hopelessly scattered and never compiled, of course.

If food fears are very much a "disease of civilization," to borrow Jean Delumeau's expression, then all of Western civilization must be included within the framework of this study. The geographical field must be measured by the yardstick of culture: it extends to all those who share the same food base in objective terms (the civilization of bread and wine) and in cultural terms, the Hippocratic-Galenic values on which confidence in or distrust of a food is based.

Since we are hostage to the provisional nature of our sources, the earliest chronological milestones correspond to the first urban regulations in the mid-Middle Ages. The *terminus ad quem* is also hard to locate. Seminal medical values gradually fell away over the course of the nineteenth century, before Pasteur delivered the final blow. I will go slightly beyond the domestication of the microbe to the dawn of the last century, when a new discourse on food began to circulate, in which the words and ideas for microbes (1877), salmonella (1888), and vitamins (1911) came into general use; when a new food policy was put into place, with the press and the welfare state playing new roles; and when a new order of food safety, which is our own, emerged.

Thus defined, the framework is large, too large. And full of risks. The first would be to take the consumer as an absolute type, when nothing could be less accurate than imagining consumer society as a smooth and monolithic whole. Another risk stems from an illusion created by the archives. Sources, the available ones, are more numerous in the Mediterranean, where a municipal socialism developed early and offers the researcher unparalleled legislative wealth, at the risk of reducing Western fears to Latin fears.

There are—there must be—in history as elsewhere, acceptable risks. We will accept them.

But we must distrust words. Fear has been distinguished from anguish. Fear entails a known and clearly identified object. Anguish, anxiety, more diffuse and more difficult to bear, is prompted by a potential risk, by the unknown. If we adopt this terminology, the vast majority of food fears would then be anguishes. Let us begin with the fear of shortage, because we know that this fear is continual, even when the possibility of dearth or famine does not materialize. This is the lesson of the hunger riots. The year 1709 in France was a year of widespread famine, but it was more marked by the death of over a million starving people than by public protests. Conversely, the year 1775 was a year of riots, and nevertheless those who unleashed the flour war were not ravaged by hunger. It was the fear of hunger that pushed them. And the historian may very legitimately wonder about the relationship between rioting and hunger.[6] Before Pasteur, eaters were hard-pressed to identify the risks they glimpsed in their food. In fact, for them, nearly everything was risk, and very little was known danger. All fear is a loose blend of well-focused fright and diffuse anxiety, and there is no need whatsoever to reread Montaigne to recognize that the imagination overleaps its object at every bound, that the rational and irrational are inextricably mixed.

We also commonly speak of real and imaginary fears. This dichotomy is even less justified than the preceding one. All fear is real, beginning from the moment when it is genuinely felt, when it pierces the imagination and excites feeling. The opposite of true fear is not false alarm but serenity or tranquillity. On the other hand, a perceived risk can be a real or an illusory danger. Thus it is a question of knowing if fears in the past were well-founded or not. Practically speaking, and despite the difficulties of retrospective diagnosis so well known to medical historians, it is not impossible for today's historian to answer such a question, to affirm or deny the suspicion and to say whether what was feared was a true threat. But is that really the historian's concern?

A history of fear falls within the history of representations. From that perspective, what interests the historian is much less the reality of things than the attention they are given, and the effort must lie in understanding why particular fears arise. Past fears cannot be judged in the light of our present knowledge. Collectively, they are rooted in the ideology of the period, by which I mean the network of beliefs, the mental and intellectual framework, that allows for the conception of fear and the channeling of the imagination. They are inscribed in the given mental structures, and they maintain ties with beliefs of all kinds: religious, medical, scientific (some would say prescientific). As for knowing if they were justified or not, that is not the focus of the research and falls outside the field of cultural history. And that is the first thing to note about the history of representations. It is legitimate. But it is not, to my mind, totally satisfactory.

First of all, it does not lead to satisfying the reader's curiosity, and, in fact, curiosity can also be legitimate. Second, if present-day knowledge about past representations can be applied badly, used in a way that results in retrospective harshness or, worse, condescending scorn, it can also be applied well. After all, if today's archaeologist is allowed to integrate the latest research techniques, why forbid the historian, similarly lacking solid microbiological expertise, to put forward a retrospective diagnosis? Such a prohibition would make the history of representations a holist history, closed in on itself—a history on air cushions, to borrow Michel Vovelle's expression—camping too high, too far from realia, unengaged with them. It is not the elevated intellectual stance that is to be regretted; it is its effects on the very notion of representation. Not to examine the relationship between representation and reality—a retrospective reality, as it were—is to be deprived of one means of defining its status.

Writers of the classical period had a wealth of expressions to denote fears disconnected from reality: chimera, hollow meat, specter, ghost, bugbear.... That was how they designated past fears, because, lacking the necessary distance from the ones they experienced, they would have been hard-pressed to evaluate them accurately, to say if the red alert was a false alarm, if it had more bark than bite.

It seems to me we may assert that fear can only be understood in the context of the society that feels it. We may also assert, without violating the principle of precaution, that any fear can be defined and classified according to its relationship to the danger. If this relationship is close, we will not marvel too much at the wisdom or pre/science of contemporaries. If the relationship is extremely distant, we will refrain from expounding on a groundless fear's ability to flourish. The essential thing is to begin to see that risks, too, have a history. Many known risks began as potential ones, but many potential risks never materialized. And there is a third possible configuration: many real and serious dangers in the past were never perceived as risks. These latter elude my work, which, in this history full of rumors and silence, has listened hard for the rumors, has caught some of them, and has missed the silence.

ONE

FORBIDDEN MEATS

July 17, 1303, the Saturday after the feast of Saint Barnabas. Philippe le Bon was king of France, and Jean de Lévis, lord of Mirepoix, a small town in Haut-Languedoc. Jean de Lévis was the successor to Gui de Lévis, a minor Francilian lord who had become Simon de Monfort's chief lieutenant in the Albigensian Crusade and had acquired as a stronghold the Montségur castle and the exclusive possession of Mirepoix in return for his good and loyal services. The lord of Mirepoix answered directly to the king, which made him Philippe le Bon's most powerful vassal in Languedoc. On this particular day, a whole tribunal had assembled in the castle's great hall. The *baile* was there, the lord's chief representative in the town; four lawyers; two professors of law, Philippe de Ripparia and André Deulesal; the four Mirepoix consuls; plus all the town's butchers. All in all, about two dozen individuals gathered for this solemn occasion, the granting of a charter.

This was Occitan country, a land that had been Cathar and was still suspected of Catharism. The heretical sect survived at the turn of the thirteenth and fourteenth centuries, and the hunt for heretics was still going on, led by two inquisitorial offensives, further west, in the country of Foix.[1] Mirepoix was relatively far removed from this track, although it could not be said for certain that there were no longer any "believers" or "perfects" within the town walls, practicing openly or in secret and identifiable by their eating habits: they never ate meat, cheese, or eggs. The Cathari were vegetarians by religious conviction. They could not eat the flesh of animals since they considered it impure, tainted by sexuality. What strengthened this ban and led to more or less radical abstinence was their belief in metempsychosis: how was it possible to eat flesh in which a believer might have been reincarnated? On the scale of Catharist food values, fish, a supposedly asexual animal, was at the top, while meat occupied the lowest rung, so scorned that they signaled their repugnance by calling it by the pejorative name of *carnasse* or *fereza.*[2]

Were there Cathari in the hall of the seigneurial castle that day in 1303? We have no way of knowing. All we know for sure is that the matter in question was precisely the one that Cathari tabooed: meat. Indeed, these men had assembled to enact a regulation involving the sale of meat in their town. Butchery was not regulated in Mirepoix. The sale of meat depended on neither the town nor the lord, and a butcher needed no authorization to open a stall, which no doubt explains the number of *mazelliers* employed either full- or part-time (there were at least of dozen of them). But freedom to practice the butcher's trade did not mean that one could sell any meat whatever at any price. That is what the text negotiated by the lawyers and Jean I clearly set forth, in eighteen articles. The proceedings were solemn, as was the gathering, and the men present were there either as parties affected by the contract or as experts. The concerned parties: the consuls elected each year on All Saints' Day, representatives of the community, and tradesmen vitally concerned with the finalized contract. The experts: the lawyers and law professors, past masters in the art of counsel and of casting proceedings into legal form.[3]

The Mirepoix Charter

In the preamble of the charter, Jean I de Lévis voiced his concerns: it was important to avoid the perils that could arise from the consumption of meat. These perils (*pericula*) were risks rather than dangers. They were unknown, uncertain, potential, they could come about in the future (*pericula que possent in futurum evenire*), and it was the duty of the lord to do his utmost to avoid them (*pro nostro posse evitare*). The first objective is clear. It is a matter of what historians of the past called public health and what we call food safety. If the wording of the charter follows some logic—which is not certain in a period when seeking a coherent order was not the lawmaker's concern—and if the table at the beginning of the document means anything, we could say that this concern for public health was the first priority. It comes before the second objective cited, which was to permit butchers to collect legal profits from their trade. There was no contradiction

between the imperatives of safety and commerce. They fell under
the ideals of justice and the common good that a Christian lord was
obliged to honor. The charter aimed at securing peace and order in
the town. But the notion of public tranquillity was incompatible with
that of competition. Business competition was considered a source of
division, a seed of discord. It was better to abolish it, by guaranteeing
that all those who sold the same thing sold it in the same place and
at the same price. Taxing meat was the lord's right, and it was also
his duty. The price of meat would be fixed by the *baîle* and the consuls
according to the cost price of the animal. In Toulouse, the nearest
large town, profits were limited to one *denier* for every twelve, that is,
8 percent.[4] But the common good also required that public health not
be threatened by "false foodstuffs," by unwholesome meats, so it was the
lord's duty to prohibit some of them. The prohibitions that these men
decided on involved a kind of thinking radically different from Cathar
doctrine. For any orthodox Christian, the distinction between pure
and impure meats had been abrogated by the coming of Christ, who
freed men from all alimentary taboos. In dismissing Jewish law, Jesus
had instituted a laissez-faire food policy: to the pure man, all is pure.[5]
From the Christian perspective, animal flesh was not ontologically
impure, but it could, under certain circumstances, be unwholesome.
This fell within the secular order of health, not the sacred order of
salvation.

The directives for butchery were not simple recommendations or
a code of proper practices. This was an ordinance negotiated between
the citizens of Mirepoix and their lord. It contained twenty-four
detailed articles, providing for market inspections, inspections of
all animals (not simply a sample), and fines in cases of infractions.
Demanded by the town's bourgeois, granted by the lords, the regulation had the force of law. It had the force of a moral obligation.

The town's butchers had convened; they were all there: Laurence
André, Thomas Auriol, Guilhem Auriol, Bernard Aybrand, Pierre
Bonaud, Bernard Terren, Pierre Vigoris, Bernard Scobilon, Hugo
Scobilon, Arnaud and Guilhem Vigoris. Their number, compared to
the population of so small a town, says much about the amount of
meat consumed in the early fourteenth century. Thus the meeting
took on an almost ceremonial quality. The public attorney read out
loud those measures that concerned them or, rather, translated the
text for the *illiterati* who did not know the alphabet, much less Latin,
and he asked them to observe the dictates of the rules faithfully. They
all pledged themselves by vow or promissory oath, with God as their

witness through the intermediary of the Gospels, and they swore, orally and on the Bible, to conform "completely and inviolably."

The text was composed in Latin and conjugated in two tenses, present and future. This was to indicate clearly the temporal dimension in which the lawmaker located himself. By establishing the rules for the present and the future, he defined the parameters of expectation, a combination of anticipation, hope, and fear. The law guaranteeing human health was only a provisional structure, built on probability, through which Jean de Lévis projected himself simultaneously into the future and into his past.

To what assumptions, what elements of culture, did these rules consciously or unconsciously relate? Projected into a very uncertain future, the lawmaker used the past as an instrument of knowledge. He started from experience, from what he did or did not know. The past, on which Lévis based his decisions, was the third tense in the charter, hidden, implicit. Since this text, like all normative texts, says nothing about the reasons behind its measures, we must try to place it within thirteenth- and fourteenth-century ideology. But how can we possibly reconstruct the entire value system governing the elaboration of those norms? Surely that is where the historian takes risks. Without written records, the general opinion of that time is unavailable to him. He has at his disposal some scant veterinary discourse, preoccupied solely with horses, and more plentiful medical discourse. It is his good luck, his only good luck, that matters of health and disease fall solidly within a well-known paradigm, a scientific perspective inherited from the Greeks and Romans that provided a framework for medieval thought.

The authorities, the Greek Hippocrates (460–377 B.C.) and the Roman citizen Galen (129–210 A.D.), were continually cited. Their discourse was echoed and repeated constantly over the ages. Fifteen centuries separated Galen and Harvey, who showed how blood circulated in the body, thus calling into question Galen's theory of humors. Over fifteen centuries, of course, ideas about certain subjects had changed, but without ever undermining the core of Galenic physiology. Galen and his Arab followers had taught Western culture that hygiene was a vast domain encompassing everything affecting health Health was determined by one's constitution, by one's nature—predetermined "natural things" over which one had no control—and by "unnatural things." These "unnatural things" allowed the body to maintain its vital functions and depended more or less on us. We could, to a certain extent, control them. Among the six unnatural things, the first three were essential. These were the ones that we absorbed and that kept us alive: the air we breathed, the food we ate, the water we drank. Air, water, solid food all belonged to the basic category of sustenance that we took in.

At the time when Jean de Lévis was legislating, a famous Catalan doctor, Arnaud de Villeneuve, was just finishing his book *On the Use of Meats* and his *Introduction to Medicine*. In these, health factors divided into three categories: natural factors (*causae naturales*), unnatural factors (*causae non naturales*), and extranatural or antinatural things. This scholastic terminology is hard to understand today, because the term "natural" has a very different and much broader meaning. The division between natural and unnatural causes of disease roughly parallels the modern division between endogenous and exogenous factors. They can cause illness, which goes against nature. Thus this framework of thought had a very long lifespan—a single horizon stretching from antiquity to the seventeenth century—so much so that in explaining questions of health, it was permissible to quote the ancients, precisely what medieval authors loved to do, and even to omit later writings, like those of the Renaissance. We must try to span the chronology without underestimating the great cultural gap, because the evidence is scanty. The problem is that the experiences that dictated such precautions could have been real, but they could also have been imaginary. The problem is that we do not know at what point medical discourse penetrated Languedoc society of the time or who, within the castle's little learned assembly, was capable of understanding and making "*ut dicunt medici*." But poorly equipped as we are, let us try to penetrate the spirit of the Mirepoix charter.

Butcher's Meat

The document treats butcher's meat or, as it says in other similar Occitan texts, *carnis de mazello*. The *mazel* was the place of sale, the booth or stall where the meat was displayed, and the *mazellier* was the butcher. In listing the types of meats offered for consumption, the document reveals a fundamental distinction between what were and what were not considered butcher's meats. What does the phrase "butcher's meat" actually designate? This was not a given that goes without saying but a constructed category, and everyone may define it differently, including or excluding, for example, horse meat.

The Mirepoix charter defined by exclusion: it makes no mention of horse meat. Undoubtedly there was no need to forbid it, since no one ate it. Hippophagia: the word is unknown, the practice infamous. The church had something to do with this, as it had condemned its consumption as barbaric, a holdover from paganism, following the prohibition campaign of Saint Boniface on a mission among the Germans, pagans and eaters of horse meat. It would be an exaggeration to speak of an actual prohibition with religious origins. If the penitentials, those penance manuals used by confessors, mention this practice, they generally declare that horse meat can be eaten, although "this is not the custom," or even "that most men do not eat it."[6] Custom and eating habits had been reinforced by the expansion of agricultural practices increasingly dependent on horsepower. The horse had become man's fellow worker, endowed with a life expectancy as long as his own. How could he consume the flesh of his dear companion? We have learned from anthropologists that there must be some distance between the eater and the eaten. An emotional bond, a familiarity, too great a proximity, blocks the phagic act. In fourteenth-century Languedoc society, the horse was more than a companion; it was a confidant. The farmer talked to his horse in the fields, the knight as he charged, the merchant in the stable, the lady as she traveled.[7]

Veterinary books of the time were the work of blacksmiths, dealing simultaneously with medicine, surgery, and shoeing for horses. Maintaining the good condition of these animals used for work, military parade, or pleasure assumed an importance equal to maintaining the automobiles we use today. These veterinary tracts sold well. They taught how to break a horse, identify its diseases, treat them and hope for good recovery with the help of nature—*cooperante natura*—just as with humans.[8] Veterinary science at that time was centered on horses. It ignored other animals, especially those destined for the butcher shop. Clerical prejudice against horse meat and natural aversion to it were so strongly bound together and so well integrated that men of the period could not say why the sale of horse in butcher shops should be forbidden. And that is why they do not. Consumption of horse meat was not even mentioned in the Mirepoix document, simply because it was unthinkable.[9]

If exclusion was implicit for horse meat, it was, on the other hand, perfectly explicit for goat meat, and only the sale of year-old kids was authorized. Unlike horses, goats were much more of a presence in the Languedoc, and goat herds were never more numerous than at the time of Jean de Lévis.[10] The basic purpose of goat breeding was to provide a food source for humans, in the form of milk, cheese, and meat. That male kids could be eaten but not the father or mother indicates that aversion to goat meat was less absolute than to horse meat. In the countryside around Mirepoix, goat flesh was considered acceptable to eat, even that of male goats. For some Montaillou shepherds, the billy goat's liver was a delicacy, more highly prized than the fish so appreciated by the Cathari.[11] But standards for food consumption in the country were different from those in the towns, and within urban circles goat meat was disdained. It is true that its status and its price were low, but was that reason enough for the seigniorial authorities to prohibit it? Or did they suspect that goat meat presented health risks? The veterinary treatises that consider horses to be the only animal worthy of care do not stoop to detailing the diseases of small livestock. It is not until the sixteenth century that we find two doctors who give evidence of fears related to goat meat. Estienne writes, "The goat is never without fever in this country." This was Malta fever, or brucellosis, a fever that Estienne assigned to the ecological niche reserved for goat breeding. "You can make no bed for this livestock; often they sleep on the tip of a rock, exposed to the blazing sun, rather than in the shade."[12]

Climate and sun were two "unnatural" things that predisposed the goat to chronic illness. And Champier fully agrees, writing that "the goat never lacks the fever, so that no one puts healthy ones up for sale." He adds that the Romans refused to eat it, "either because they detested this lascivious and foul-smelling animal (the male goat) or because they were afraid of its illness. In fact, according to Plutarch, it seemed the goat suffered epilepsy, among other things, and that those who tasted it or touched it contracted this disease." And further on, citing another authority, Champier asserts that goat meat "is rather bad, acrid meat, besides which it is hard to digest, causes belching, and provokes cholera, according to the renowned doctor, Hippocrates."[13] Between fever and cholera, it was probably fever (Malta fever) and its potential transmission to humans that worried the Mirepoix legislators. The animal was considered "hot," and they mistrusted this "hotness," repugnant in its male version (the propensity to be in rut) and pernicious in its female version (the fever). Why did the goat's voice tremble? Because it had the fever, of course! And since it constantly quavered, it was constantly feverish.[14] Goat did not appear in official butcher stalls because it was suspected of carrying the remittent disease Malta fever.[15]

A question remains: why forbid goat meat but not kid meat? This lopsided prohibition may seem to be a provisional victory of taste over health concerns. It is also true that milk-fed flesh was believed to be harmless, since milk, through its freshness and humidity, tempered flesh that was hard and dry by nature. An entire tradition dating back to antiquity conveys doubts about the wholesomeness of goat meat.[16] André Deulesal and Philippe de Ripparia, present as legal experts, were steeped in Roman law and drew their inspiration for article 4, concerning goat meat, from a Diocletian edict forbidding the sale of goat in the Roman Empire. Nevertheless, the charter allowed the sale of this suspect meat in second-rank stalls called *bocaria*, though not in public butcher shops. That the word "*boucherie*" has a strong etymological link to the meat of the *bouc*, or goat, is good evidence of the vague and shifting status of this meat and the way its consumption carried with it precautions.

Since the classification of butcher's meat responds to criteria that are never explicit, we can simply conjecture that some of them stemmed from deeply rooted anthropological markers, like the distaste for horse meat, and others stemmed from reasons of health safety. In the end at Mirepoix, three categories for consumption were retained: ovine, bovine, and porcine.

That They Dare Not Sell Unwholesome Meat

Thus mutton, beef, and pork were sold, but under one condition: that their flesh was "good," "useful," "not diseased" (article 8). The diseased meats that were forbidden were listed at the beginning of the charter, first mutton, then beef and pork. Provided, once again, that the order of the list is not arbitrary, we have here a ranking for the fresh meat consumed in southern towns at that time.[17] The regulations were written in Latin, the language of lawyers but also the universal language of science and of doctors in particular. Thus it is surprising to see the Mirepoix jurists abandon Latin each time they mention a disease, resorting to the vernacular language, a dialect of Middle Occitan.

We could attribute this bilingualism to inadequate terminology. Latin was a poor and imprecise tool for speaking about animal diseases. In texts contemporary with the Mirepoix charter that remain restricted to Latin, two collective nouns are used, *peste* (or *pestilence*) and *morie* (or *morine, murie, murrain*). These very comprehensive terms for animal diseases are catchalls, concealing more than they clarify, and applicable to dozens of more or less serious pathologies.[18] The vernacular words are more precise and more in accordance with the spirit of thirteenth- and fourteenth-century laws, as well as those of the following centuries. The objective of those writing these local laws was not to elaborate a beautiful law, in elegant and flowery language; it was to make a good law. A good law was demanded by the populace and blessed by the higher authority, and it resulted in a consensus, a point, as I have noted, that had already been reached. A good law was also formulated in short, simple, and useful rules; it was applicable, in a word. That is why shepherds and butchers were not addressed in Latin when it was a matter of diseased meat but rather in their own language and words.

Prohibited among the ewes and sheep were those that were *marranos*, *galamutos*, or *capmartinos* or sick with *picota*. Local terms were used, as if the diseases that plagued the Haut-Languedoc did not strike elsewhere. The rich popular taxonomy for animal diseases makes retrodiagnosis very difficult. Only one disease is clearly identifiable, ovine "*picote*," so widespread throughout the Languedoc. In his 1567 treatise on the plague, Joubert, the famous Montpellier doctor, spoke of an animal plague that was rampant around Montpellier, commonly called the "*picote*." To each region, its *picote*. Elsewhere, it was known as *clou*, *claveau*, *clavin*, *clavelle*, *clavellière*, *glave*, *clousiau*, *vérole*, *petite vérole*, *vérolin*, *vérette*, *picotin*, *rougeole*, *caraque*, *rache*, *bourgeon*, *pustule*, *gamise*, *gamadure*, *liare*, *pest*, *bête*, as well as *marandra*, *magagna*, and *chas*.[19] All these diverse terms share the characteristic of confusing the disease with its main symptom. It was an eruptive disease, characterized by the appearance of pustules called *piqûres* (*picouta*) in southern France and *clous* in northern France. This confusion between the disease and its symptoms recurs in the scholarly discourse, where all the nosology based the name of the disease on the major symptom or syndrome. Thus a goat could transmit the "fever," the fever being the disease itself, characterized by an uneven, elevated temperature. This metonymical linguistic construction attests to a very common thought process, which mistakes the effect for the cause. Today, this ovine variola, recognized as nontransmissible to humans, is designated by the single term of *clavelée* (sheep pox). It is endemic in the Mediterranean region, rarer elsewhere, and English herds have long been free from it. But, in the thirteenth century, it reached England through Northumberland, and the British Isles became part of the European microbial system. English sheep retained only one privilege over their fellow creatures: they could graze peacefully without danger of encountering wolves.[20]

The second ovine disease denounced by the text is perplexing: the *marrane* sheep appears in no official nosology. The adjective *marrane* is familiar, however. It is a borrowing from across the Pyrenees, and in the Castilian language it designates a pig. To understand this species crossover, we must remember that the word underwent certain semantic shifts, passing first from animal to man. Its primary shift: it also designates a Jew or Muslim. Tell me what you do not eat, and I will tell you what you are. To call Jews or Muslims by what they abstained from added insult to injury. Anti-Semitism often resorted to this process, language finding itself aligned with iconography here. Artists made the animal disdained by Jews one of the symbolic figures used to designate them.[21]

Its second shift: in the mouth of a Gascon native in 1300, *marrane* was the word used to designate in an unfriendly way one who lived on the other side of the Pyrenees. "In the time when we other French were enemies of the Spanish, we called them *marranes*, just as they called us *gavaches*," said Marot. Between the pig, the cursed infidel, and the sick sheep, semantics established links that tell us more about the bad reputation of the pig—which is transmissible—than about the disease of sheep. Etymological dictionaries meant to help historians understand old texts are not much use. According to Mistral, these sheep are languishing, skinny, weak. As the verb *marraner* means to work with difficulty or to balk at working, it is clear that such sheep have trouble staying on their feet and walking, but what is their scrawniness and languor attributed to? If we must risk a retrodiagnosis—risky, since we know that the diseases of animals, like those of humans, can appear, disappear, or mutate and that in 1300 those animals could have suffered a plague that no longer exists—we might guess that these forbidden sheep had tuberculosis (*marranes*), that the rams had anthrax (*galamutos*), and the sheep with head rot (*capmortinos*) were afflicted with dizziness—unless they suffered from trembling? In any case, scabby ewes and mad sheep would not be found on the hooks of the butcher stalls in Mirepoix.

Cows banned for consumption had neither clearly named diseases nor external clinical signs; at least, they were not described, and diseases were only discovered during post mortem inspections. On examining the carcass, it was observed that "the marrow was fluid and uncoagulated in the bones" (article 3). We do not know if the brain was also liquefied and quasi-spongy. According to a very archaic conception of the mental apparatus, the signifier *medulla* covered three signifieds—the spinal cord, the bone marrow, and the medulla of the brain—that were considered to be closely related and similar in nature. In Toulouse, those cow carcasses lacking "good and sufficient marrow" were equally suspect.[22] Bovine disease had no name. It remains a mystery.

Last on the blacklist were pigs that the text calls "leprous." Leper or leprous: that the same words applied equally to humans or pigs indicates immediately what a vague and menacing aura surrounded the animal. "Leprosy is the disease of medieval France par excellence."[23] Leprosy prompted fear. Moreover, was only "lepromatous" leprosy true leprosy? It is difficult to discern Hansen's bacillus in the monstrous clinic that constituted the Middle Ages. While all ovine diseases capable of destroying human health were grouped under one article, porcine leprosy, all by itself, warranted three regulations. Three regulations were better than one. To detect the disease, all pigs were to be examined. While sheep only had to submit to one inspection, before slaughter, and cattle also only one, after slaughter, pigs had to submit to a double exam, ante mortem and post mortem. For the first one, the pig was knocked down, turned on its side, and immobilized. Its mouth was then held wide open with a wooden stick so that its tongue could be examined by sight and by touch. By looking at it and by passing a finger under the tongue, one could see or feel if it bore the sublingual pustules that signaled leprosy in an "evident and manifest" fashion. The task was assigned to specialists, called *langueyeurs*.

But the charter did not confine itself to external clinical signs. It demanded verification that an apparently healthy animal was not infected; hence a second inspection was required at the time of cutting up the carcass. The examination was done carefully, because, a priori, infected meat looked as good as healthy meat, except for the presence of "grains" in the flesh, that is, encysted larvae in the muscle mass. It took a trained eye and keen attention to recognize among the fascicles of muscle fibers cysticerci that took the form of minuscule white cysts, the size of one "grain" of millet.

These were rigorous measures. In sum, six types of reputedly unwholesome meats were excluded from consumption. Were the risks exaggerated? Risk measured uncertainty. In 1303 certainty was minimal, uncertainty oceanic.

The Leprous Pig

We cannot expect a normative text to be full of observations to support the rules it proclaims. We know what meats were prohibited; we do not know on what grounds they were prohibited. The statutes for Florentine butchers were hardly more explicit than the Mirepoix charter when they claimed that all animal meat was capable of transmitting disease.[24] Yes, but which disease? Theoretically, meat could be banned for human consumption because it was believed capable of transmitting the same disease from animals to humans. It could also be banned because the flesh of a sick animal was thought to be of poor quality and harmful to humans. In such an exchange, so subtle it escaped the comprehension of people at that time, couldn't our flesh become like the flesh we absorbed, if the latter was unhealthy? Incorporating fresh flesh involved the risk of ingesting the disease it carried or some other disease. And how to know if the dreaded diseases were zoonoses, illnesses common to humans and animals, or just the digestive disturbances, diarrhea, or poisoning that reputedly unhealthy meat could cause?

Leprosy in pigs does not exist. The expression porcine leprosy designates a disease that has been known since 1760 to be, in fact, a parasite and since 1865 to be spread from animals to humans and vice versa. The parasite exists in the pig in the larval state, encysted in the muscle mass; on penetrating the human digestive tract, it develops into a tapeworm. All things considered, it is an ailment hardly related or comparable to the fear that it provoked.

To understand the cultural and psychological environment out of which the fear of porcine leprosy arose, we must first consult the medical discourse. On the disease of the animal, it says nothing. On the human ailment, since it dominated the whole pathological landscape until the sixteenth century, it is infinitely more verbose. The prestigious and nearby school of medicine in Montpellier then had a professor, Arnaud de Villeneuve, who taught there in 1300, and two authorities, Galien and the Arab doctor, Avicenna.

In 1303 Arnaud de Villeneuve, a Catalonian, was sixty years old. He had had a very full career, with a prestigious clientele, since he was called on by the pope and by kings alike. Thus this perpetual traveler sailed between Catalonia, Marseilles, and Nice, a nomadism that encouraged the circulation of medical ideas. He was putting the finishing touches on a book about healthy diet, one of many in a generous opus that included a treatise on leprosy and a nosology concerned with worms in humans, especially intestinal worms. Villeneuve was the first to classify these strange animals—even while doubting their animal nature—and he described the tapeworm that one of his patients had vomited, one or two arms in length. As this was the longest that he had taken to be observed, he qualified it as *solium*, not "solitary," as it is too often, wrongly, translated, but "sovereign." Did this enormous king of worms come from eating pork? Neither Villeneuve or his emulators ever say anything about that.

How could one imagine such a relationship between the "grain" in the pig and the "worm" in the human? There was no need, moreover, to imagine it, since the origin of intestinal worms was "known": since similar creatures were unknown in the open air, it was deduced that they engendered themselves. Like all the worms of this foul micro-fauna, from snake to frog, they were born through spontaneous gen-eration. The corruption of the humors in the stomach was enough to make this sovereign worm appear, which was too common to be truly formidable.[25] This worm was a familiar tenant in human intes-tines, and one lived with it through long cycles of cohabitation, five or eight years, with a renewable lease. One tried to avoid them by means of an annual cure each year in May, consisting of garlic and new butter.[26] One did one's best to get rid of them through empiric methods, like the one advised by the surgeon Ambroise Paré in the Renaissance: "And to flush them out still more and get rid of them, you must anoint the seat of the disease with honey and sugar, because they flee the bitter and run to the sweet; and leaving, go out instead from the stomach."[27]

The origin of leprosy in pigs, on the other hand, was not known. The disease was so widespread that it was believed to be hereditary. Even so, it was suspected that it was somehow related to the pig's inti-macy with humans, because it was observed that the wild boar never had leprosy. We do not know if the pig's reputation for being dirty was at the origin of this permanent infection, this unhealthy and con-tinually renewed cycle. The ecological niche that humans assigned to the animal was filth, and it wallowed there, absorbed human waste, the tapeworm included, and returned it to humans. In the country, the pig was associated with the manure pile. In the towns, it fed on all the urban refuse. That was where the real, though unrecognized danger lay: getting parasites. Nevertheless, the pig was very much considered the animal of risk par excellence in butchery regulations. But exactly what risk? Leprosy, of course.

Let us return to Arnaud de Villeneuve, the most reliable contem-porary guide in matters of health. On leprosy, he produced a short treatise in which he reviewed all the factors, "the second causes," that could provoke the eruption of such a contagious disease:

Now one becomes leprous when one sleeps with a woman with whom a leper has just coupled. Also at the moment of conception itself, as when one is nurtured by impure blood or conceived by a corrupt sperm, or as when one is conceived during menses. One also becomes leprous through bad disposition and quality of air, by immoderate use of melancholic or phlegmatic foods, and by the meat of the donkey, bull, or cow, by the meat of unhealthy pigs and other similar impure meats. One becomes leprous through the abuse of dishes flavored with garlic and pepper, immoderate use of pure wine, as the inhabitants of Gaul abuse it, and also the Burgunds, and because of that, many of them are leprous. Likewise, one becomes leprous by spending too much time with lepers.[28]

Summing up the misconceptions of his time, Villeneuve left the choices wide open. Of course, consuming pork could bring on leprosy, but that was only one factor, lost among others in this incredible etiology in which the variety of the parameters responds to the diversity of forms of leprosy thought to be observed, this polymorphic disease that varied from one individual to another. In alluding to the unhealthy pig, Villeneuve's text contrasts sharply with the medical tradition: he does not adopt the discourse of his teacher of diagnosis, Galien. To find the reasons for this infidelity, we might look in the direction of the School of Salerno via the Italian Platearius, who taught a mistrust of the leprous pig, or even to Jewish medicine. Villeneuve read Arabic, and his nephew, Armandgaud Blaise, read Hebrew and translated the *Regime of Health* by Maimonides. Maimonides, a Spanish rabbi, justified the prohibitions of the Talmud by citing the dangers inherent in consuming an animal fed on refuse. He found proof that the pig was an unclean animal in the French cities of his time, where the houses, he said, resembled latrines: "If eating pork was permitted, all the streets and houses would be even dirtier than dung heaps and latrines, as we see in Gaul today."[29]

In disputing the causes of leprosy, each doctor proposed a long list of predisposing causes, which included all types of alimentary pollution but not necessarily the fear of pork flesh. Bernard de Gourdon, another prominent Montpellierite, implicated other dangerous foods, for example, an excess of lentils, but not pork flesh.

Apparently, Villeneuve's version became the commonly accepted one. His text is repeated, almost word for word, in the encyclopedia of Bartholomaeus Anglicus: "It [leprosy] can be caused by corrupt air or by the consumption of bad and melancholic food, too cold and dry, like the meat of bull, donkey, and bear. It can sometimes come from excessively hot foods: if, for example, one constantly consumes onions or pepper and similar substances. It is also caused by the ingestion of corrupt foods, like the meat of leprous or diseased pig or even like spoiled wine."[30]

The doctors represented two traditions: one, a Spanish and Jewish tradition (*marrane*, to use the Gascon term), suspected pork of transmitting leprosy. The other, descended from Greek rationalism, did not. It can be eaten, Aristotle said.[31] Between those two traditions, one alarmist, the other more reassuring with regard to human health, the doctors wavered. The debate continued for a long time, and in the century of the Enlightenment eminent specialists like Paulet and the abbot Rozier still argued over the presumed dangers of leprous meat.

We can find traces of this possible link between porcine and human leprosy in the diagnostic procedures. The detection of human leprosy was a very delicate thing. Thrown off by polymorphous symptoms, lumping together more and less severe dermatoses under the name of leprosy, the surgeon was charged with sending those declared leprous to leper houses, that is, condemning them to civil death. To ensure his diagnosis, he had at his disposal a battery of symptoms or signs, ranging from equivocal signs, which implied a presumption of leprosy, nothing more, to univocal signs, which condemned one to the leper house permanently and without appeal. In 1275 the surgeon Guillaume de Salicet evoked one such univocal sign in his diagnostic procedure: "A very sure sign, when there is doubt about a case of leprosy, ... is that, if the doctor holds the patient's tongue tightly between his fingers, he sees at the base of the tongue, or on the uvula or the palate, small pustules, white, red, or yellow, and foul-smelling."[32]

For Gui de Chauliac, another prominent surgeon, there were six univocal signs of leprosy and sixteen equivocal signs. Among the sixteen equivocal signs, "the seventh is grains under the tongue, under the eyelids, and behind the ears."[33] This confusion between the vesicles of porcine leprosy and dermatoses in humans is completely explicit in this report by Ambroise Paré, who declared leprous a man whose "tongue [is] swollen and black and above and below are found small grains, like one sees in leprous pigs."[34]

The medical examination for detecting leprosy bore a resemblance to the *langueyage* of the pig. That it was practiced by surgeons and not by doctors is not irrelevant. Surgeons, those paramedics disdained by doctors, inferior to them, and endowed with know-how rather than knowledge, risked being closer to popular beliefs. They could serve as a conduit between the learned world and the general public.

Within this framework, a transmission was invented between a nonexistent animal disease and a monstrous but poorly defined human disease. The unobservable was observed, and, what is more, the invisible was seen. The invisible was the internal flesh of the leper, which had to present "grains" similar to those of the leprous pig. There is, again, no discourse, but, for example, there is a 1410 exchange of insults, as reported by Françoise Bériac. It involved a quarrel, a man's death, and legal proceedings in which the murderer recounts the abusive exchange including this, the most horrible insult: he was called a leper, a *mezel*. His aggressor threatened: "He would hit him so hard in the face that it would make such a big wound that the grains of leprosy would appear on the surface so that everyone could see and realize that he was a leper."[35]

The allusion to the grains of leprosy that pepper leprous flesh is clear. One inferred from what was seen in the pig what must be visible in the body of the leper. The body and its representations are very much shaped by the imagination, to echo the words of Jacques Le Goff.

The pig became the focus of all fears. Was that because it was the only animal raised exclusively to feed humans? Was it because humans were made like pigs? That was an opinion shared by many, common folk and scholars, such as Henri de Mondeville, who wrote, "the lower stomach of man—these are the bowels—is like the stomach of the pig." By his viscera, man was very closely related to mammals in general, and to the pig in particular.[36]

With diseases in sheep or cows, one observed, compared, extrapolated. With the pig, one fantasized. The general view produced no discourse. It operated, protected itself, and was expressed through the aid of normative texts. Urban regulations were quite suggestive on this subject, for example, when they forbade the ingestion of pigs raised at leper houses or when they ordered the flesh of pigs recognized as leprous to be given to these same leper houses.[37] In Mas d'Agenais, lepers were condemned to eating only what they produced, and they risked having their sheep and pigs killed, with no legal recourse, if the animals happened to be caught wandering about.[38]

It was in such regulations that the fantasy of leprosy took shape, and, thus inscribed into the law, it became the norm.

Science and Knowledge

It is impossible to know if what was taught at the university in Montpellier reverberated at all in Mirepoix. The town legislators nevertheless drew on some knowledge when they agreed that animals known to be diseased, through evidence or through knowledge (*evidenter seu scienter*), would be eliminated. Such evidence was presented publicly: that was what revealed all the external and visible signs of the disease, according to a topology that allowed for locating the disease in a precise location. As the leprous pig was recognized first by the tongue, so the *picote*-stricken sheep was recognized by pustules under the belly, the *galamuto* ram by anthracic tumors. The law implicitly distinguished two stages of the disease, stated or not. If the external signs were not manifest, one "would know," nevertheless, that the animal was suspect. To what knowledge was Jean de Lévis alluding here? Perhaps one sensed the beast was sick, because this knowledge was intimately tied to the senses, smell in particular. Furthermore, Occitan commonly uses "*savoir à*" in the sense of having a taste, an odor, an air of, that is, some trace that recalls something known.[39]

This "science" undoubtedly borrowed nothing from academic knowledge but much from the empiricism of professional expertise. In the Paris slaughterhouses reorganized in 1810, one paid attention to the "odor of fever" in meats "that smelled hot."[40]

Article 5 of the charter launched directly into this sphere of empirical knowledge with the injunction: "Let no butcher dare to blow." This prohibition appeared again in many other butchery regulations. Those of papal Comtat, in the same period, were particularly definite on this subject. In Carpentras, it was even specified that the desired goal in blowing was to skin the beast and that human breath had to be avoided. In Bédarrides, the 1413 town statutes prohibited blowing "*cum ore nec canono.*" In Barroux, on the other hand, it was permitted to inflate with a cannon—that is to say, with a reed.[41] In Italian cities, all legislation related to the sale of "*bona et pulchra*" flesh condemned calf inflated with breath.[42]

What did this practice of blowing, so unanimous and so unanimously condemned, consist of? We might recall a technical process associated with the preparation of slaughtered sheep. To skin them, one made an incision at the base of one leg and blew air into it: the animal inflated to bursting, and the skin, detached from the carcass, was easier to remove. Certain specialists, like Louis Stouff, are inclined to favor another explanation: causing meat to swell up would be a way of disguising it, of making it appear better by adding to its volume or its weight. The statutes hardly provide us the means to decide between these two interpretations. Some are linked exclusively to the blowing of ovine meat, others to all kinds of flesh; in some, the actions of skinning and blowing are found in close semantic proximity; in others, to blow and to cheat are nearly synonymous. Let us leave the question unanswered for the time being. What matters are the presumed risks. The procedure was denounced because it was considered harmful. By inflating and blowing into the flesh, the butchers "filled them with bad air and pernicious winds."[43] More positive, the regulations of the sixteenth century advocated the use of a bellows "to obviate the dangers that can follow" from injecting human breath.[44]

The potentially dangerous situation evoked here was communicating an ailment from human to human, through the intermediary of animal flesh. We might think here of tuberculosis—what we call, since Koch, tuberculosis—which was attested in the early Middle Ages, when it was communicated from cattle herds to humans. But there is no reason to believe that the citizens of Mirepoix, who were trying to avoid imaginary zoonoses, were thinking of this very real disease. Academic knowledge and university medicine taught that only the miasmas of the air were responsible for the propagation of epidemics. All the same, the notion of contagion was not foreign to people of that time, and it seemed more conceivable when it was a matter of animal diseases.[45]

An anonymous work from the fourteenth century, *The Surgery of Horses*, shows how contagion and its mechanisms were conceived:

> 7. When a horse catches the disease, *roigne* or *farcy*, from another horse, then it corrupts the air with its breath. And this corrupt air is very capable of subtly transforming the bodies of men and animals.
> 8. That is why philosophers forbid children to draw near to a man stricken with the fever, because children are so tender that they are immediately stricken.... Children attract to themselves the air that is corrupted by the sick person's breath.[46]

These two articles offer a good opportunity to fathom how contagion was conceived in all its configurations. The first (article 7) deals with the diseases of horses, one of which is glanders, called *farsins* here, the most disquieting because it is fatal. The second recommendation concerns interhuman contagion. We may note that the mechanism for contagion does not differ for human and animal and that, in both cases, the privileged carrier is the ailing one's breath. The stench of the breath signaled the disease, and it was by the sense of smell that the health risk was detected. That contamination could take place through the air was a recognized fact, and there was no need for a theory of bacteria to explain it. The theory of humors was just as effective. The disease was attributed, at its deepest level, to a derangement of the humors, the blood in particular, "which has more seignory in the beast."[47] Contagion resulted when a volatile product originating from the blood and transported by the breath was transmitted from the sick subject to the healthy subject. This anonymous horse surgeon was a good Galenist.

Thus there is no need to speak of pre/science. To forbid blowing was a precaution that fit within an intellectual framework in keeping with the officially accepted theory of miasmas. Nor should we speak of precursors. It would be a mistake to consider this measure a prefiguration of the discovery of contagions that marks the beginning of modern epidemiology. The Mirepoix legislators were not ahead of their time. They were of their time.

In the end, if they took such elaborate precautions with regard to consuming meat, it was because they were convinced of or, worse, obsessed with the danger for humans of contracting animal diseases. Of course, the "horse surgeon" did not mention pathogenic agents circulating from one to the other, but, proposing a homology between animal and human constitutions, he facilitated such thinking. Since the human and the animal body functioned in comparable ways, they could similarly dysfunction and spread their disorders to each other. Wasn't rabies the oldest and cruelest known example of such transmission? Experience could confirm the idea that the barrier between species was easily crossed. Associative frenzy did the rest. Many human and animal diseases presented symptomatologic affinities. The vocabulary clearly demonstrates this: *galeux*, *marrane*, *capmartino* (mad), the same adjectives that applied to sheep could be applied to humans. The eruptive disease sheep pox resembled measles, so much so that it was sometimes called the smallpox of ewes! In 1411 Pasquier signaled the presence throughout Europe of a *tac* epidemic, an eruptive disease common to humans and sheep. The clinical descriptions make today's veterinarians think it was a matter of a sheep pox epidemic, concomitant with an epidemic of measles. But the people of the fourteenth century had a functionalist conviction and a chronological diagnosis. They thought that the similarity in symptoms was not a coincidence, that there were secret, internal correspondences between human and animal diseases. That the two diseases appeared simultaneously presented a strong case of communication for them. The simultaneity was interpreted as a relationship of cause and effect. "Post hoc, ergo propter hoc," was the decisive maxim that took the place of reason and won the day.

Zoonoses existed; people knew that but believed them to be more numerous than, in reality, they were.

The Mirepoix charter appeared at the juncture of three spheres of knowledge: rationalist and individualist medicine, local veterinary practice, and popular beliefs. It cut across two experiences, one real and one imaginary. When these two were not compatible and diverged on the assessment of danger, the legislators bet on the worst: they took the maximum precautions.

TWO

POLITICAL MEAT

Butchering under Surveillance

Between 1200 and 1500, the texts regulating the sale of meat were numerous. The Mirepoix charter is only one example of the regulations many towns provided for themselves in this period. Far from being a pioneer, it closed a cycle of economic legislation that ran through the southern towns of the realm throughout the thirteenth century. The trend started in the largest towns, organized into municipalities early on. In Toulouse in 1184, the elected *capitouls* in charge of the city took three archetypal measures regarding butchering: the profit of the butchers, here called *macelliers*, must be limited to one *denier* out of twelve (that it, 8 percent); partnership between two butchers was forbidden; and selling the meat of sick animals was likewise forbidden, unless the buyer was warned. Control of profits, limited trade arrangements, respect for health: subsequently, these three principles would continue to assert themselves and would be adopted and developed in later texts. The Toulouse charter on butchering, for example, renewed in 1394, was a very long document with sixty articles, nineteen of which are devoted to health safety.[1]

Let us cross the Rhône, the border between the realm and Provence. According to Louis Stouff, it was with the period of the consulate and the emergence of a certain autonomy among communities that the first rules for butchering appeared.[2]

The Republic of Arles provided statutes for itself at the end of the thirteenth century, including four articles that dealt with butchering.

❋

All the urban statutes of the thirteenth century, those of Montpellier (1204), Avignon (1246), Marseilles (1253), and Salon (1293), included instructions on butchering. In the following century, in the villages of the Rhône valley where a municipal butchery trade was established, the urban model was adopted, and community statutes also contained measures regarding the sale of meat in villages. In papal Comtat, the 1400 statutes of Sarrians forbade the sale of diseased or even suspect meat. According to the 1468 statutes of Pernes, blowing was prohibited. In Châteauneuf, meats were to be sold "with no suspicion of disease."

Putting meat under surveillance was not a peculiarity of the Languedoc and Provence. In the entire country, wherever urbanization and the community movement spread, this kind of legislation emerged between the twelfth and thirteen centuries and was particularly prevalent around the Mediterranean arc at the time of the first municipal rights. It would be a mistake, however, to draw an absolute link between urban emancipation and the concern for healthy meat. The example of Mirepoix serves to remind us that, where he had authority over the market, the lord enacted measures in this domain. In Languedoc, the earliest regulations are contemporaneous with the southern feudal system, with the Lévis family in Mirepoix, the last Guilhem in Montpellier, and Gaston VII in Béarn. In matters of economic policy, many powers claimed to have control and exercised it concurrently or successively. In addition to the laws enacted by lords and municipal magistrates, we must consider professional regulations, established by the butchers and the food trades themselves.

To see our way a little more clearly through this normative maze, we can draw a broad outline of two models: the municipal model of the Mediterranean towns and the professional model of the north.

In southern France and in Italy, health regulations were voted on by the cities and recorded in the statutes. Consular power in matters of policy was exercised either directly, through regulations, or in an oblique way, by controlling the elaboration of statutes involving the food trades drawn up by trade associations.[3] The food trades were regulated trades, and supervision was particularly focused on the butchers, fishmongers, and bakers. This southern model—we must be precise here—was a Mediterranean model and was found again in Italy as it was in Spain, where the municipal officers played a predominant role in matters of health policy. The municipal magistrates considered themselves, and were effectively considered by the public, to be the natural guardians of public health. In the coffer of their archives, the Avignon consuls guarded two precious collections: one contained all the city statutes; the other was the set of registers where municipal regulations were copied out and all the proceedings on market policy appeared. They called these huge registers the *livres de la politique* (the books of policy). Consulting the books of proceedings, it becomes clear how many sessions were devoted to the problem of fresh food supplies, meat in particular. "Policy" was not a minor affair in the life of the city.

If the food trades were well supervised in the south, in the north, they were organized autonomously. These were the trade guilds. The statutes of these guilds were primarily preoccupied with the interests of trade. They were aimed at limiting or avoiding unfair competition, since a trade shared a monopoly. Another of their aims was to establish rules of good conduct with regard to the buyer; the quality of goods and services offered had to meet specific, uniform standards. Thus trade association measures enumerated—broadly—the rights and privileges of the producers, as well as standards of production, and consequently obligations with regard to the consumer. Something close to the idea of public service was imposed on artisans and, a fortiori, on the food trades. Whatever trade one practiced, it had to serve the city.[4] Northern butchers swore obedience to the guild regulations, just as those in Mirepoix took an oath on the charter.

These two regulatory systems were not equivalent. Municipal law generated stricter and more precise standards. The professional statutes forbade the sale of unhealthy meats or "faulty foodstuffs," but without being more specific. In their 1381 statutes, Paris butchers devoted only one article to the question, establishing that anyone among them "who sold bad flesh" would be liable to a fine of sixty *sous*, payable to the guild, which enforced its own professional policy. This terseness did not necessarily signify less protection for the consumer. It expressed the obvious: that men of the trade knew what they had to do and that a monopoly had been granted to them in exchange for certain responsibilities toward the buyer. Municipal law was also more precocious: Jean de Lévis granted the charter to Mirepoix at nearly the same time that the Paris provost, Guillaume Thiboust, introduced the first measure involving the meat trade. There was only one: "For the common profit of good people, that all flesh that dies not by the butcher's hand be burned." Thus all carcasses not butchered in the city would be incinerated.[5] It was not until 1462, with the Tours edict, that Paris had regulations as detailed as the those in the Languedoc village.

And what was the king's role in all this? He played a part, certainly, but here, as in the domain of public health in general, his involvement was limited and late in coming. To find that astonishing constitutes an anachronism, because one would hardly have dreamed then of asking him for what he was not able to grant. For a local policy and inspection process, who was better able and equipped than local authorities and the trades involved?[6] The prince was preoccupied with health, but primarily his own, which explained the presence of the court physicians, who were in charge of tasting dishes, looking after the royal constitution, and on occasion, in times of epidemic emergencies, consulted as experts. But he did not have a prophylaxis applicable to his entire realm. The Capetians were interested above all in Paris, though they did not succeed in making the capital's butchers answer to them. The Parisian Grande Boucherie constituted the most powerful trade guild, and its 1381 statutes established that the property of the butcher stall and the right of being received as master butcher belonged exclusively to the male offspring: the trade was transmitted to the eldest son, like the French crown. The Grande Boucherie of Paris was rich with wealth, members, and also ambition. In the face of it, the king oscillated between protection and exploitation, being more interested in its wealth and potential capacity to bail out the treasury than in the quality of the merchandise it offered. The Great Plague of 1348 redirected royal attention a bit. In 1351 King John the Good intervened to limit profits to 10 percent; in 1363 real health provisions were added to the edict.

Food law in the ancien régime did not come about with a single wave of the legislative wand. There was no single source at the time for issuing the law, and legislation was fragmented and scattered. In fact, there were as many regulations as there were markets. Texts with diverse names—statutes, drafts, customs, charters, orders, capitulations—composed what was called the law, what we would more likely call regulations. They restricted the food trade and put into place an economy of the market, which is very far removed from the market economy we speak of today. First, the market itself was a privilege. The urban market was an official and obligatory place, regulated and supervised. It had to be authorized, which was not to be taken for granted. In the 1780s, the royal power authorized only 40 percent of the requests for holding fairs and 35 percent of those for markets. The market was not a place of freedom; it was a place carefully watched over by whomever controlled economic policy, the lord or the city.

Thus there existed no single law on food safety but scattered rules, dispersed throughout the texts that determined how the towns would secure their food supply. It was in the law constructed around the problems of provisioning, of quantity and regularity, that those rules concerning quality appeared.

That They Be Killed in the City

The normative activity regarding the food trades, intense and multifaceted as it was, produced a plural but quite uniform urban law. That is, the measures taken to guarantee the safety of edible foodstuffs found their way from one text to another, so much so that they create the impression that, inspired by the same concerns, they were copied from one another. The statutes regulating butchering in Carpentras were echoed, more or less, in the regulations of villages in the flat country. Parisian legislation on the trades, formulated by the provost Boileau at the time of Saint Louis, was adopted elsewhere. It could be found in Rouen as well as the towns of the northwest.[7] Solidly established on this shared fund, modern legislation broke little new ground, adopting the old, sometimes in an allusive way: it was necessary, said the Toulouse magistrates, to sell meat according to the old statutes (orders of the Toulouse magistrates, 1422).[8] And the Avignon consuls imitated them, referring to the ancient wisdom (*Antiquitas sagax*).

Let us not exaggerate legislators' respect for the old rules or their tendency to imitate normative models. In fact, they had few solutions for guaranteeing the healthiness of foods. If a new risk appeared or, especially, if a new precaution became feasible, they were perfectly willing to alter and add to their meager legal arsenal. Between 1200 and 1400, a sort of *Codex alimentarius* was developed, which constituted the common core of multifaceted and long-lasting legislation. Along with bread, two foodstuffs were particularly controlled: meat and fish. Butcher stalls furnished fresh meat only on the weekdays when the church allowed meat to be eaten, about 215 days a year, and the fishmongers worked especially during Lent and on those days when meat was not allowed, about 150 days a year. Meat, along with bread, was subject to a kind of supervision that made it a "political foodstuff."[9] Within this legal framework, we can generally discern the shared, obligatory standards, the ones repeated like a theme from one text to another and from one market to another.

The most insistent standards concerned slaughtering. The sacrifice of animals involved the whole of the ancient city-state; likewise, the slaughter involved the whole town during the ancien régime. The two essential injunctions were that the animals must enter the towns on foot and be slaughtered after having been subject to a health inspection.

It was specified in the Mirepoix charter that the animals must come on foot to the butcher or public butchery before being slaughtered. And this was repeated and expanded in statutes throughout the south, regardless the place or time period: animals must enter the town on their own feet (*eorum propriis pedibus*).[10] The northern, professional variation was formulated in this way: "Let no butcher be so bold as to sell flesh at the door if it was not seen to be alive by two or three men who testify to it by an appropriate and sufficient oath, and even so they can only sell what the masters have seen and established as good."[11]

One did not speak of slaughterhouses but of *taudou* and *affachoirs* or, in modern French, *tueries* and *echorchoirs*, the places animals were killed and skinned. It is hard to know if they were located exactly in the towns.[12] In Sisteron in 1401, slaughtering and selling were forbidden outside the *mazel*. In Verona, the statute of 1450 required butchers to slaughter in their own storefronts.[13] The statutes provide a further indication of the confusion when they name the one who does the slaughtering: it is the butcher himself. To name the action of slaughtering the beast, many words existed, all of them related to the lexical type *macellare*, from which is also derived *mazel* and *mazellier*. Suffice it to say that slaughtering and the sale of meat were two closely related activities, performed by the same person at the same place. Some regulations forbade butchers to do the slaughtering in their own homes. They thus anticipate a more developed system, where physical separation between the slaughtering and the sale replaced the slaughter-stall conjunction. Municipal, public slaughtering grounds were set up, where the butchers were required to bring their beasts. They were conveniently located, often close to a river or stream into which the blood and all the butchering wastes could be discharged. If Italian cities were glad to banish their slaughtering grounds to the outskirts of the urban areas, even outside the city walls, the French cities preferred to keep them in their centers, near the large markets.[14] In Paris, despite Charles VII's attempts at reform, the slaughter grounds remained annexed to the butcher shops, creating a large red stain in the heart of Paris, dominated by the steeple of Saint-Jacques la Boucherie. Thus the slaughter–butcher shop complex was firmly established at the heart of the city, breaking with the ancient or early medieval tradition of banishing to the outskirts those lowly occupations soiled by the blood of beasts.

The reason for this norm and this localization is very clearly health related, even if historical anthropology allows us to link the obsession with meat on foot to the horror of *morticine* meat, that is, any meat from animals that died without being butchered. The penitentials inform us that clerics ranked such meat among the unclean meats, and consuming it was punishable by forty to one hundred days of penitence.[15] The animals arriving on foot at the heart of the town represented an essential guarantee for the consumer, giving him the opportunity to verify that the animal was healthy, without visible signs of disease. The sheep was not to turn around in circles, the calf was to be "lively and solid on its feet," not newborn and certainly not stillborn, because the meat of an animal extracted from its mother's belly was suspect. Furthermore, meat on foot had skin and entrails, both necessary for the double health examination, internal and external, to be effective. In Alès, an early-fourteenth-century ordinance from the seigniorial court that had been requested by the consuls determined the fate of a suspect cow. As the animal had been killed after having been brought into the town on a cart, which seemed to indicate that it could not move on its own, it was decided that the butchers could not sell the meat at the *mazel*.[16]

Beginning in the fourteenth century, another concern preoccupied the town councillors and strengthened their desire to maintain the slaughtering within the city walls: this was the cities' need to increase their taxes. The urban tax system uniformly took the form of taxes levied on food products, meat in particular; henceforth, each animal was taxed at the time it entered one of the city gates, which facilitated tax collection and avoided fraud. Thus the fiscal system served as a powerful rationale for maintaining the old rules of slaughter, extended over seven centuries.

The standards also unanimously proclaimed that all perishable foodstuffs must be sold promptly. For meat, this injunction seemed to go without saying, since storage was impossible and one worked according to demand, slaughtering when and as much as need dictated. Before being sent to the slaughter grounds, the herds stayed in the semiurban meadows that the city made available the butchers.

The oldest-known Provençal regulations, dating from 1262 in Grasse, allowed pigs to be sold as fresh meat only on the day they were slaughtered and the day after; beyond that, the meat had to be salted and converted into "bacon," not the English specialty but a salt meat that was very widely eaten. In Auch, which established regulations at the same time as Mirepoix, one could sell the meat "of one day on the other." According to Louis Stouff, who knows the Provençal regulatory corpus best, the time limits for selling meat after slaughter were, according to the place, two or three days. Sometimes they were stricter, especially during the summer: the statutes of Mazan from 1381 allowed fresh meat to be sold only on the day of slaughter and the next day until three o'clock, from Pentecost until the Feast of Saint Michael, except on holidays, when sale was authorized the whole next day.[17]

But let us not be too quick to invoke the constraints of the Mediterranean climate. Parisian butchers could not keep meat long, either: "no butcher will keep killed flesh for more than two days in winter, and in summer, a day and a half at the most" specify the fourteenth-century statutes. The sale of meat took place very quickly everywhere.

Reading the statutes and ordinances is enough to shatter that old myth that attributes the medieval taste for spices to the habit of eating very stale and nearly rotten meat. Eating rotten, putrid meat was completely contrary to the medieval conception of disease, as something counter to nature that resulted from internal corruption. Eating corrupt flesh would inevitably lead to the same phenomenon in the body, besmirching the machine. Nevertheless, it is possible that the myth contains a bit of truth, because the meat sold in the public butcher shops was fresh, too fresh—too hot, as one said then—according to our own standards and our own gustatory requirements. The meat of the day is soft and tasteless; meat killed the day before is much tenderer after cooking. Could we hypothesize that the "hot," twitching meat of a retired beast, sent to the butcher only when it could no longer serve in the field, was the meat of choice? Even if the animal had first been put out to pasture to fatten up, it was middle-aged. The consumer was a gerontophile by taste or necessity; he ate beef that was never less than thirty months old and more often five or ten years old and mutton that was three years old. The flesh was not really old; regulations forbade that, especially from old sow and old cow, which were both given horrible nicknames. But mature bulls were eaten. This practice offered the additional guarantee that older animals had had time to develop symptoms of diseases perhaps undetectable in younger animals. But this fact remains: a time limit on sales did not guarantee a time limit on consumption.

Though, as we have said, the moderns developed few new standards otherwise, they did, nevertheless, create standards for time limits. But it was a matter of a minimum date of sale. In sixteenth-century Avignon, slaughtering took place every day at the municipal Calade slaughter grounds, and meat was sold at the nearby butcher shop at the palace square *no less* than four hours after slaughtering. In Valréas and Bédarrides, animals killed in the morning had to be put on sale by evening, and those slaughtered during the vesper hour had to be sold in the morning, so that the flesh would still be cold at the time of delivery.[18] The leases of modern butcher shops repeated the invariable formula: it was necessary to kill in the evening for the morning and the morning for the evening "so that the meat had time to dry out." How are we to interpret such legislative laxness that approaches our current standards: Less fear of the putridness that was an obsession in medieval times? A change in taste? It really seems that health precautions and putrid meat were still the concern, but the moderns perceived the risks of meat that was too old as well as meat that was too fresh, too humid, that threatened to provoke "dangerous fermentations." In 1559 three Paris butchers were sentenced for having sold "flesh that was too hot, which is contrary to health."[19]

The freshness of fish and seafood, as well as tripe, preoccupied the town councillors. In Geneva, fish had to be sold within one day in the summer, two days in the winter, and three days for large trout, pike, and perch. In Ornans and in Dole, the tripe butchers "will not keep or permit to be kept those tripe more than twenty-four hours after they have been cooked."[20] In all the Paris markets, oysters were not sold from May through August, that is, only during the months with an R in them. As for milk, it was sold "upon leaving the udder of the animal" and in any case within a day at the most.[21]

Flesh Unworthy of Entering the Human Body

Unhealthy meat is given the place of honor in the texts. The oldest ones use the comprehensive term *morie*, which has given rise to a small lexicographical debate: Does it designate all infected meat?[22] An epizootic disease?[23] Most of the ordinances specified what category was to be excluded from human consumption. Depending on the place, the qualification was in Latin, "caro infirma, morbosa, morbifera"; or in Occitan, "ni carn estissada no pudenta ni crabot ni anhet" (Lectoure, 1280) or "ni auze vendre en lo dich mazel comun

carns de moria o feldas o botadas o remolhadas" (Montpellier, 1368);
or in the language of the French king, denouncing meats that were
"gravides, morbifères, glaireuses or morveuses, mélancoliques, chaudes,
infirmes." From this wide spectrum of a fluid and variable nosology,
let us try to isolate two categories: meats with parasitic diseases and
meats with bacterial diseases.

Suspicions were particularly strong with regard to leprous pigs. In
Carpentras in 1437, butchers were ordered not to sell pig flesh without
having had it examined to see if the pigs were leprous.[24] This precaution was almost ubiquitous. Leprosy was identified by leprous vesicles,
called grains. Thus flesh that was "grainy," "seeded," or "leprous" fell
into one and the same category, banned for consumption. The pig's
visit with a *langueyeur* was mandatory. One could not just suddenly
become a *langueyeur*, and a decree from the provost of Paris established
the conditions necessary for being named that kind of expert: "Let no
one act as pig *langueyeur* until the master butcher has testified that he
is an expert and knowledgeable in this."[25] Once the diagnostic examination was over, the *langueyeur* decided if the pig was leprous in the
first degree, in which case he marked the ear, or if it was definitively
leprous, in which case he cut the ear. This ear marking facilitated
"traceability."[26] That the pig came from nearby, that it issued from the
flourishing urban stock of animals, fed on the wastes and by-products
of the urban artisan class, did not reassure the legislators; in fact, quite
the opposite.

One measure was adopted in some cities like Marseilles and Arles
in the early thirteenth century and spread throughout France and
Italy following the Great Plague. It forbade the roaming of pigs in
the streets. It is generally interpreted as reflecting another type of
health concern, a concern for clean air. That, however, reduces the
town pig to its single organic function of leaving refuse in the streets
or its reverse, of serving as refuse collector. The legislators may well
have recognized another aspect of letting pigs roam and may have
considered how pigs ate: if they ate badly, consuming unclean food,
didn't that present a danger for human consumption? An ordinance
from John the Good is quite suggestive. In 1363 it was forbidden
"to kill flesh of no matter what kind that was fed in the house of
the oil maker, the barber, or the leper house."

Here we have an abstract of fears: the taboo of blood, the blood
of sick humans that the barbers, who were surgeons and bloodlet-
ters, disposed of from their shops; the suspicion of leprosy among
those who lived in the leper houses; and, above all, the question of

the quality of food for livestock, itself a guarantee of the quality of human food. It was indecent, for example, for omnivores to be fed on animal flesh. There was no question of raising pigs in the vicinity of the slaughter grounds, where they could ingest the remains left from butchering.[27] Swayed by this fear of animal feed, the legislature went a long way when it forbade not only lepers, who were perpetually ostracized, from raising urban livestock but also certain tradesmen: barbers everywhere; surgeons and apothecaries in Troyes; blacksmiths in Angers, Saumur, and Pontoise; fishmongers; and oil makers.[28] Here was compiled a blacklist of dangerous animal foods: human blood, flesh, the oil cakes and residues from oil pressing, fish scraps. Omnivores were not allowed to eat just anything, not even cultivated plants like hempseed, a variety of hemp.[29] Leprous or drugged, the pig might transmit that condition to humans through blood or pork sausage.

Ultimately, the only by-products of urban industry considered safe for poultry or pigs were the leftovers from bolting flour. Bakers profited from this, feeding pigs on flour and its wastes in their backyards. It was an essential complement to their occupation. "The trade," said the bailiff of Langres, "might decline and be abandoned if the tradesmen could not keep and fatten pigs to use up their bran and other waste products."[30] Force-fed in this way, the pigs were so fat that they could hardly move, often making their last journey by cart—thus in defiance of the well-known rule requiring arrival on foot.[31] Some bakers expanded this backyard livestock business to almost industrial levels, like Jean Griffon, who raised sixty pigs right in the heart of Amiens in 1475. But, once on the market or the fair ground, city pigs were not on equal footing with forest pigs. Nonleprous pigs were divided into two groups: in the first group were pigs fed on beechnuts, acorns, and chestnuts, that is, those wild and natural foods that made for prize pork flesh; in the other group were the other pigs, all just as healthy, but fed on grain and bran. This dual selection, between leprous and healthy and then between rural foraging and urban force-feeding, shows how precautions increased.

Was animal pathology different beyond the Loire? In northern regulations, we see the appearance of a disease rarely mentioned elsewhere (Narbonne constitutes an exception) and involving "large animals." It is le fil or fy, or sometimes la pommeliere. Du Cange, the great French scholar whose authoritative dictionary of Late Latin is reputed to have helped historians read charters, interprets fy thus: "elephantiasis, disease of cattle, a type of leprosy." Du Cange was undoubtedly the victim of the leprosy obsession. In contrast, most veterinarian researchers have translated *fy* as tuberculosis. In 1363 King John the Good banned bulls and cows stricken with *fy* from the capital. In Normandy as well, suspicion was directed toward meat from cows whose blood did not clot, as the butchers said, no doubt tubercular in some form or another. In 1487 Rouen butchers prohibited the sale of meat from cows "*entichées de fy*" (*entichées* here means intoxicated). The same prohibition was applied in Evreux and Caen. Tubercular meat had to be seized and burned or thrown in the river. Burning was more effective. For a long time, infected meat was swept along in the Seine, the Rhine, and the Rhône. In Avignon, the provisions masters spotted rotten meat in the butcher stalls that had been fished from the Rhône upstream, washed, and offered once more to the consumer. Discovering this antituberculosis legislation in the 1930s, a veterinarian marveled: "Regarding tuberculosis, [medieval] legislation proves truly fierce: total seizure in all cases.... Compared to the measures legislated in the decree of January 24, 1934, total seizure seems draconian to us. But can the legislator be blamed for his extreme prudence, dictated by philanthropic concern?"[32]

Uncertain about the dangers of tuberculous meat, still not totally clear in 1934, the medieval legislator took extreme precautions, and the republican veterinarian remained skeptical.

The last element in this regulatory nucleus: butchers were forbidden to sell cooked meat. This was in order to defend the monopoly of the "*chaircuitiers*," the only ones authorized to sell *chair cuite*, cooked meat. As a corollary, only butchers had the right to sell raw meat, and it was from them that delicatessen owners and other "sausage makers" had to get their supplies. The law traced complex, fragile, and fluid boundaries between the various food trades, with consumer health appearing as part of its rationale. The monopoly was thus justified by the desire to keep unhealthy meat from being recycled: "A butcher cannot sell cooked meat, because then it would be too easy for him to cut up meat of poor quality; for the same reason, innkeepers, pastrycooks, roast meat sellers, and caterers must not practice the trade of butchering, because then one has no assurance of the goodness of the meat that they cut up."[33]

The sale of salted meat at fairs was forbidden in certain places "because it is impossible to recognize the disease when the skin is removed."[34] Without skin or entrails, it was impossible to detect a possible disease. Evidently, it was the whole animal, living and walking, that could reassure the consumer.

The statutes of 1475 for Paris charcuteries recommended covering "said cooked meats with clean, white, linen cloths."[35] The tripe sellers in Besançon had to present their products in baskets covered "with beautiful drapery, very white and very clean ... to protect it from flies and all other filth."[36] This is one of the rare instances that flies are mentioned. One can read hundreds of southern statutes and never see a word about flies. The fly was so present that it was invisible. Other sources tell us that it was present, omnipresent, and pervasive. In the kitchens, for example, they never left "as long as there was grain or sugar."[37] But, as ubiquitous as they were, they were felt to represent no danger. Maggots were considered the product of spontaneous generation. Why protect oneself from flies when one knew that they were not the mothers of maggots? Parisian delicatessens took unnecessary precautions.

Attention to cleanliness and hygiene within the trades appeared after 1350, with the wave of plagues, and only in northern regulations. Besançon butchers had to be "healthy and clean of body, having nice, clean hands," their aprons were to be very clean also and scraped each day.[38] As for customers, they were forbidden "to touch with their hands or handle said flesh, except with a very white and very clean stick that said butchers must have before them in their aprons." Beginning in 1450, bakers in Rennes were required to have their hair and beards cut once every three week, to wear clean shirts, and to avoid kneading bread if their hands were "infected with ulcers."[39] In Chartres, to become a butcher, one had to testify to being free of scrofula and epilepsy, by which, it was believed, tuberculosis or undulant fever could be transmitted through the intermediary of handled meat.[40] Thus the risk of contamination, in all its forms, was implicitly recognized.

Such precautions against a different kind of food pollution were absent from the southern urban regulations: we can no longer speak here of a common normative fund or of a widely shared hygienic culture. Of course, the lack of standards does not signify the lack of cleanliness in actual practice, and perhaps some butchers did shoo flies off meat, like Jean Trouvé, the butcher friend whom François Villon names in this list of legatees:

Item: to the butcher Jean Trouvé
I leave *The Sheep*, fat and tender,
and a swatter, to keep the flies off
The Crowned Ox, which is for sale,
and *The Cow* too.[41]

Untouchable Foods

The urban *Codex alimentarius* offered a selection of preventive measures, falling within the sphere of health and safety, that were reassuring, familiar, and rational. But all things are not equal, and sometimes the standards varied. That was the case in certain Mediterranean cities where Jews and Christians lived together.

That Jews had to have special meats posed problems that were reflected both in urban regulations and in the statutes Jewish communities issued for themselves, intent on observing the distinction between permissible meat—kosher—and impure meat, called "treif."

In all the cities where Jewish communities existed, two separate butcher shops were provided for. "Let the *mazel* of the Jews be separate from the *mazel* of the Christians" is the usual regulation.[42] This segregation was confirmed in Arles about 1200 and in Montpellier in the fourteenth century: "Henceforward let no *mazelier* or the other have the audacity to sell or have sold in the public butcher shop of Montpellier any *viande sagatée*, but in a separate place."[43]

Viande sagatée was the meat of animals slaughtered following Jewish ritual by a *sagataïre*. Since the technique for ritual slaughter demanded an entire apprenticeship and could not be practiced by just anyone, it was rarely the rabbi who performed it in Comtat communities but rather a specialist who came from outside, sometimes from very far away, from Italy or Poland, for instance. Thus the rabbi, the *sagataïre*, and the butcher were three distinct figures.[44] But the word *sagater*, which always appears in the regional languages, was charged with weighty connotations. In a more general and very pejorative sense, *sagater* meant to spoil, to degrade, almost the equivalent of "botch" or "bungle." That was exactly the ambiguity inherent in this segregation rule for butchers that admitted so few exceptions. On the one hand, as a separation demanded and accepted by both communities, who saw it as a necessary affirmation of their identities, it seems only natural. On the other hand, the word *sagater* introduced an image of Jewish food and meat fraught with tensions. Meat "according to the law" was characterized in certain texts as "unclean" or "sordid." Those who sold it were perfidious Jews.[45]

Two factors heightened the conflict, both clearly alluded to in the preamble of an important legal text: "So that there be no communion between the Christians and the Jews, let the Jewish *mazel* be separate from the *mazel* of the faithful, so that the meat prepared following Judaic custom—being understood that this is necessary to them—which exceeds their own needs and which is put on sale, not be bought by Christians."[46]

The first difficulty was a practical one: when the Jewish community was very small, it was difficult for them to maintain a butcher shop. And, if there was one, it was difficult to dispose of all the meat, not to mention the hindquarters of the slaughtered beasts, considered improper for consumption but nevertheless in need of an outlet. Thus there was the potential for exchanges between Jewish and Christian butcher shops or for mixed clientele, which greatly displeased the city magistrates. "It is said that they [the Jewish butchers] sell in the Christian *mazel*."[47] The rumor reported here was from Arles but was also encountered elsewhere.

The first difficulty led to the second one. If there was no systematic segregation of consumption, then both communities were threatened by the risk of commensalism. The text uses the word "communion," which has clear religious connotations. Noël Coulet has shown how this Christian requirement to separate the two butcher shops and the two paths of consumption related back to recommendations from the church. Ecclesiastical policy was established by the Council of Albi in 1254 and the Council of Nîmes in 1286. The Midi bishops categorically forbade all Christians from using Jewish foods and beverages, since the Jews refused some Christian foods and beverages.[48] The Christian prohibition was meant to respond to another prohibition. The statutes of Pernes explicitly demonstrate this: "As it is prescribed to each person to keep his distance in any contact [*contagio*] with Jews and in sharing their meals, … just as those Jews keep their distance from us, we rule that no Jewish merchant dare to slaughter according to their ritual animals either large or small within the walls of the town of Pernes."[49]

We are thus in that ambiguous cultural context where each community seems to be trying to protect its identity through the principal markers, which are food and clothing. Rabbis expressed their own desire that fellow Jews be distinguished from the rest of society at the same time that the Council of Latran sought to require Jews to wear *la rouelle*, a round, colored piece of cloth. It seemed as though acculturation was taking place, except that it prompted reaction and resistance on both sides, from the church as well as the rabbis.[50] It would be anachronistic to say that twelfth-century urban statutes addressed this concern for distinction, that civil regulations thus distilled the church's recommendations. The first rules on untouchable foods preceded the demands of the clergy, and with heavy consequences for the very spirit of the law.

To enforce respect for the separation of butcher shops, the laws created a food border. The first regression: rotten meat and meat "of the law" were classed together. In 1243 the statues of Avignon assigned to the same category flesh from diseased animals and flesh from animals slaughtered by Jews. In this move of counterseparatism by Christians in opposition to Jewish separatism, Christians forgot they had no food taboos, that meat fell strictly within the worldly domain. They invented categories of acceptable and unclean meat that replicated the kosher/treif duality. But the regression continued, and from untouchable meat came the untouchable Jew. In 1221 Narbonne quite clearly forbid Jews to do commerce in lost girls and meat, rotten meat in particular.[51] It was around food, not just meat, that the image of the scapegoat Jew was constructed. In Avignon, the statutes recorded in the mid-thirteenth century and repeated in 1441 ordered "that Jews and prostitutes not have the audacity to touch with their hands either bread or fruit that is offered for sale." More specifically, these impure ones were required to buy what they had touched.

Expressed here was the widespread belief that Jews transmitted, through contact, an unhealthy defilement. This conviction was shared in many Mediterranean cities, where we find the same injunction, even in the same terms or sometimes embellished. In Salon, the contaminating duo of Jew/prostitute was replaced with a formidable trio, prostitute/Jew/leper, completing the confusion between moral and hygienic defilement. In Gerona, in Catalonia, the list of foods susceptible to being tainted by Jewish hands grew longer: it included bread, cake, meat, fresh cheeses, fresh or salted fish, fresh fruits, grapes, figs, onions, cabbage, and spinach. The way this confusion systematically appeared in Catalan regulations and more sporadically in Provençal regulations gives the impression of a "feature of social psychology" very widespread in popular thinking.[52]

Let us compare the role of dirty hands in the butcher shops of the House of Burgundy and of southern France. We can discern a similar intuition about the role of touch in contamination, of course, but the moral frameworks are not comparable. The Burgundy law, cited previously, was located within the realm of rational precautions, the other in the world of fantasy.

In these anti-Judaic regulations, it is never apparent how such contact would be harmful to the food. By touching the product, did the Jew poison it, in the same way as, later, he was accused of poisoning water in the well? The textual proximity of Jew and leper would make one think of contagion. But the affinities between Jew and prostitute suggest another course. The prostitute was an impure woman, as all women were on certain days of the month, according to deeply rooted belief. On those days, their presence, their contact, or their breath in the cellar or at the salting tub could provoke alimentary catastrophe. "If one wants to kill a pig, one does not kill it that day, because all the meat would turn." The list of female curses was very long. Here is one: "The woman being in her month, walking by beds of melon, squash, and cucumbers, makes them dry up and die; the fruit that survives will be bitter."[53] The mysterious power of women exerted itself against fresh, moist, and perishable foodstuffs, like pork, melon, or cucumber. Its nature was to putrefy. By making what they touched or even what they passed "turn," menstruating women accelerated the natural process of decay. Perhaps it is not too far-fetched to connect the food prohibitions regarding women with those involving the "impure" Jew. The female in heat was quite lawfully spurned in butchering regulations. It was forbidden to butcher or offer for sale cows or sows in heat or even ones that had just given birth. A legal waiting period had to be observed for "the heated beasts to cool off," providing the butcher with healthier meat. The waiting period varied according to the species and the place: it was anywhere from nine days to six weeks long. If Jews had the same power as impure women, it was apparently more potent, since, in Gerona, they contaminated not only fresh produce but also raisins and dried figs.

One contamination hides another. Another kind of contamination seems to have emerged from the imaginary danger of food contamination through impure touch. The sacred seems contagious. Through contact with the Jewish community, Christian legislation forgot its own perspective and invented taboos. Drive away your demons and they will return to haunt you. Why else would a secular food culture find it so difficult to dispose of the sacred entirely, to relegate the notion of cleanliness to the kitchen or the backroom of the butcher shop? The sacred seems contagious; certain popular beliefs became part of the Christian faith. The Christian woman was impure on certain days, so she had to be extra cautious in her contact with food, indeed even avoid it. Certain plants were good for one's health; consider, for example, sage, the plant that saved. But beneficial foods did not, paradoxically, guarantee eternal salvation, only good health. This was the revenge of the sacred, and the strong comeback of the notion of defilement in regulatory texts was negative proof of it.

In terms of food, a Judeo-Christian culture did not exist; there are two cultures. In the thirteenth century, they clearly confronted each other, perhaps even collided. It is not certain if local laws echoed popular opinion, or if, on the contrary, they tried to create a pollution phobia that paved the way or accompanied the accusations of poisoning leveled against Jews during the Black Death and the first pogroms.

Nor do we know if townspeople believed in their regulations, especially when the strictness of the law was meant to compensate for the difficulties of implementing the butcher shops' separation. Documentation of daily life shows that these measures were very rarely observed and that transgressions were common. We find butchers of the two religions cooperating without shame, and Nîmes prostitutes with their hands white from kneading pastry for the town officials to offer to the poor for the Feast of Ascension. Neither Jews nor prostitutes rendered the food they touched untouchable, and marginal status did not imply marginal economic means.[54] In reality, in the marketplace, proximity had the edge over segregation, despite efforts to draw lines. Here we see the limits of our sources: regulatory standards were not simply translations of everyday behavior. Between the law and actual practice, there might have been harmonious agreement, or great discrepancy, or anything in between. In the case of rules regarding Jewish butcher shops, transgressions occurred because the law was not credible. For other health precautions, the law was a matter of the *normal*, that is, of respectable—even if not always respected—norms.

THREE

THE BIRTH OF THE CONSUMER

The word *consommateur* (consumer) appeared in the French language in the twelfth century. At that time, it was used rarely and inconsistently, applied basically to big eaters: "It is a devourer and consumer of food to excess."[1] Is it risking an anachronism to extend the term to the new type of eater just then emerging, whose main characteristics were that he was a city dweller, a carnivore, and more or less protected by the laws of his town?

The new consumer was situated at the end of a long process that he recounted to himself thus: at the very origins of man and his history with food, we do not find the dark mists of time but a luminous golden age. The humans of the past—a past before the Flood—lived close to nature, consuming what mother earth provided for them. They ate healthily, equipped with primitive and tough stomachs that allowed them to digest an uncultivated and crude diet of milk, acorns, and berries. They were not subject to diseases, and they died at a very old age. This belief was drawn from a good source: the Old Testament is full of aged men, nine hundred or more years old.[2] But there is also this, from Genesis: "the Lord said, 'My spirit shall not abide in man for ever, for he is flesh, but his days shall be a hundred and twenty years.'"[3] The doctor Laurent Joubert established the natural life span of modern man to be "six twenty years," and people of his time considered a full life to resemble Christ's, dead at thirty-three years old.[4] Through difficult circumstances and the passing of time, humans experienced a decline, obvious in their longevity, their stature, and their digestive capacities.[5] And, bemoaning his sad human condition, a life condemned to death, man sought the means for prolonging his existence.

The consumer of the ancien régime knew that he was smaller and more fragile than his ancestors and that his was a worn-out stomach. In addition, he had to seek his food farther and farther afield, and thus, having become urban, *he no longer knew what he ate.* It was this anguish that pierced the modern consumer and nourished his fears.

The Long Route

There were, and for a long time there would be, two food circuits. For those who lived in the country, the route was short. Those consumers were also producers; they knew what they ate, as their food came from their own labor or followed a direct route involving their family or village. The country dweller nearly always kept livestock, sometimes tended sheep, and occasionally acted as butcher when he slaughtered a pig or sheep, alone or with others. But, as soon as the urban market was established, the assumptions underlying food stocks were fundamentally altered. It happened sometimes that the city dweller remained a producer, the town being a place where fruits and vegetables were grown in enclosed gardens and where very fat pigs were raised. But most of the time, he was reduced to the status of passive consumer. As for the city, it did not stand idly by waiting to be supplied. It organized what it drew from the surrounding countryside to best provide for itself and carved into the flat lands an alimentary basin. Foodstuffs came not just from the country nearby but from a supply area that expanded when the population grew or in times of shortage. During famine, Toulouse imported wheat from Sicily, England, Limagne, and Burgundy. For meat, the route also lengthened. Although they were regional centers and home to fairs, small cities like Carpentras or Grasse had trouble being self-sufficient. Their appeal to Haute-Provence established a whole circuit of exchanges between the mountains, the true reservoir of meat, and the plain, a circuit strengthened by the seasonal movement of livestock between the highlands and the lowlands. Marseilles appealed to livestock producers from Marvejols and Vivarais.[6] Haut-Dauphiné specialized in raising sheep, and entire herds of livestock left from Briançon, destined for the Piedmont, the Po river plain, Turin, or Genoa.[7] Cities sometimes sought provisions from very far away; Venice, for example, with more than one hundred thousand mouths to feed, sought beef cattle from as far away as Hungary. The pastoral regions of the Pannonian plain supplied Austria, Poland, and especially the large Italian ports. An international market was thus established for livestock, not to mention other long-distance importation circuits, whether of salted cod, sugar, or spices like the so-called seed of paradise coming from so faraway and almost legendary a source. The city created a new eater, reduced to the status of consumer and very far removed from the sources of provisions. Destabilized, cut off from the country, the urban consumer no longer knew what he ate and no longer ate the same things as his rural counterpart. The urban economy created a new model of consumption.

Among other ruptures, the transfer from the country to the city disrupted eating behaviors.[8] In 1837 the Academy of Medicine launched a major inquiry in France on health in rural areas, complete with questionnaires. All the mayors were invited to respond to a certain number of questions, including the following: specify if the place has a sufficient number of inhabitants to consume fresh meat.[9] This was the essential question: it was impossible to have a butcher shop, to slaughter beef cattle daily, without assembling a large enough contingent of consumers. The rural eater was condemned to salt pork and mutton. Consuming fresh "green" meat was the exception, dependent on a collective holiday or an individual misfortune, like an animal's getting injured. One fifteenth-century document from Béarn cites that a cow and two kids were killed for a funeral feast.[10] Where there existed the right of *carnelage*, which consisted of confiscating and slaughtering a strange animal that came to graze in the community pasture through accident or malice, the slaughtered beast was divided up among all the parishioners on Sunday, after the church service. With ten thousand mouths—the population figure many cities attained in the thirteenth century—the urban privilege of regularly slaughtering large livestock became common practice.

The high levels of urban consumption attained in the early fourteenth century are striking. This was the century of many herds and few humans, decimated by recurring plagues. We can speak of a carnivorous Europe according to the numbers given by Abel, who estimated that in fifteenth-century Germany, the annual meat ration per inhabitant was one hundred kilos, or over two hundred pounds. This was a prosperous time, when a kind of physiological optimum was achieved. After that, carnivorous Europe declined, to varying degrees, according to place and environment, as we can see by figuring and refiguring the calculations we can make thanks to the bookkeeping of town butcher shops. The annual ration seems to have been closer to twenty-six kilos per inhabitant in Carpentras in 1472, and twenty to forty kilos in Touraine.[11] Let us not quibble over annual rations. What matters is the high number of butchers: there were 177 in Toulouse in 1322, and a good dozen in the little town of Mirepoix. What matters is that abundance was the rule in the marketplaces, that prices were low, so low that sustenance on the days one ate meat was a third less expensive than on the days one did not, so low that even the poor, or the less poor, could take part in this carnivorous feast. In 1348 in Sicily, a worker in the slaughterhouses received, in addition to his monthly salary, a basket of three loaves of bread a day and two to four kilos of meat a week.[12]

A model of urban consumption was established, in which meat constituted the basic value. City dwellers consumed less and less salt meat, which had been the prime meat for everyone in earlier centuries. They ate fresh meat, the rich preferring beef and veal, the less wealthy settling for mutton or pork, but always fresh, which distinguished them from countryfolk. It was the quality of such meat, as well as the quantity consumed, that constituted an urban privilege. Another privilege was consuming bread and forsaking gruel made from secondary grains, which remained the standard base of the rural diet. The urban diet was indisputably superior to the traditional diet. The urbanite ate meat daily, sometimes twice daily in the wealthiest circles or most prosperous times, regularly drank wine, ate fish and fresh bread.

While traveling in his native region of the Cévennes, one city dweller heard locals repeatedly tell him, "I don't like fresh meat," or more precisely, "I don't like the smell of fresh meat." He noted that habits determined tastes: "The inhabitants of our mountains have a natural aversion to that kind of meat."[13] The matter was settled: fresh meat was for ogres and urbanites. As a social symbol, it was perfect. As food, it was ambiguous: good to eat, certainly, but humid in nature, perishable, its putrid fermentation capable of rapidly spreading to the whole human body. Flesh was a high-risk food.

There is a close tie between the emergence of rules on food quality and the first urbanization trends in the West. The explanation is not to be found in municipal autonomy and the appearance of elected officials, which were neither necessary conditions—the lords could do all this just as well—nor sufficient: autonomy provided the legislative tools, nothing more. These means served a political will, that of the oligarchy who ran the cities, representing the "fat people," the carnivores, well-fed and nervous about the contents of the dishes on their plates. The reason for the laws lay in this anxiety and in the desire to protect themselves from food risks.

A Two-Speed System

The fat people and the little people. There were two categories of city dwellers, and the local laws not only took into account this fundamental social division, they reinforced and solidified it by organizing two types of butcher shops and, even more important, by distinguishing two types of consumers.

We speak of butcher shops as one thing, even though an entire former system of butchering carefully distinguished between the public butcher shop, on the one hand, and the lower butcher shop, on the other, with transactions between them being strictly forbidden. In southern areas, *mazel* and *bocaria* were not equivalent terms. In Carpentras, the *mazel* and the *boucherie* were found on either side of the cathedral. The 1455 regulations explicitly stated that these two designations corresponded to categories and qualities of different meats. At the *bocaria*, one could only buy inferior meats, like those from male and female goats (*bouc* and *chèvre*). This distinction between the town butcher shop and the common butcher shop was very widespread, although not the norm.[14] Sometimes the shops were separated into two markets or two locations, sometimes they could coexist at the same site: at the big market in Marseilles, forty tables were set up for the *mazel* and seven for the *bocaria*, and, in Tholonet, there were twenty-nine and twelve, respectively.[15] Known as the *banca parva*, or the *petit reng* in Normandy, or the *Freibank* in the Holy Roman Empire, the institution of the *petite boucherie* spread throughout Europe and even beyond, when the Spanish exported it to Latin America. The *carn de rafali* of Spanish town ordinances was transposed into *ollo del pobre* in Santiago, Chile.[16]

The small shop butcher was inferior to the *macellier*, since he sold lower-priced meats, not the cheapest bits, over which the tripe dealers had a monopoly, but less noble flesh than beef, mutton, and fresh pork. He offered goat, sow, bull, ram, and, depending on the time and place, other meats.[17] In Auch, the small butcher shops were "stocked in the requisite seasons with pig, lamb, salted and lean sheep, kid and gosling."[18] There, as in all of Gascony, the big butcher shops were equipped with stalls or permanent "benches," while the small ones had more temporary, mobile installations, also called benches, but in the feminine form (*bancs/banques*). Here, as elsewhere, the transition from masculine to feminine indicated a pejorative.

For the common folk, second-rate meat was less expensive and also less abundant: small butcher stalls were less numerous, for a clientele of theoretically more numerous "little people." But the common folk had access to a third market, mentioned in but not regulated by the statutes, a free market where rotting meat could be procured. When the magistrates said, "we have decided that leprous or unwholesome meat will not be sold in the butcher shop," they added, "we want it to be sold in a place far away from the public butcher shop." In Alès, the sick cow, arriving in a cart, was solemnly forbidden from being sold in the *mazel* and no less officially offered for sale in another part of the city. The severity of the regulations regarding butcher shops went hand in hand with an almost absolute liberalism regarding what took place outside these establishments. The sale of sick or hurt animals was not formally prohibited: it could be done in certain places; the seller and law officers were only obliged to see to it that the buyer was forewarned.[19] The Avignon statutes of 1243, the Grasse statutes of 1262, and the Mazan statutes of 1381 provided for places where such meat could be sold. Throughout the fifteenth century, the council proceedings of Barjols repeated that the meat from sick animals had to be sold in one specific town square.

The fate of the pig illustrates this two- or three-speed system. Declared healthy, the pig was found in the public butcher shop stall or, after cooking, in the stall of the *charcutier*. Declared leprous in the first degree, it was sold in Paris's central food market after an appropriate treatment: "The pigs with flesh only seeded with a few leprous grains can be repaired ...; if the flesh is not yet corrupt, salt can correct the malignancy, one can then use it without risk ...; the flesh of seeded pig should be put in salt for fourteen days ...; then sold in a particular corner of the market, [indicated] by a post and a white flag."[20] If it was recognized by the *langueyeur* as leprous in the last degree, "of twenty-four carats," and thus absolutely harmful, the pig was given to the prisoners of the king, under Louis XI, or thrown into the Seine, under Louis XIV.[21] Elsewhere, it was given to lepers or even included in the charitable offerings distributed by town magistrates. This official benevolence extended to all confiscated meats, when they were not either thrown into the river or burned: "If meats are neither good nor healthy, let them be seized and distributed to the poor."[22] In Gascony, those scraps seized by the police constituted a category called *escarpits*. *Escarpits* were generally distributed "for the love of God to the poor and destitute people,"[23] and it was rare, given the economics of shortage, for them to be thrown into the Adour or the Garonne rivers. Beginning with the first attempts to get the poor off the streets, public distribution was replaced by donations to assistance organizations. Thus charities and leper houses recycled rotting or parasitized meat and enjoyed the privilege of benefiting from the blood of the slaughter.

While one part of the meat business was very carefully supervised, conducted within a strict network of prohibitions and inspections, another part was conducted in total freedom, by virtue of health laws that were not the same for everyone.

The Myth of Digestion

We must consider municipal legislation in the context of its cultural climate. It is significant that urban legislation came into being at a time when medicine was making its appearance in the universities. It was around the great university towns of Montpellier and Bologna and under the influence of their medical and law schools that the earliest municipal legislation flourished, as well as in the shadow cast by Rome and the thirteenth-century papal court, so extraordinarily interested in medicine and eagerly rewriting the myth of prolonged life and rejuvenation.[24] There was certainly a gap between learned discourse and what the scholars called popular ideas, and one would have to look hard to see the point at which scholarly thinking did nor did not influence popular images. Here it is enough to consider the widely held conception of health as a context for the health measures adopted in the towns.

What did the urban magistrate and lawmaker know about human physiology? His body was a black box, impenetrable to him. How the body itself was made, its bone structure, the arrangement of the organs, was not well-known, and it would take men of science much longer to complete the exploration of human anatomy than it took them to map the vast oceans. As for the functioning of the body, which, with Fernel in the sixteenth century, came to be called physiology, it could only be understood through hypotheses that allowed current medical theories to be received and interpreted. Knowledge was created through the analogical method. The invisible was reconstructed beginning from the visible, from the known. Two images in particular structured the representation of the body.

The first metaphor was the machine. The body was a machine, in which the heart and brain, the liver and testicles struggled for dominance, except that there was also a well-defined hierarchy of organs. Another organ, connected directly to the liver, was considered the king of the viscera. This was the stomach, one of this corporal machine's three motors, since, along with the heart and the brain, it was one of the vital heat centers. When warmed, it transformed what was eaten into four humors, liquid or moist, that permeated the body and maintained it in good health. The stomach was first represented as a soup pot where foods were cooked. In the Renaissance, another image took over, via the alchemical method and the success of distillation. The cucurbit, equipped with tubes and a spout, gave the best idea of this gastric alchemy, this distillation that transformed foods into chyle and then into humors.[25] The imaginary machine also took the form of a mill, with a millstone for crushing and grinding, or even an oven: "We also see how that very excellent alchemist our good Lord built his oven (which is the body of man), with so beautiful and so right a structure, that there is nothing to redesign: with its necessary vents and registers, which are the mouth, the nose, the ears, the eyes; in order to retain in this oven a temperate heat and a continual, aerated, bright, and well-regulated fire, for performing all his alchemical operations."[26]

The second image, directly related to the first, used the kitchen as the explanatory model for digestion. At the end of that mysterious transformation produced by "successive coctions," or repeated cooking, ingested foods became humors. Phlegm, cold and moist in nature and centered in the brain, was a poorly cooked humor. Blood was the model of a perfectly cooked humor; bile and melancholy were overcooked humors.

Provided with this medical imagery, one could understand many things about internal operations: how the humors rose or fell with age and the rhythm of the seasons; how one humor predominated in the body of each individual, determining one's temperament or complexion to be phlegmatic, sanguine, bilious (or atrabilious), or melancholic; how all sorts of receptacles or "vessels" (another term borrowed from cooking) contained and transported the four precious fluids in the body. If this or that humor became too abundant or too thick, if it became corrupt, then the pipelines backed up, the digestive tubes became blocked, the residues could no longer be eliminated, and they rotted. This rotting released noxious vapors that poisoned the brain and the heart, and thus the machine broke down and disease took over.

The success of the humor theory stemmed from its implications for the healthy body as much as those for disease. Health was conditioned by *eucrasie*, or the equilibrium of the humors, while their disequilibrium, or *dyscrasie*, caused illness. For two thousand years, people knew that disease was a disturbance of the humors, resulting from an interaction between an individual's constitution and an exterior factor, whether the climate, diet, or exercise. In the worst configurations, the interaction between "something unnatural" and someone's "nature" resulted in that "thing against nature" that was disease.

That was the generally accepted representation, powerfully bound up with the Galenic paradigm.[27] We can understand what gave it its power and its capacity to resist any discoveries contradicting it for two thousand years. It was a system of perfect clarity for explaining an internal world that was perfectly obscure. The secret of its longevity lies in the intellectual disposition of men who, confronting scientific uncertainty and the unknown and presented with two theories, always choose the one that is more intelligible and easier to represent visually and reject the more complicated or less decipherable one that, nevertheless, would have a better chance of adhering to the complexity of the living thing.

People in the thirteenth and fourteenth centuries focused their attention on the phenomena of digestion and nutrition in this human machine. By the same token, they attached much importance to food. Of course, the air one breathed was more necessary to life and more dangerous, since it penetrated the body unmediated, but how could its quality be controlled? Foods prompted more interest because one had some say over them. Between 1250 and 1300, the style of medicine that developed and began to be taught in the universities in Paris, Montpellier, and Bologna seized on that question. Far from being limited to medical disputations, the debate extended far beyond the medical schools and informed a vast interdisciplinary (or rather nonspecialized) field in which the physical and metaphysical were intertwined. Physicians dealt with it, as did theologians and preachers. All the important scholars of the period discussed food issues to a greater or lesser extent: the English Franciscans, Roger Bacon, Ockham and the Oxford Circle, Arnaud de Villeneuve and Bernard de Gourdon of the University of Montpellier. Nutrition nurtured philosophical debates that struggled with the question of assimilation: ad-similare. One assimilated food, but at the same time it became one's body and similar to it. "If food is, at the beginning, different from the eaten, it must be that it divests itself of this difference and, through various changes, is rendered like the eaten, in order that it can be food."[28]

This was a mysterious phenomenon, very worthy of the attention and reflection of thinkers, physicians, and metaphysicians, because, between this mundane transubstantiation and the Eucharist, one could imagine points in common, even an impious comparison.

The other debate that sparked research at the time bore on the transmission of original sin. Was it possible for this gene to be transmitted from Adam the father to us through nutrition? This was to pose the question of the nature of human flesh. The most widely accepted proposition considered humans to be a mix of two kinds of flesh, an essential flesh in which nutrition played no part and a material flesh that maintained the body's innate heat. Only the essential flesh would be resurrected.[29] Of course, here we enter sophisticated, scholastic debates, but they have the merit of showing what bright intellectual incandescence the questions raised by the "little fire" of the stomach had sparked. For Gaston Bachelard, the myth of digestion was a major feature in what he calls prescientific thought.[30]

"You are what you eat." This simple statement, acknowledged by all, was reduced to other, more mundane terms, directly connected to the problem of health. The disquieting relationship between the digested thing and the digesting body led to a particular orientation in all branches of the medical arts. Clinical care thus centered on digestive problems. Nearly all of Arnaud de Villeneuve's therapeutic arsenal was devoted to the disorders of the stomach.[31] In health strategies, the diet occupied the place of honor. Along with surgery and pharmacology, it constituted one of the three branches of preventive medicine—actually, the most important branch, since it was more valuable for preventing than for healing in a time when medical competence was limited and therapeutic resources ineffective. The branch of preventive medicine involving the "regime," or diet, included a good number of dietary prescriptions. Doctors advised the powerful: prince or pope. At court, they were the archiaters, the taster physicians. In the cities, they were asked about the same questions of diet, and they wrote books on dietetics: "In order to content the great number who never stop asking the doctors when they are eating, 'Is this good? Is that bad or unhealthy? What does this do? What does that do?' so much so that the poor doctor, who often has a good appetite, is abruptly interrupted and diverted from eating by these demands, and leaves the table hungry."[32]

To respond to this social demand, the doctor as theoretician made himself into a teacher and health educator. He wrote on "health regimes" or "health conservation," or he compiled food dictionaries. Between 1270 and 1320 was a period when such literature flourished, on the model of the diet drawn up by Aldobrandino da Siena in 1256.[33] These diets were drawn up by well-known doctors for medical students and powerful figures, but they could also be found in merchants' libraries.[34] After 1350 there was not a doctor who, in a treatise on the plague, or in a *Practica*, or in an *Antidotarium*, did not give advice on healthy eating.[35] Faithful to the teachings of the old masters, even while neglecting to cite them, the doctors of the Renaissance followed in that tradition.[36] The dawning of the age of print expanded the success of health books. Written in a clear, vernacular language, accessible to all readers, sometimes in verse to make the precepts easier to remember, these diet books were educational. They taught simple and practical rules:

We are our bodies, our temperaments, but they do not inevitably determine us; we can increase our chances of good health by governing our bodies.

We must be attentive to the digestion, that marvelous and delicate process that allows us to live, but we must be just as attentive to its opposite, indigestion, the source of many diseases. If the digestion, activated by gastric heat, is a "little fire," there is very good reason to control it, foods must be "as proportional to the capacity of the stomach as wood is to the hearth."[37]

We must exercise vigilance over our diet. In all the health books, it is always the chapter entitled *De cibo et potu*, on drinking and eating, that is the longest. Feeding oneself is taking care of oneself. Hippocratic aphorisms are quoted; others are invented as necessary: "one shortens his life by the contents of his bowl, one digs his grave with his teeth." One can lengthen one's life with prudence. Saint Clement of Alexandria's adage is repeated: We must not live to eat but eat to live.

Flesh is the best "meat," used in the wider sense of the word to mean "food." According to the anonymous author of the *Régime de vivre*: "Among all other foods, flesh is the very best nourishment, because it corroborates, comforts, feeds, and fattens the body and is of the next conversion to blood. That is why those who eat great quantities of meat with wine for beverage are very fat and sanguine."[38]

Assimilation is most rapid from one flesh to another, thus making flesh the best of foods. Language underscores this superiority. For a long time, the word "meat" (*viande*) had a very broad meaning, applying to everything that served life (*vivenda*). Urban usage narrowed the word's meaning, reducing it to simply the flesh of animals. In the seventeenth century, the first dictionaries ratified linguistic practice. In passing from plural to singular, meat confirmed its preeminence.[39] Finally, nothing is more logical than the bourgeois diet.

The preachers—the last in this convergence of interests around nutrition—denounced the horrors of food and readily named the responsible party: the butcher, now subject to public condemnation. In Jacques de Vitry's exempla, many of the moral anecdotes related to the dangers of butcher-shop meat. For example, there was one about the butcher of Saint-Jean-d'Acre, who was taken prisoner by the Saracens and whose life was spared, on the grounds that he had killed more pilgrims than infidels by selling them bad meat and rotten fish.

Preachers, doctors, and theologians attest to a hypersensitivity to alimentary accidents, contemporaneous with the flourishing of urban standards for the healthiness of food. Those most powerful, like the prince, could secure themselves the services of a court doctor who was also taster and tester of meats served at the princely table. *Facere periculum*: in medical Latin, this meant very precisely "to detect the danger." His was not a subordinate position, Jérôme de Monteux boasted, reminding his royal patient that he had tested the prince's milk when he was small, and, later, he used to slip healthy substances (*aliquid salubrium*) into his mouth.[40] The rich and the less rich, those fat, carnivorous classes, read the advice about health regimes, possibly followed it, and incorporated it in the municipal legislation they devised as part of preventive medicine.

The Stomach of the Rich, the Stomach of the Poor

The fear expressed through the medium of legislation was not uniform. The same magistrate who forbade the sale of rotting meat in the public butcher shop, who was so careful not to eat it himself, distributed it as alms to the city's poor. Nevertheless, his good faith and his concern for the public good should not be called into question. He believed that what was not good for him was good for the poor. And the science of nutrition confirmed his conviction.

In theory, health regimes were a matter of individual medicine. They prescribed diets *ad personam*, adapted to the temperament of the individual. Theoretically then, there ought to have been the same proportion of phlegmatic or sanguine temperaments among the bourgeois and among the common folk, and the risks ought to have been the same for everyone. This goes without saying. But a kind of reasoning factored in here, which began with an old tradition before eventually diverging from it. It went as follows: physical exercise and rest, *motus et quies*, were cofactors that influenced health, indispensable, unnatural things that controlled the elimination of what had been ingested. Physical exercise was linked to one's occupation, and occupation to one's station, to social status and power. Since eating according to station was declared a physiological necessity, the social status of the individual became a major criterion.[41] The argument continued: there were two types of stomachs, for which two different diets were suitable. Men of study and leisure fell into the "tertiary" category, which included the prince, the merchant, and the cleric. All those whose occupations involved hard physical labor fell into the other. The society of eaters formed an axis with two poles: at one extremity, the figure of the scholar, the intellectual; at the other, the rustic, whom the urban poor greatly resembled.

In this ideal configuration, the intellectual occupied the summit. The man who thought the most digested food the most poorly. Plagued by literary intemperance and a sedentary lifestyle, the scholar had to ingest wheat bread, white wine, and the white meat of chicken and poultry, all subtle and light things that would facilitate the work of digestion. The activity of the brain, that cooler directly connected to the stomach, threatened to drain off all the vital heat, so it was necessary to treat the stomach with care, to limit the work of the digestion, and, in a general way, to economize on all related activity that consumed energy, like physical or sexual activity. Soft muscles suited the intellectual, according to Arnaud de Villeneuve. And Marsile Ficin listed the enemies of the man of study: staying up late, too much or too heavy food, and sexual exercise, since copulation was as exhausting as forty blood lettings.[42] The fragile constitution of learned men was one of medicine's favorite themes, producing a narcissistic literature that conflated author and subject. But it was more than a cliché; it was a category of thought. Even in the nineteenth century, medical encyclopedias addressed the diseases of the learned separately. Thus, with regard to food safety, a specific social category stood at risk.

At the base of this dietetics of class was the man in need. He was absent from the health books, which addressed a different clientele, a clientele that could choose its diet. Moreover, only the idle could be vigilant about their health: "No one can follow a suitable health regime if he is constrained by an occupation. It is best, in fact, if he has at his disposal the things necessary for life, without having to do physical work, and if he is generally free."[43] Nevertheless, we know about food suitable to men in need thanks to the *Treasures of the Poor*, those manuals compassionate doctors devoted especially to them. The first *Thesaurus pauperum* was compiled by Peter of Spain—the future Pope John XXI—to be used by poor students and masters. From these booklets, we can glean a portrait of the *popolo minuto*, the little people, their needs and risks. It is a portrait of a group with solid stomachs:

> Coarse foods are only suitable for those who work all day long, from morning until night, like harvesters, gravediggers, and fighters, for whom heavy exercise increases their natural heat. Because the great weakness, and the evacuation from the whole body proceeding from this labor, and likewise the profound sleep that follows it, are the reason that such coarse foods are digested. In addition, when one is accustomed to them, and when they are taken in small quantities, they are more familiar in nature and better digested. Such coarse foods also suit those who have endured hunger out of necessity, and from lack of provisions, provided that they be taken in small quantities. Individuals of good constitution ... however, will be much better off if they abstain from such foods for their health.[44]

The medical reasoning here follows directly from Galen: the unnatural thing—here, the professional activity—generated greater vital heat. Toughened by work, the stomach was not more solid mechanically, but it was better able to "burn" ingredients difficult to digest. Moreover, these foods were easily assimilated because they were familiar. Each social category was locked into a nutritional model. Heavy foods, earthy and inexpensive, were for heavy men, performing hard labor and used to such sustenance. The medical grid adjusted itself perfectly to the social reality, with one exception: students, who were intellectuals but poor and difficult to throw into the procrustean bed of dietetic categories.[45]

We could give countless examples of these providential coincidences between eating habits and their effects on health. Coarse red wine was the drink of rustics and the poor? Even better, it was good for wine-growers and laborers, "because being at once digested by the strength of the stomach and by work, it provides more firm and more copious nutrition and renders the man more vigorous when necessary."[46] White bread did not appear on the tables of the poor? No matter, since rye bread "is more proper for rustics than for city dwellers, who are more delicate."[47] In justifying segregated food standards, doctors were impeccable. Of course, they did not really say that infected or rotting foods could pass through the stomachs of the masses without ill effects, but by approving a long list of vile foods that were good for laborers to eat, such as grass snakes ("well voided and skinned ... well washed, cleaned with lye"), viscera, innards, even tendons, nerves, and bones, dogs (preferably small and young), cats, and rats, they gave the legislator wide latitude and a clear conscious.[48] Men with nothing will be content with scraps, wrote Massimo Montanari, citing as support the *Ordinacions* of Pierre IV of Aragon, who stipulated that turned wine, moldy bread, rotten fruit, rancid cheese, and all sorts of similar wastes had to be set aside as ritual alms for the poor. That practice closely resembled the *escarpits* of the Gascons.[49]

Beginning with Galen and unnatural things, the doctors diverged from both Galen and Avicenna, who made the individual constitution the central axis of their studies. Now there were no longer just particular cases but also certain categories at risk and others that were hardly at risk at all. In rationalizing this dietary inequality, dietetics perfectly legitimized a system of consumer protection that operated at two different speeds.

FOUR

THE VIGILANT CONSUMER

During the Renaissance, seven women of quality gathered in a Venetian palace: Leonora, Cornelia, Elena, Adriana, Corinna, Virginia, and Lucrezia. These seven friends formed a kind of feminist tribunal, very determined to demonstrate *il merito delle donne*, their capacities compared to men. The chosen field of competition was a difficult one, nothing less than the great book of nature about which, by rivaling each other in erudition and knowledge, these women could prove their equal competence. In centering their conversation on the natural sciences, they reserved a special place for food, which became their fundamental theme. It was not a matter of cooking, a lowly task these ladies delegated to their cooks; it was a matter of observing nature, of the wealth of things it offered humans, in the three natural kingdoms. These Venetian women listed the animals, fish, fruits, grains, and dairy products known in their time in a very-well-informed catalog that would have been exhaustive if it had not omitted roots, bulbs, sheep, and pigs, all foods they failed to consider for social reasons that are easy to discern. For each product nature offered, the question of its comestibility was posed, as well as its virtues and, alternatively, its vices, which were the same as food risks. The discussion thus unfolded following the naturalists' classical approach to the properties of foods. Like all natural science of the time, theirs bore the heavy mark of anthropocentrism and utilitarianism. And their quasi-encyclopedic food science was wholly preoccupied with the problems of health.[1]

The knowledge of food that these ladies displayed was not a theme for women scholars or an ornament for Venetian salons, like the ice mirror or the Bergamo tapestry. Such training was not reserved for women. Even without considering professional cooks, men were not excluded from everything related to food and securing provisions. A famous treatise evokes the long history of men's participation in the domestic economy. In *Le Mesnagier de Paris*, written about 1390, a older, experienced middle-class man addresses his young wife, who is perfectly ignorant about matters of housekeeping, heaping upon her moral and practical advice. But male or female, it was still a matter of the middle class and an urban context. Nevertheless, must we believe that this health-conscious food culture was not shared in the least among the social classes and that those who knew nothing of it represented "almost all the inhabitants of old Europe, the infinite multitudes of paupers and rustics"?[2] That claim seems excessive and underestimates an oral tradition well established at the end of the fifteenth century that circulated the latest dietetic aphorisms by means of food proverbs passed around like small change.[3]

In the face of risks, in the face of fears, surely neither the patricians nor the poor went unarmed. The law did not protect them equally, thus making it all the more necessary for them to protect themselves. And they had the cultural means to do so.

The Health Contract of the Ancien Régime

The food laws in effect until the early nineteenth century were explicitly intended to preserve the public peace and implicitly intended to look after public health. In Lucques, for example, laws were enacted "in the name of the public good and the health of the population."[4] It was never a question of consumer rights. Public health was based not on the right of the citizen and the correlative duty of the state but on the general, primary interest of the state to ensure its own existence by imposing rules on communal life.[5] According to this legislative logic, the buyer was not a protected and passive individual; he had to know how to protect himself. Moreover, he had no reason to leave matters blindly to the power of the law and the vigilance of his town's authorities. The market inspectors had at their disposal only the simplest means of examination and detection, and that would be true until the advent of chemistry. The experts' authority was based solely on their experience as tradesmen. Enforcing professional regulations was entrusted to guild masters chosen from among the food trades. Municipal law enforcement was no different insofar as experts were recruited from among the tradesmen, older butchers, or pastry cooks. We may wonder about regulations being enforced by those who were both the judges and the judged. People of the time certainly did, and accusations of laxness were raised. An attempt to circumvent the problem in fifteenth-century Avignon led to electing and paying two provision masters from among men not belonging to the profession. But adopting recognized incompetence as the principal criterion for recruitment was not the best solution. The inspection circuit became long and complicated because all foodstuffs suspected but not verified by the provisions master had to be taken to the town hall to be inspected by experts chosen by the city. Thus, when asked to examine two leg cuts and two loin cuts seized from Madame Clop, a butcher, Monsieur Bonnet, master pastry cook and sworn expert for the city, pronounced his decision "according to God and conscience and the experience of his age" and declared that, considering the red and green color of the said legs, it seemed to him that to eat them would be "to risk getting some disease."[6]

The consumer had to be in a position to protect himself. The law gave him the means to do so by establishing a major principle: the consumer had to be able to see the "good and faithful" product. In fact, public inspection was characteristic of the whole craft and trade sector, and all who passed the artisan's window or the butcher stall counted on it. The application of this principle led to a particular topography for the food trades. Just as the slaughter grounds had to be located within the city, so the butcher shops had to be clustered in one central spot. There was a single point of sale, or else it was split into public and small butcher shops, under the eye of public and municipal supervision.[7] In well-populated cities, the seafood trade also had reserved locations for selling fish. In 1212 Montpellier built a fish market, and Toulouse did the same in 1351. Salted fish, on the other hand, could be sold anywhere, as could cooked meats.[8] The consolidation of the markets was not dictated only by a concern for protecting the consumer; it also offered other advantages, such as "giving the appearance of abundance," which was another way of reassuring the city dweller, as well as allowing prices to be controlled and taxes to be collected.[9]

The visibility of products was the great principle that governed relations between merchants and consumers. All meat was displayed, as whole carcasses or in halves hung by nails, nets, or pegs, displays made easier by the low weight of animals, sheep and lambs weighing thirty-five pounds (about fourteen kilos), goats weighing about eight kilos, quarters of beef cattle weighing sixty kilos. The buyer had to be able to examine them in the light of day. This was not a minor point, judging by the authorities' ongoing struggle against the very widespread practice of lighting shops with candles in broad daylight, thus changing the appearance of the meat, which constituted a merchandising trick.[10] In the same spirit, the law granted consumers the right to enter the innkeeper's cellar to verify that the wine sold really came from the right cask.

What happened in cases of violation? In the statutes, each rule included the penalty applied in case of transgression, penalties that varied from place to place. The penal imagination was very much in power. In Narbonne, regulations limited the penalty to corporal punishment, a good whipping "with sheep tripe" in front of the stall.[11] The Italian statutes provided for a range of penalties, from flogging to the pillory to banishment, but fines were by far the most frequent punishment. Monetary penalties sometimes took another turn. In Arles, if the butcher "did not tell the truth," if he sold one kind of meat for another, he had to reimburse the buyer. In 1204 in Montpellier, custom required a reimbursement of twice the amount paid in such cases.[12]

This type of penalty raised the question of what qualified as an offense. The notion of deception was broad and ambiguous; it involved two ethical concerns: public health and honest transactions. The drafting of regulations made parallel and comparable infractions as different as cheating on the weight, selling female meat for male meat, and selling contaminated meat as healthy meat. No distinction was made between falsifications that amounted to trivial adulterations and those that could threaten consumers' health. When reparations consisted of reimbursements, only the individual was considered the injured party, even if everyone's health was threatened. The underlying notion was that of fraud, or even theft. Thus English custom likened deception about meat to theft; it had the "flavor of theft" (saporem furti).[13] On the other hand, in other provisions, the threat to public health was taken much more seriously. One paid a different penalty for attaching testicles to a sow to pass it off as a boar and for selling a leprous or contaminated sow. The statutes of Comtat, which are full of fines and their fixed rates, demonstrate that a simple theft was punishable by a few sous in the fifteenth century. When it was a matter of selling meat unsuitable for consumption, the fine was increased ten times, thus reaching the theoretical maximum the law provided for.[14]

More than a quantitative leap, this marked a change in the nature of the offense itself; it bordered on the crime of poisoning. The law followed moral standards of the day. Berthold de Ratisbonne, the Franciscan preacher, maintained that fraud by the cobbler, the tailor, the blacksmith, or the merchant "only involves goods"; on the other hand, the butcher who blew with his mouth, the innkeeper who added certain substances to drinks "strikes a blow at life" and risked losing his soul.[15]

Carnivorous Consumers

The best guarantee for the consumer, the one that could calm fears prompted by the lengthy route meat traveled, was the proximity and visibility of the slaughter. To those who called for the slaughtering to be done outside the city walls, the magistrates responded that meat then risked arriving in the city already corrupt, and one could not know or see that it was unhealthy.[16] Slaughtering *intra muros* was the urban counterpart to butchering the family pig. Thus the eater was in a peculiar situation. Each day he saw and heard whole herds crossing through his city. An inhabitant of Avignon living near the gate of Saint Michael could count the sheep: in 1772 he saw an average of 606 sheep and 23 cattle parade by each week. From the Châtelet, a Parisian could witness perpetual bovine traffic jams; sometimes he complained of being assailed by mooing and bleating. He hated the nuisance and the assault to his senses, the noise and the foul smell. But never did the visual assault of seeing these animals slaughtered enter into the grievances submitted to the city authorities, at least not until the eighteenth century. In the order of priorities, it was important to be able to verify *de visu* that the animals crossing through the city were not suffering, because a suffering beast plainly meant that its meat might be less fresh and thus less healthy for the consumer. As for the slaughter, for so violent and spectacular an event, it remained mundane and acceptable. It took place in the streets: "From the beginning, the street was a place where one could see beasts having their throats slit."[17] The public spectacle of the slaughter was violent and led to the general opinion that butcher's trade—since the butcher was also the knacker—was unworthy. The French eater demanded that, in processions, the butchers march behind the main part of the parade, and the English eater demanded that butchers not be members of juries when a decision had to be made about putting a murderer to death. But no one questioned the public nature of the slaughter itself.

The relationship to animals was not the same as it is today. Or, more accurately, yesterday's consumer had a direct relationship to animals that we have lost, which expressed itself through a certain image of the domestic beast. Weren't domestic herbivores created by God to sustain men? Sheep, cattle, and pigs had no rights except to nourish us, and they lived the long, fruitful life of the ruminant in the open air. There was no kind of attention or pity for "our brothers the animals." A forerunner with regard to the attention he gave animals, Francis of Assisi only recently acquired his role of patron saint of nature and beasts, in 1966, under Pope Paul VI. On only one point are we less sensitive than our forefathers: they could not bear to see a horse slaughtered to be eaten.

The very creatures the city dweller saw slaughtered he found that same day in the butcher stalls. For him, meat had a history. It had an age. It had a gender: he bought ram or ewe but ram especially, because male meat was considered better than female meat. For him, meat was not anonymous, harmless flesh; it retained a very strong tie to the living animal. He ate *mouton* or *porc*, the same word designating the living animal and the ingested animal. Only the English language introduced a distance between the eater and the eaten by distinguishing the animal and the meat with the dual cattle/beef, sheep/mutton, pig/pork. Elsewhere, the vocabulary did not enact that disjunction between living animal and dead meat that we, as twenty-first-century urban consumers, have generally achieved. To adopt the neologisms coined by Noélie Vialles, they were *zoophagous*, and we are *sarcophagous*.[18] Two logics exist with regard to eating meat. The sarcophage ingests anonymous, deanimalized meat. For a long time, another kind of behavior prevailed: the zoophage liked to recognize the living creature he consumed.

For the zoophagous eater, there were no unworthy pieces. Every part of the pig or the sheep was good: the feet, the tripe, the liver, the brain. The Mesnagier could list all the pieces that were grouped under the generic name of *fressure*, or "pluck": the liver, lungs, and heart in a pig, that is, three pieces, but four pieces in the sheep or calf, seven in the cow.[19] If the live meat was a man's domain, the sale of tripe was virtually a woman's monopoly. At each urban intersection stood the tripe sellers who soaked in tubs of lye the already cooked entrails that they "sold to the poor people for breakfast." Noting this taste for innards, Champier, the doctor, sought to limit its use: "Those who are born with a solid stomach or who perform arduous work can eat it without too much risk."[20] The taste for offal was just as pronounced: "Nearly all the French like the feet of sheep and eat them cooked in water, with vinegar and sprinkled with very green parsley. Some fry them or sometimes grill them on the coals. They fry to perfection boiled cows' feet, which are quite hard. As for the feet of calves, they eat them boiled and add pepper and saffron. They also roast on the grill pigs' feet cooked in water and eat them with vinegar, sprinkled with onions and minced."[21]

"Those who lead a brilliant life" appreciated calf's head, sweetbreads, cow or sow udders. They feasted on marrow, which they sucked out of the bones they broke or spread on bread slices. On the other hand, they rejected bull, ram, and billy goat testicles, the spleen and the liver, and they left the kidneys and their "horrid intestinal odor" to the porter and companions. The latter bought fresh, half-throbbing, the hearts, testicles, and kidneys. Even the lungs, considered light food, were consumed. It would not be for another century that they would become food for cats, which were themselves clandestinely recycled into human food.

Market Vigilance

The oldest cookbooks in English opened with an obligatory chapter: how to know what to buy? The answer was simple: use the five senses, those cognitive powers—as the scholastics called them—present in each person's brain.[22]

The market offered a sensorial atmosphere, a world of odors and colors in which buyers did not make decisions blindly but by putting their five senses to work, apparently in the following order:

Smell performed the first test. The buyer breathed in the aromas but could also detect contamination. The smell, a sense that we have nearly lost in comparison with the keen olfactory sensitivity of earlier centuries, was the first to be called on.[23] Backed up by Hippocratic medicine, this was precisely where bad odors and infection were directly linked. "Everything that stinks kills," was a saying before Pasteur. What stank was corrupt and a source of corruption for the stomach, capable of creating digestive disasters. Consequently, the market was one of those places where olfactory vigilance was exercised, attention to what was fetid and putrid. The nose signaled corruption, demanded the buyer be repulsed by what was perishable or rotten. In 1784 in Châtillon-en-Bourgogne, public outcry caused two baskets of foul-smelling herring to be removed from the market. The seized baskets were examined by the town expert, a master surgeon who "examined the said herring and reported that the odor of those herring was due to their being old, and that he did not believe they were spoiled, and that he did not think that they would be harmful to the health of those who could make use of them."[24]

Sight was also decisive: butchers bought animals on the hoof, eyeing them for weight, and they were never off by more than five kilos.[25] They sold the meat not by the pound but by the estimate. Everywhere, public authorities responsible for verifying weights and measures did their best to impose the use of the Roman scale. They succeeded in Paris when, after 1540, the scale system was imposed, but the practice of estimating survived elsewhere, especially in the small butcher shops and in the sale of mutton. Sellers and buyers shared this preference for sale by sight, since the price fixed by the authorities was the same, no matter what the cut. If they could not haggle over the price, they haggled over the cut. Leg and collar cuts were not equal.

Sight was the means of detection for the inspectors, whom the authorities told "to keep a close eye" on the markets. These inspectors were often called by suggestive names like *regardaïre* or *regardator*, "regarders of things that are sold."[26] If the eye entered second, it confirmed or denied the risk that the nose allegedly discovered.

Touch gave the hand a major role in the act of buying. All food products could be touched all buyers, with the notable exception of Jews and prostitutes. Sale "by sight" was just as much sale "by hand." One weighed items in one's hand rather than on a scale. At the fishmonger's, every buyer had the right to inspect the baskets of seafood "over, under, and in the middle as they saw fit."[27] On the subject of fish, domestic tracts were not sparing with advice on how best to choose fish in general and each type in particular. One verified freshness "by pressing with the thumb, and if the gills were red." For dried cod, it was recommended to "try it with the teeth."[28] Likewise, one tested chicken by feeling the wishbone, the rabbit by breaking a back leg. It was very rare that a manual gesture did not accompany a visual inspection, with the exception, already indicated in the Franche-Comté regulations, of choosing bread, because of the suspicion that butchers and buyers "do not always have clean hands."[29]

Taste played the final role in determining the good and salable quality of products. Consumers had the right not only to touch but also to taste, especially oil or wine, according to a custom that the French civil code of 1804 perpetuated by establishing sale by sampling: "With regard to things one customarily tastes before buying, there is no sale as long as the buyer has not tasted them" (art. 1587).

We might think that buying and selling practices are trivial matters and predictable, since human sensory equipment has not changed. Yes, except in these choice-making procedures, yesterday's consumer demonstrated a more acute sensitivity, totally different from our own. Maurice Aymard noted this acuteness in travel accounts: "Let us follow these travelers: they never failed to compare the quality of the bread, wine, meat, and fruit, as we compare those of our modern cuisines. But who among us, tasting salt, would be able to discern the fine distinctions of origin, taste, color, and salting power?"[30]

In the act of choosing foods, the five senses were set in motion, but in an order and according to a hierarchy that is no longer our own. It was the nose's job to alert and reject. In a world of smells, detection was done by the nose, but decisions were made through confirmation by the other senses. The consumer was the man with the psyche described by Robert Mandrou, whose sensorial hierarchy was different from our own, sight ranking third, after hearing and touch.[31] Hearing also played an active role in making choices. The normative texts make it clear that purchases were never done in silence or in secret. They gave rise to heated bargaining. Legislators intervened to keep verbal exchanges within civil boundaries, with two specific professions in mind: the fishmongers and the butcher boys. In 1570 the latter were called into line: "Do not mistreat or malign the Ladies and Gentlewomen ... , do not use against them any words of derision or mockery, and gently accept the offers they make for their purchases."[32]

The laws in general convey a distrust for the food professions, and, in a parallel fashion, they encourage the act of buying not to be passive. Bargaining was ubiquitous and obligatory. Regulations limited oral advertising but required verbal exchanges. They subjected merchants to the negative obligation not to deceive but also to the positive obligation to inform consumers about the quality and origin of their goods. If they wanted to sell contaminated meat, it was possible, but "the butchers will sell no suspect flesh dead of *morie* without first notifying the one who wishes to buy it and keeping it away from the table of the aforementioned butcher shop."[33]

Notification was done orally. Under Louis XVI, a Parisian regulation added that the butcher was required not to do the customer the
injury of "having painted in large characters one's name in front of
or in the most obvious spot in one's butcher stall." That was in 1782.
The portion of the population who knew how to read had grown
considerably, or at least the number of those capable of deciphering
large characters, having had one or two years of schooling. The move
toward another system of communication occurred slowly, a system
in which labeling, and thus sight, would play a prevalent role.

The System of Colors

The visual dimension in cooking is not the exclusive domain of
eastern culinary cultures. We know by reading their cookbooks that
medieval eaters were passionate about colors and sensitive to the
aesthetics of the plate.[34] On the medieval table as in the market,
all the senses were called upon. Spices such as saffron served to add
color as well as enhance taste. *Le Mesnagier de Paris* taught that a good
mistress of the house ought to know how to prepare a blue jelly
from a sunflower, to cook a pear dish with an infusion made from
hay to turn it red, and to transform white wine into red by using
wildflowers.[35] The sauces that accompanied dishes had to delight
the eye.

Certain colors predominated, those that were technically feasible
and in keeping with the chromatic preferences of the time. In the
English kitchen, saffron was added to obtain yellow, parsley juice for
green, sunflower for purple. The color held in highest regard was red,
for which one did not hesitate to buy at the apothecary that exotic and
expensive product, sandalwood.[36] The Mesnagier liked yellow, which
gave dishes a golden tinge, and eagerly topped recipes with *jaunet*, a
saffron sauce. He was fond of *genesté*, a ragout the color of broom.[37]
In cooking, yellow was valued. On the other hand, the Mesnagier
recommended serving good white lard rather than yellow, a color
he here considered repulsive: "ugly as yellow lard," according to the
proverb.[38] Butchers used a sales strategy that played on color. In their
stalls, they lit many candles in full daylight, and the lighting "made
yellow, corrupt, and withered flesh be taken for very white and very
fresh flesh."[39] Yellow was valued in one case, disparaged in the other.
In cooking, saffron yellow was a much appreciated value enhancer,
a gastronomic alternative to gold. In the pantry or at the salt-meat
market, yellow was repulsive, a sign of rancidity, even rot. Thus the

same color had a different cultural status according to whether it appeared in a prepared dish or in a raw product.

We are in the presence of two chromatic systems. One of them was strictly culinary. It permitted judging at first glance the art and the success of the cook. It could bring several colors into play for a single meal, following a hierarchy of preferences that varied according to region. The English put red at the top; Europeans disdained it and preferred white. The other system was strictly alimentary. It involved raw products, which it also permitted to be judged at first glance for freshness and integrity. It constituted a guarantee of safety. Theoretically, the two systems were antithetical: while the aesthetic pursuits and creativity of chefs resulted in sauces and toppings featuring completely artificial coloration, at the market, concern for the natural took precedence. In matters of gastronomic preparation, tastes and colors could be disputed; in matters of market produce, there was no dispute: everyone agreed.

We have access to the chromatic language of freshness through certain regulatory texts. Regulations in Avignon, for example, prohibited "soaking in the street," that is, soaking dried cod in the drainage ditches that ran through the market streets. In Paris, there was also a rule concerning this foodstuff, so important in times of scarcity. It forbade "spoiling it and boiling it," that is, artificially blanching it with lime. In 1396 the Paris provost forbade modifying butter to give it a yellower color by mixing it with marigold flowers "or other flowers, grasses, or drugs."[40] Yellow butter meant good butter: the adage held for all of butter-eating Europe. In Amsterdam in 1641, the town took measures to prohibit adding annatto to butter, which allowed good but very pale cowshed butter to mimic pasture butter, more highly valued and more pronounced in color.[41] The coloring used here was derived from the seed of the annatto tree, imported from the West Indies. In French markets, the most widely used formula was as follows: annatto, turmeric, and seeds from Avignon, thus a mixture of imported spices and indigenous dying plants that were ground with oil or fat and added to the butter to color it. As saffron was too costly, it was replaced by substitutes or even by false saffron. False saffron was made of grasses of the same color or of strands of recooked and colored meat, imitating the stigma of the dried flower. The Parisian authorities became alarmed. They wanted consumers to be able to buy foodstuffs as nature made them. But consumer tastes sometimes drew them toward colors alien to what nature produced.

The language of food colors was inconsistent: that grass or vegetable should be green, ham pink, lard white is understandable. But why should bread or cod be white? Why should butter be yellow? When we look at the other chromatic system, more natural than the one applied to culinary preparations, we find that it was not based on objective perception alone. It seems that, for certain products, the natural color had to be revised and corrected by culture. Historians who have studied the chromatic symbolism revealed in many objects cannot explain why, in cooking but especially in market products, white was so highly valued.[42]

The doctor and humanist Marsile Ficin offers us a possible explanation for the privileged status of white. In 1489 Ficin dedicated the three-volume *De la vie* to Lorenzo de' Medici (how the two men were related does not concern us). In the first volume of this triptych, Ficin devotes much space to one of the humors, black bile, also called melancholy or atrabile. He focused on it because his concern was the health of men of study, and excessive intellectual work led to an excess of black bile. Black bile was not like the other humors: cold, dry, earthy in nature, it was like sediment, a deposit of blood that had to be purged. Arnaud de Villeneuve called it "the enemy of joy and of open expansiveness, akin to old age and death"—which is to say that it was the worst of the four humors.[43] There was unanimous agreement on its decidedly pathogenic nature, and, in learned circles, everyone considered it the worst enemy of the vital equilibrium. To counteract the harmful effects of melancholy, Marsile Ficin proposed a medicine of opposites. Allopathic medicine was the most classic, but the scholastics turned it into a dogma. They were so set on resolving contradictions that their intellectual efforts tended to reconcile opposites at any cost. Ficin forbid anything black and dry, all hard, acrid, burnt food, "and all that is black." Conversely, "all dairy products are good, like milk, fresh new cheese, and sweet almonds; and similarly, the flesh of birds, hens, capons, kids, and other small beasts who still drink their mothers' milk, fresh-smelling eggs, and the soft brains of young animals ... good clear light wine with a good sweet odor."[44]

The struggle against deadly melancholy led to extolling the virtues of white foods. We cannot judge the impact of Marsile Ficin and his somewhat fuzzy Neoplatonism, but we can certainly acknowledge that his theory of universal correspondences may provide justification for the color system then in force. It was undoubtedly with the same allopathic intention that Arnaud de Villeneuve gave the almond a place of honor in the eighteen recipes included in his *Régime*. He recommended it in three forms, the fruit, the milk, and the oil, and attributed to it two virtues: it cleansed, softened, and whitened the skin by removing freckles, and it clarified the humors. Cooking for the sick and convalescent took the color system one step further and proposed dishes that "clarified" the black humors, like capon "*au blanc*," which was served with an almond sauce, or dried cod in a white sauce.[45] The leading recipe in international medieval cuisine, the one that met with the longest and widest success, was blancmange. Arnaud de Villeneuve mentions it, as does the Mesnagier, and an anonymous recipe book from the fifteenth century gives this version of *albus cibus*: "Make as follows: take rice and grind it into flour with a mortar. Then, take the well-cooked flesh of young animals, finely cut, and cook it in milk; next, add the rice flour and boil. In Gaul, this dish is called *le blanc mangier*."[46]

The blancmange's fate was extraordinary. All European cuisines included it and offered two versions, either with white chicken for the days one ate meat or with fish pulp for the days one did not but always with exclusively white ingredients. It was passed down through the ages and through cooking styles and trends. In 1816 the great cook Beauvilliers served his own version of it, with a veal and chicken base, carefully making sure that these two meats "be without color."[47]

In the passage cited, Ficin alludes to a category unknown in the butcher trade: white meat. White meat was a composite that blithely crossed the boundaries between species and grouped together four-legged and winged creatures according to a single shared trait: their color. Thus certain terrestrial animals regained favor, like young goat, which we know was suspect if eaten in the adult form. They were young and unweaned; this was "milk" meat. The reference to milk, to its whiteness, is one of the keys to understanding why a white food is inevitably on the side of health, of the pure and innocent.

Let us return for a moment to the case of fevered goats, suspected—rightly—of transmitting brucellosis to humans. There were two possible means of transmission through ingestion: milk and meat. It is consistently true that all fears at that time were focused on the flesh, adult flesh in particular. It was this deep mistrust, combined with other reasons, that severely limited goatherds in rural southern France. From the sixteenth century on, each community took draconian measures against the now undesirable "poor man's cow." The statutes of Pernes, for example, established strict dairy quotas and only allowed enough goats to provide milk for the region's "children and sick." A few decades later, their fate was sealed. Goats occupied a much smaller place in the livestock tradition, goat meat no longer appeared in the small butcher stalls, and salted goat meat, widely eaten two or three centuries earlier in the Pyrenees and the Provence Alps, disappeared from the diet. On the other hand, the success of goat cheese never flagged, from the Piedmont region to northern Spain.[48] In the case against brucellosis, goat meat, with the notable exception of "milk" flesh, was indicted for every sin; milk itself was found completely innocent. Now, according to our present knowledge of brucellosis, the opposite is true. Food fears missed their target by making goat meat their scapegoat.

Milk, said Champier, was "blood digested, uncorrupted, a radiant and admirable white."[49] What better way to express this domination of white? Behind excessive regard for whiteness lay the comfort of the maternal breast and obscure infant desire. All kinds of values have been attributed to white, including a hygienic value, more present today in our bathrooms than in our kitchens. Then, though, white, the sign of purity and innocence, white, the sign of cleanliness and sterility, reigned over food. It functioned as a guarantee of safety and health.

Galenic Cuisine

The whole policy of domestic precautions consisted of choosing and preparing products well. But doesn't cooking well mean, first of all, satisfying the demands of taste? Here we touch on a sensitive point, at the dangerous crossroads of medical writing and culinary discourse. Because taste was not ignored by the discourse on health. On the contrary, the eater's sense of taste was considered indispensable for maintaining his health. Just as one had to be able to evaluate the wholesomeness of fresh produce with the help of the five senses, so one could use taste to determine if prepared dishes were good for one's health. As the sense of senses, taste's primary function was to elect foods that responded to the specific needs of the individual and were adapted to the individual stomach. Second, it allowed toxins to be detected through flavors. Those in high positions benefited from the services of official tasters who helped them avoid being poisoned. Others had their own tasting abilities at their disposal. Thus taste was an important tool in food vigilance, the final sounder of the alarm.

All that was a matter of a theoretical inspection, performed individually and after the dish was served. More interesting was what happened beforehand, in the warm and mysterious privacy of the kitchen, where the acts of culinary preparation incorporated hygienic standards. When, for example, one practiced "double cooking," by boiling before roasting, could that be considered a prudent health precaution or rather a clever technique for creating a new flavor that rendered the original product unrecognizable? When each soup had to have its boutonniere of clove to stud the onion or the meat, was that for the clove's alleged disinfectant virtues or rather for its powerful aroma? No book from that time answers these basic questions, simply because they were not asked. Their agreeable dietetics did not consider *Sanitas* and *Voluptas* competing values, or, if so, there were ways of reconciling them. They postulated synthesis and combination, which was the very essence of the art of cooking. For any food that was fundamentally dangerous, they proposed a compromise, a practical recipe that permitted the cook to use it without being offended by it. This took place within a complex, codified system, and some of the keys to it are missing. We must give up on discovering the reason for culinary acts and be content with finding among them those that also seem to be health precautions.

The essential precautions were no secret and needed no recipe. They were common practice: to eat the freshest food possible, always cooked. A concern for consuming very fresh food, very close to living, introduced an element of barbarianism into cooking. With something of a guilty conscience, English historians have recounted the cruelty that the first English recipes demonstrate: beat the living fish to soften the flesh, rip the eyes out of the live cuttlefish, roast the crayfish alive, hang the hen and bleed it, take a rooster that is not too old and beat it to death.[50] These methods were not an English monopoly. They were used throughout European cooking in the international medieval style that included among its most popular dishes recipes for eel and lamprey, in which squeamishness could play no part in the preliminary treatment. In the *Mesnagier*, lamprey preparation demonstrated explicit concern for health: "We must note that some bleed the lamprey before skinning it, and others skin it before bleeding and scalding it. Before bleeding it, wash your hands very well.... If your fingers or hands are soiled with blood, wash them; also wash the wound with vinegar."[51]

The toxic effects of blood serum were known, as were the antidotes. For lamprey, it was immersion in boiling water; for the cook, it was washing the wound with vinegar. Making vinegar was the only trade open to lepers; that says everything about the faith it inspired in its prophylactic power.

Did the rule of consuming foodstuffs in all their freshness also apply to meat from the butcher shop? The meat sold was fresh—too fresh before the gustatory turning point of 1550 that required more aged meat. But if sale date limits were mandatory, actual consumption dates are unknown to us. Quite extensive delays between sale and consumption have long been suspected. Certain sources attest to deferred consumption, given the practices of salting and hanging meat in pantries.[52] The Venetian cook Bartolomeo Scappi recommended hanging all older animals for a few days to make them more flavorful but cooking young animals without delay.[53] The hanging practice has excited the imaginations of certain historians, leading them to believe that spices were used to mask the taste and disguise rotting meat. This idea has been refuted, at least with regard to the diet of the rich and powerful. Let us simply consider this fact: spices were not native herbs but exotic products brought long distances by boat, and some part of the dream of the East entered into the extraordinary attraction they held for eaters. They were expensive and reserved for the urban elite, who made them into a mark of social distinction. If only the elite used them until the Age of Discovery, how can we imagine that only the elite also ate rotting meat? The absurdity of such a proposition is clear. The use of spices returns us, once again, to the system of humors, which recommended consuming foods that were moderately warm and humid. For example, beef was cold and dry: better to readjust it by boiling it and consuming it seasoned with hot spices, pepper or ginger, available to the rich, or mustard, for everyone else. So far as it was possible, one ate fresh foods and also spiced foods, according to one's means.

The need to cook is the very foundation of the art of cooking. According to anthropologists, we can read in the cooked one of the basic mental categories that, as opposed to the raw in Western consciousness, has structured our collective unconscious. Since raw and cooked are in the same relationship as savage and civilized, we end up with a mythic, linear vision of history, in which we pass from the savagery of the raw, through the barbarianism of the grilled or roasted, finally to reach civilization, with the boiled, the steamed, the simmered.[54] Nevertheless, it is not clear that humans themselves share this single, progressive and comforting vision of the evolution of humanity. As we have said, they recount their food history in another way, centering on a lost paradise and the Fall. No feeling of superiority over those ancestors with the solid stomachs turns up in this pessimistic schema. In short, in the discourse that they use among themselves to explain their distaste for the raw, humans provide other explanations: "Nearly all that gives nourishment to man, save milk, is harmful, useless, and unfit to eat, if it is not first seasoned by art, as in the bakery, the confectionery, or even the kitchen, in order to give it flavor, for all that the stomach cannot very well cook badly prepared meats. Why (as Plato says) such flattery for arts like cooking, which is a subject, like a servant, to Medicine."[55]

Let us put aside that last claim, which affirms through *petitio principii* and pious hope the imperialism flaunted and reiterated by doctors confronting cooks who objected to their intrusions into their kitchens.[56] The essential point remains that medicine and cooking spoke the same language and shared the same pivotal idea around which the whole question of food turned: digestion was a slow and gentle cooking. This postulate had a converse one that was equally important: all prolonged cooking was a kind of predigestion. Digestion began in the kitchen, which ensured a preparatory cooking for the marvelous coction that the stomach completed. So there was nothing worse than the raw, understood here as those raw and noxious humors produced by uncooked or badly cooked foods. "Blend and pass through a cheese-cloth, mix everything and boil." These instructions from the *Mesnagier* were repeated. Cookbooks, which for a long time did not specify proportions or times, demonstrated three solid facts: all recipes required cooking; the cooking method of choice was boiling; cooking was slow and often combined methods.

Cooking times (when, by luck, we come across them) were particularly long. Anne Wecker, from Basel, Switzerland, who left us her recipe book, boiled veal and sheep brains from one to three hours, before cooking them a second time in the oven, with butter.[57] A detailed study of verbs designating the action of cooking in medieval recipe books reveals that all sorts of precooking methods were distinguished by different words. These were used especially for meats, in order either to tenderize, or to clean them, or both.[58] To plunge meat into boiling water before roasting it, or to "parboil," would be less a first cooking that a first boiling to "blanch," but can the symbolic necessity of this precaution be debated? With blanching, we enter a murky realm where notions about purification and protection against diseases all get mixed up. Harmful foods like oysters were boiled in their shells, then shucked and fried. Mushrooms were prepared in a similar fashion.[59]

Recorded cooking times were long, and it was best if the meat finally fell off the bone. Red, so appreciated as a sign of freshness in the butcher stalls, was detested at the table. Rabelaisian cuisine shunned red meat, with the exception of lobster and crayfish: "The redness of meat indicates that it is not cooked enough, except for prawn and crayfish, which redden in the cooking."[60] Nevertheless, the French had a reputation for eating food less well cooked than their neighbors preferred it: "The Germans say of the French that they put themselves in great peril by eating their carp so poorly cooked." If they had the misfortune of being served carp "*à la français*," they scurried to put their share back on the fire.[61]

In Rabelais's time, the first exotic tinctorial plants appeared in Old World markets, like the "ember" red wood, or brazil wood, for which the small but widely read tract *Le Secret des secrets* gave a novel use: "To make well-cooked flesh appear completely raw." It indicated how to proceed: by dusting meat cooked as usual, that is, very well cooked, with a little brazil wood powder. This was the very model of the fine culinary joke, capable of triggering the worst reactions in dinner guests and the greatest mirth in their hosts, and, considering the popularity of *Le Secret des secrets*, this "recipe" undoubtedly met with success.[62] The table companions of the Embrun chapter in the Alps complained to their bishop about their cook, who put ewe or veal in the soup in place of mutton and, what was worse, served it "half-cooked."[63] Stew was consumed here as a single-dish meal; this was the rustic *pot-au-feu*. On distinguished tables, it appeared as an entrée, in the form of soup. Whatever it was called, *pot-au-feu*, *minestrone*, *olla podrida*, depending on the indigenous version, it was the basic dish everywhere. And for a long time, lacking forks, the essential nutritive act was to soak one's bread in the soup and swallow great quantities of boiling, salted water, accompanied by a few swigs of sometimes nearly fizzy vinegar water, tart but free of pathogenic germs. From the health point of view, this was not so bad.

According to present scientific thinking, there are two good reasons for cooking food well: cooking makes foodstuff easier to assimilate, increasing the digestibility of vegetable fibers and softening the collagen of meat into gelatin. That was what Monteux, quoted earlier, said, in the words of his time. The second reason is that boiling destroys a certain number of germs and parasites. Monteux may also have had some intuition about that when he wrote: "The true remedy for all corrupt and evil water is to boil it to half the quantity, and for the reason that fire has the property of separating out all things strange and of another species."

It is a long way from prescription to practice. Was water often boiled? Was milk? We know the sayings on the subject of milk. The first piece of advice was to "increase with a little water" the milk before cooking, since it always overflowed when boiled. The second piece of advice was to cook over a low flame to avoid the rapid boiling that inevitably made the milk overflow. Watering down and cooking gently were two practices dictated by those "two secret reasons of the common opinion" connected to the horror of wastefulness in a society with shortages. But, if people knew how to cook milk, they did not tell us why it had be boiled.[64]

Thus the virtues attributed to boiling remain obscure. We must add that the doctors hardly mentioned it, and, when they considered disinfection necessary, the designated agent was salt or vinegar, rarely water. For example, they indicated what precautions to take to make dangerous flesh, like goat or leprous pig, comestible. For goat, the treatment consisted of water and spices, used here in their original role as remedies: "Cook it in a pot covered with a great quantity of water and strong spices and clove and then eat it only after it has cooled."[65] This cooling was a supplementary precaution considered indispensable for hot and feverish meat.

For infected pork, we know today that an hour and a half of cooking in boiling water or a correct salting over twelve days is sufficient to render it edible without risk. Urban regulations tell us that it was standard practice in the markets to leave leprous but not completely unhealthy meat in salt for forty days to "remedy" it. Salt was considered the principal antidote for infection—which, parenthetically, sheds a certain light on the question of the *gabelle*, that salt tax despised in the French countryside: any fiscal increase affected the healthiness of food. A quarantine in salt was especially effective on the symbolic level: forty days—*quarante* means forty—was the canonical time allotted for a disease to break out. According to cooking tracts, all salted meat was washed and then boiled, hence subject to a double purification by salt and then by water.

Why, in the end, were these acts performed? In accordance with medical prescriptions? Or because experience demonstrated that such precautions were not in vain? And what if, conversely, habits and customs dictated medical prescriptions, doctors being content to legitimize well-established practice? Because of a natural aversion to things raw? "It is a thing that arouses nature and horrifies, eating meat raw. The taste and sight of it only becomes bearable after long cooking, which conceals from the senses what first appears as inhuman and disagreeable.[66] Out of concern for the gums in a time before dentures?[67] For all these reasons combined, as Rabelais the doctor suggests with regard to cooking beef in the monastery kitchen? "The more it was cooked, the more tender it became, the less it damaged the teeth, the more it delighted the palate, the less it upset the stomach, the more it nourished the good monks."[68]

Given the stockpile of preconceptions that informed practices in the kitchen as well as the market, it is impossible to say that conforming to the current health model was entirely conscious or following the dictates of necessity and luck entirely unconscious. If such practices were effective, no one could say why.

FIVE

THE PHOBIA OF NEW PLANTS

The Conquistador's Neophobia

In conquering the New World, the conquistador faced many dangers, a hostile nature, and human enemies. He took on every risk, except one: the food risk. The food habits that he discovered in pre-Columbian America provoked in him a whole range of reactions, from simple repugnance to absolute aversion. The discovery of cannibalism, that transgression of an absolute taboo, prompted horror but also relieved him from any doubts about categorizing these humans—since he had to admit, in accordance with the papacy, that they really were humans— as savages. Many other things shocked him, like the poisoned arrows of the Caribbean Indians. Well established since Socrates, the Western tradition of poisoning relied instead on ingestion of the toxic product. The conquistador regarded the poisoned arrow as a coward's weapon, even though, in the crossbow that drew many arrows at one time, he had at his disposal a decisive weapon that shot more powerfully and farther, worlds beyond the native bows that were powerless against Spanish armor. The other's food was disquieting. The first Americans encountered in the Caribbean, the Taino people, ate no grains but roots like manioc and sweet potato. They also ate "all sorts of wild and venomous beasts," including dog, snake—served at feasts on the islands near Cuba—tapir, and opossum.[1]

Even beyond these nonfoods, the foodstuffs that the conquistador considered edible amounted to very few, fish primarily, more in keeping with the Mediterranean diet, and fruits like banana, quickly accepted since it satisfied an avid and frustrated taste for sugar, sugar being a rare and expensive spice. "They have neither bread, nor wine, nor salt." This simple remark by a missionary tells us nothing about native customs, but it speaks volumes about the conquistador's prejudices. A seaman like Jacques Cartier—and sailors were more accustomed to salt meat than most—refused food offered by the Americans in the end: "Because the aforementioned provisions were not to our liking and they had no taste of salt, we thanked them, making signs that we were not hungry."[2]

To say that in matters of food the conquistador did not succumb to the exotic is to put it mildly. Let us consider the role of taste in the acceptance or rejection of new foodstuffs. Innately appealing, sugar is a powerful aid to neophilia. Sugar has traditionally served to hide bad tastes and to help with ingesting anything new or repugnant. For example, pills are sweetened or sugarcoated to make them easier to swallow. An acquired taste, salt prompted a strong aversion to bland foodstuffs. Without bread, wine, or salt, the conquistador had much difficulty forcing his way into new territories, and we now know that the business of reprovisioning, beginning from island or inshore bases, was a constant concern. When supplies were no longer forthcoming, the conquistador had trouble advancing. Food habits caused a temporary slowdown in European expansion.

The first phase of the European conquest found the conquistador on the brink of starvation and in danger of being poisoned. By approaching America through the West Indies, the Spanish did not enter the culture of corn but the culture of manioc, providing "the mediocre and dangerous cassava bread."[3] It figured into the first accounts about the Taino people of the Greater Antilles, which informed the Old World that the Indians were hunters, fishermen, and gatherers and that they also grew an enormous root, the manioc. The manioc was easy to grow, resistant to predators and to the hurricane winds that devastated other crops. The Tainos and their close neighbors in the Caribbean, the Arawaks, prepared this root in various ways, boiled, roasted, in a tapioca cake, or even ground into flour and made into cassava bread. But in its wild state, the skin of one of the two varieties of manioc, the bitter variety, contains strong doses of prussic acid, a form of cyanide. The Tainos knew this, peeled the root carefully, collected the toxic juices for their arrows, and processed the pulp according to a method designed to detoxify it. This technology was vital. In a good chapter entitled "The Science of the Concrete," which opens his book *The Savage Mind*, Claude Lévi-Strauss writes that "to transform weed into a cultivated plant, a wild beast into a domestic animal, to produce, in either of these, nutritious or technologically useful properties which were originally completely absent or could only be guessed at; ... to work out techniques, often long and complex, which permit cultivation without soil or alternatively without water; to change toxic roots or seeds into foodstuffs or again to use their poison for hunting, war or ritual—there is no doubt that all these achievements require a genuinely scientific attitude, sustained and watchful interest and a desire for knowledge for its own sake."[4]

Were the Spanish urged by hunger or blinded by a clear feeling of culinary superiority? Did they display scientistic arrogance in the face of the Tainos' science of the concrete regarding their manioc? They consistently disregarded the Indians' expertise. This negligence had a price, and the transition from wheat bread to manioc flour proved to be a catastrophe. A few decades later, Champier reported on an experience so traumatizing that everyone knew about it, even he, a doctor from Lyons who had barely traveled beyond his country's borders: "When they first tasted the manioc root, it was fatal to them. But after a certain amount of time, perceiving that the poison was only to be found in the root's juice, they boiled it in water and roasted it on the fire and then began to taste it. Because thus rendered less unfit to eat and less harmful thanks to this preparation, they made so bold as to eat it. That was why, after having dried it very well, they attempted to preserve it and to keep it for making bread. Thus experience taught them that it provoked no stomach trouble."[5]

Later, converted to the preparation techniques of the pre-Columbians, the Spanish and Portuguese offered manioc a fine future. Cassava bread, which kept for a long time, became a staple for expeditions and long missions. The Spanish propagated it in South America, the Portuguese, who discovered it in Brazil, did likewise, as did the French in Martinique. The success of the manioc accompanied the monoculture of sugar cane. Everywhere where a plantation economy was established, this root became the food-producing plant. Of course, it was the basic food for the slave, not for the planter, who cultivated nostalgia, and watermelon, cantaloupe, and peaches in his garden. In the end, once the Creole diet stabilized, it was a mix of the imported Mediterranean diet and the hunting-fishing system of the pre-Columbians.

The conquistador was a neophobe, his neophobia reinforced by the cruel experience of the manioc. This aversion to new things is, first of all, a biological reflex. It is inscribed in Western genetic inheritance. Until two or three years of age, children put everything in their mouths. They are neophiles open to all alimentary experiences, sometimes dangerous ones if their conduct is not monitored by their parents. After these early years, they enter into a neophobic phase that lasts into adulthood.[6] We should add that food at that time did little to test one's neophilic potential. Children in the ancien régime were raised on mother's milk for a more or less long period. According to the custom in Montpellier, girls were nursed for eighteen months, boys for twenty-four, before switching to harder "meats," in reality, milky gruel.[7] The alimentary repertoire of early childhood was extremely limited; introduction to different flavors and new products took place very late. Only nutritionists could say if such late weaning left lasting marks, a greater sensitivity to the strangeness of foods that lacked the scent of childhood, and if such a diet contributed to making that age less capable than ours of facing food's otherness.

Genetic neophobia was reinforced by cultural neophobia, which was very powerful at the time of the American conquests. Any change in the alimentary regime was suspect a priori. The accepted dietetic wisdom taught that health could only be maintained by leading a steady, well-regulated life and eating a diet based on consistency and balance. An abrupt change in diet was fraught with digestive troubles; it threatened the balance of the humors, that is, one's health. "Nature cannot without great violence endure sudden changes," warned Rabelais.[8] And another doctor, Jérôme de Monteux, subtly argued why eating counter to one's food habits, these having become "second nature," had to be avoided: "Because considering that nutrition is nothing other than repletion of lost substance, which is similar and familiar to that of the party, it must necessarily be the case that what at present nourishes him also be similar and familiar.... Long use and custom renders foods familiar to nature [even if one knows] that they are bad in and of themselves. And consequently less harmful than those one is not yet accustomed to."[9]

Such reasoning made the stomach's familiarity with the ingested ingredient the foremost factor and led the medical therapist even to the point of dismissing a food's intrinsic unhealthiness. In the alimentary equation proposed above, familiar food is equivalent to healthy food. What certainty in support of conservatism! Neophobia was a medical recommendation widely circulated by the *Régimes* on health: "The meat that one is accustomed to eating, whether in and of itself it is bad or harmful, is nevertheless better and more suitable to the body than good meat to which one is unaccustomed."[10]

Thus food risk arose with every new food. Each time, it was necessary to be sure the product was edible and, once assured of that, to know its food value. On this point, humans could not, like animals, rely on instinct. In 1492 there were a few cultural truths. They found their support in the ancient authors, whose works were republished and thus translated: Pliny, Dioscorides, and the naturalists of antiquity who had classified the plants and defined their properties. The herbaria of the late Middle Ages and the Renaissance that established the nomenclature for useful plants, their uses, and their virtues—that is, their medical properties—were known to everyone, scholars in their studies or humble village women who practiced herbal medicine without knowing it. Therefore any new plant caused a disruption in the food repertoire. It could certainly be integrated, but only after examination.

Food expertise fell into the domain of medicine, a vast and ill-defined field, the *physicus* having at his disposal two sciences that he considered auxiliary, botany and cooking. Among those doctors preoccupied with new foods, two were French, Jean Bruyérin-Champier and Jean Liébault. In collaboration with his father-in-law, Charles Estienne, Jean Liébault wrote *L'Agriculture et maison rustique*, published in 1569, an enormous best-seller, having gone through eighty editions by 1700. Champier, a Lyons doctor, was the author of a history and encyclopedia of food, originally published under the title of *De re cibaria* in Lyons in 1560. One passage from *De re cibaria* reveals its tone: "It should come as no surprise that every day new diseases declare themselves, unheard of in the last century and spread from one country to another. In effect, we are adopting a new lifestyle that we are importing from another world. Because if we go looking for foods in the Indies, must we not expect them to be contaminated?"[11]

It was this mistrust, much more than wonder, that seemed appropriate in the face of the vast botanical abundance of the New World. Among the new and suspect foods, Liébault cited the cucumber. The cucumber was not American, but it had just arrived on Western tables, and its cold, aqueous nature made Liébault doubt its digestibility by the human stomach. Liébault condemned its use as totally pernicious. It was a food, he said, "to dedicate to mules and asses." He did, however, recognize its one virtue: "It is said that a cucumber placed lengthwise near a child who has a fever, the same size as the child, relieves him entirely of that fever." To treat hot with cold was indeed standard allopathic medical advice, as treatments drew on opposites. New food was not good food, but it could be good medicine.[12] If the cucumber was pernicious as a food, what about the potato? For two centuries, the potato would feed social fears.

The Omnivore's Dilemma

This is the dilemma of humans torn between the necessity of finding other food sources and the danger of ingesting toxic substances. As formulated by sociologists, the dilemma affects all points in time and all countries. It is perfectly reasonable to propose that, in the modern age, humans experienced it intensely, for at least three reasons: (1) The discovery of the Indies, first the West Indies and then the East Indies, introduced them to a new, unparalleled botanical world. (2) Neophobia was inscribed at the heart of the culture of the time, which squarely rejected novelty "no matter what visage it presents" or else accepted it only if it signified a return to the tradition.[13] (3) The need to supplement the diet became very strong with the "beautiful sixteenth century," when humans began to multiply like "mice in a barn" (Bodin)[14] and a frightening gulf opened between available resources, which remained steady, and a population experiencing rapid growth. A certain decline in the European diet followed, beginning in the 1550s. If sixteenth-century navigators went in search of spices, eighteenth-century navigators, at least until the mutiny on the *Bounty*, dreamed of the mythical breadfruit tree. Charles de L'Ecluse was at the heart of the dilemma.

Born in Arras in 1526 and called Clusius according to the humanist fashion, Charles de L'Ecluse was one of the great botanists of the second half of the sixteenth century. He was the author of a history of plants, the first great botanical work in French. His circumstances and renown brought him to the summit of a network of naturalists, travelers, and the simply curious who sent him living or dried plants, seeds, and bulbs, which he cultivated, described, had drawn, and, most important, classified: because the first task of a naturalist was to name any new plant, to give it a double Latin patronymic and then to assign it to the family to which it corresponded. On January 26, 1588, Clusius was overseeing the imperial gardens in Vienna when he received two strange roots from one of his correspondents—two tubers, in scientific language. They had been sent to him by Philippe de Sivry, lord of Walhain and prefect of the city of Mons-en-Hainaut. In the letter attached to the shipment, Sivry wrote to Clusius that he had gotten this "fruit" from a person who had accompanied the papal legate in Belgium and who had called it by the name of *taratoufli*.

The plant posed a series of problems to Clusius when he examined it methodically. Had it really come from Italy? He thought that it came instead from America, via Spain and Italy, like all those other unknown varieties he received and that were "a mob come from Naples and from Spain."[15] It was, he said, a new plant. He was mistaken. In the absolute sense, that term can only be applied to vegetables resulting from human manipulations. If L'Ecluse acclimated, grafted, crossed, and selected in his imperial garden, he never truly created a new plant. All plants were known and cultivated in some corner of the world. Moreover, L'Ecluse knew this very well. If, on the one hand, he stooped to a placid Eurocentrism by qualifying a non-native plant as new, on the other hand, he did strongly suspect its origin. He had little doubt that this was the plant Pierre Cieça mentioned, in the fortieth chapter of his Spanish chronicles of Peru, published in 1550: "In areas neighboring Quito, the inhabitants have two other plants along with corn that serve to sustain their existence, one of which is the *papa*, with roots much like tubers, lacking any hard husk. When they are cooked, their pulp is nearly as tender as puréed chestnuts; dried in the sun, they are called *chumo*, and they are conserved for use."[16]

It was clear to L'Ecluse that the *papa* of Peru and the *taratouffe* of Belgium were one and the same root. The problem was that the ancient authors did not mention it, under either name. At first, he thought he could relate it to the *arachidna* described by Theophrastus, but the description was so vague that he had to reject that theory. Thus neither Theophrastus nor Dioscorides nor any other ancient naturalist spoke of it. For a humanist such as Clusius, who thought of himself as a dwarf perched on the shoulders of giants, the lack of any reference in the naturalist corpus inherited from antiquity created confusion. This uncomfortable situation was nonetheless more and more common, because the scholars began to be nearly overwhelmed by the wealth of new information. In the *Herbarum* compiled by Otto Brunsfels, a German, at the height of the Renaissance, 258 species of plants were listed. Less than one hundred years later, in 1623, the Swiss naturalist Gaspar Bauhin listed 6,000 in his *Pinax theatri botanici*. Faced with this expansion of the vegetable world, Bauhin and L'Ecluse were among the first scholars to learn to do without the authority of the ancients and to stop drawing from their corpus as though it were a lending bank with unlimited funds.

But how should he classify it? Clusius proceeded according to the only method he knew: by comparison with indigenous plants. Attempting to define the unknown beginning from the known: that was the only scientific process possible. And it was laden with consequences, because, according to the relationships and affinities thus established, a plant's status was predetermined. For Clusius, the leaves recalled those of the horseradish, the flowers had the scent of linden, and the roots were "round apples, quite similar to that of the mandrake." To begin by calling this strange tuber a *pomme de terre* was a just and creative intuition; to compare it to the mandrake was an excellent deduction but fraught with repercussions. In effect, it connected this well-traveled plant to the rare and formidable *Solanaceae* family. The family was unknown in Europe, except for henbane, belladonna, and mandrake. Henbane and belladonna were very ordinary plants that grew on village walls, and mandrake was cultivated in vegetable gardens.[17] But they had a bad reputation, and they smacked of heresy and witchcraft, an old rumor that a scholarly work, *Natural Magic*, had just confirmed. *Natural Magic*, the work of the Italian naturalist Giambattista Della Porta, had appeared in Lyons in 1561 and had met with immediate success. Della Porta considered poisons at some length in it, and the period was haunted by the theme of poisoning. Nineteenth-century authors presented the fear of poisoning as a kind of court fashion imported from Italy. But we now know that it permeated the whole social fabric. Who did not consider himself the target of a poisoning attempt, quite happy nevertheless to have survived it and to tell us about it, like Ambroise Paré? Who had not endured the threat of poisoning, all the more frightening since one did not know how to keep it from actually happening? Poisoning was the most common verbal threat in the sixteenth century.[18]

Renaissance Italy, considered rightly or wrongly to be the promised land of poisons and drugs, nurtured well-known poisoners but also toxicologists like Della Porta. To tell the truth, Della Porta was a little of both. In his classical description of plant poisons and their effects, he granted first place to the *Solanaceae* family. The root of the *solanum manicum* prompted "quite pleasant visions"; henbane gave the one who consumed it the feeling of being whipped all over his body and made "him stammer and wail like a donkey and then whinny like a horse." Those who consumed belladonna "believe themselves changed into animals; some swim on the ground like seals, other walk like geese, others graze on grass like cattle."[19] The slyest sorceresses could resort to a very common *Solanaceae*, the morel, or nightshade. The drug extracted from it was concealed in gorgonzola, said the learned Neopolitan, and the unsuspecting consumer found himself transformed into a beast of burden. One section in Della Porta's work, the one that assured him his dubious success, contained certain recipes for using these poisons in the form of potions or "poisoned boxes." These poisoned boxes contained hemlock, belladonna, or henbane, crushed and fermented. On opening the box, the vapors escaped and were so deadly that they asphyxiated the one who breathed them. Thus the most common members of the *Solanaceae* family were all plants with bad reputations. As for the mandrake, because of its anthropoid appearance (this was the "little planted man"), it undoubtedly inspired the richest phantasmagoria of all the plants. Here, botanical science no longer simply crossed paths with humble country herbology in search of medicinal plants with therapeutic virtue; it ventured into the terrain of witchcraft itself. A recent study on the hallucinogenic properties of belladonna and mandrake might explain the ecstasies and frenzies of the witches. Mandrake was the witches' favorite plant for its psychedelic properties; it was all the rage at sabbath parties.

The potato's scientific career got off to a bad start. As a fruit of the deep earth, it shared the bad reputation of underground plants. They all had the drawback of "engendering phlegm," those cold and aqueous humors that were believed to come from growing far from the air and sun in the cold, humid soil. Thus it followed logically that the nature of the earth reappeared in the nature of the plant, which in turn passed it on to humans. As the little cousin of henbane and mandrake, used only for particular purposes and completely suspect, we can understand how it aroused the confused distrust of Clusius.

What he sought was the quintessence—what else to call it?—that secret property of plants that made them edible or else poisonous. The potato no doubt contained bad juices, what we would call toxic molecules, but in what doses? Because, in old medicine, poison was known to be a matter of dose. The same word was used for medicines and poisons, this semantic unity clearly showing that they shared the same nature and that the difference between them was only a matter of degree. The effects—from ecstasy to poison to therapeutic benefits—depended on this dose, which was impossible to determine. Let us note that the *Solanaceae* primarily caused hallucinations, a fact of which Charles de L'Ecluse was well aware. In other words, with regard to the three degrees of toxicity—narcotization, insanity, and death—they were only toxic in the first degree. Actually, at that level, it was a matter of drugs not poisons. But, in the end, was the potato even edible?

The connection Clusius made between the mandrake and the potato was scientifically based. Bauhin confirmed it, and Linnaeus ratified it: the potato belonged to the *Solanaceae* family. But the comparison was so rife with potential risks that Clusius had reason to be tempted to stick to the old medical principle: when in doubt, abstain, take refuge in precaution-abstention. And nevertheless Clusius continued to observe and even to experiment with the plant. If it was impossible for him to assess this unknown, probably harmful food, he could still assess its effects. As Montaigne said about the quintessence, "only practical usage can tell us about that."[20] L'Ecluse navigated between certainties and uncertainties. Through Cieça and other Spanish voyagers and missionaries, he knew that the *papa* was edible and that for the Indians it was a standard food, one that compensated for "their lack of bread." But he also knew that plants traveled alone, that they landed in the Old World without their symbolic system and especially without expertise, those ancestral methods of preparing them, all the more necessary as a plant could be toxic by nature but edible if prepared correctly (the case of manioc was still on everyone's mind). He also knew that what Indians could eat without risk was not necessarily safe for others. That was another trait of the ambient neophobia: the belief that certain foods were good in one's own country "but, in another place, venom."[21]

In addition, Clusius was not satisfied with remote evidence. He was part of a new generation of scholars who had ears but who also had eyes. He pressed beyond observation to performing his own experiments and to recording the results in a botanical report. There he first described his experimental cultivation and the extraordinary yield that it produced. This was truly "a prolific plant," he wrote, which produced more than fifty tubers on a single plant. He weighed them: the biggest weighed thirty to sixty grams (spleenlike in form but of a doughy, floury consistency). He peeled them, pleased that they only had a skin, a thin layer—very different in this way from the chestnut, to which they were so often compared! He braised them, undoubtedly "between two dishes," covered them with a rich turnip and mutton sauce, and ate them: "I certainly found them no less tasty and agreeable to the palate than the turnips themselves. But I judge that they cannot be eaten raw, because then they are almost indigestible."[22]

The essay was reassuring. Clusius suspected some pernicious juices, dangerous to one's health, like those the mandrake contained (these are our modern alkaloids), but he was convinced that they were destroyed by peeling and cooking the tubers. Indeed, cooking, with its power to transform the nature of the raw product, was very much the necessary and sufficient precaution.

As a modern botanist, L'Ecluse distanced himself from received knowledge. That was one of the first lessons of the potato. It led ineluctably to thinking that the knowledge of the ancients was obsolete; it opened a way to naturalist observation freed of all accepted authority. As a traditional botanist, he considered his role not to be limited to identifying and classifying plants. It was still necessary to speak of their virtues and, conversely, their harmfulness, in short, to take a stand in the domain of human health. With him, botany was more than botany; it was the key to food heaven or hell.

But what did the doctors themselves think? In fact, they did not think about it, and that came as a great surprise to the naturalist, who wrote: "One nevertheless has reason to be surprised to learn of this plant so belatedly, since it is said to be commonly used in Italy, where its tubers are eaten, cooked with mutton, like turnips or carrots, and where it is even fed to pigs. But what is still more surprising is that, nevertheless, this plant was still unknown in the School of Padua, which I learned through friends who studied medicine in that city and to whom I had sent some tubers from Frankfurt." But we should certainly not rely too heavily on this single piece of evidence, which would lead us to think that the doctors were all silent or very reserved.

Finally, we come to the vital question: was this wandering fruit innocent or guilty? Clusius's response was not too decisive: edible but no more. That opinion was accurate. It was confirmed in 1596 by the Swiss naturalist Gaspar Bauhin, who classified the tuber in his *Phytopinax*, giving it the scientific name of *solanum tuberosum*, by which it is still known. He also attributed three qualities to it: it caused wind, "incited Venus," and provoked leprosy. Thus he both gave the plant a definitive taxonomic status and cast doubt on its food value. Indeed, the food status of the potato was variable and uncontrollable. It evolved in autonomously, independent of scientific discourse. At first, the potato seemed to be adopted, without waiting for the opinion of naturalists. Subsequently, between around 1650 and 1760, it was avoided and even rejected, without regard for the opinion of scientists.

Between Neophobia and Neophilia

Clusius's research did not constitute authorization for putting a new food on the market. It served no official purpose, as no institution had called on his expertise. Even if this had been the case, approval would have been very belated and useless in any case. At the time when Charles de L'Ecluse was writing, the potato was no longer just a horticultural curiosity, grown in botanical gardens, which were, of course, urban gardens. It had already won its place in the field.

For the farmer, it offered many advantages over the plants that it could compete with or replace, like the chestnut. This American was a good sort, requiring little in the way of soil, tools, or labor. It reached maturity in three or four months and then provided abundant offshoots. It was astonishingly productive, "prolific," as Clusius said. A century and a half later, Adam Smith estimated its yield at six times that of grain. "Allowing, however, half the weight of this root to go to water, a very larger allowance, such an acre of potatoes will still produce six thousand weight of solid nourishment, three times the quantity produced by the acre of wheat."[23] An acre was enough to protect a whole family from hunger. This was the striking argument of all potato promoters, a convincing argument in those times of recurring shortages.

Those were clear advantages, but they only became apparent later. They must not make us forget the initial drawbacks, both technical and ecological. The plants brought back by the conquistadors yielded tubers quickly when farmers tried growing them in the summer. Harvested green, potatoes have a higher content of solanine, which can increase further if they are inadvertently stored in sunlight. Ingesting green or immature potatoes must have caused a number of mishaps, too sporadic to be recorded for posterity but serious enough to leave lasting memories.

Despite its original failings, it served to feed man and beast, as the Tuscan example mentioned by Clusius showed, as well as the supply accounts from the Seville hospital beginning in 1573; this is to say that it had entered human consumption long before and largely outside of any scientific opinion. Still, there were strong connections between the approaches taken by the botanists and by those experimenting in the field. Initially, they posed the same questions: what do you resemble? what do you taste like? and thus what can you replace? The same principle of familiarity, the key value for neophobia, determined the course of scientific research as much as it did popular inquiry into this American gift that, as far as anyone knew, might (or might not) be poisonous.

In this use of reference to reduce the unknown to the familiar, it seems we can discern two cultures. One was the Latin culture. In general, the Spanish compared the *papas* they brought back from

Peru and later from Chile to chestnuts (minus the husks). As for the Italians, they used a different comparison, which the given name makes clear: it was the truffle, which shows up in a variety of forms in different languages, Italian (*tartuffo*), German (*Kartoffel*), several French dialects (*tartifle, tarteufe, tartoufe* ...). In other words, it was immediately identified with foods that were recognized as edible, even though they occupied the lower echelons of the food hierarchy. Growing in the earth, engendered by the soil like the truffle, the potato acquired the status of an earthy, humid, and thus inferior plant. Like the truffle, it was classed among the viscous mushrooms that were nutritious for empty stomachs.[24] But let us beware of overstating another of the tuber's flaws. The status of an inferior plant was reversible, as the astonishing trajectory of the truffle amply demonstrates. Because of its gastronomic virtues, the truffle rose in the eighteenth century from the rank of an earthy, common food to the dignity of a fine, aristocratic herb, a social ascension that the potato never managed to duplicate.

For the English, since Walter Raleigh, if we are to believe the official hagiography, the same plant was known as the "potatoe of Virginia," labeled about 1640. More than a comparison, here was a confusion with another tuber, the sweet potato, which was brought back from America in Christopher Columbus's holds and enjoyed wide popularity. Its sweet taste had much to do with that (I have already noted that sweetness encouraged neophilia in those Europeans deprived of sweets, except for honey). The comparison to this other potato enhanced the tuber's status, since the sweet potato was not in the *Solanaceae* family and fell into the category of sweet foodstuffs, which were rare, precious, and expensive. Potatoes were treats, tasty delights for holidays. "Let the sky rain potatoes; let it thunder to the tune of Green Sleeves, hail kissing-comfits and snow eningoes," cried the Merry Wives of Windsor.[25] Raining potatoes and other sweets was a dream of milk and honey, a true English-style eating spree. No doubt this confusion between the two potatoes favorably disposed the English toward the Virginia potato. Of course, when eaten, its doughy taste, more bland than sweet, dispelled the confusion. Nevertheless, it retained the mark of its good reception in its name. English naturalists who cultivated it confirmed the spontaneous approval it received. In his *Herbal*, which appeared in 1597, John Gerard distinguished the Virginia potato from the Spanish potato, later called the white potato and the sweet potato. But he granted them equal nutritional value: "the common Potatoes, being likewise a food, as also a meat for pleasure, equal in goodness and wholesomeness unto the same, being either roasted in the embers, or boiled and eaten with oil, vinegar, and pepper, or dressed any other way by the hand of some cunning in cookery."[26] And the great Francis Bacon went even further: "One-quarter starchy roots, like those of the potato, mixed with three-quarters grain, produces the healthiest and best beer for prolonging life."[27]

Good to eat and even good to drink. Clearly the reception for the New World plant and its initial reputation were much better on the other side of the Channel. Acclimatization was certainly successful, especially after plants arrived from Chile, from Concepcion or Valparaiso, that were better adapted to Europe's temperate climate. But how to move from acclimatization to acculturation? Acculturation presumes a transposition of taste, an integration into the culinary landscape. And for the potato, that was still far off.

Flour for Pigs

Why did the potato's conquest come to a halt after the Thirty Years' War (1618–1648)? From then on, its expansion proceeded in fits and starts, impelled by wars and shortages. Michel Morineau observes that it consistently arrived in the company of dire poverty: the English wars in Ireland, Louis XIV's war in Alsace and Lorraine, the War of the Spanish Succession in Flanders.[28] Once the phase of curiosity and experimentation was over, the potato struggled to find its place in the agricultural and food landscape. Curiosity turned to aversion, it seems, and neophilia to rejection.

War always favors the cultivation of substitutes, but it does not affect their status one iota. During the Thirty Years' War, it was true that the potato became common, especially where devastation was greatest, in the Germanic countries. It became the ideal substitution crop in times of hunger, the answer to shortages. It was also the ideal plant in times of pillage, because it had the great advantage of growing underground and could be stored in the earth. Marauding bands of roughneck, mercenary soldiers pillaged everything, chickens, sheep, sacks of grain, daughters. Only the hidden provisions, the potatoes, might escape the army rabble. But what were advantages in time of war quickly lost their charm when peace returned. As famine food, the potato had no pedagogical value. Necessity determines the law but not taste. The potato contradicts the Pavlovian theory of conditioned reflex, because the impression of satiety that it provided in times of hunger and the pleasure associated with being full should have resulted in an indelible, acquired taste. Nothing of the kind happened. A share of the high mortality may even have been attributed to its ingestion. Once the crisis passed, the potato's status was determined, a status much lower than when it was first introduced, at least in most of Europe.

Many factors contributed to this lower status. First, we know that, despite repeated attempts, the potato could not be ground as a grain and thus could not be made into bread. It would never be more than a starch that could possibly replace gruel. Second, it became established practice to use this underground crop as animal feed. In Glux, in the Morvan region, "they sow many potatoes, or *treuffes*,' which, cooked, mashed, and mixed with any kind of flour, but especially with buckwheat flour, fatten all types of beasts marvelously."[29] Occasionally, it could feed humans, like all crops with a dual purpose concealed in fallow ground: meant for animals in normal times, for humans to supplement their diet when necessary.

It is not certain that all animals were fed potatoes everywhere, as in the Morvan region. Elsewhere, there were clearly attempts to make potatoes fodder for cattle, but it turned out that the green stems were toxic to ruminants, and they caused some mishaps. This was not good fodder, it was concluded; only the tuber could be used, and only pigs could eat it. Also, it was observed that, rather than letting the pigs unearth the potatoes themselves, as they did with truffles, it was better to cook the tubers before using them as feed. From there, it was only a short step to suspecting the potato's ill effects on human health: "We have noticed that the children in our provinces fed on these roots have large, hard stomachs and are subject to swollen glands. Pigs that have eaten many of these roots recently dug from the ground get so drunk on them that, for a few hours, they cannot walk."[30]

The potato found favor in poor, wooded areas where pigs were raised extensively, largely on acorns. When the wooded areas devoted to raising pigs, hunting, and gathering shrank and with them the possibility of raising pigs on acorns, the potato appeared as a last resort, the only means of maintaining pig herds threatened with decline. That was what happened in the Jura and Auvergne in the seventeenth century and later in Limousin under Turgot's intendancy. In 1760 lumber merchants in Bordeaux began investing in oak from Limousin to fill the growing demand for wine casks, at the same time reducing the grazing area for pigs in the Limousine mountains. In wooded country, the progress of the potato compensated for the loss of wild acorns.[31]

Use created, or else reinforced, prejudice. For two centuries, the potato remained animal feed, good for pigs. That this animal wolfed down tubs of boiled potatoes was clearly a sign of its foul omnivorous appetite. Potato flour was only an animal flour or, more precisely, a vegetable flour for fattening pigs. If in 1613 the tuber figured as a royal food on Louis XIII's table, a generation later, its fate as fodder for pigs seemed sealed. What a demise!

Can a food for beasts be good for humans? That was a fundamental question. Lévi-Strauss formulated it very expressively: for a food to be good to eat, it must be "good to think."

The Fear of Leprosy

In 1620, in the notice where he gave the potato its scholarly, definitive patronymic of *solanum*, the Swiss naturalist Gaspar Bauhin ended his eulogistic report with a strange rumor: "I have been told that the Burgundians have forbidden the use of these tubers at present, that it is food that causes leprosy, and that they call it the artichoke of the Indies."[32]

Was this prohibition of a legal or more informal nature? For the neighboring Franche-Comté, Ernest Roze cites, without providing sources, a ruling prohibiting the cultivation of the potato by the Besançon parliament, or possibly the Dole parliament, in 1630, regarding the territory of Salins.[33] Certainly, the potato's unwholesome image became very widespread after 1650. The rumor took firm hold in those regions where the potato had found its niche: poor lands with acid soils, mountainous topography, and long winters, that is to say, Limousin, Burgundy, Franche-Comté. Here we see the old specter of leprosy resurfacing, even though the disease itself, "true" leprosy, had been in clear decline since the sixteenth century.[34] Leprosy continued to haunt the Western imagination even though the last French leper houses had closed their doors in 1693, and the occasions of actually seeing lepers were exceedingly rare.[35] The old fear attached to old suspicions found new life in new syndromes. On the blacklist of foods that could predispose one to leprosy, drawn up in the Middle Ages, pig meat occasionally appeared, but figuring more frequently were cold and earthy foods like the mushroom and the *tartuffe*.[36] From the truffle to the *tartoufle*, or potato, from one food risk to another, was an easy transition. The disappearance of leprosy went hand in hand with the persistence of an umbrella word. The term remained, forever labile, ready to adapt to a new pathological configuration. Thus it came to designate complex, often benign syndromes, such as the "little leprosy" that rumor accused the potato of transmitting, recognized today as possibly psoriasis or scabies.

The fear of leprosy was only one aspect in a whole imaginary construct built around the potato, the factors of which are difficult to sort out. Let us remember that the potato was not the first food suspected of transmitting disease. During the Renaissance, German doctors attributed leprosy to excess cabbage, cheese, or beer in the peasant diet—but they did not blame the tuber. Johann Zimmermann, of Bern, attributed grave disorders to the intemperate consumption of greasy substances. According to him, one had to avoid using both vegetable oils and pork lard. "It is for this reason," he wrote, "that scabies prevails nearly constantly in the northern Scottish Isles."[37] In Burgundy, where the rumor was pervasive, the potato was accused of causing leprosy, but so was wine, at least wine made from the gamay grape. In the late fourteenth century, the gamay, a vine newly introduced in the vineyards, raised so many questions that the Duke of Burgundy, Philip the Bold, forbade its cultivation. The governor of the city of Besançon specified why the plant was condemnable and condemned: "the bad vine is of such a nature that it ... is always the cause of the perdition of the former and whoever drinks it continually for one or two years, that would be sufficient to make him leprous, as has been attested by good and faithful doctors."[38] Now why reproach the gamay, pejoratively nicknamed the "fat gamay"? For one thing, it seems, it "pissed wine": it provided abundant juice of mediocre quality. The same criticism, that of being too productive, was leveled against the potato. In other words, the potato's high yield, which could appear as a comparative advantage, was not considered a positive factor at all according to the thinking of that time. That it did not require much labor, certainly less than a traditional grain, was not to its credit, either. On the contrary, the accounts of miraculous plants in the Indies that were not even sown and grew wild lulled the European imagination but hardly captivated it. No one believed in the return of the golden age or a time of abundance. Paradise was lost forever, and everyone knew that henceforth man had to earn his bread by the sweat of his brow. The true foods, the noble foods—and wheat was at the top of the list—required much blood, sweat, and tears. That was the price to pay, the added human value that rendered the food good for the stomach. On this subject, Champier quotes

Ecclesiastes: "One toils only to eat."[39] When it came to agriculture, no one believed in miracles or miraculous plants. The argument for quantity, made by the agronomists and then the physiocrats, confronted three centuries of agricultural attitudes shaped not by any inaptitude for figures—that skill was as developed as it is today—but by a vision of the postlapsarian world.

Popular images associated human leprosy with leprosy in pigs. This association is not surprising when one considers that the potato was most often eaten recycled in pork. Limousin pigs with dark rumps, fattened on potatoes, were all leprous.[40] This lamentable sanitary state stemmed from the filthiness of the stables and the pigsties. The pervasive filth fostered the disease, but breeders were eager to believe that it was hereditary: a leprous sow bore very leprous piglets. If the uncleanliness in which animals were kept led to leprosy, then human uncleanliness might explain the frequency of skin diseases like scabies. "Our peasants still do not understand that cleanliness costs nothing and that it ensures the health of humans and animals. Indeed, it is not unusual for them to wash their faces only once every eight days: Sunday. And they must do so again if they want to go to town or to some sort of gathering in a neighboring village. But if they remain at home, they muck about the whole day, as they do all week, in cow dung and pig manure, their bare feet in clogs; the manure and mud are stuck like putty up to their knees, but they will happily go to bed without washing their legs or feet."[41] Certain skin diseases were endemic, like ringworm, for example, which was transmitted by animals to the workers who cared for them in Auvergne, Limousin, and Languedoc.[42]

According to the circular analogy that linked the feeding of pigs to leprosy and porcine leprosy to human leprosy, the potato became part of a fantasy that far exceeded the relatively minor role it played in the human diet. Medical topographies from the Enlightenment shed some light on this relationship linking physiological destitution, uncleanliness, skin diseases taken for leprosy, and the consumption of the potato in certain impoverished areas of Europe, from Scotland to Limousin.

Cultural Prejudice

In modern times, it seems that the only culture to be widely converted to potato consumption was the Irish culture. Arthur Young, who traveled there in 1777–1779, gave this startling testimony: "One sees among the Irish a great dish of potatoes placed on the ground, the whole family crouched around it, devouring an unbelievable quantity of this food, even the beggar invited to eat, the pig having its share, as well as the family, the roosters, hens, turkeys, geese, the dog, the cat, and perhaps the cow, and all share from the same plate. One cannot have witnessed such a scene and not be convinced of the abundance and, I might add, of the gaiety that accompanies it."[43]

This praise for the potato must be read with much caution, coming from an avid potato flour promoter like Young. Our witness presents as acquired taste what was perhaps initially only necessity. The Irish peasant, subjugated by his landlord, could not choose between potatoes and bread, even dark bread, and he endured, rather than demanded, this transition to a new culture. The potato was one of the changes imposed by English colonization: the good land held by English landowners was devoted to exportable grains, the plots left to peasants to potatoes, their sustaining monoculture. From the perspective of the land quality/yield quantity relationship, this was the best solution for maintaining the proletarian agricultural workforce. Of course—and we will come back to this—what was good for the Irish was not good for the author, a wealthy English landowner. If this Irish eating scene delighted Young, it was shocking enough to those on the Continent. Of course, Irish table manners were a bit peculiar. But to eat squatting was a custom found in other Celtic countries, Brittany, for example. Also in Brittany, as in Léon, in the area of Saint-Pol, it was still the custom for humans and animals to live under the same roof, without separate living quarters.[44] But what a French or Latin reader would have found most shocking was the familiarity or, more, the warm intimacy between man and beast. If solidarity with their creatures was the one thing all rural livestock breeders shared, promiscuity, on the other hand, was no longer acceptable. In England, the cottages built or rebuilt between 1570 and 1640 all had stables that separated the animals from the humans.[45] Throughout Europe, the long coexistence with animals had come to an end, and, in the eighteenth century, farmhouses and cottages, as humble as they were, were divided so that the animals were sheltered on one side, the humans on the other. Even if the partition was tenuous, even if it consisted of a simple screen, that did not matter: the segregation between humans and animals was the essential thing. On the other hand, the animals themselves were rarely separated from each other. Most farms were not equipped with sheepfolds, cowsheds, stables, henhouses, and pigsties. Very often, the stable brought large and small animals all together under one roof. In every case, the humans resided well apart from the beasts, with the exception of the farm-hands on large farms, whose beds were often set up in the stable or the cowshed. If one no longer lodged with the beasts, a fortiori it was unimaginable that one should eat with them as they did.

Here we confront an old taboo, which the medieval peniten-tials clearly evoked when they forbade humans to share their food with animals or to eat after or like animals.[46] This kind of prohibi-tion became relevant again with modern education.[47] The combined efforts of two Reformations, Protestant and Catholic, to make the perfectible Christian into a civil and civilized man, the widespread distribution of small tracts peddling the ideal model of the decent and honorable man, all this tended to impose new standards of social behavior and to condemn any behavior associated with animality. In this new regimen, table manners occupied a privileged place. To define the appropriate behavior, etiquette manuals used a whole bestiary as foil: a child must not, for example, attack his food like a wolf, or slurp his soup like a beast, or gnaw on bones like a dog. Avoiding making noises while eating was the first mark of civility. Thus it was forbidden to sniff meats, to blow like a salmon and click the tongue like a badger when clearing one's throat at the table. De civilitate morum puerilium, by Erasmus, denounced other bestial attitudes, such as drinking with the head back like a swan, and warned that only cats, not humans, licked bowls or plates that had held sugar or something sweet. One must not lick one's lips while eating, like a horse, or gnaw on bones, like a dog, or open one's mouth, like a pig. The animal world har-bored a whole repertoire of archetypal behaviors that constituted the code of prohibitions for a man who knew how to live. Nature, and thus animality, was presented as the counterexample for the world of culture. The boundary between man and animal had to be strictly maintained. This was the period when statues judged indecent, like those representing Saint Anthony and his pig, were removed from the churches.

The reasoning was clear: one must not eat like a pig, which implied that one must avoid both gluttony as well as tubers and acorns. Only the most extreme need could reduce one to the foods of beasts. To eat pigs' food gave a feeling of degeneracy.[48] Psychologically, one oscillated between the feeling of regression and, worse, the feeling of breaking a taboo. Only in periods of extreme poverty was it accept-able for humans to act like animals and eat tubers meant for ani-mals. By doing so, they made themselves wild, like the Indians, who were "similar to pigs."[49] In times of sufficient food, people refused to be thus identified with beasts. Finally, it was a question of dignity. Each charged with cataloging local resources in his own county, the investigators for the First Empire clearly understood this when they explained why people balked at eating the starchy food. "A great number of Solognese believe it a disgrace to eat potatoes, which grow very well in their sandy soil."[50] Eating potatoes threatened one's honor, or one's health, or both.

Boissier, an academician during the Enlightenment, compiled Occitan words used in his native Cévennes. In the article "Tartifles," the word for potatoes in Languedoc, he gives this single acceptation: "*Tartifles*, a term of low and common usage by which one responds to indiscreet or inquisitive questions one does not want to answer: 'de tartifles,' one replies, which means the same as these words: *de la merde*, which people who are brought up well avoid using."[51] Defying decency, Occitan expressively formulated the most common and the most popular representation of the potato.

But the Irish? The Irish were not the exception that proves the rule. The Irish did not eat like pigs, because their pigs, except during festive and convivial meals like the one Young describes, were not fed principally on potatoes. In a country where grass was plentiful, the pig was an herbivore, and boiled potatoes did not constitute its daily sustenance. Humans, on the other hand, had been consuming potatoes since 1650, and they were great potato consumers, their daily ration rising to two-and-a-half kilos a century later. The Irish could season their boiled tubers with butter and salt, two ingredients that were rare in other countries. This diet, completed with dairy products, seemed to suit them. Adam Smith testified to that: "The chairmen, porters, and coalheavers in London, and those unfortunate women who live by prostitution, the strongest men and the most beautiful women perhaps in the British dominions, are said to be, the greater part of them, from the lowest rank of people in Ireland, who are generally fed with this root. No food can afford a more decisive proof of its nourishing quality, or of its being peculiarly suitable to the health of the human."[52] And a whole wave of Anglo-Saxon historiography supported Smith and related the fertility of the Irish people to their diet based on the potato and dairy products.

Subject to more extensive research, it seems that around 1800, with the great famines of the empire that assured the potato's integration into the human diet for good, the tuber entered into two distinct food systems.[53] In the Hercynian lands of France and in the Apennines, it was a food for pigs, and thus it inspired only aversion in humans. In the other system, the potato was a food accepted by humans. Rhizophagous (root-eating) Europe stretched over a whole arc of cold lands, from Ireland to Prussia. In these countries, the omnivorous pig was fed in the traditional way, rooting out its sustenance in the fields or the undergrowth. It is possible that its rations were supplemented with kettles of cooked potatoes, especially if it was being fattened, but perhaps we must take a closer look at what that kettle contained. Were these potatoes the same variety as those found on people's plates? The distribution of different potato varieties and also perhaps their various uses is a difficult but no doubt fruitful path to follow.

Let us pause briefly in Alsace, a good observatory and outpost in this rhizophagous European realm. Human and animal potato consumption could create illusions and confusion. But the Alsacians had very specific ways of using and preparing the tuber. It was most often used in combination with the noble grains to make bread: "To substitute potato flour for wheat flour to make bread is, with all the difficulties that entails, a sign of ingenuity."[54] Here the potato was only a stand-in for a more noble and higher-calorie food. That demonstrates how it was stripped of its own identity. Thus the Alsacians consumed it in the form of a mixed bread or else recycled in animal protein, pork being their principal food. In Haute-Alsace, potatoes were eaten whole, baked in their jackets, with a bit of milk curd.[55] The variety used was reserved for human consumption. Beginning in 1747, Alsacians distinguished between potatoes meant for animals—the *Erdäpfel*, much like the Jerusalem artichoke—and the *"poires de terre"—Grunbieren*, reserved for people.

We are very familiar with the primitive potato, depicted in the first botanical plates, the object of curiosity and description. But once established in the field, the potato escaped observation. Nevertheless, a kind of green revolution, a silent revolution, took place there. Between the tuber represented in Gerard's herbarium of 1597 and the beautiful American that was actually consumed two centuries later, there were great differences, and it would be wrong to imagine a clone of the Chile's purple-red potato forever identically reproduced. What is more, it would be better to speak not of the potato but of potatoes, the cultigen brought back from America had been so transformed. This was the result of the long, patient, furtive work of country biotechnicians. Their genetic tinkering allowed varieties lower in solanine to be obtained, thus exonerating the potato of one of its serious flaws. Around 1780 Parmentier selected a dozen varieties from the several dozens he had received from his Vilmorin friends.[56] In 1817 Vauquelin analyzed forty-seven varieties of potatoes presented to him by the Agricultural Society. He classified them according to their starch content. At the top of the list was the *orpheline*, followed by the *décroisille*, the *petite hollandaise*, and the *brugeoise*.[57] At the same time, Beauvilliers, in his *Art de cuisiner*, decided that the only potatoes acceptable for distinguished tables came from Holland.[58] Thus the most common classification divided the varieties into two groups, one meant for animals, the other for humans, or, even more simply, distinguished the "good species" from the "bad," which included potatoes "with centers penetrated with reddish circles, which could be used only for beasts."[59] Between the pig that devoured the entire tuber, including the skin, and the human who ate specific varieties, the skins removed, a symbolic stage appeared that made the potato "good to think," for man, and thus "good to eat."

The Art of Reassuring the Public

Can one combat a fear when one senses, when one knows, that it is groundless? That was a problem confronting almost anyone interested in issues of land use and agricultural progress in enlightened Europe. From the scientific and medical point of view, the question was resolved and the elite were convinced of the plant's harmlessness. This certitude was confirmed by the decision of the medical school in Paris, consulted by the abbot Terray, inspector general for the realm. At ten o'clock on Sunday morning, March 2, 1771, after the mass, the assembled doctors solemnly declared that "the food of potatoes is good and healthy, not at all dangerous and even very useful." From then on, fear was no longer justified. It was a popular error, a prejudice, a sign of ignorance. An Italian doctor deplored it: "The popular error, that potatoes engender phlegm, results from the bad habit we have of decrying anything that has not been hallowed by custom. And in the meantime, good things continue to be discredited."[60]

According to the historical botanists, it was almost at this same moment, 1768, that a nonevent of great importance took place. The distribution paths of two primitive species of potato crossed on the Continent, opening the way for a burst of biodiversity. It is not insignificant that the potato's propagandists had new varieties at their disposal, less bitter and less toxic than the early ones. The struggle against prejudice was the business of all enlightened administrators and agronomists of the eighteenth century, but history charts only a few key figures in this pioneering avant-garde, such as Battara and Occhiolini in Italy and Turgot and Parmentier in France. Anne Turgot and Antoine Parmentier: two men, two different methods for vanquishing fear.

A doctor with expert knowledge of the Limousin countryside wrote: "For at least half the population, the chestnut makes up part of the basic diet in our area.... A minister whose memory will always be dear to the French but who has been justly reproached for being too devoted to method had planned to destroy the chestnut in Limousin, to replace it with the potato, but this would have ruined the whole province."[61] That minister was Anne Jacques Turgot, named intendant to Limoges in 1761. For thirty years, Turgot generally administered with one great plan: to reformulate and experiment with physiocratic theories on this very broad mass of French people at the end of the reign of Louis XV. In his assigned territory, Turgot the Parisian would preach the good agronomic word and cultivating the potato.

But how to convince this population of chestnut eaters made up of all social classes, especially the peasants, who consumed more than the others for four months of the year? Could he change the food system by changing the people? Turgot did not believe so. The province presented to him was peopled "with Limousin fools," to use his expression. These men were slow, apathetic, fixed in their routine. Physically, they had weak constitutions and were small in stature, only an average of 1.6 meters in height. It was a population of dwarfs that Turgot had to govern. To understand the physiological woes of his charges, the intendant accepted the medical explanation then in vogue, which readily linked disabilities with diet. This link was not groundless. In these lands poor in grain and also in livestock, the diet was very unbalanced, characterized by an excess of starchy foods, chestnut flour and gruel galore, and by an extreme scarcity of animal protein. The peasants' frailty demonstrated how the traditional food system had reached its limits. It had entered into acute crisis in which the tension between humans and resources surfaced sporadically through shortages and most dramatically through the diminished average human height that characterized Europe during this time. Continuing his analysis, Turgot wrote: "The peasants of the country are naturally lazy and recalcitrant, because they are used to living on chestnuts, which provide them subsistence without cultivation or work." Here, the diagnosis blurs nutritional causes with moral causes. Turgot denigrates the chestnut in no uncertain terms, reproaching the "bread tree," as it was widely called, for providing peasants food without effort. Using the same reproach we have seen directed at the potato, he takes it and turns it around, the distrust of a yield that "comes in its sleep" here operating to the advantage of the potato.[62]

But Limousin inhabitants remained stubbornly attached to the chestnut. Shown the advantages of the potato in the field, they considered the advantages of the chestnut in cooking, which they knew how to prepare in many different ways, its taste suiting them, and they considered it superior to the bland potato. They liked the chestnut simply because, for them, it was more agreeable to the palate.[63] For Turgot, to be attached to this stodgy food was only an additional sign of mindlessness.

Thus it was not the rustic eater to whom he addressed himself but the producer. Turgot arrived "devoted to method," as the previously quoted author wrote, meaning he used technocratic methods to serve an ideology of agronomic reform. He was convinced that the food system could be changed only by establishing an agricultural alternative. He spelled out his program completely in the letter he addressed to his colleague, the intendant of Auvergne, when he wrote, "the state of poverty and mindlessness of the farmers in our provinces can only be combated with the expenditures and intelligence of wealthy, educated landowners."[64] That was to apply, to the letter, the physiocratic maxim: change can only come from landowners, "sensible men," and "zealous citizens." These men would never eat the potato, but they had the means to impose its cultivation, for example, by requiring in their leases that tenants and sharecroppers devote plots of land to it. That came very close to the colonial method, practiced by English landlords in Ireland to impose the potato or plantation owners in the West Indies to impose the manioc as the requisite staple crop. Unfortunately for Turgot, Limousin was a country of free peasants. And important figures, when solicited, did not always react as Turgot wished. A prominent member of the local agricultural society, M. de Feytiat, assured his colleagues that the intendant's tuber was not good for fattening pigs, "which he had proven by having given more than twenty sacks of potatoes well prepared with bran to two pigs that he meant to fatten, and not only had they not benefited from it, but he even had reason to suspect that this food had shrunk their entrails."[65] Rejection on the part of peasants, reticence on the part of the influential: we can understand how, despite the intendant's efforts, the tuber's progress was nearly nil during the 1760s.

Parmentier relied on other weapons in his fight for the potato. His coveted victory should not be called agricultural revolution but food reform. He began at the other end of the economic circuit, judging the consumer to be the one in charge. A military pharmacist, Antoine-Augustin Parmentier enlisted in the Seven Years' War when he was twenty years old. Five times he was taken prisoner in Westphalia. There he experienced the potato. Called the *Kartoffel* there, this fruit was considered, as in France, good for pigs and prisoners of war. Returning from captivity and grateful to the food that had saved his life, Parmentier devoted himself to promoting the potato, taking advantage of two opportunities: the official opinion of the Paris medical school, declaring the plant no threat to health, and the competition proposed by the Academy of Besançon in 1772, "Les Végétaux qui pourroient suppléer en temps de disette à ceux que l'on emploie communément pour la nourriture des hommes," which prompted him to write *Recherches sur les végétaux nourrissans qui, dans les temps de disette peuvent remplacer des alimens ordinaires, avec de nouvelles observations sur la culture des pommes de terre*, published by the Imprimerie royale in Paris in 1781.

In presenting to the academy the advantages of starchy foods in general and the potato in particular, Parmentier identified his objective: "My plan, as I pursued it, was to find out if these tubers truly contain some particular element capable of producing the harmful effects they are accused of in many of our provinces. What I am presenting is the simple examination of a long despised root still subject to prejudices; I will have fulfilled my intentions if I can help to destroy them."[66] Thus this fight against fear involved the destruction of two prejudices, one health-related, one cultural.

To discredit the health-related prejudice, Parmentier became an experimenter. As a chemist and physician, he was more convincing in his studies on chocolate, by which he discovered the laws of calcium balance, or on the American stew pot, which he improved beginning from Denis Papin's model, than in his studies on starchy foods and starch, all of which constituted what he called the stomach's "ballast," or on the flour substitutes that he proposed for times of shortage, a hodgepodge of potato and mandrake root. Apparently, he had no new scientific argument, only an experiment concocted in Paris's Hôtel-Dieu where he was pharmacist. This set off a serious conflict with the nuns who cared for the sick there, one of those repeated conflicts that set doctors and nurses against each other and that arose from questions of diet for the ill and hospital dietetics. We know from the *Mémoires de La Reynie* that the well-known poisoner of the 1680s, the Marchioness of Brinvilliers, was a visitor to the hospital, less in the spirit of charity than to try out a few concoctions of her own creation. That was how Parmentier proceeded, but with a product he was sure was innocuous. Another oversight by our passionate propagandist: to use the potato as food, he created dozens of recipes—the famous shepherd's pie, or *hachis Parmentier*, among them—but without necessarily including the method of preliminary preparation recommended by others: to cook the unpeeled potatoes in water and then remove their jackets and "throw them to the hens" before preparing the pulp in various ways. Based on reliable intuitions, these two actions were a good precaution.[67] At the most, he advised using the Papin stew pot that he had perfected, preferring cooking with steam to cooking with water.

It was through the methods he used to stimulate cultivation of the new crop and fight cultural prejudice that Parmentier showed his full worth and made use of his best talents, those of publicist, conducting various publicity campaigns. In this process of promotion, strategy and means were considered. Parmentier knew that "good taste, leisure, and other factors are often more a part of consumption than actual needs." No doubt he had noticed the growing trend toward yeasted bread. Even though he condemned this process, siding resolutely with the *anti-mollistes*, Parmentier watched powerless as this phenomenon transformed a luxury product into an increasingly democratic consumer good. Parmentier's dream was to replicate that process of cultural ratification with the potato, which would finally put this New World fruit on the tables of the working class. From which arose his strategy, cast in the social logic of downward imitation.

For the image of the potato to change, for it to become a refined product, Parmentier knew he had to appeal to two groups, the opinion makers and the medical consultants. The opinion makers were Parisians, men of the court or those holding power such as the governor of Espagnac, the lieutenant general Lenoir, and scholars of renown like Lavoisier, Arthur Young, or Benjamin Franklin, who feasted or claimed to feast on tubers prepared in various ways at widely publicized banquets. At an even higher level, the most illustrious promoters were recruited from the royal family. Marie-Antoinette ordered hats from Rose Bertin, the fashionable milliner, decorated with potato blossoms, and ate potatoes "disguised" in the mashed or hashed forms that bore her name. What better way to say that the potato was fashionable? The medical consultants who could influence opinion were more traditional. These were the doctors who had just declared potatoes innocent and the large landowners to whom Parmentier spoke at each meeting of the agricultural society. "Accustom your vassals to it through all sorts of means," he repeated, "except through authority, but especially preach by example."[68] The message both groups sent was loud and clear: eat potatoes—it's fashionable and healthy.

Parmentier's efforts, his new techniques for promoting a model of consumption that ran counter to acquired habits and thus to consumer expectation, were equaled only by his failure. The publicist established the rules for food promotion, but at the same time he circumscribed its limits. His consumer model was not adopted until much later and then only out of necessity. The long, hard work of persuasion by the elite might have been necessary, but it was not sufficient.

Among the opposing factors, the social barriers in a society with fixed social classes played a large part. The problem with the rich was that they looked favorably on the potato ... for the poor. The big landowners, like Young or the French agronomist Duhamel de Monceau, recommended that farmers grow potatoes, but for their own consumption and for their farmhands and domestic help. Moreover, they considered the potato, if it was not fundamentally unhealthy, to be badly suited to their delicate stomachs and refined palates. This social prejudice was openly displayed in the article in the *Encyclopédie* devoted to the potato: "This root, by whatever method it is prepared, is bland and starchy. It should not be counted among pleasing foods, but it provides abundant and healthy enough nourishment to men who ask only for sustenance. The potato is justly accused of producing gas, but what is a bit of gas for the vigorous organs of peasants and laborers."!

This was a medical opinion, the opinion of Gabriel-François Venel, a Montpelier doctor in 1742 and a personal friend of Diderot. Let us consider the two potato articles by these Languedoc encyclopedists, this article by Venel in the *Encyclopédie* and Boissier's article, cited earlier, in the *Dictionnaire languedoncien-françois*. They suggest a paradox: if the potato was unhealthy and indigestible, was it equally so for everyone? Enlightenment doctors such as Venel remained faithful to the physiology and differentiated dietetics inherited from the Greeks, and they still considered the peasant stomach to be more solid. But was this class prejudice tenable? The Cévannes peasant, on the other hand, in passing an absolute judgment, believed that a food was good, or not, but that it was the same for everyone. Parmentier attempted to break down this class barrier, but without success.

If the rich and powerful did not consume Parmentier's potato as they consumed leavened bread, how could the process of social imitation that he had envisioned take place? The less powerful were not duped by the uproar of publicity orchestrated by "Monsieur Parmentier and other so-called scholars."[69] Governing the palate is an impossible task, and this rule offers no social exception, because the poor, too, have taste buds. That is what Parmentier discovered during the shortages in 1815. With his Philanthropic Society friends, he opened forty-two kitchens in Paris, charged with distributing bowls of bouillon for a cent. The recipe for this popular soup was English, and it was thickened with gelatin and called "Rumford soup." But the philanthropic cooks had to adapt it to the taste of Parisians, not partial to gelatin: "The poor," noted Parmentier, "like others, are discriminating in what they like."

With regard to the potato, we must undoubtedly speak of aversion more than fear. Collective aversions are more long-lasting than fears. But the basic question of the conditions required for a food to be accepted and for food behavior to change has not been resolved. That economic logic did not impose its cold law of comparative advantages until the dawn of the nineteenth century is more an observation than an explanation. To blame atavistic peasant resistance is just as pointless, since, here and there throughout the Old World, rural cultures had integrated the potato plant before the Revolution. And, finally, couldn't time itself be one of the keys to this mystery?

It took the potato more than two centuries to escape from purgatory, surely the term necessary for its consumption to be sanctioned by custom, for the neophobic reflex to diminish gradually, to be replaced by familiarity, that principle on which all peace of mind regarding food entirely rests.

SIX

BREAD ON TRIAL

"In my father's time, they had meat every day, meals were ample, and they drank wine like it was water. Today everything has changed; everything has become expensive; provisions for the wealthiest peasants are worse than those of servants in the past."[1] Those are the words of Gilles de Gouberville, a small landowner in Normandy in the 1560s. That everything was better in the past, in our fathers' time, that the golden age is behind us, has been such a commonplace since Cato the Elder that historians have looked there before giving Gouberville the benefit of the doubt. His nostalgia was well founded. The food situation of the French, and of Europeans in general, deteriorated beginning in the mid-sixteenth century. According to the calculations of the German economist Abel, the average meat consumption curve began to fall in the 1550s.[2] The phase of overabundant livestock came to an end. Thus, between the fourteenth and eighteenth centuries, the Germans went from an apex of one hundred kilos to meat annually per capita to fourteen kilos. Abel's figures have been debated and adjusted; nevertheless the downward trend in meat intake remains incontestable, except in pastoral regions. In Avignon, between 1610 and 1736, the annual allocation of beef and mutton fell from seventy-six pounds per inhabitant to fifty-nine pounds. The butchers, so numerous in the southwest in the late Middle Ages, occupied an ever-diminishing place in urban life. In the town of Montpezat in Quercy, there were eighteen butchers in 1550, ten in 1556, six in 1641, two in 1660, and one in 1763. Even if the number of inhabitants had held steady or declined, as Braudel says, it was not in the proportion of eighteen to one.[3] With the fall of meat intake, a period of personal happiness ended for the food culture.

As animal protein consumption declined, bread consumption increased to compensate. In northern and central Italy, the standard intake rose to 650 grams per day in the fourteenth century. In seventeenth-century Sienna, intake amounts were generally between 700 and 900 grams, with a peak of 1200 grams. France experienced an even more appreciable increase. In March 1662 the doctor Gui Patin was worried about the rising water level of the Seine, wheat was no longer arriving from Rouen, and he lived in fear of "tumult," that is, a popular revolt.[4] Thus the bread question was a crucial one, and this was more true in France than in any other country. The French had become "the biggest bread eaters anywhere in the world."[5] It was in France, in the capital, that the queen's bread affair exploded in 1668, at the beginning of Louis XIV's reign. The remarkable thing about this was that it was not connected to a grain crisis. As grain production determined the price and dependability of the city's food supply, administrators were particularly attentive to it, and, for them, governing the city meant being informed about the availability of grain and the outlook for future harvests. They distinguished among four different situations: times of abundance, meagerness, scarcity, and famine. The grain situation set the tone for the year to come; it determined the security of the food supply and the cost of living. The bad periods, those of shortages, were called la disette, scarcity, or, metonymically, la cherté, high cost. The harvest year of 1667–68 came in a time of relative security between two great grain crises, one in 1662 and another in 1692–93. This was a period of calm, even abundance. An essential given: it was because the issue of quantity was not a problem that another issue arose, one involving quality and health.

Good Bread

The fear of no bread is formative: in Paris, it dictated the organization of the bakery trade into a figure that Steven Kaplan describes as a triangle. At the base of this triangle of bread—or of fear, if you prefer—were found the frightened and threatened people; next came the bakers, often threatened; at the top, the police who governed the city.[6]

Daily bread was provided to Parisians by the city bakers, organized as a guild and constituting one of the most regulated and supervised trades. Additional bread supplies were provided by bakers who traveled from Gonesse and the surrounding area. These arrived from the suburbs two times a week in carts filled with big loaves sometimes weighing more than twelve pounds, popular because they were good and less expensive. Gonesse bread was "a light bread that has many eyes, which are the marks of its goodness."[7] This twice-weekly bread delivery was indispensable for feeding the lowest working classes. Paris's poor population under the reign of Louis XIV consumed about 1,500 grams of bread per person per day. Theoretically, that is the right amount of calories.[8] In practice, we must take these numbers for what they are and be wary of extrapolating. This intake of 4,000 calories a day was a statistical unit;[9] in other words, it did not exist in reality. Raw averages are without social significance. In 1668 there was no average Parisian who ate an average of one-and-a-half kilos of bread a day; there were bread eaters corresponding to different levels. Daily bread is not everyone's bread.

Bread not only served to nourish, it also marked social identity: tell me what bread you eat, and I will tell you who you are. We are aware of the opposition between white bread and dark bread, the famous mirror of social division. For a big city like Paris, that binary distinction was too perfunctory, and, in fact, bakery shops had to offer three types of bread to conform to guild statutes: the white bread of their guild, white-brown or bourgeois bread, and *pain de brode*, a loaf of rye and bran. The prices, too, were set by the guild.[10] The scale went from one to three: when white bread cost three *sous*, average bread cost 18 *deniers*, and inferior bread cost one *sou*.[11] If the hierarchy of breads was a measure of social stratification, then it revealed a Parisian society divided into three classes. In reality, though, urban society was infinitely more stratified, and the tripartite division no longer corresponded to the needs of social differentiation. The play of demand was more subtle, and, to respond to it, bakers were permitted to make other breads besides the three fixed-price types:

"Nevertheless, making other kinds of bread like Gonesse-style bread and bread called queen's bread will be permitted." This little sentence, article 15 of the statutes, allowed room for the bakers' creativity and freedom and provided them the opportunity for lucrative profits. But "queen's bread," especially, was the response to a demand for refinement from the upper classes. It represented a new way of making bread as well as being a new bread. As the *Journal des sçavans* reported to its distinguished readers:

> For clarification on this question, it is necessary to know that there are two kinds of leaven. The most commonly used one,

called French leaven, is only dough made with water and flour and kept until it becomes sour, as everyone knows. The other, which is called yeast, is the foam released from beer when it ferments. French leaven acts more slowly, causes the dough to rise less, and makes a heavier, denser bread. Yeast ferments dough more quickly, makes it rise more, and the bread it makes is light, delicate, and very soft. It is this second type of leaven that Paris bakers are in the habit of using to make rolls.[12]

The family of well-risen rolls was called upon to grow, but, under Louis XIV, it already included many varieties, among which the best known, incorporating salt and yeast, was called soft bread or, when milk was added, queen's bread.

Which queen was this? According to the *Journal des sçavans*, the bakery invention dated from the beginning of the century, when Henri IV married Marie de' Medici. This novelty was considered an Italian import, attributed to the queen's Florentine entourage. Queen's bread was a part of the Medici revolution that occupies such a major place in the official history of French culinary arts that it is one of the founding myths in the history of French cuisine.[13] The French debt to Italy seems large, in terms of gastronomy as much as table manners. Thus queen's bread can be classified among the many inventions that came from Florence, along with the fork and preserved fruits. But it must also be linked to a tradition that took shape in the French court a century earlier. For each wife of the king, there was a product named after her: the bread for Queen Marie de' Medici, the plum for Queen Claude, the soup for Queen Marguerite de Valois, the herb for Queen Catherine de' Medici (but, in this case, the name was shared with Jean Nicot, the man who introduced tobacco to the court around 1560, from which came its other name, *herb à Nicot*).

In fact, this genealogy forms only one branch of culinary mythology. The example of *potage à la reine*, the queen's soup, may help us understand the expression. The soup that delighted the Valois court was nothing other than blancmange, which had been appearing for decades on the tables of princes and the bourgeois. The delicacy, lightness, and color of the queen's soup are traits found again in the queen's bread. On aristocratic tables, the queen's chicken was also served, the most refined of all poultry, with tender, white flesh, closer to chick than hen.[14] Thus *à la reine* seems one of those uncontrolled *appellations d'origine*, used to describe what is most noble and best in the food order—the best, of course, inevitably being light and white.

For queen's bread to rock the city, causing the commotion we are about to examine, it had to move from the court to the city, and it could no longer be just an urban luxury bread, reserved for a minority. To what social depths did its consumption descend? According to Pocquelin, one of the experts summoned on this occasion, queen's bread consumption involved "an infinite number of inhabitants of the largest city in the world."[15] We must be content with this qualitative appraisal. It indicates a widespread shift in taste. All Parisians experienced the same desire for good bread. But what is good bread? There are infinite responses, and thus some historic ones, to this question. For today's child, bad bread is a slice full of holes that let the jam drip through. Yet that was exactly the ideal bread for a seventeenth-century Parisian, who wanted a light, spongy crumb, good, for example, for absorbing sauces without falling apart, since various hearty stews were then fashionable throughout the city. So much for texture. For taste, this whiter bread was not necessarily more bland, seasoned as it was with an unusual ingredient, salt. The eater found the taste "delicate," much preferable to that of sourdough bread, which, because of acid fermentation, was often sour and poorly risen. Its eyes and its whiteness made queen's bread strikingly superior.

The Queen's Bread Affair

In 1668 a lawsuit was under way before the Paris parliament, one of those repeated lawsuits that set related trades against each other and required the judges to study the questions of boundaries within the food market. The controversy involved the Paris bakers on one side and the innkeepers on the other.[16] It was the bakers who had lodged the complaint, arguing that they had a monopoly on bread sales to the innkeepers but that the innkeepers, in defiance of regulations, were buying bread from outside. Like the taverners—which constituted a different trade—the innkeepers had the right to sell wine by the glass. Thus many inns used the sign of *la galère*, the galley, an allusion to the rolling and pitching gait of some of their clients. But, unlike the taverners, the innkeepers also had the right to set out food, to offer bread slices for eating and for sale. They were in the habit of stocking up at the markets from the traveling bakers and serving their clients Gonesse bread, made with "French leaven." Was that their right? It was precisely this right that the judges had to decide on, since the Paris bakers adamantly insisted on their monopoly.

A careful reading of the statutes of both guilds suggested that the bakers were within their rights. Conscious perhaps of their legal handicap, the innkeepers then counterattacked in another area. They could not buy bread from the city bakeries, they argued, because it was made with yeast and was unhealthy. Thus they were obliged to order it from the Gonesse bakers, who used good water, water from the Crould, an affluent of the Oise, and sourdough starter. There was no place like an inn for spreading a rumor: queen's bread was bad for one's health! And the rumor also spread through the markets when Gonesse bakers in turn got involved in the lawsuit. What had begun as a minor dispute between trades over their market shares had turned into a major health crisis.

But this was not a plot, as some suspected, only a kind of nasty complicity between certain consumers, enthralled with the whiteness and appearance of queen's bread, and certain guild bakers, who could produce it at less cost and especially with less work, because kneading yeasted bread took only about a third as much time. The result was an unhealthy alliance between one group's gluttony and the other's greed. Queen's bread was seductive, of course, and wasn't all seduction the work of the devil? And how was one to know if this loaf with "eyes and a good appearance" was not in fact "filth … quite revolting and capable of making the human body writhe"?[17] Actually, the innkeepers did not invent this rumor. But they made much of a March 24, 1668, decree issued by the medical college, a decree solicited by La Reynie, the new and very powerful police lieutenant for the city of Paris. Among his other tasks, it was La Reynie's duty to be the "king's journalist," perfectly informed about all that was said and done in the capital. With regard to the queen's bread affair, he soon got wind of the rumor. He took it seriously and decided to consult the doctors on the subject. The early scientific expertise of 1668 was informal in nature. La Reynie invited several doctors to his house and explained to them that it was a matter of protecting the consumer. One could take precautions, he said, against bread made of bad flour or poorly baked. "Its taste and appearance easily reveal both these faults. It is not the same with fermentation, which makes the dough rise, which refines it and makes it lighter. Because the worst is sometimes what gives bread the best appearance of goodness." He solicited the advice of his guests: did adding yeast to the dough present certain health risks? After some discussion, opinion was divided. La Reynie then asked the medical school to take up this question and study it in depth.

On March 24, 1668, all the doctors of the medical school assembled. There were seventy-five medical school professors to listen to the report given by four of them, charged with examining how bakers made their leaven and how they used it. The majority of the experts—forty-five out of seventy-five—declared themselves against the use of yeast: "We the undersigned doctors of the School of Medicine of Paris, asked to declare what our feelings are regarding the yeast or beer foam that Paris bakers have put in their bread since the beginning of this century, deem it not only not useful or necessary for making bread but also, if it is considered as much for itself as for its effect, harmful to health and detrimental to the human body."[18] This opinion was made public. The information circulated through traditional channels in the city: the work communities; the food trades, which served as an essential link, since these were commercial trades, with clients and shops that served as centers for socializing and communication. Through the inns and taverns and shops, the rumor spread.

As the rumor grew in the summer of 1668, the magistrates decided that, before they passed a law, six famous doctors and six citizens of the city would give their opinions. To this end, they convened a conference on bread on January 3, 1669. What made this conference singularly modern was that it included simple consumers as experts on food safety, and on equal footing with doctors. In truth, these consumers were not chosen randomly. They had to represent public opinion as it was understood among the ruling classes, which was radically different from the lower social strata, so changeable, so prone to passion and emotion that they would be incapable of expressing a stable, sensible opinion. From the perspective of public administration, one could only rely on "wise individuals and testimony from those one can be sure of."[19] The spokespersons chosen had the double distinction of being old (letting experience speak) and noteworthy. These good gentlemen were Robert Ballard; Jean Rousseau; André Le Vieux, director of the hospital; Charles Le Brun; Guy Pocquelin, clothes merchant (and related to Molière); and Antoine Vitre, retired printer (he was eighty-one years old). Let us consider the testimony of the elder Vitre, because it is representative. Like the others, he took his job seriously. He listened to the doctors and claimed to be surprised and troubled by their differences. He had surveyed the bakers and understood that kneading yeasted dough was less arduous work. He had traveled and observed that in countries like England and the Netherlands bread was made with yeast and even that "there are whole towns in France, like Saint-Malo, where all the bread eaten there is made with yeast." In Paris, at all the great tables, this light bread was eaten, and in all the religious communities: among the Jesuits, the Oratorians, at Cluny.... And his report ended with the irrefutable evidence that, throughout his long life, he had hardly eaten any other bread besides the queen's bread. His sober testimony conformed perfectly to what had been asked of him:

> To declare without flattery
> What to make of the bread
> That even those with no more teeth
> Had chewed for sixty years.[20]

The opinion of the eldest of the experts matched those of his colleagues, with only one exception: Le Brun. Thus their final recommendation was one of laissez-faire: let the bread be made, let the consumer choose.

But the doctors, with sixty-seven-year-old Gui Patin at the head, were not of this opinion. Gui Patin, illustrious dean, *caput facultatis*, head of the medical profession, as the statutes read, challenged the arguments of experience and "good sense": "To say, as those who defend it do, that they have not seen anyone drop over sick or dead from eating this bread is not a good way to clear it of the faults with which it has been charged. It is like sugar refined with lime or alum, or heavily salted, peppered, and spiced meats, or wines in which one tosses lime, fish glue, or other things bad in themselves, which men concerned about their health avoid, even if none of these things causes death or threatens one's health on the day it is ingested."[21]

For him, the sum of individual experiences was not an epidemiology. To deny the pernicious long-term effects was to deny the possibility of risk. Whereas risk did exist; the doctors were convinced of this. They did not list yeasted bread among those products recognized as dangerous but among the adulterated, "sophisticated" ones, to use the expression of the time. The list of such products was long—Gui Patin only gave a brief survey—but their effects on health were difficult to assess. If yeast was not actually a poison in the proper sense, it was an additive that had to be forbidden. It made bread into an altered, falsified product, in no way "good and faithful."

The arguments exhausted, it came time to vote. Of the six doctors, four followed their senior authority and declared themselves opposed to the use of yeast and two came down in favor of it, providing that the yeast was prepared and used well. The Paris gentlemen had agreed that they would go along with the scientists' opinion, and yeast was condemned by a wide majority.

Health decisions followed; in July 1669 La Reynie pronounced himself in favor of prohibition. One year later, in March 1670, the parliament rendered its decision. In the end, after hearing the public prosecutor's conclusions, the court permitted the use of yeast in the making of rolls. Perhaps for the first time, a food risk was submitted to a democratic vote and then to a judicial decision.

The Judge and the Police Captain

What had begun as a mundane lawsuit had precipitated a real crisis, to the point that, if the queen's bread affair was not an affair of state, at least it mobilized the highest political authorities in the capital.

It took place within a particular context: the complete reorganization of the Paris police, required and sponsored by Jean-Baptist Colbert. A year earlier, the superintendent had established the position of first lieutenant of police, a police captain, appointed by the king. The Cobertian reorganization, which, in typical ancien régime fashion, added without cutting, had not standardized the Paris public health inspection system. The competent authority in matters of food supply and safety remained a many-headed monster, which numbered three institutions of justice and an administrative authority: the Châtelet, which controlled Paris's central market; the merchants' provostship, a jurisdiction consular who had his seat at the Hôtel de Ville; the parliament; and the lieutenant of police, this captain who was named directly by the king and who, overriding the judicial authorities, embodied the modernity of the state.[22]

Beyond the overlapping domains, which prompted rivalries or forced cooperation, all the decision makers shared the same conviction with regard to food supply and health: to secure abundance and guarantee good faith in transactions were their two obligations.[23] That the Paris parliament, the greatest tribunal in the realm, was concerned with food safety may seem astonishing, especially if one refers to the maxim: *De minimis non curat praetor* (minor affairs are not the business of the judge). Either the maxim was not a permanent feature of French law, or the long-robed judges did not consider affairs that concerned human health to be minor. In 1631, at the request of the public prosecutor, alarmed by certain medical reports, the parliament had forbidden the use of smoking tobacco in a public place: the king's prisons. The court deemed tobacco harmful to the health of those who smoked and others as well. Later, in 1752, as a result of a lawsuit involving delicatessen dealers and grocers, a ruling by parliament granted rights over the Bayonne ham label. The judges were concerned with public health, a concern both heightened and tainted by political consider-ations in the eighteenth century, when the legal profession sought to cultivate its popularity with Parisians. Thus the parliament and the lieutenant were engaged in a symbolic competition for the esteemed image of the capital's nurturing guardian.

After the parliament, the second decision maker was the police lieutenant. His intervention in this matter might initially seem just as odd, if one thinks of the popular "dung, street lamps, and prosti-tutes" slogan, which, in the eyes of the public, summarized the main duties of the capital's new strong man. But the new administrative regulations just taking shape were defining new roles for the police. The police lieutenant was, first of all, the king's man, responsible for helping to propagate the royal mythology. Pierre Goubert has high-lighted the popular images that supported the notion of an absolute king. The dispenser of justice, the worker of miracles, the king of war: these were successive or simultaneous images that constituted His Royal Majesty. With the Sun King, and especially after him, one aspect faded, that of miracle worker, healer of scrofula, which hardly anyone believed anymore, including the king himself. But another mythic image developed concomitantly, the figure of the "baker king." The ideology was simple: as father of the people, it was the king's duty to see that his subjects were fed. And the sovereign's obligations implied no constraints for his subjects. On the contrary, this ideology valorized their rights, which were not those of the citizen but of the consumer.

Steven Kaplan has shown that until 1760 a kind of social contract existed between the monarch and the cities. The cities promised to remain peaceful and faithful, and, in exchange, the king looked after their provisions. This implicit pact did not prefigure the welfare state, insofar as the role of the state was not "to feed the people but to see that they were fed."[24]

In Paris, it was the job of the lieutenant of police to keep this royal promise. How did the lieutenant conceive of his function and what place did he assign public health? We know the answers to these questions thanks to La Reynie's colleague and successor, Nicolas Delamare. Delamare compiled a *Traité de police*, a true reference manual for enlightened administrators. For him, police commissioners, who were the "assistants" and the "eyes" of the magistrates, were to see to it "that the low life be contained, the vagabonds driven out, the poor pro-tected, and that the good people live in security and peace." That was the first part of their mission, the best known, and the one summarized by the amusing triad of "dung, street lamps, and prostitutes." But their responsibilities went far beyond collecting garbage and maintaining the moral code: "Having thus first looked to regulating the people's conduct with regard to mind and heart, the police must then devote himself to ... providing them also corporal goods.... Health, which is the first and most desirable of these corporal goods, thus precedes all others of this nature." Among public health concerns, Delamare lists clean air, pure water, wholesome food, and medicine.[25]

This was not just a declaration of intent. In sum, half the *Traité* was devoted to the sale of provisions. Delamare assembled a whole regulatory corpus on this subject, including old ordinances coming from various sources as well as recent measures. Clearly, public health was very much a major preoccupation for the lieutenant. In 1697 the growers who cultivated the marshes around the city and provided it with vegetables and other market products were prohibited from using the fecal matter produced by the city to fertilize their gardens. This was a courageous measure, since, in the name of public health, it eliminated an easy and profitable outlet for urban sludge sold as manure.

But let us return to bread, which, in police vocabulary, constituted a basic necessity and not simply an edible as, for example, vegetables did. La Reynie exercised his right to control the bakery trade, making sure that no bread sold was "rejected, spoiled, hard, burned, scorched, or badly turned," as forbidden by guild statutes.[26] But his supervision went even further, and in 1668 he added a health component to the notion of bread quality.

La Reynie and the parliament managed the crisis according to the consultation model, although appealing to experts appeared to be a means to delay a decision, a stalling technique in the face of an awk-ward situation. In fact, the lieutenant aligned himself with the opin-ions of the experts, specialists and nonspecialists alike, and adopted a prohibition measure long before the parliament came to its decision. A man like La Reynie, aware of the importance of public opinion and attentive to its vagaries, could not ignore it on so sensitive an issue and could not seek beyond it for a second opinion.[27]

Modernity values consultation, the appeal to experts and nonspe-cialists alike, and it values the media. The debate over queen's bread first echoed in the buzz in the inns and public squares, and then the rumor found its way to the newspapers. Particularly important to this spread of information was the *Journal des sçavans*, a newly created periodical meant to link the republic of letters to an enlightened public. The newspaper reported on current scientific controversies, which were sometimes quite specialized. A good example was the exchange of views between Philippe Hecquet and Raymond Vieussens over the physiology of digestion (1712). Beginning from the moment when information appeared in this high-caliber publication, undoubtedly supervised by La Reynie, the affair took on the air of a scholarly debate. Contrary to the standard claim, information in this case did not cause great anxiety. Rather, it deflated a fear into a worry, and then into a scientific controversy.

The Experts

By putting officially recognized doctors and nonspecialists on the same footing, the scientific tribunal convened by the king's judges demonstrated a crisis of confidence regarding certain official medical doctrine. Between 1550 and 1650, Galenism had entered into a crisis, and, if it had passionate defenders like Gui Patin, it was increasingly assailed as dogma. In 1668 a current theory threw the medical school into even more turmoil than yeasted bread. It was the theory of blood circulation, formulated by the Englishman William Harvey three decades earlier, which they refuted and rejected with every last ounce of their energy. Patin called Harvey a *circulator*, a bad pun on the Latin words for both circulation and charlatan. One of the rare therapeutic victories of that century was quinine. Now this antipyretic was rejected by all the Galenists, Gui Patin at the head of them. Patin was the sworn enemy of all new drugs like opium, quinine, and the whole exotic pharmacy. He stubbornly confined himself to proven medications, to the 125 phytotherapic remedies of the botanical repertoire, copious purgation, and merciless bloodletting.[28] Those who claimed to cure in other ways were only Arab cooks. Patin *dixit*.

What quinine proved to the gentlemen of the courts was that, in order to approach a "scientific" truth, one had to combine the two approaches offered by the medical tradition, and both had to be confirmed by experience. The first experience (*experimentum*) was one's own, what one observed with one's own eyes. The second experience (*experiencia*) was the experience of others, that of past generations, reported and compiled in books. *Experiencia* required a historical knowledge of the subject one studied, a narrative, a *history*.[29] Some contemporaries gave voice to the need to take individual experience into account, among them, the surgeon Jean Devaux who, in a pamphlet written in 1683, declared that everyone must become his own doctor: "When I see a man who is otherwise quick-witted ask a doctor if a food he has often eaten is good or bad for his health, I would like to ask him if he is not insensitive to himself, if in eating it he has not felt its effect, good or bad.... You do not have to be a doctor to conclude that, if a food is agreeable to the taste, if it is easy to digest, without leaving the stomach feeling too loose or too tight afterward, it is a good food." The Parisian surgeon was not alone. A number of thinkers of that time, readers of Montaigne, rehabilitated the notion of instinct, otherwise known as the ability of each person to have a valid opinion on what he himself uses.[30] The two types of experience were essential and complementary bases for making a sound judgment, and that was why the judges convened a scientific jury composed equally of Paris gentlemen and doctors. The first group provided their personal experiences, the second their historical memory, and the two together guaranteed a kind of scientific rigor that was nevertheless very difficult to conceptualize.

Did the judges' distrust extend beyond official doctrine to the entire medical profession? This was a decade when Molière met with success on the Paris stage. His plays *L'Amour médecin* (*The Amorous Doctor*), *Le Médecin malgré lui* (*The Doctor in Spite of Himself*), and *La Malade imaginaire* (*The Imaginary Invalid*) all aimed satiric wit at the incompetence of doctors. Molière denounced their bankrupt cures, all the excesses of a medical practice based on bloodletting and purgations, which, according to public opinion, weakened the sick person rather than curing him. Moreover, Molière's critique was effective; it made people laugh because it touched the heart of their collective experience, a deeply held popular opinion. For a long time, doctors had been reproached for their methods of treating the sick. And, conversely, doctors reproached the sick for their "vulgar errors." In the sixteenth century, Joubert declared war against popular errors and prejudices, denouncing "the absurd ignorance of those who completely trust the doctor except with regard to the quantity of food." "Stubborn and contradictory," patients contested the diets prescribed to them, particularly fasts. The common folk considered eating, eating well, even overeating, to be good treatment, said the doctors. They thought that ten capon were better than the light foods Joubert proposed, like a good bouillon, which he advised them to drink or to inhale, which was "the same thing, as long as the food entered the stomach." This accounts for the doctors' bitter bedside battles over the sick, to prevent their near and dear ones from stuffing them, or in the hospitals, against the nursing nuns for whom the best medicine consisted of forcing bread, herbal teas, and meat on their patients and making them drink a pint of wine each day. But this miscomprehension was limited exclusively to rations, to quantities for the sick. Joubert was very precise about that: "As for foods, there is much to contest, but not concerning the quality—which is still the most important and most difficult issue—but the quantity."[31]

Joubert's reservation is significant: with regard to the quality of foods, no one denied the competence of the doctors. Judging the "goodness" of foods was a matter of health maintenance for healthy people, that is, a kind of preventive medicine that doctors, very aware in other respects of the limits of their therapeutic arsenal, always considered the main branch of medicine. Gui Patin was the author of the *Traité de la conservation de la santé par un bon régime* (Treatise on conserving health through a good diet), which met with the kind of success reserved for that literary genre. Evaluating food risks was at the heart of the doctor's vocation. On this point, medical authority was never questioned. Even Molière did not dismiss physiology or the whole of medical doctrine. His comic doctors, M. Purgon and Diafoirus, offer idiotic cures, calamitous treatments, but good diagnoses. In a certain sense, Molière and his audiences took them very seriously.[32] We must view the public's skepticism toward doctors as relative: they were only discredited to a limited extent. Effective professionals, no, but honest men, yes, and, as such, they were worthy of public esteem. With regard to food risks, they were credible authorities.

The information then available for evaluating food risk was very rudimentary. This was the time of quite primitive baking and milling technology and the predawn of nutrition. If physicians felt entitled to define the roles and virtues of foods, they were incapable of analyzing their composition. In the earliest phases of chemistry, one man attempted this, a doctor named Nicolas Lémery who was born in 1645. In 1675 his *Cours de chymie* (Course of chemistry) met with great success; it was reissued several times in French and translated into many languages. Lémery separated everything into three distinct groups: mineral substances, vegetable substances, and animal substances. That was a first step, but not sufficient for advancing the science of nutrition. His son Louis, who also taught at the Paris Medical School, published in 1702 a *Traité des aliments* (Treatise of foods), which included this definition: "Anything capable of repairing the loss of the solid or fluid parts of our bodies merits the name of food. According to this definition, the air must be regarded as a true food and even as the most necessary one of all."[33]

This remark might point to an extension of the doctor's domain, toward the "aerism" of Enlightenment physicians, but, in food matters, the younger Lémery did not go beyond the old questions. The programmatic title of his treatise provides some sense of this: "Treatise of foods, in which one finds in order, and separately, the differences and the choices that one must make for each of these in particular; the good and bad effects that they can produce; the principles by which they thrive; the climate, age, and temperament to which they are suited." The analytical grid that Lémery provided for each food came from the treatise of Pisanelli, which appeared in 1584 and was itself derived from the medieval *Tacuinum Sanitatis*. Thus this was a phase of trial and error, halfway between the old science of virtues and the elements of Lavoisier.

The limits of scientific knowledge restricted the medical debate in the bread trial to the proven thesis/antithesis formula. The final opinion, communicated to the public, took the form of a dissertation on the risks of fermentation.

The fermentation process was one of the mysteries all pre-Pasteurian researchers struggled with. They knew that fermentation produced agreeable foods, like cheese, or even healthy beverages, like wine or cider. Nevertheless, the changes that took place in the fermentation vats remained the work of mysterious powers, impossible to harness. Beer "worked"—that was why brewing was forbidden in some Protestant countries on Sunday, the day of rest—and fermenting beer released more heat than fermenting wine, to such a degree that French brewers could not always control their overflowing vats. The phenomenon of fermentation was compared to decomposition and putrification, through which things deteriorated and were transformed. What linked these processes was the cycle of life and death; life, through spontaneous generation, participated in the work of death. The chemists had nothing to say about fermentation. It was the alchemists who practiced it, but in an occult and dubious fashion. Medicine was also aware of theories formulated two decades earlier by a doctor in Brussels, Van Helmont, who claimed that this obscure chemistry also took place within the human body and that digestion called into play the juices and fermenting agents that decomposed the bolus. The gastric juices, he said, were acid, and they were necessary to the digestion. For Van Helmont, the digestive phenomenon was not mechanical; it was essentially chemical. But, since the Brussels doctor maintained that a non-noble metal could be transformed into gold, his kind of chemistry was still too close to alchemy, and the medical school did not much appreciate it. Then, too, rather than holding forth on causes that escaped them, doctors preferred trying to anticipate effects.

In the two public debates we know something about, the discourse differed. The first was a debate between doctors who opposed each other but agreed on the essential thing: remaining faithful to Hippocrates. The first Hippocratic premise was that poison was a matter of the dose. Everyone agreed on the distinction between substances that were intrinsically harmful, like arsenic, and those that were merely suspect when used in small quantities. According to this reasoning, to forbid the use of the latter seemed as stupid as forbidding lemon juice, the acid administered as a medication in cases of scurvy, albeit in small doses. Yeast was considered an additive, a suspect additive.

This first Hippocratic premise was countered with a second Hippocratic idea: the doctrine of contraries. Yeast, it was argued, like all harmful substances, could be reduced to a harmless state by mixing it with its opposite, and it was not so dangerous when it was mixed with good flour. The idea was that the combination ought to minimize the potential for harm. So was that a yes for the queen's bread? It was a no, obtained both through a democratic vote and in the name of a third Hippocratic principle that subsumed all the others: *primum non nocere*. The majority of experts voted together, mindful of the maxim "first do no harm," and pronounced themselves against the use of yeast.

The second debate, which brought together doctors and worthy citizens, departed from strict doctrine. The first medical argument was to challenge the first category of experience, the kind that all could share and that could have the effect of completely exonerating queen's bread from all suspicion. To deny any effect was to deny any risk. Once the argument from individual experience was dismissed, the doctors deliberately established themselves on other ground, shifting the focus of the debate: the issue was not the yeast from beer but beer itself. This discursive shift permitted the debate between scientists and laymen to take place on common ground and to move from the invisible and uncertain to the visible and better known. Concurrently, it permitted the doctors to play on the beverage's bad reputation. And what were beer's faults?

There were two levels of criticism, a scientific one and a more practical one stemming from actual brewing conditions. The medical school's report took the form of a historical record, since history was the collective memory and that transmitted memory constituted "true" experience, which transcended the experience of each individual, considered "false" because much too short and too limited. Also, it should come as no surprise that the doctors tried to outshine each other in their erudition, in turn calling on any among the ancients who considered the subject of beer, beginning with Dioscorides and Galen. They passed quickly over Pliny, who praised beer, preferring to cite Tacitus: "this sad drink made of hops, barley, or spoiled wheat and bad water." They always chose quotations that supported their thesis. Many pernicious effects, in the end, were attributed to beer: headaches, bad nerves, a longer and more tiresome drunkenness than wine produced, sometimes leprosy as well. Really, what could one expect of its "foam," produced from "rotten barley and water" and mixed into bread?

Beer was less healthy a beverage than wine, the doctors concluded, because its fermentation released too much heat and because it was badly prepared. On this point, medical prejudices were confirmed by other doubts arising entirely from the techniques of French brewers, who were often unable to control their overflowing fermentation vats. In countries where it had become the national drink, beer was subject to various brewing standards. Bavaria set the example in 1516, when Duke William VI proclaimed the "edict of purity," authorizing only the ingredients of water, barley, malt, and hops (an edict still in effect today, though now it applies throughout Germany). Paris went no further than the statutes of 1269, which required that beer be made with barley, mixed grains, or *dragées*, which were secondary grains, but without ryegrass because of "the disorders that this grain causes in human organs."[34] Made with secondary grains—oats, lentils, or vetch—and without hops, which gave the brew aroma and clarity, French beer remained a barley beer. According to Rozier, brewers continued to add dangerous grains like ryegrass to the brewery vats or to substitute absinthe for hops to save money.[35] In Flanders, where beer was the favored drink, its production was carefully controlled. It had to be made from a specific variety of barley and from hops, to give it bitterness and guarantee that it would keep, and other unhealthy additives, such as coriander seeds, lime, and fish glue, were forbidden. In Lille, inspectors, or *eswardeurs*, were responsible for verifying that brewers respected set brewing standards. In Paris, Delamare renounced the idea of regulating an indefinable mixture: "It is adulterated by mixing lime into it to make it stronger or by using soot in place of hops, which gives it a little touch of bitterness, and many other ingredients are also added under the pretext of making it more pleasing."[36] Was that because hops were almost never grown in France? In any case, the French did not direct their efforts toward updating regulations but toward denigrating foreign products. German beer? It was made with polluted water: "poisoned and reddish water that runs through the middle of cities, where it receives every infection."[37] This was simply the Roman Tacitus's opinion of Germanic barley beer transferred to the German beer of the sixteenth century. Flemish beer? It was made with what they called *ratten bruick*, rat grain, and so no doubt contained arsenic.[38]

This anecdotal detour serves a purpose as it can lead us to something fundamental, to what went unsaid in the debate over yeast in terms of the ethnic and cultural dimension. The case rested on an argument of civilization: wine and "French" sourdough bread had to be preferable to beer and its yeast, both foods of inferior status by default. One drank beer for lack of anything better when wine growing was impossible and when one lived in a northern country, and, similarly, one mixed flour with yeast there. If beer was a drink, wine was a food. It was good for one's health. In French hospitals, it was served to poor patients in great quantities to reinforce their failing bodily functions. Was there any better diet for the sick than the daily ration of a liter of wine and a kilo of bread offered them in almost all large urban hospitals? The argument of civilization was not always explicit. It was hidden behind the old principle of familiarity: "we were brought up on sourdough bread and wine, why change?"[39]

This attitude was reinforced by the situation of grain cultivation, where beer could be seen as competition for bread. To drink beer might mean doing without bread, since both were made from grain. It was not beer's harmfulness, which was hard to prove, that so convinced the experts. It was the powerful ideology of bread and wine, indissolubly linked, and from a perspective that was not just eucharistic. Between the two, there was truly an affinity of blood.[40] The debate shifted from scientific to cultural grounds. But it ended with the same conclusion: "Death flies on the wings of the queen's bread."[41]

The Judges Facing Risk

Judges and doctors were very familiar with each other, and the intrusion of doctors into the courts was as old as criminal medicine. Between 1450 and 1500, doctors' expert opinions were solicited with regard to autopsies, injuries and blows, and miraculous recoveries.

The courts called on their expertise in cases of sterility, impotence, and poisoning. In 1520 the parliament consulted the medical school regarding the dangers of pollution from the use of coal as a combustible fuel. In 1631 it was the doctors' negative report that led to the prohibition against tobacco smoking in the prisons.[42] The decade from 1660 to 1670 was a period of sustained collaboration, and the domain of legal medicine, although it was not yet called by that name, became more expansive. This was the decade when, prompted by Colbert and Pussort, the courts relied heavily on doctors in cases of witchcraft. Distancing themselves from demonological culture and magic, many magistrates embarked on a campaign against accusations of witchcraft and possession, and they found their best allies among doctors, who provided decisive arguments. Patin, for example, did not believe in the devil, or possession, or miracles—listening to his remarks made in symposiums (behind closed doors), it was not really clear if he believed in God—and he was a great friend of Lamoignon, the highest magistrate of the time. After being set back by cases of poisoning in which doctors were obviously consulted, this cooperation finally resulted with striking the crime of witchcraft from French law in 1682.

Despite this long history of collaboration, the judgment of the law courts in the yeasted bread case did not concur with the recommendations of the various expert committees. We may certainly formulate a few hypotheses here to explain the judiciary logic involved and why it prevailed.

The king's judges ruled over the debate and added an ethical dimension to it. They reasoned in terms of moral philosophy. Now, on the normative level, what value was to be accorded the voting process, even when a large majority agreed? It was absurd to count votes to discover where an elusive truth lay. The judges undoubtedly felt that they could not leave such an important question to the chance involved in a semielectoral process. Their intellectual stance probably differed from that of the politicians and prominent citizens, who witnessed the lack of consensus and open disagreement among doctors. While this contingent saw such "contradictions" among medical experts as grounds for questioning their expertise, the judges saw a debate, a true philosophical controversy in which, in the absence of certainty, one thesis outweighed another. Also, wanting to keep the scales balanced, they listened attentively to the two opposing parties. The yeasted bread supporters were the minority, of course, but they had strong arguments and important key figures to defend them. Claude Perrault, their leader, transformed the debate into a quarrel between the Ancients and the Moderns, presenting himself as the archetypal modern as opposed to Gui Patin, the archaic academic.[43] To demonstrate their arguments, queen's bread partisans invoked in turn the experiences of foreign countries. They stressed the fact that yeast was rarely used alone in breadmaking, that it was generally combined with sourdough as an extra agent to enhance the effects of the latter. Above all, the defenders of the queen's bread expressed the strong conviction, strong enough to convince the judges, that yeast was not intrinsically bad. According to the conditions of its production and transport, it could sometimes be good and sometimes be bad. That was the real snag. The yeast that bakers used at the time was not like the cultured yeast bakeries now use. It really was the wild "foam" that came from the breweries. At the end of the long journey from the Flanders breweries, it might easily arrive in a more or less obvious state of autolysis, and, at the very least, it could give bread a very bitter taste. On the other hand, fresh foam collected from local brewery vats presented no danger.[44]

The judges' decision was clearly a victory for the queen's bread proponents.[45] It could also be interpreted as the outcome of a certain judiciary logic that would help shape the judicial attitude in the face of risk. "When the question is uncertain, take the less forceful stand" was the old adage. This had been reinforced to some extent by the recent medical-judiciary reconsideration of witchcraft. To put it simply: one could no longer condemn without proof. Producing proof became essential, whether it was proof of witchcraft or possession for the courts or proof of nobility within the royal administrative offices. According to this new jurisprudence, yeast could not be condemned without certainty, solely on the basis of adverse criticism. This legal principle ran counter to the medical principle of precaution, and it translated into an acquittal based on the benefit of the doubt, but with one condition. The judges authorized the making of yeasted bread but forbade "the use of any yeast other than what is made in this city of Paris, fresh and uncontaminated, under penalty of a fine of 500 pounds."[46]

In doing so, the judges did not deviate from the classical contract on health. By leaving the freedom of choice to consumers, they respected the balance established between consumer vigilance and policy measures, both of which were necessary to guarantee public health.

The judges' decision settled the dispute on the commercial level. It did not completely resolve the controversy. A hundred years later, there were still Parisians like Robert Ducreux who deplored the judges' authorization and railed against them: "They were as ignorant as gluttons. They were afraid of displeasing women or were as fussy as women; they wanted pastry bread. For their poor judgment and gourmand attitudes, I consider them effeminate wimps."[47]

Ducreux attributed to yeasted bread a whole list of typical, if minor, urban ailments, such as constipation. Wouldn't the remedy here be to drink some water from the Seine, famous for its well-known laxative qualities, especially among tourists? This text, written in the 1760s, proved that yeasted bread was still a hot topic. The debate continued, and we find echoes of it in the *Journal des sçavans* and the dictionaries of Furetière and Savary. All the old grounds for latent distrust remained, cleverly exploited by people like Parmentier, who led a crusade against yeasted bread parallel to his campaign for the potato. In this "soft bread" controversy, the opposition raised their voices and made themselves heard over their adversaries. We must not be deceived by their discourse. The field of the debate had shrunk considerably. Henceforth, it was limited to what could be called the official forum: the medical school and a few scholars, who nevertheless remained divided in their opinions. In fact, both sides had been heard, and Savary pronounced the other verdict—the one handed down by the public—in 1740: "It seems that experience has since decided in favor of the citizens and against the doctors."[48]

Experience—once again! This time it referred to the growing use of queen's bread in Paris and all the other cities of the realm. Yeasted bread consumption spread throughout all the urban social classes to such an extent that it lost its status as social symbol in the large cities. To change one's bread was to change one's life. Besides the statistics, there were other indications of this food revolution. Witness, for example, the furniture: the bread bin disappeared when city dwellers began buying all their bread from the bakers who made queen's bread.[49] Peddlers could be seen in Paris making their rounds balancing tin cans on their heads, like milk deliverers, but these cans contained the precious fresh yeast they sold to the bakeries.[50] Also witness the evolution of language. Through a semantic shift, the word *blé*, which had designated all kinds of grain used in breadmaking, henceforth was applied only to wheat. White bread was no longer an elite privilege. It was the soldier's bread and the Parisian worker's bread, who considered it an earned benefit. The poor bought it, too, out of defiance and because this refined, porous bread was better for dipping in soup and soaking up gravy.

Two pacifying forces were at work in the cities of the eighteenth century. The first was the phenomenon of social imitation, and, in the end, it was an undeniable victory for the Paris working class to gain access to white bread. The second was taste, that increasingly significant value that accompanied the expansion of French—which is to say, Parisian—cuisine. In 1668 the experts accused Paris bakers of wanting to "appeal to the tastes of *friands*."[51] *Friands* were the predecessors of gourmets, and there were many of them in the following century, both men and women, since women were at the heart of the new bakery demand. White bread was a necessary part of a recently invented food practice: morning breakfast with café au lait. And did the most ardent opponents of yeasted bread avoid eating it? Nothing is less certain. "No doctor today does not eat yeasted rolls with lunch," insisted Mercier, and there were many cases of what Morin called "winking reason" among the learned experts whose tastes and habits conflicted with their opinions. Among those nonpracticing believers, there was the famous case in 1699 of a doctor presiding over a thesis on the dangers of tobacco for the nose. Throughout the examination, he had his snuffbox in hand, and he punctuated each argument he presented against the use of this toxic plant with a vigorous pinch! It was said that his nose was not in agreement with his tongue.

That the question of yeasted bread could dominate urban public debate on food risks signaled the obvious fact that a food revolution was under way in French cities, equivalent to the meat revolution that transformed the English diet at that time. The white bread revolution was considered a positive thing. And, in fact, with his kilo and a half of white bread practically guaranteed each day, the city dweller could consider himself satisfied. After all, that assured him a comfortable supply of 3,500 to 3,750 calories. In 1942 the ration of bread per adult was limited to 275 grams. In 1946 those French entitled to the "A" rationing card were only entitled to 1,300 calories. By comparison, a caloric ration before 1789 is generally considered sufficient. Nevertheless, people ate badly: eliminating the husk through bolting deprived white bread of a share of its nutritive matter, and the diet overall provided too much vegetable protein and too many glucides, too little animal protein and fat. Today, such an increase in bread consumption would not be considered a dietary improvement; very much the opposite.

The yeasted bread controversy overshadowed other realities that hardly concerned affluent Parisians at all. Consider, for example, this

1670 report by Gui Patin on an epidemic that then raged through the capital's hospitals: "In my opinion, it seems that this disease is *morbus totius substantiae*, a disease of poor and badly nourished people.... Good bread, a bit of wine, white linen, good air, and a mild purgation at the onset of this illness would do enormous good.... The Germans have written much about it. I think I have seen more than two hundred theses on it in my lifetime, but the disease will not be cured by Latin words or secrets of chemistry. Curing people's poverty would easily cure scurvy."[52]

A good diagnosis and a beautiful text. Patin observed what had long been a disease of seasoned sailors, deprived of fresh provisions and thus of vitamins. As it was not clear the two diseases were the same in nature, "sea scurvy" was distinguished from the "land scurvy" that ran rampant in large Paris hospitals beginning in 1663, which says much about the malnutrition of the Paris population, deprived of fresh foodstuffs during the long months of winter. Patin had clearly sensed a deficiency disease, without knowing exactly what deficiency it involved. How could he speak of a vitamin deficiency when the vitamin—the micronutriment as well as the word—dates from 1911? The bedside remedy that he prescribed—lemon juice—was the right one. So was the basic prevention that he advised, but that type of treatment was beyond the scope of doctors. Gui Patin should not be scolded for bringing false charges against yeast. He knew too well that diet could lead to dangerous deficiencies, which developed quietly, never rousing the fears of the well-nourished.

SEVEN

SILENT FEARS

Societies of the classical age were not free of the major risk: the risk of famine. A bad harvest, whatever the causes, inevitably unleashed shortages and stirred up the governing and the governed. Administrators feared high prices and the riots they could engender. The clergy dreaded the decline in morality and charitable tendencies. The king feared for the health of his subjects. A short time after his accession, marked by a terrible food crisis, Louis XIV wrote in a memorandum for the intendant of the Dauphiné region that shortages were so formidable because of the diseases to which poor nutrition led. The king was aware that food-related hardships rarely occurred alone and that the problem of food quantity gave rise to the problem of food quality. Before famine, the final stage of privation, there was the risk of malnutrition. Sporadic or chronic, too little food generated deficiency diseases. At the time, they were known as diseases of poverty. The problem with the diseases of poverty was that they unleashed unheard-of fears: one hardly heard the victims complain.

The Dangers of Rye Bread

"In that time, the disease of the ardents blazed among the Limousins." Thus the pen of Ademar de Chabannes, writing in 997, cited one of the well-founded fears of the year 1000. The epidemic was known by forty different names in six different languages, the most common being Saint Anthony's fire or sacred fire, or the disease of the ardents, the "ardents" being those who burned with an internal "fire" that consumed them before causing their limbs to swell up and dry out. "May Saint Anthony's fire burn you!" was the worst curse that one could wish on an enemy, because the pain was horrible, and in the end it killed you.[1] It took a long time to make a sure diagnosis, to distinguish gangrene in its two forms, dry and convulsive, from the other "fires." Ademar de Chabannes would have to wait seven hundred years for a likely etiology to be established, linking the disease to food, and eight hundred years for the scientific world to accept the relationship between gangrene and the ergot fungus of rye. The cause supplanting the symptoms, it was then that the gangrene would take its current name of ergotism. As for ergot itself, Candolle, a botanist working at the beginning of the nineteenth century, would identify it as a parasitic fungus, a cryptogam of the rye grain.

When it appeared in the Middle Ages, the fire was like the plague: sudden and invasive. And it was like leprosy: polymorphous (the name hid beneath it perhaps two or three gangrenous diseases). But it was not contagious like the plague, and it was not as deadly as the plague. Nevertheless, it was debilitating enough to provide past societies with a large share of disabled, maimed, armless, and legless cripples and sufficiently widespread throughout the Continent and in every social stratum to elicit prayers to Saint Anthony for a cure. There was a religious order of hospital workers, the Antonians, who served the sick. And there was an abbey, Saint-Antoine-en-Viennois, at the edge of the Dauphiné region, that served as both pilgrimage site and hospital to welcome and care for the ardents.

When, after a long lull, the disease reappeared in 1638 in France, the monastery experienced a resurgence. Two Benedictines visited it in 1639: "The monks have charitably reopened their hospitals, so long closed, to the destitute who have been stricken; with much compassion we viewed twenty of them, some without feet, others without hands, and a few without feet or hands, because this disease can only be cured by cutting off the limbs that it first attacks. There was a very skillful brother there, who lacked nothing. He showed us feet and hands cut off a hundred years ago that were just like those he cut off every day, that is to say, black and completely dry."[2] Any visitor could see, exhibited ex-voto in the door of the abbey church, mummified limbs resembling dry wood.

In 1638 the collective memory remained vivid enough for the resurgent disease to be quickly recognized as a nonconvulsive form of Saint Anthony's fire. Gangrene ran rampant for two centuries and was particularly virulent during "those tempests of hunger," as the bishop

Esprit Fléchier called them, that ravaged Louis XIV's France.[3] Beyond France, there were signs of epidemic crises throughout the empire: Alsace was affected, as was England in 1661, and Sweden as well. If this disease recalled Saint Anthony's fire, it was clearly less democratic than the disease of the ardents, which struck men and women from every social stratum. "It treats the poor worse than the rich," and, among those poor, this gangrene especially affected country folk: it had become a rural disease—*morbus ruralis*. It was the peasants who "burned" from gangrene, and particularly the peasants from the poorer countries, from Silesia to Saxony to Sologne.[4]

Beginning in years 1630–1650, Sologne was generally considered the center of the epidemic. Sporadic outbreaks of gangrene kept devotion to Saint Anthony alive. In 1682, when the prior of Sennely decided to remove the saint's statue from his church, he met with strong resistance. The statue was "ridiculous and shameful" with its pig, but the faithful faithfully brought it offerings, in the form of gift pigs.[5] Not only did gangrene rage, but so did fevers, comparable to malaria. The Sologne fevers, the Solognots' gangrene, not to mention the red disease peculiar to Sologne sheep: all this explained the notoriety of this poor region of marshes and sandy soil.

For scientific circles in the classical age, it became something of a privileged observatory for rural pathologies, conveniently close to Paris. There, each theorist could try out his own methodical system. The aerists thought that the marsh air, the bad air (*malaria*, as Italian doctors called it, after Ramazzini, the great Padua university professor) was responsible for the intermittent fevers. Fagon, the king's doctor, stubbornly maintained that the atmosphere was responsible for the selective grain disease that attacked certain ears and spared others: "There is fog that ruins the wheat, but, for the most part, the ears of rye are protected by their barbs. In those that the malignant humidity reaches and penetrates, it blackens the skin and alters the grain."[6] The nutritionists thought that the gangrene originated with food, following the lead of German doctors, who attributed the disease to the consumption of "horned rye." Those who fell into neither school of thought considered gangrene a disease with multiple causes. They attributed it to the peasants' scanty diet, their lack of cleanliness, and the excessive cold.

The theory that linked gangrene to rye ergot was presented for the first time at the Marbourg Medical School in 1597 in Paris, in a report to the Royal Academy of the Sciences. The academy had sent one of its own, Perrault, to investigate "this strange disease that almost exclusively attacks poor people and in years of scarcity."[7] The multifaceted Perrault—anatomist, architect (his most beautiful work, the Louvre colonnade, was close to completion)—after studying the question of wheat bread, was confronted with the question of rye bread. Upon his return to the capital, he noted in his report that he "had learned from the doctors and surgeons of the country that rye sometimes went bad, in such a way that those who consumed bread made with large quantities of the bad grain would lose body parts to gangrene, some one part, some another; that, for example, one lost a finger, another a hand, another a nose, etc., and that this gangrene was not preceded by fever, or inflammation, or considerable pain, that the gangrenous parts fell off by themselves."[8]

This was in 1672. The academician drew his information from the humble knowledge of local practitioners and from patient observations by doctors in the Hôtel-Dieu d'Orleans, which accepted the most severe, and often desperate, cases. A surgeon in Montargis told him that this disease attacked rye crops almost every year, especially crops grown in light, sandy soil, that there were few years when it did not happen, "but that the harmful grain naturally made no one sick when not found in great quantity."[9]

Others had observed that over the course of particularly humid years, rye developed a parasite that the Gâtinais called *bled cornu* and the Solognots called *ergot*. If Berry, Blésois, and Gâtinais were attacked nearly every year, it was because the ergot developed in poor, wet soils. Sologne was the "province that unfortunately produced more ergot all by itself than the whole of France" according to the abbot Tessier. The Solognots were big eaters of rye bread. Cases of gangrene appeared mid-August, after a few weeks of consuming rye flour, and slackened through autumn, when, with the buckwheat harvested, grain consumption did not rely exclusively on rye.

This interpretation, factoring in food, was not immediately accepted. The academicians were not convinced by the series of deductions that led from spring rot to summer heat to food poisoning. The fact that all the Solognots who consumed the same bad bread were not all victims of gangrene greatly increased their doubts. Finally, nothing definitively proved that gangrene was a result of poisoning. Was ergot something to fear? In an attempt to dispel the uncertainties and provide a definitive answer to the question, two men well known in learned Paris circles, the abbot Tessier and Parmentier, resorted to experiments on the living. By running trials—Tessier on a beautiful glossy pig, Parmentier on dogs—they obtained different results: the pig died of convulsions; the dogs survived. Parmentier thus proclaimed ergot innocuous and denounced the worry over food, "the absurdity of the fears regarding this so-called poison."[10] In the face of Parmentier's skepticism, Tessier responded that the dose administered was not strong enough and that one could not reasonably be reassured by tests done with such small quantities of ergot. After 1776, following demonstrations done by Paulet, Jussieu, and Tessier, most members of the scientific community admitted that the gangrene originated with food. No one could deny that ergotized rye was a risk, but no one could prove that it was a known danger. The result was a unanimous recommendation to the government: that tests be ordered on criminals condemned to death—in other words, that the bread served in prisons be more or less tainted with ergot. And they added, "This is a way of rendering crime itself useful to humanity."[11]

"Deaf to the Cries of Danger"

All those who, like the abbot Tessier, had gone to Sologne to research the problem and were convinced that the disease originated in food remarked that "the indifference of the native is notable; those who thresh the rye are not concerned about it, and neither is the miller."[12] The millstone ground rye and ergot, grain and parasite together, and it all was turned into flour. Grow something else! said Tessier. Why not switch to the potato, which would thrive in the poor soil, with much higher yields? The answer was no surprise: to abandon grains and dark bread, whether rye or buckwheat, "many Solognots seem to believe a disgrace."[13] Thus Tessier, disgusted both by such resistance to novelty and such resignation to gangrene, drew a rather severe portrait of the Solognot. Physically, he was a pale and sallow figure, under five feet tall, with a weak voice, languid eyes, and a slow gait. Morally, he was ruled by ignorance, stubbornness, routine, stupidity, and imbecility, these last two terms used according to their medical definitions. Undernourished people had weakened mental faculties.[14]

Basically, the Solognots were more stupid than their chickens. Because unlike the Solognots, some pointed out, the chickens had a good regime: they got up early, ate when they were hungry, were happy, went to bed early, and never ate anything adverse to their constitutions. And they were wary of eating ergotized grain: "However cleverly it is mixed into their feed, they prefer to go three or four days without eating."[15] Ignorance, when it was a matter of the food risks of ergotized rye, was vigorously fought. There was a relentless information campaign to combat it throughout the eighteenth century. Where the epidemic raged, both the intendants and the agricultural societies seized any opportunity for warning people. The population was informed through billboards posted on walls and memoranda distributed to parish priests, lords, and other "charitable persons."[16] The whole food safety policy was a preventive one, aimed at informing people of the dangers incurred by consuming ergotized rye flour and urging producers to sift the grain better to separate it from the parasite. In 1762 Duhamel du Monceau wrote: "It is always easy to separate out the majority of the ergotized grains with the help of a sieve, because most of the diseased grains are much larger than the healthy grains. Sologne peasants sift their grain in the years when it is not expensive, but, in years of shortage, they are careful about wasting ergotized grain. And that is why they are stricken with a dry gangrene that makes their extremities fall off."[17]

In fact, the information campaign was successful; the Solognots seemed to be perfectly well-informed. But although they heard, they did not listen. If it was not ignorance, then what prompted the Solognots to continue braving the danger of ergotized rye? That question baffled most observers. And asking the question also elicited answers. Here is a brief sampling of such testimony:

Abbot Tessier wondered, "By what fate does it happen that these men, convinced that ergot can make them sick, have no difficulty leaving it in the grain they eat? Because I cannot doubt the way the inhabitants of Sologne think about ergot. All those I asked in that country gave me examples of its grievous effects on individuals in their families. What can be the cause of their indifference on so essential an issue except their extreme poverty, which renders them deaf to the cries of danger?"

An Orléans doctor noted, "Finally, is it not surprising that the inhabitants of Sologne who, knowing the bad effect of this food, continue to get food poisoning, fully aware of the cause? ... But we must consider that Sologne produced hardly enough grain to feed its inhabitants. There is great poverty there. Thus, to satisfy hunger, nothing must be wasted. And the only means of preventing them from using this bad food would be to provide them the equivalent in good grain."[18]

All the observations agreed on two points. Eating rotten rye was a survival technique. The peasant found himself in a double bind: he could not sell ergotized rye, which was not marketable; he had to eat the grain or go hungry. The second point was that the risk was acknowledged universally but assessed relatively: in years when rot did not affect the whole harvest, one avoided ergotized rye; in years of shortage, one did not, and the threshold of vigilance dropped to zero.

Let us look beyond these basic observations. Was such risk accepted with no forethought? The fate of poor imbeciles trapped by necessity who had no choice? Was it not also calculated, resulting from a more or less conscious, more or less rational choice?

The Solognots took into account various factors that made the risk acceptable. The parasitism varied according to the degree of maturity of the grain, and it was rare for all the ears to be parasitized. And Solognots recognized that the effect somehow depended on dose. "The harmful grain naturally makes no one sick when not found in great quantity."[19] But how to define this absolutely vital threshold? Tessier and Parmentier both tried, by mixing healthy and ergotized flour in proportions of about eight to one. In this attempt at a quantitative assessment of the risk, Tessier approached the truth, but he was unable to define a maximum dose having no effect on animals or to extrapolate to humans. Now, defining an acceptable dose was perhaps what the villagers were attempting with their limited means, based on memory, their entirely empirical methods, and the hope that the quantity of ergot absorbed would not be enough to produce anything more than the earliest effects of ergotism: a certain sensation of drunkenness and pins and needles in the limbs.[20] The other variable was, indeed, the effects. Dry gangrene developed according to different pathological stages, following a course that was not at all inevitable and causing mutilation only in the final stages. It was rare for the disease to prove extensive, requiring amputations. To lose a limb was not fatal, and to die from the disease was rare. In bad years, when the Solognots with ergot numbered in the hundreds, only a few dozen were hospitalized in Orléans, where the most serious and desperate cases were treated. The others escaped with a few minor afflictions, vivid hallucinations, and occasional spasms. Let us not underestimate this variable. The villagers had enough experience with the disease to know the clinical effects very well. On one particular point, they knew more than the doctors. Noting early on a relationship between the ingestion of ergot and the frequency of spontaneous abortions, Sologne midwives (and those in Germany, Tessin, Lyons) discovered one of ergot's virtues: it prompted uterine contractions. They administered it to women giving birth, at the beginning of labor, thus accelerating the delivery. The practice was included in the 1782 *L'Albert moderne*, but it was either unknown or rarely adopted among the learned medical community. Obstetricians introduced ergometrine, one of the alkaloid extracts of rye ergot, in the maternity wards one hundred years after the last gangrene epidemics. Urban medicine was a century behind simple rural practice.[21] This all relates back to that unrecognized expertise, that knowledge of plants and their properties, that "science of the concrete" that learned circles scorned, rendering them generally incapable of understanding the behavior of the poor in times of food crises.

Rustic Drugs

Now that we have entered the hidden genetic world of the parasite *claviceps purpurea*, we know that it contains alkaloids and its composition is quite similar to that of LSD. Thus we can better understand the disorders provoked by the gangrene in its early stages. All ergotism began with a phase of psychological troubles, described by classical age clinicians as: "drowsiness and dreams," "vertigo, din, dizziness," indeed even "a frenetic delirium," "it is certain that made into bread, it [ergot] provokes vertigo, and feelings similar to intoxication";[22] "as soon as the peasants ate this harmful bread, they felt almost drunk."[23] This was ergotic drunkenness. Did it cause fear? For some, it took the form of "very laborious sleep and disturbing dreams"; for others, the intoxication could be gentle and prompt hallucinations quite unlike the nightmares populated with strange and monstrous beasts caused by that earlier form of gangrene, Saint Anthony's fire.[24]

Quibbling over the effects of spoiled rye returns us to the blunt question of rustic drugs. We could avoid it, hide behind some great historian, postulate with him that the range of available dope in the country was quite limited, practically nothing outside of "the simple and rough high of wine and alcohol—and, in any case, not the gentle dreams of oriental drugs."[25] Artificial paradises were not yet available to the poor. The silence of documents seems to confirm this opinion. In their books, the naturalists treated "stupefying" plants with timid prudence. These learned gentlemen did not want to know, or, if they did know, it was inadvertently, thanks to experiments made "by mistake" or "by accident." Thus the one who "ate some mandrake root mistaking it for licorice" experienced drowsiness and delirium, and that was how its narcotic effects came to be known.[26] In written accounts, the consumption of rustic drugs was always involuntary, when it was not unavoidable, as in the case of ergotized rye. Nevertheless, it is impossible to confirm this received idea. Unsuspected artificial paradises were indeed available to the underfed. We see drugs only as physiological stimulants for escapism. They can also respond to other needs. "There are certain drugs that are not at all nourishing, some of which appease hunger for a short time; such is the case with smoking tobacco, which, by making one spit a lot, gets rid of a share of the humor that causes hunger."[27] Lémery, the author of these lines, shared the opinion expressed by Fuchs, one of the first naturalists to study tobacco: "The aforementioned smoke received through a cornet appeases hunger and thirst without otherwise intoxicating, a fact ratified daily by sailors."[28]

Tobacco was widely introduced in rural France as early as 1629, the date that marked the creation of the first royal tobacco tax. Since we know that fiscal policy never follows far behind consumption, this is an invaluable indicator of its widespread use. Considering tobacco solely as a substance consumed for pleasure and a good stimulant for the intellect will not explain its success. There had to have been stronger psychological drives to make it so popular. Lémery provides us a key here. As a stimulant, tobacco had little initial appeal. As an appetite suppressant, it had every chance of success. The need to suppress hunger, to fool it, was just as strong as the need to satisfy it. More precisely, the drug was another means for combating shortages, as it neutralized the sensation of hunger or, even better, created compensatory dreams filled with lands of plenty. In a climate of insecurity over food supply, it responded to a physiological need first, more than a need for pleasure.

Without access to luxury drugs, the poor could draw on the infinite repertoire of local plants, wild or cultivated, stupefactive substances that were less distinguished but just as effective. The narcotization of the countryside was achieved well before the arrival of tobacco. Rustic drugs were denounced by dieticians and administrators, offering us good opportunities for spying on these furtive practices.

In a chapter on edible seeds in his *Traité*, Delamare mentions wild mustard seed, which "fortifies the stomach and facilitates digestion," and likewise hemp seed, called *cannabi* in Provence: "The seed of hemp was formerly among a number of vegetables that were served fried for dessert, but at present this evil stew is entirely banished from the table.... Whoever ate much of it would alienate his mind; the dry leaves or its flour mixed in a drink would render those who consumed it drunk, stupid, and dazed."[29] Delamare speaks of its consumption in the past tense, as a thing of the past; Champier, writing a hundred years earlier, presents it as a current phenomenon, although reserved for times when securing provisions was difficult.

Seeds and grasses of all kinds, with questionable virtues, were part of a certain peasant culture. Let us be clear in our understanding of rustic drugs. The word "drug" itself, with its modern-day resonances, invites error on our part. The very narrow category of "drugs" established in the nineteenth century does not correspond to those native stupefactive substances that the poor had found in nature or culture. They did not prompt social fears, because they were ambivalent, remedies according to one aspect, poisons according to another—but isn't that the very definition of all medicine, depending on the dose? They were not ranked with those substances consumed for pleasure, they were not taken through the nose but through the mouth: in our sources, they were classified with edible seeds and foods. Edible seeds, coming from secretly cultivated cereals or wild grasses? Of course, the peasant, that frugal eater, knew about them. In a chapter on cereal diseases in his *Histoire de l'alimentation*, Champier drew up a compendium of the knowledge of that time, highlighting how diseased grain could be harmful to eat. When flour from such grain tasted good, it produced bread that tasted as good or even better than bread made with healthy flour, so the threshold for perceiving risk fell: that was the case with ryegrass, and that was the case with ergot. And there was the added problem that the first—and often the only—effects were sensations not wholly disagreeable. By means etymologically eccentric but medically justified, Champier related the two words, *ivraie* and *ivresse*, ryegrass and drunkenness, signaling the gentle euphoria or, at worst, the visual hallucinations that accompanied its ingestion: one "saw things" when one ate ryegrass bread.[30]

In central Italy, ryegrass, that self-propagating plant, grew with wheat, was harvested with it, and milled with it, finally becoming an ingredient in those "ignoble" breads with toxic effects denounced by the botanist Pietro Mattioli: "The bread, when a notable quantity [of ryegrass] enters it, makes the men who eat it become stupid, as if they were drunk, and they fall into a heavy sleep; that is why in Tuscany, we are very careful to separate the ryegrass from the wheat, to avoid the harm done to the head by such intoxication and sleep."[31] This was a Sienese, a city dweller, speaking. In the cities, the police supervised grains. It was their responsibility to "watch particularly that the flour and bread meant for human consumption not be full of ryegrass, so as not to disturb the stomachs or the minds of those who eat it."[32] Countryfolk behaved differently. Targioni carefully observed them, and he denounced the damaging effects and the "malice" of bread with ryegrass, because it tasted sweet, so much so that it was difficult to distinguish the poisoned flour. He spoke of his great astonishment at seeing ryegrass cultivated around Camugliano and the inhabitants putting it in their bread (a sixteenth of the flour—subtle dose!) to enhance the flavor, without the slightest effect on their health.[33]

Ryegrass bread, rye bread: beyond Paris's pure wheat bread, we have hardly any idea what breads were made from. And the mixtures varied, moreover, from one region, one year, or one season to another. Before the French Revolution, Taine drew up an incredible catalog of these mixtures, and no regional historian since has failed to mention region-specific grains.[34] Bretons on the island of Batz, for example, ate a bread made of barley, three-quarters rye, and one-sixteenth wheat.[35] This universal practice of mixing bread flours led to unbelievable compromises. In the country, stupefactive seeds were added or, rather, not removed. A doctor in Grenoble named Villars noted the dangers of a certain lentil variety cultivated in Champsaur and Dévoluy to feed animals, and humans when necessary: "The poor peasant, afraid of lacking grain for the year, has observed that a dozen or more such lentil seeds mixed with the rye that he uses for bread makes the bread harder and heavier and that his children and servants eat less of it."[36] (The Alpine peasant's solution was no worse than the remedies proposed by certain scientists in times of shortage. In the indigestible repertoire that Parmentier drew up—six hundred pages long—listing all the substitutes for bread, he cited grasses, legumes, and roots. Postulating that the starch was the most nutritious part of the grain, the pharmacist traced starch in all the vegetables. He found it in the horse chestnut, the tuberous vetch, the colchicum, and even hellebore and mandrake, and he did not hesitate to advise mixing them with good flour in times of shortage.)[37]

This variety of lentil was both toxic and rich in protein, let us say, poisonous and nourishing, which called for cautious behavior. The precise amount shows that such mixtures were not necessarily improvisations made in response to great urgency but products resulting from calculated risk. Must we continue to think that, threatened with food shortages, people ate anything they could? Nothing is less certain. These doses, arrived at by trial and error, mean something. A dozen lentils in Dauphiné bread responds to our current notion of an additive: a substance added intentionally; it is understood that one knows what one is adding and in what quantity.[38] With a sixteenth part of ryegrass in Tuscan bread, we are approaching the weak dose, the homeopathic dose of the poison recommended by Paracelsus in 1530.

The Solognots ate rye bread in summer; the less poor could resort to a mixed bread of rye and wheat and then to buckwheat bread or rye and buckwheat, once the buckwheat harvest was in. Thus their bread contained varying proportions of rye and varying proportions of ergotized rye as well. The main precaution was not making bread from 100 percent ergotized rye. And since this bread did not taste bad, it diminished any fears: the disease could be avoided, Solognots thought, as long as one did not eat rye bread all the time. And, in fact, attacks of the gangrene lessened as the grain diet evolved. These supposedly imbecile peasants had, in the end, their own alternative policy of prudence. Unable to achieve zero risk and eliminate ergot from their diet, they sought to limit its harmful effects. The desperate need for sufficient quantities of food could accommodate a calculated risk. Between the certain danger of dying from starvation and the probable risk—not always proven or proven to varying degrees—of gangrene, the Solognots chose the lesser of two evils. The effects of these self-intoxication practices in terms of mental health have yet to be evaluated. They could be enormous, leading to an imaginary universe "where images of monsters and nightmares ferment, described by poems, ballads, stories, and legends in countless situations of fear, astonishment, ecstasy, wonder, feverish excitement, and irrational emotion."[39] Not long ago, a large segment of popular culture discovered such a universe through domestic drugs.

After 1850 Solognots no longer had to make this difficult choice. Pine plantations took over the drained marshlands, and cultivation of the potato, perfectly adapted to the poor soil, allowed the food system to be diversified. Thus gangrene lost its hold and ceded its territory.

Doctor Ramel's Files

Rural food fears were refracted fears. They did not emanate directly from those threatened by the risk, either because they were unconscious of that risk or because they did not express their distress. The poor laborer did not complain. It was through the intervention of others that one knew the risks, that one measured the distance between the actual risk and the reaction it caused. Borrowing an expression from the sociologists, let us call such individuals sounders of the alarm. Among the alarm sounders, there is one group the historian holds dear, because they were skillful both at observing and describing; these were the country doctors.

The country doctor is a recent invention. He emerged in France during the "first medical crusade," between 1770 and 1830.[40] He is invaluable because he wrote up not only personal prescriptions but also medical topographies, memoranda, and reports in response to requests by the authorities. This new practice seriously questioned the way medicine was practiced within the framework of the profession. Until then, the medical relationship was a very private one between doctor and patient. Henceforth, in addition to this narrow, private sphere, a public sphere, beyond the framework of the hospital, opened for medicine.

Young Ramel was a doctor in Aubagne and a correspondent for the Royal Society of Medicine. To call him a country doctor is inaccurate, as Aubagne was a large town near Marseilles. Ramel's practice, however, extended into the surrounding country, from the Mediterranean coast to the interior of lower Provence, thus providing him a solid knowledge of the various professional circles—fishermen, carters, weavers, farmers—as well as the various bioregions. Between 1783 and 1792 he wrote forty-three letters to the Royal Society, which included research reports, various solicitations, and requests for long-distance diagnoses. Among his correspondents were such notables as Vicq d'Azyr and Fourcroy. Ramel was one of the links in the lively network between Paris and the provinces that much reduced the isolation of the countryside.[41]

Ramel's concerns, as expressed through his correspondences, were very diverse. They involved not only human health but also that of animals. He was greatly upset by a case of glanders that struck two mules in 1783. After an evaluation by two of the town's blacksmiths, he was called in for consultation. If there was no licensed veterinarian, the doctor played the role of expert for animal diseases. Glanders was an extremely serious zoonosis, and Ramel undoubtedly knew that, but his fears all revolved around the economic consequences of an epizootic spreading in a country of cart drivers. Transporting merchandise by mule, he wrote to the gentlemen of the Royal Society, was "one of the major branches of commerce in this country." Arranging for the suspect mules to be sequestered, he kept the disease from spreading, to everyone's relief.

As for human afflictions, he consulted Paris only regarding communal diseases or isolated phenomena. Intestinal worms constituted both simultaneously. Ramel had a thorough knowledge of them. He classified them according to the families he observed—lumbrical, ascaride, cucurbitain (this last thus named because the segments resembled "seeds of squash or melon"). But one particular worm, emitted from the mouth of a young man in Roquevaire, posed a problem for him. He observed and sketched it and sent four very precise drawings to Paris. What was this monstrous worm, whose head was adorned "with two horns and two ears of a bat," which was still moving as it came out of the poor young man's mouth? An anecdote no doubt, but it recalls the common truism regarding digestive parasites that "take the man in the cradle and only abandon him at the tomb," a kind of parasitism so intense that it resulted in vomiting up the tapeworm.[42]

Ramel's colored illustrations show how the imaginative etiology of Enlightenment doctors went hand in hand with extreme precision and a fine sense of observation. Ramel was the very model of the new doctor the Enlightenment introduced. This new doctor was not a man of new knowledge: he still lacked investigative methods and therapeutic tools. But he was a man with a new function. Like his colleagues, Ramel no longer considered health to be only a private affair. It was also a public affair, and, as a doctor, he had to be committed to the service of the medical magistrates.

On two occasions, Ramel was called on by the municipal authorities: first, in the previously mentioned case of glanders and then on the subject of bread. In 1785 the mayor and the consuls of Cassis were worried about the quality of bread provided by the city's bakers. They asked Ramel to consult the higher authorities—that is, the Royal Society of Medicine—regarding the way the bakers used seawater or the brackish city well water for their bread. The main motive for using salt water was clearly to avoid paying for salt. The crime of lèse-gabelle was quite widespread along the French coasts, and Cassis bakers were not the only ones guilty of it. But in Cassis, following Mayor Roux, an enlightened freemason, this common abuse was perceived for the first time as more than simple fraud that only hurt the economy; it constituted a possible health risk. Ramel served as Cassis's spokesperson: could it be that the poor quality of this heavy, bad-tasting, badly risen bread was responsible for certain prevalent diseases, especially the pulmonary tuberculosis that was almost endemic? A memorandum was sent to the Royal Society on January 27, 1785, accompanied by a vial containing a sample of the offending brackish water. As this report was supposed to be exhaustive and objective, it covered all aspects, the worrisome ones as well as the reassuring ones. At the very least, the quality of the water was doubtful. The consuls noted that the seawater was drawn from the port and was "more murky and muddy"[43] than the water of the open sea; as for well water, its degree of salinity varied according to the rainfall. The bakers, too, had plenty of arguments demonstrating the harmlessness of their products. Theirs was a subtle, proven technique: whatever the degree of salinity in the water, they were careful to obtain the ideal proportion of salt, that is, two pounds of salt for three quintals of dough. Thus the bread met the required standards—which was not always the case, because if bakers had to pay for their salt, they were often inclined to economize. Besides, wasn't good flour, from the heart of the country, enough to make good bread?

As for Ramel, he seemed divided between two views. His observations in Cassis were rather reassuring. Those who ate bread made from seawater did not seem to suffer from this daily consumption; the fishermen, in particular, had vigorous constitutions and good health. We know that doctors concentrated on the peasants' physical aspect and profile, that the topology of the rustic body emphasized or exaggerated distended, relaxed stomachs or, worse, *hydrosfamelicus*, the stomach inflated in times of shortages. There was none of this among the fishermen, whose "sound lower stomach muscles were more firm and more prominent."[44] The other view was drawn from Ramel's reading, which provided him with historical knowledge and inclined him toward prudence. He had read translations of Manningham and Zimmermann, the sad lists they had compiled of bread adulterations in the big cities. Paris was no longer the center of food horrors; London had supplanted it. "A few years ago, London bakers noticed that one method of making white bread caused constipation; they took it into their heads to toss jalap into their flour, and their bread eased bowels by acting as a purgative."[45]

Torn between this conflicting evidence, Ramel left the question to the society's chemists. Fourcroy himself and three other specialists studied the problem of Cassis saltwater bread in their Paris laboratory. No one knows the results of their evaluation.

Not all the town's fears were equally shared. In 1790 Ramel complained to the society: "It is worth noting to you that the same citizen who charged me a few years ago to consult you on defective bread-baking methods is still the mayor at this time and that he does not think of asking me to consult you on the prevailing epidemic, a much more important subject than bread." Does this mean that Ramel was less sensitive to the dangers of foods than infections? Not at all. But he classified risks according to urgency. The immediate risk of the epidemic had priority. Food risks had long-term effects that were difficult to measure: "Bread does not suddenly give rise to diseases.

But can't it quietly predispose us to them, and doesn't the good of humanity demand that this dangerous abuse be corrected?"[46]

The problem he confronted was what he called slow poisons.

Slow Poisons

Samuel Tissot was the best-known Swiss doctor of his time: his *Advise to People on Health*, published in 1761, met with enormous success. It was translated into seven languages and reissued ten times in six years, without counting pirated editions. For Tissot, among the main causes of diseases, two were at the top of the list, overwork and true exhaustion. "True exhaustion" manifested itself when one's strength was not restored, for lack of sufficient or wholesome food. He added, "But this case is very rare in this country; I believe it to be most frequent in a few French provinces."[47]

To read the reports addressed to the Royal Society or all the administrative correspondences on the subject of epidemics that came into the Versailles offices via the intendancies, pockets of poverty really did exist where the problems of grain quality and quantity arose simultaneously. Ramel's Provence, which had access to "sea wheat," or imported rice, was protected from shortages. But other regions, such as Brittany, were particularly vulnerable.

At the time of the "fevers" that ravaged the parishes around Landerneau, a Doctor Vigier wrote to the Brittany intendant: "You ask me, Your Lordship, what is the cause of these diseases that devastate our countryside? I confess to you that I can only attribute them to the bad quality of our wheat. Last year, there was too much rain: it was impossible to dry the wheat before gathering it and storing it in those great wooden bins that serve as warehouses for this foodstuff for all the inhabitants of the country. The wheat warmed up, fermented, and developed a moldy taste; it was ruined, and most of it went bad. The farmers sold the best wheat and kept the worst for themselves, out of which they made flour for bread or gruel."[48] This buckwheat gruel, thickened and cooked with butter as a pancake, was the Breton *galette*. Now, in 1769, the *galette* was bad, and, if it did not directly cause the epidemic, it promoted it by lowering the body's resistance. The administrators shared this analysis. In 1774–1775, following the terrible epidemic that threatened to depopulate Brittany, thirty-nine Breton subdelegates sent a report to the intendant. According to all of them, the epidemic was linked to the high price of grain. Thirteen of them were more explicit and blamed the impoverished diet of country folk and especially the poor quality of the badly preserved grain they ingested.

If there was no good grain, what could doctors do? That was why they despaired and revolted against a kind of official medicine that, for example, advised a starvation diet for the sick: "I have only to forbid bouillon with meat, when there is no meat and when the bouillon, if there is any, hardly differs from clear water," wrote one Alsacian colleague. Another wrote, "They have nothing in their stomachs but worms."[49] Another heresy of the rich man's dietetics: to be afraid of foods that might be heavy or cause gas, that might obstruct the digestive canals. Whereas, as Villars said with regard to Champsaur, why speak of the danger of indigestion "in a country where indigestion is nearly as rare among people as it is among animals?"[50] Let us feed them first; then let us treat them: that was what one doctor after another wrote.[51]

Italy constituted another privileged observatory for common diseases. Italy's prominence was explained by the tradition of the doctor *condotto*, bound by a medical pact to a city or a district.[52] The Italian doctors' discourse closely echoed that of their colleagues across the Alps, discourse that revealed their impossible task of trying to distinguish poor eating from undereating. It was all one pathogenic complex they observed, in which food was both insufficient and unhealthy.[53] Even for a disease like malaria—which could definitely be linked to air quality—food factors were also suspected. Meat coming from livestock that wandered in the swamps, grains rooted in marshy soil, vegetables growing in stagnant mud, all these foods were accused of being corrupt and corrupting influences, of provoking the putrefaction of the humors that unleashed the fevers.[54]

All slow poisons were not of the same nature, and they did not all equally require the intervention of public authorities. Doctors divided them into two categories: those created by nature, like ergotized rye, and against which the administration could do nothing except issue multiple warnings; and those created by humans, like the "falsified" bread of Cassis. For this second category, doctors asked the state to intervene in the name of medical policy, a concept just invented by Johann Peter Frank.[55] "The greed and ambition of those who sell basic foodstuffs is so great that men (and especially soldiers, artisans, and the poor), instead of finding food a substance they can assimilate and which restores them, find nothing more than a slow poison that gradually undermines and devours them, a poison that withers the useful arms of the state, that dissolves the armies meant to defend it."[56]

Against the cupidity of men capable of adulterating bread, guilty of numerous frauds that transformed food into slow poisons, Ramel appealed to the vigilance of the beneficent state: "On the contrary, our investigations, having food substances as their subject, will shed light on a beneficent government always attentive to the interests of public health. From the denunciation of these abuses will spring useful and coercive regulations. Doctors will zealously supervise the enforcement and the handling of those regulations."[57]

Ramel assigned the doctor a new objective: social supervision, which he conceived as an extension of preventive medicine, but this time at the level of the whole population and not just the individual. He was not alone in this kind of thinking. Michel Darluc, his colleague in Aix, became Provence's naturalist. Throughout his travels to the country's interior, he continually denounced those practices and manipulations, voluntary and involuntary, that compromised the quality of food. But what could policy do? That important question had no clear answer in this decentralized realm where the cities had all the supervisory authority in the area of food safety. Consider, for example, the oil mills in the country of Aix, which provided a product with an excellent reputation, although it was produced under filthy conditions. The enemy here was not human greed or "malice," but routine and bad habits. Against these two tendencies, Darluc called for intervention and constraint. "Is it not of the least importance that the police in these places watch a bit more carefully than they do that good order and cleanliness in oil mill practices be maintained and that, when they are lacking, such negligence be severely punished?"[58] Unapologetically repressive, Ramel and Darluc called passionately for a rational medical policy that would give doctors responsibility for defining the rules of prevention and possibly supervising the implementation of health standards.

In rural areas, conflicting fears were obvious: the "learned" fears of enlightened gentlemen and the fears of the common people rarely matched. This resulted in the struggle that doctors led on both fronts. On one side, they sought to calm unfounded fears, especially with regard to the innovations they encouraged: the potato is a good example, as demonstrated by the disputes between Poitou doctors and farmers over accepting this new crop. Thus, on the one hand, they tried to reassure, encourage, and stimulate progress. On the other hand, they sought to warn, increase awareness, and instill fear when danger existed unrecognized. In their fight, the doctors used fear as a double-edged sword.

Instilling a fear of slow poisons was a difficult task, because it was promptly refuted. How to demonstrate the risk of disease or death when the effects were not immediate? The fear provoked by the idea of poison was generally associated with the short term: whether the poison was "cold," like hemlock and mandrake, or "hot," like arsenic, it inevitably had a stunning, spectacular, immediate effect. People were familiar with poisons; they used them. And, as new substances like arsenic spread, country folk were no less vulnerable to all too "familial" accidents; their popular nickname for this poison was "the powder of succession."[59]

Long-term effects, or "predisposing causes" for diseases, are hard to understand. And to admit, because, if the cost is not immediate, it becomes highly improbable. Over the long term, repeated ingestion of certain foodstuffs posed the risk of death, but the standard retort was that something else would no doubt kill you before that happened. Apprehending such risk was complicated because, not only was harmfulness hard to prove, but slow poisoning very often involved foods that were normally good to eat, which circumstances rendered dangerous. Out of necessity, they had been harvested too early, when they were too green, or they had spoiled after the harvest or rotted from being badly stored. Now everyone understood that familiarity with a food guaranteed its safety. This distinction doctors made between the "radical vice" of poisonous foods and the "relative danger" of otherwise healthy foods was decidedly too subtle![60]

In the epidemiology that first appeared during the Enlightenment, many like Ramel put the food factor first and advised a healthy diet as the first remedy. But others named environmental factors as the primary culprits and granted air quality the place of primary importance. This group—the aerists—was more numerous, louder, and, above all, supported by official authorities like the Royal Society of Medicine. The aerist doctrine was then in vogue. It was behind all field studies, and it led to the compilation of local medical topographies. Of course, Ramel was aware of the dangers of bad "effluvia." He even described the emanations from the shallow ponds in his region. But, on the whole, he believed more in the harmful effects of adulterated foods and undrinkable water than in the inconveniences of bad air and the "epidemic constitution" of a place. The meteorological medicine then in fashion annoyed him: "The doctors of our age would do well to abandon research on the air, research that can never correct and improve the air's influence or moderate its effects, and turn instead to analyzing the solid and liquid foods that people eat." And later, driving the point home: "Accurate analyses of food and especially of drink would be infinitely more useful to humanity and would contribute to the progress of medicine in a much more vital way than trivial, bland meteorological observations that can never convert medical meteorology into a positive science."[61]

Ramel said what he thought, and he wrote it down. He fumed against the "meteorological whole" of such hegemonic thinking and was nevertheless naive enough to wonder why Félix d'Azyr, the society's ideologue, showed him so much "coldness." As if he did not know that these gentlemen were real sticklers about the declared orthodoxy and quick to take offense if their authority was undermined.[62]

In the end, Ramel recognized his own responsibility: "I have shown my poor taste in challenging an opinion that it [the Society] seems to have embraced since its establishment, and that it cherishes." Country doctors felt flattered, of course, to be included in the Parisian network, but, by factoring food so heavily in diseases, they found themselves at odds with it. The medical thinking of the Enlightenment, which favored the emergence of a kind of environmental medicine, resulted in a regression and a retreat. By selecting texts and impoverishing the Hippocratic corpus in order to retain only what related to theories of air and place, such thinking minimized the food risk and marginalized those who made it their concern.[63]

But perhaps the sounders of the alarm during the Enlightenment were heard, and more or less understood. The emerging medical policy granted a place to food, though it was a very small place in the immense project of public health as it began to unfold.

EIGHT

THE PÂTÉ AND THE GARDEN

Hollow Meats

During the reign of Louis XIV, in the bookstore of Charles David in Aix, a little book written by one of the city's doctors, Michel Bicais, sold for three francs. *The Method for Regulating Health by What Surrounds Us and by What We Take In*—that was the book's title—was packed with practical recipes and advice on what to eat and what to wear. In the chapter on fabrics, Bicais insisted on the purity of clothes. He had observed cloth under the microscope, seen "the filaments interlaced like window screens," and discovered that, in the interstices of the fabric's weave, foreign bodies, possibly foul ones, could be lodged. He inferred from that the need for strict rules of hygiene, that is, in times of epidemic, looking for tightly woven clothes to limit the miasmas' means of entry and, in ordinary times, resorting to "perfumes with sharp particles that pass through the threads like scraping knives or awls, loosening and removing the trapped matter."

Among all fabric fibers, silk seemed to him the best for its health qualities. He considered its nature to be vegetable and not animal, since it came directly from the mulberry leaf, thus conferring on it certain virtues: "Thus this restored herb has excellent qualities, it is cooling and cordial, it is good for erysipelas and angina, if a piece of it is used in which one has strangled a snake." Silk's properties were truly astonishing. Thanks to its "vegetable nature," it could sprout in a humid and nourishing spot, for example, on the wound of an injured man. "A wild plum tree has been seen to flourish on the stomach of a shepherd, and green peas have been drawn from some ears."[1] We may wonder why a plum tree and not a mulberry, since silk, according to Bicais, was only mulberry regenerated! With spontaneous generation, anything was possible, and others, whose scientific authority was incontestable, maintained that silkworms could be procured by killing a bull fed on mulberry leaves for twenty days.[2] The theory of spontaneous generation, which the Aix doctor fervently supported, left the range of possibilities wide open.

The equipment Bicais used to observe fabric fibers belonged to the first generation of microscopes, and his investigations were exactly contemporary with those of Antoni Van Leeuwenhoek, who discovered microscopic organisms in a drop of swamp water and opened the way to micrography and histology. A simple, mediocre instrument with a single lens, it only magnified one or two hundred times, which resulted in chromatic aberrations. But the faults that distorted observations were less significant than aberrant reasoning. Basically, as modern as the instrument was, it hardly mattered. What mattered was one's perspective: we see only what we can conceive. For a long time, before and after Descartes, people had a sense of the impossible. That explains a major difference between contemporaries of Paracelsus and Paré and ourselves: "They did not believe that there were possible things and impossible things in the mixed lot of what they observed."[3] Thus ideas we find preposterous and illogical held sway in the learned world, which granted nature omnipotence, a nature that created and produced without limit or law. As for popular thinking, it was open and receptive to all food fables.

The elite of classical times, who began to acquire some notion of the possible and to distinguish fact from legend, had an expression they used to label and discredit food fears and unfounded fantasies: those who experienced them, they said, gorged themselves on "hollow meat." It would be better, of course, to cultivate good reason and nourish oneself on certitudes. But how many others fed on fantasies and hollow meat, opening wide the field of the marvelous? The alimentary imagination operated between two poles, one reassuring, the other disquieting. Rumors clustered about the disquieting pole.

Rumors in Times of Crisis

Food fables are rarely positive. Rumors that spread generally sound the alarm, alarms more or less urgent, most often false, but how does one verify a rumor, which is, by nature, unverifiable? Rumors circulate within temporal and geographic parameters. Some are intensely regional; for example, potatoes were thought to transmit leprosy, especially in the western frontiers of the Massif Central. Others are more sporadic and resurface in times of crisis.

Rumors accompanied epidemics. All epidemics implied that those stricken ingested something in common, like air or foods. Writing his *Traité de la peste* in 1568, Ambroise Paré first incriminated bad air and then food, noting that all kinds of epidemics appeared "after having drunk corrupt wine and putrid water, or after having eaten bad food like rotten grain, herbs, wild fruit, and other adulterated things." And he concluded: "Such foods engender obstructions and putrid humors, from which follow galls, abscesses, ulcers, and putrid fevers that are the first symptoms when contracting the plague." That was a very reasonable etiology. As for the primary causes, "the plague is a disease coming from the ire of God, furious, tempestuous, hasty, monstrous, and appalling, contagious, terrible, a savage beast, fierce and very cruel, the mortal enemy of life, man and many animals, plants, and trees."[4]

With Paré, we enter fully into that twilight zone where the rational and the irrational exist side by side, where fantasies fan out from observations that are not in themselves false. The implication of food took place within the strictures of the humoral paradigm, which conceived every disease as a kind of intoxication. It also derived from the commonplace observation that shortages and epidemics were often conjoined, one dragging along the other. If those beset by shortages would eat anything, was it any wonder that serious pathological disorders resulted? That was why, during the 1590 epidemic, people were convinced that Paris inhabitants had been sold flour ground from human bones.[5]

In 1706 a series of sudden deaths spread panic in the Eternal City. Not knowing which way to turn, the public attributed the epidemic either to an unknown poison supposedly circulating in the city, or to the poor quality of tobacco sold to nicotine users, or to the excessive use of a new food, chocolate. Giovanni Maria Lancisi, the pope's doctor and a good specialist in cardiac pathology, diagnosed a wave of aneurysm ruptures, but that hardly matters.[6] What does matter is that the list summarized the most common food accusations: a food of poor quality (here, tobacco); a new food with unlikely effects (here, chocolate), and, finally, deliberate poisoning (here, the specter of the unknown poison). Listing the accusations in this way makes them all seem equal, as if they shared one plane, but, in fact, they were perceived very differently. If the risk of rotten or naturally unhealthy foodstuffs was acceptable, the risk resulting from human malice was not. Deliberate poisoning was intolerable, because it targeted each and every one in its hatred of society, and because it testified to man's wickedness, to his malice, in the worst sense of the word, and to some men being possessed by evil.

Unintentional or deliberate, the vector for collective poisoning could either be water or else solid food: for instance, fish.

Italian doctors observed that during the recurrent influenzas and plagues in Palermo and Cagliari, the poor represented the first and the greatest number of victims. Today's historian would link this undeniable fact to conditions of working-class life, to overcrowding in squalid neighborhoods and the ongoing physiological wretchedness that offered attacking bacilli little resistance. Observers at the time blamed, instead, the working-class diet, composed of food that was too often salted and sometimes spoiled. In particular, they accused "the corrupt flesh of cheap, stinking tuna on which the common folk stuff themselves."[7]

When extraordinary diseases appeared, fish was often blamed. In 1249, when scurvy attacked the Crusaders outside the walls of Cairo, it was reported that the men had eaten fish, a food that was undoubtedly unfamiliar to them. When syphilis struck and ravaged the ranks of Charles VIII's army as it lay siege to Naples, the water was blamed, the stars (a fatal conjunction between Saturn and Jupiter), and women—this last hypothesis, that it was a sexually transmitted disease, being justified. A fourth theory circulated: the direct source of the epidemic lay "in the corruption resulting from eating human flesh, which had been publicly displayed and sold as tuna while the French lay siege to Naples."[8] Fish meat, abundant and cheap, was the most available fresh food for the soldiers. But was this meat really tuna? Was this food a bit too unfamiliar? The French thought they had consumed something else, something that made them, literally, sick, because it made them cannibals. The poisoning was compounded by the transgression. No other complicating factors seemed to be involved. The French could not point to a cowardly attack, to vengeance on the part of the Neapolitans through the intermediary of food, because the disease struck soldiers in both camps. Thus it earned its double name. The French called it the "Neapolitan disease," while the rest of Europe knew it as the "French disease." God's ire? Human malice? In the interpretive schemas for great epidemic catastrophes, there are many intersecting levels of explanation. The one involving food does not implicate just any food. For the fable to be credible, it must conform to commonly shared perceptions, agree with dietary beliefs.

Fish was the scapegoat in times of epidemic. It had a bad reputation among doctors, as did all produce that was fresh and aqueous, being eminently corruptible and corrupting. The water it contained was suspect, pernicious, perhaps like the water of the manioc with its sinister reputation.[9] Popular opinion mistrusted this animal species—as cold and humid as the environment from which it came—and considered it as dangerous as its homophone (*poisson/poison*). A number of proverbs attest to this: "All fish is phlegm," "flesh makes flesh and fish makes poison."[10] *Advice to the Bourgeois of Paris*, widely distributed in anticipation of the plague, recommended a strict dietary hygiene, avoiding drinking water from the Seine and fish, rejecting the meat of animals not butchered on the same day, seasoning all foods with vinegar, lemon or orange juice, or even crushed sorrel.[11]

Fables are long-lived. They owe this to their adaptability, to how easily they can be transposed from one calamitous episode to the next. The epidemic outburst of the nineteenth century reactivated food fears, and cholera took over from the plague. But side by side with traditional fables, new fables emerged. During the cholera epidemic of 1832, many believed in deliberate poisoning, in a plot against the destitute by the rich or even against the hospitalized by the doctors. But a new legend also took shape. The risk of "coated candies" and "poisoned cakes" offered to little girls surfaced for the first time. It was Louis Blanc who reported this rumor. Within the given framework, the motifs changed, and the spectrum of oral vectors for poison evolved. Fresh meat and fish lost their hold, tied as they were to the medicine of humors. By the nineteenth century, progress in chemistry made the risk of bioterrorism more conceivable. From that time on, that fear accompanied and intensified every threat of crisis. In the French part of Lorraine in 1914, parents advised their children not to pick up the candy they found, which they feared was poisoned and distributed by the enemy. The poisoner was always compared to the enemy, though all the more cowardly for being invisible and for victimizing those most vulnerable. His image has evolved over time. The enemy responsible for bacteriological warfare was first the religious enemy (for example, the Jewish poisoner of wells) and then the class enemy, before nationalism prevailed, making him the enemy from across the border.[12]

The True Story of Cat Pâté

Among food rumors, certain ones are not sporadic and tied to times of panic but persistent, engendering chronic or continual fears. These are urban legends, stories that are brief, structured, and true to the extent that they report a misadventure of someone close or, rather, that one heard from a friend of a friend, or ..., the mode of transmission being considered a guarantee of the anecdote's authenticity.[13]

Today, this kind of anecdote is only conveyed orally, whereas, if we can track down the legends of former times, it is largely because they were granted written status. At one time, these "words without an author" found their way into print. It might have been, for example, in a work as serious and respectable as the *Dictionnaire de commerce*, compiled by Savary in the early eighteenth century to instruct merchants. In the article on beer, he reports a popular rumor that explains why porter, a beer popular in England among porters, was so strong: "The French believe that, to make their beer stronger than all other European beers, even those from Mons or Bremen, the English toss a skinned dog into the brew, all the flesh of which is consumed by the cooking of it." This practice, adds the reasonable Savary, is hardly plausible.[14] He does not believe it, and nevertheless he reports it. Like other enlightened authors, he no doubt assigned himself the additional mission of destroying prejudices. In this case, the encyclopedist adopted the basic posture of scientific positivism advocated by Francis Bacon: "When you encounter a common misconception along your way, do not hesitate to destroy it in passing, like a traveler cuts back brambles."

In these legends, it was less the food itself that came under indictment than certain trades, precisely those that dealt with foodstuffs and transformed them: brewers, innkeepers, confectioners. Among the food trades, consider the figure of the confectioner, who prompted mistrust throughout all European countries and beyond.

A confectioner, or pastrycook, was a specialist in *pâte*, dough, pastry crusts, and his main product was pâté. According to Furetière, pâté was "a baked pastry made of cooked meat, chopped or larded, and stuffed with many small ingredients and seasonings in order to make it more tender and flavorful or to help it keep for a longer time."[15] Pâtés or tarts were an urban specialty since they required a professional's oven. In the Middle Ages, only the filling was meant to be eaten; the crust was hard and inedible. The modern version made it edible. The two characteristics attributed to pâté that Furetière noted, that it disguised the meat and helped it keep longer, were double-edged. They gave rise to all sorts of rumors.

We can group these legends into two types. In the first, the harsher ones, the dough was stuffed with human flesh, and the provider, innkeeper or confectioner, was portrayed as a serial killer. In the second, the most common, the meat was cat meat, and the pastrycook, if not a dangerous neuropath, exposed the consumer to grave risks. The rumor assumed various modes of expression. There was a sung version of it, to the tune of "La Mère Michel," in which Père Lustucru, a cook, has the audacity to say "for a rabbit your cat is sold." There was a legal version: in a 1500 Paris lawsuit, a certain Gillet de Bailly accused Philippot Malquis and Jacques Le Page of making him eat "a pâté of cat brain, from which he had never recovered." The victim's particular infirmity? From then on, it was impossible for him to eat meat.[16] There was a philosophical version: in the ironic and skeptical tone of one who does not believe it, Montaigne used this rumor as proof in his demonstration of the power of the imagination. The credibility of such stories, he said, came "from the power of the imagination acting mainly on the more impressionable souls of the common people." And he continued: "I know of a squire who had entertained a goodly company in his hall and then, four or five days later, boasted as a joke (for there was no truth to it) that he had made them eat cat pie; one of the young ladies in the party was struck with such horror at this that she collapsed with a serious stomach disorder and a fever: it was impossible to save her."[17]

The examples cited here are all French and do not do justice to the legend's latitude, which was both very restricted and very wide. It only circulated in cities, but it circulated in all European cities and beyond. The seventeenth-century English ballad version of it bore this programmatic title: "News from More-Lane; or, The mischievous tricks of a tavern boy of this place who, having bought a fat foal for eighteen pence, the mare being dead, and not knowing how to raise the foal by himself, killed it, and had it cooked in a pâté, and invited many of his neighbors to the feast, and, telling them what it was, made them all sick, as you can hear in the following song" (end of title).[18] We find a Portuguese version reported by the Jesuit Viera in his *Art of Cheating*, and a Swiss version.[19]

The cat, a semidomestic, semiwild creature, with suspect nocturnal habits, was the favorite target of culinary myths. According to certain beliefs, its flesh was poisonous. The spinners of the *Distaff's Gospel*, so invaluable for understanding a certain kind of popular culture, warned against eating a number of things: one could not eat food touched by a wolf—which was equivalent to sharing a wolf's food—without risking the loss of one's voice, or a very painful death if the wolf was not already dead. Similarly, it was dangerous to eat foods soiled by mice. This transfer by absorption applied to all harmful or worrisome animals, and the cat was included among those ranks. One had to avoid eating the head or the flesh of a cat for fear of being paralyzed "in the head or back."[20] At the same time, the cat, in particular, the black cat, had many medical uses; it relieved hemorrhoids and gout, cured epilepsy, and prevented hair loss. But the pharmacopoeia especially valued its blood and excrement. Its flesh and brain, on the other hand, had the reputation of being true poisons.[21] During the Renaissance, the cat's brain was the object of paradoxical fascination, since, according to Champier, some considered it a delicious dish, while others believed it to be poisonous.[22] Champier himself did not reveal his personal opinion, but we know of his prejudices concerning brain in general. It was a food he advised against as too phlegmatic and difficult to digest. The other question raised was less a matter of the wholesomeness of this foodstuff than of its effects. The fear existed, and one worried about its psychosomatic effects, convinced like Montaigne, that food fear could cause death.

Rumors survive for as long as they retain the appearance of plausibility. The numerous regulatory documents concerning pastry production confirm that fears about bad pâté were not simply a matter of legend. Pâtés prompted deep distrust.

We must add that the pastrycook's art itself was questionable. It was primarily the art of chopping and grinding. Wanting to prepare a "house" pâté, the Mesnagier de Paris enlisted a professional. The meat that he boiled beforehand was taken to the pastrycook's back room, where he alone could "cut and mince it very fine."[23] His expertise was formidable: he chopped so fine that the original materials were no longer recognizable; he skillfully mixed ingredients; he masked them in the pâté. Mixed and disguised, the pâté was potentially dangerous.

In Paris, famous for its pâtés, professional supervision came late. Until 1440 the trade was largely itinerant and poorly organized. The first statutes for pastrycooks, dating from that year, included seventeen articles. Ten of them involved food safety and prohibited pastrycooks from concealing in their products foodstuffs "not worthy of human consumption." They forbade stuffing pâtés, turnovers, and rolls with "seeded and foul flesh, rotten fish, sour milk, moldy and stinking cheese, foul or corrupt flesh, eggs bought from brotherhoods." This represents a fine inventory of the varieties of possible fraud, from leprous meat to eggs left as offerings on altars. Pâtés were truly the masterpiece of the food-scrap-and-leftover trade.[24] As for the Saint-Quentin pastry-cooks, they vowed to "dress no meat for human consumption that they would not want to eat themselves."[25] Pastrycooks in Lima, Peru, were also strictly supervised to protect the health of those early fast-food (*comida corrida*) aficionados: "This day, the alcaldes and the magistrates have decided and ordered that henceforth no one can make cakes or turnovers unless he shapes and rolls the dough in front of his door, where the oven in which they are baked will also be located, so that they are made, baked, and displayed for sale publicly for everyone to see.... This decision has been ordered to be rendered public, as well as the requirement to stuff such products with meat bought from the butchers."[26]

Pâté was a way of accommodating leftovers, meat leftovers, in particular. Thus suspicions abounded regarding the use of bad-quality meat rejected by the public butcher shops, for example, stillborn calves or fetuses found in the bellies of slaughtered cows, as well as already cooked and not "new" meat or unsold cuts that had passed their date. Pâtés were suspected of masking the taste of turned trimmings, and here another legend, invented by the histori-ans of the past, managed to resurface: the use and abuse of spices as a way to hide the taste of rotting meat. In fact, it was true that spices were used excessively in making pâtés. The Paris innkeeper's pâté baked in a crust was made of tongue, cinnamon, clove, and pepper.[27] English "pies" included eight ingredients: beef or mutton, dried fruit, and lard, in addition to spices. But those were the luxury products.

For ordinary, away-from-home eating, cheaper pastry shops did not use exotic spices. Their business strategy was to sell in quantity at a low price, and using exotic spices hardly meshed with their concern for profits. In the role of diluter or dissimulator of taste, the regu-lations mention native ingredients such as onions, garlic, shallots, or even mint. Especially mint: it was used so heavily for this purpose that, if we are to believe Aulagnier, it was often called *pasté*.[28] On the other hand, the use of cats can also be viewed from this commercial perspec-tive. The cat was worth nothing, except for its fur. Eighteenth-century France did a considerable business in cat pelts, and nothing tells us how the carcasses of the skinned cats were eliminated or recycled.[29] So the story is plausible. Is it any wonder, then, that modern France maintained an instinctive, wary distance from pâtés?

The pâté legend was not an impervious cliché, immune to the influences of the times through which it endured. It had to adapt to the dominant behavioral values. The sixteenth century, for example, introduced two new aspects. First, it designated the chosen target of possible pâté poisonings. Listed as "public cooks," roast-meat sellers and pastrycooks were "always supposed to have meat cooked or ready to cook to satisfy the immediate or unforeseen needs of the inhabitants and also those of strangers."[30] These impatient customers had no precise identity at first. Not included among them, of course, were those with a cook, or even simply a housewife, at home. It was the working classes who grabbed a quick snack, but they were a mix of all ages and both sexes.

In the sixteenth century, hurried workers, eager for a quick bite, were very numerous in France, especially in Paris. Jérôme Lippoman, a Venetian ambassador, testified to this in a famous text dating from 1577. There, he remarked that, "in France, more than elsewhere, pastries are popular, that is, meat cooked in the pan," that food bought cooked and prepared cost less than food bought fresh at market, and that, thanks to those food trades, "the poor worker" could eat on meat or meatless days as well as the middle class.[31] Was it the proliferation of fast-food places that made regulations even more stringent? In 1522 the statutes for Parisian pastrycooks were very precise: "No man or woman may sell and display for sale, in covered baskets, small pastries for three, two, or one cent, of corrupt and foul flesh, not worthy of human consumption, into which is put onion, removing the taste of said corruption, which young children of the house and other persons are more inclined to buy for their cheap price, and use and eat them, by which means they often engender in themselves corruption and disease."[32]

The Paris police would throw such pastries into the river if they suspected them of poisoning children or, rather, youth, that ill-defined age class that was just beginning to come into its own. Adolescents, in particular, adolescents "of the house" (meaning, from good families), were promoted to the rank of a "vulnerable population." Royal legislation began to protect them and to bring negligent and infanticidal parents before the courts. They also had to be protected from the vendors who wandered the streets crying their wares, little pâtés, hot from the oven, that had become the "great ragout of schoolboys."[33] In the urban microcosm, loud with the cries of hawkers, some advertising, as enticing as it was, could be false. The iconography attested to that.

In an engraving by Abraham Bosse, a boy pastrycook holds out a plate of pâtés to another boy hardly younger than himself:

> This pastrycook is shrewd and has a pleasant manner
> For swindling money from that little boy
> But he for his part is no slouch
> At wolfing down the pastries offered.

Another engraving shows another scene of peddling on the streets:

> Thus they hawk the little tarts
> In Paris for the spoiled children
> They sneak off into its alleys
> To push them under their noses.[34]

Street youth were portrayed as the designated prey of the swindlers in the food industry. This notion would not disappear. It cropped up again in 1914 with the shameful distribution of poisoned candy.

The urban legend underwent a second metamorphosis. Pâté, the lone suspect among prepared foods in the Middle Ages, gained a rival: rabbit stew. Medieval consumers did not eat much rabbit, which was generally wild rabbit, reserved for the lordly tables. On the other hand, there is evidence of cat consumption in the modern period. It seems to have been common and even legal in the Germanic countries, where the cat was given the nickname of *Dachhase*, "rabbit of the roofs." In France and Italy, one spoke of the "gutter rabbit" but did not consider the meat of this carnivorous hunter to be edible, except in cases of dire necessity.[35] The legend experienced a minor shift, dictated by new eating behaviors. It focused on tomcat/rabbit stew, a dish with a composition just as difficult to control as pâté.[36] Nevertheless, urban regulations attempted to define standards and see that they were applied. Vendors had to sell rabbits with heads as verification. Confirmed by a ruling in 1631, Parliament pronounced a sentence against the Pères Lustucru. They had to make amends on the banks of the Seine by throwing in the skinned and decapitated cats that they had stored in their larders and crying out in repentance: "Brave people, it is not due to me and my perfidious sauces that the tomcats you see here were not taken for good rabbits."[37]

The post-Revolution period marked a decline and an abatement in those legends constructed around the themes of pâté and rabbit. The image of the pastrycook distinctly improved as he abandoned street sales as an extension of his shop business and turned to a new type of production favoring the sweet over the savory.[38] Tomcat stew was still denounced, but the taboo concerning cat meat consumption fell away; henceforth one no longer had to fear dying from it. The emotional charge defused, it remained only a paltry danger, one of deception.

The Serenity of the Garden

Fear always plays on a fundamental ambiguity: accidentally or deliberately, through human malice, a food that is usually good can become bad. Pâte was a perfect example of this. It was ubiquitous throughout the food culture of the ancien régime. It was the food of the poor. It was also a dish for the king. La Mettrie, an Enlightenment philosopher, died of indigestion—some said suffocation—in Berlin, at the court of Frederick the Great, having overindulged in a pâté of pheasant and truffles. Who would not love to taste this pâté with Prussian truffles? Or the pâtés *à la financière* served at the tables of generous farmers, with their garnishes of calf sweetbreads, cockscombs, and rooster kidneys? Or a pâté from Périgueux, made from partridge?

They tasted delicious. And, even better, their composition was not a mystery. One knew who prepared them and where the ingredients came from. Being homemade made them reassuring. The reassuring aspect was the short food circuit. Conversely, the little pâtés of the city engendered urban fears. The city violated two kinds of familiarity: food sources became distant and anonymous, and the phenomenon of eating away from home increased the gulf between the eater and what he ate. Pâté production was also a fast-food industry. That is how contemporary food images represented the situation. They oscillated between the two poles that defined the field of the alimentary imagination, fear at one end and serenity at the other, following a cursor that moved in that symbolic space measuring the length of the food circuit. Serenity was best represented by its most enduring image: the garden.

The garden (meaning here the vegetable garden) was a place that perfectly encapsulated certain values. It was a place of freedom where, protected by high walls from outside eyes and fiscal supervision, individual initiative could express itself, experiment, and innovate. It was a place made for pleasure and serenity, and for food security as well. It is not surprising that the garden completely eludes our best sources of information, urban codes of standards. We could scan the entire *codex alimentarius* of the past and find nothing related to food supplies from gardens either inside or outside the cities. When the consuls of L'Isle in the Comtat listed their powers with regard to foodstuffs, they stated their authority over "bread, flesh, fish, and other meats and fruits for eating that are sold and resold in said city of L'Isle and its territory," a wide jurisdiction, but one that left the garden outside its legal domain.[39] Without standard or supervision, all that was for autoconsumption or exchanged outside the market was considered intrinsically healthy.

But was this security simply a matter of appearance, a feeling, an illusion? Was the garden just a metaphor for food safety? We must pause here for a brief inquiry into the essential question of autoconsumption, which, though it sometimes turns its back on reality, is usually attuned to it.

In 1600 Olivier de Serres presented autoconsumption as the ideal in his *Théâtre d'agriculture et mesnage des champs*. His model householder "managed" a good-sized, versatile operation and sold his surplus grain at market. There, he also bought what he lacked, which was not much. At the very most, his wife, the good housekeeper, had to supplement the family provisions by procuring from the city "anchovies, sardines, herring, tuna, hake, cod"—that is, essentially, fish, dried or marinated—oil, groceries, and dried fruit.[40]

The Pradel operation that Olivier de Serres managed and that provided him a theoretical model proved that, in fact, autoconsumption was not a utopian dream. The stories of the operation he related tended to show that it very nearly approached the autarkic ideal. Salt and sugar were bought from outside. As for everything else, the Ardèche domain provided nearly all the household needs. We can observe the same pattern in the Norman manor of Gilles de Gouberville and in many other estates—there is no point in listing the numerous examples—where supplements from the city were both necessary and minimal.[41]

Autoconsumption existed—though to what extent we do not know—in the villages. It was also a reality among certain city dwellers, the powerful or well-off who owned land in the country. Opening the records of any lawyer to the file on land rentals contracts is sure to reveal a whole variety of annuities in grain and in money, as well as little payments in hens, capons, game, fresh cheese, butter.... The concern over fresh provisions can be read in these contracts signed before a lawyer. If it was a matter of sharecropping, the city dweller sometimes secured for himself in addition a supply of fresh produce, to be delivered to his home. If it was a matter of tenant farming, small approbations were provided for, additional payments destined for the larder of the urban dwelling (this practice being prohibited in France since ... 1946!). In 1545 one Avignon landowner on the banks of the Durance rented the gardens below his mansion to a gardener, stipulating complex and precise conditions. He demanded sixty florins a year, fixed a low sale price for all the vegetables he would need, left the gardener the grapes, and secured for himself exclusive rights to the roses. As for the all-new production of artichokes and chard, it was "retained by and reserved to" him. The Piedmont bourgeois farmed out calves to the peasants of the flat country with rental clauses guaranteeing their food supply. A calf was raised with great care "in a particular fashion."[42] Direct fresh food supplies were also popular in the parliamentary circles of Bordeaux. These gentlemen, which is what they called themselves, were amply provided with products of the hunt, the farmyard, the warren, and the pond. State resources provided food for the nobility, the gentry of southwest France constituting one of the most successful models of autosubsistence.[43]

To drink one's own wine, eat one's own chickens, eggs, and cheese. The possessive can be laden with all kinds of values: patrician ostentation, the pride of ownership, nostalgia for the family land. But it also conveys the full assurance of knowing what was on one's plate. One could eat and drink with equal peace of mind if the products did not come from one's own land but from a known source. Past society did have a third way of acquiring food in addition to producing it directly and buying it at market. A whole barter system was in operation, though we only know about the part that revealed itself on the surface. In the villages, gifts of pigs were a ritual.[44] Among the nobility, gifts and countergifts circulated: "I dined with Mademoiselle Desgranges, rue des Cordeliers.... I had delivered there a young hare, a young rabbit, two woodcock, eight snipe, and six partridge, three red and three gray."[45]

In these circles, the garden was not a myth. It became one among the urban working class. Some cultivated—in every sense of the word—a very reduced form of a garden in their windowboxes or on their balconies. The 1450 Verona statutes prohibit inhabitants from this type of gardening, for fear of falling water, soil, or manure.[46] In large cities, the first sources for fresh produce were the gardens within the city walls. The taste for urban autoproduction was widely shared. In Paris, it affected those who had land as well as those who did not. L. S. Mercier speaks of his contemporary, his kindred spirit, the Parisian who "raised a little garden three feet long in the open air;

he placed a flower pot in his window; it was a little tribute that he sent to nature from afar. A fruit tree grew in the narrow enclosure of the window box.... Despite prohibitions by the police, this homebody was attached to his flower pot, his boxed garden. He hid it when the inspector went by and replaced it when he had passed."[47]

These hanging gardens were truly a "tribute to nature"; the longing for nature and the desire for a direct food circuit were closely connected.

The Autoconsumption of Scraps

Edmé Rétif owned the La Bretonne farm in Sacy, Burgundy, and his fifty hectares produced a substantial share of the daily food. "Each year, I kill four pigs, ten of my oldest sheep.... I get (from the butcher shop) five pounds of meat, steer or cow, each week; in the summer I sell twelve dozen eggs each week and keep the rest for the household. My walnut trees provide me with salad oil all year, and walnuts for snacks and desserts in winter for everyone. As for my wheat and my wine, everyone here eats his fill."[48] In so varied a polyculture as La Bretonne's, there was a surplus that went to market and a supplement that came from market, meat from the butcher shop, in particular. The market being close, the food circuit was short and thus reassuring.

Small producers in the country resorted to the market more frequently than we might imagine. In fact, the majority of the population was obliged to sell in order to buy grain, with unfortunate consequences for their food security. The logic of the market itself held that one sold one's best products there, to make the largest profit. Champier's Perrette sells a can of pure milk at the market. She and her family make do with curdled milk or whey.[49] She makes money from the best products of her farmyard, the fresh eggs, young chickens, and fattened capons and keeps for her family's consumption the duck or turkey eggs, the aged rooster, and the five- or six-year-old hen that has become a poor layer and gets thrown into the stew pot, because it will only be edible after long cooking. The same was true of the preserved foods: once turned into goose or duck conserve, the Gascon farmer sold the thighs and kept the rest. Throughout, the small farmer kept for his own use the leftovers.

Salt pork merits a moment's pause, emblematic as it was of domestic autoconsumption. The sacrifice of the pig, or the *tuaison* or *tuaille*, is the subject of abundant, if discordant, discourse. Or, rather, it would be better to say that there are two versions of it. The first is urban and can be read in the treatises of urban policy and regulations. It is primarily a question of the processes preliminary to the slaughter, of the required "visit" for the tongue and ears, of all the health inspections to which the animal was subject. In the midst of this discourse, the figure of the *langueyeur* looms large. The second version is rural and literary. It recounts the slaughter as an event and a rite. It stresses the domestic liturgy and celebrates the meal of pig meat that followed the slaughter, to which neighbors and relatives were invited, on the condition of reciprocity. This was almost the only occasion for eating fresh meat. All the rest was destined for the salting tub. Were health precautions taken? In these accounts, the *langueyeur* is noticeably absent from the ceremony. *Langueyage* took place, said Liébault, if the meat was "displayed for sale at the markets and fairs in the big cities."[50] It was, in fact, the city dweller who paid attention to the quality of pork and sometimes noted in his account book the precautions taken: "December 23, 1669, I paid 18 pounds 4 sols for a pig that cost me 8 pounds 5 sols a hundredweight, 2 sols to have it verified as healthy and 5 sols to the one who killed it."[51]

Nevertheless, rural folk were not unaware of the risk. That is what Liébault suggests in a somewhat oracular fashion: "and believe that this was the reason our fathers did not ordinarily do it." The phrase is very enigmatic. Does it mean that the forefathers, from the dark ages of the fifteenth century, abstained from eating pork for health reasons, and their sons ate only salt pork, actually, salt pork that was then boiled? That would have been a wise precaution, as salting destroys germs and bacteria.[52]

To describe the killing of a pig as the culmination of a closed-circuit food network would be an exaggeration. It omits the role of the outsider, because the one who sliced the pig's throat was always a specialist recruited from outside the family circle. And it obscures the role of the market. The rustic, that great eater of pork, knew neither the taste or color of sirloin or filet mignon.[53] Hams (*jambons*) were traditionally made from the four legs (*jambes*) of the pig, but city dwellers were sold hams made from the front legs, which were preferred by gourmets. In the pig, everything was good, of course, but here, again, the best found its way to market (or to the manor, or to the presbytery).

And, of course, only the successfully salted meat was taken to be sold. Often salting was not successful, because salt was expensive, and "it is rarer to encounter the good larder than the good granary or the good cellar; you hardly find any in which the flesh of pigs, even bacon, has not turned rancid and yellow . . . so much so that one hardly knows which corner of the house to give over to the larder for it to be well-situated, so difficult is this matter."[54] Everyone had his own technique for salvaging salt pork that had turned: for example, removing it from the salting tub and placing it in the chimney, "where it will recover."[55] If it recovered poorly, it was still not thrown away. Thus Parmentier claimed, "Bad salt meat has killed more men than shipwrecks and wars." Statistics being unavailable, we must take Parmentier's word for it. But what a harsh blow for the reassuring image of salting tubs overflowing with pork and beams hung with hams!

Jacques Léonard, among others, has clearly delineated this paradox: the food-producing class, up to their necks in financial difficulties, kept for themselves only foodstuffs of inferior and sometimes even unhealthy quality.[56] In times when it was hard to make ends meet or when shortages threatened, the situation of the autoconsumer got worse. It was then that the Solognots sold well-sifted, market-quality rye, keeping for themselves the ergotized grain, that the Bretons brought their unfermented buckwheat to the city, keeping the wheat that was cut quickly and too early. The unmarketable remained in the country, where it was recycled, which is to say, ingested.

The market played the role of health regulator; what was good left for the city, what was bad or merely questionable remained with the producer. Urban regulations constituted a second filter, returning to the outlands those foodstuffs not worthy of human consumption. (Fortunately, humans who lived in the country were known for having more robust constitutions than city dwellers.) In the process, these two supply circuits created a cultural gap. Patrician, and, later, bourgeois, cuisine based its reputation on "good" products, meaning safe and healthy. Rural cuisine was not so fortunate, and, for it to be transformed into "regional" cuisine, no longer scorned by city dwellers, "good" farm products had to remain on the farm. This metamorphosis would eventually take place, but not until the agricultural industry altered the conditions of production.

NINE

HUNGARIAN CATTLE DISEASE

One fear pursues another. The terror of the plague subsided when, after a last surge in 1663 and 1669, the scourge vanished for good from northwestern Europe's epidemiological landscape, and from the entire Continent after one last foray into Provence in 1720–1721. But people neither let down their guard or stopped being afraid. With the great waves of the plague past, it was the epizootic that caused fear.

Men of the eighteenth century had much experience with epizootics. They had to confront grave crises, they created new methods for fighting them, and, finally, they invented the word "epizootic" itself.[1]

Specialists in veterinary history estimate epizootics to be the cause of 200 million deaths among cattle in Europe during the Enlightenment.[2] Any estimate in this age before statistics must be regarded cautiously, especially this one, since it is counts together those animals that died of disease and those slaughtered as a preventive measure. Preventive slaughter was, in fact, invented in that century. It was novel and extreme, and, before linking it to fears prompted by contagion, we should consider the context in which it was adopted.

From the Epizootic to the Panzootic

Not only were epizootics frequent, but they also traveled quickly. In 1683 Wincler described a contagion "that travels at a steady pace, covering about two miles of Germany in twenty-four hours without sparing a single parish."[3] Gradually, many epizootics became panzootics, at

❉

least on the European scale. Evidence of continentwide microbial unification appeared repeatedly over the century: rinderpest raged in several waves, from 1711 to 1714, from 1742 to 1748, from 1769 to 1775, and in 1796; hoof-and-mouth disease appeared sporadically in 1662, 1680, 1695, 1707, and between 1763 and 1813. Classically, the spread of diseases was blamed on war. Epizootics followed the routes of military campaigns. Any movement of troops set in motion herds of horses and horned beasts, that indispensable stock of meat-on-foot needed for provisions. But the view commonly accepted by veterinary history must be reconsidered. In the eighteenth century, epizootics were more frequent than wars. In 1774, when the French army—its infantry and cavalry—was put at the disposal of the intendants to establish quarantine lines, and in 1775, when troops blockaded Gascony and Béarn, these were very much times of peace. War was a factor that contributed to the spread of epizootics, but it was only one factor.

Let us be brief: propagation does not have a single cause, as thought in the past, when war and war alone was held responsible.[4] That misconception is explained by the fact that, for a long time, veterinary attention was focused on horses, saddle horses in particular. The first students graduating from the veterinary schools in Lyons (founded in 1762) and Alfort were trained only in equine pathology. In the same period, the first public health workers focused on the health of military camps and the army. Neither were epizootics the result of productivist agriculture, as some believe today. They resulted from a combination of factors that stemmed directly from the way livestock raising and trading were practiced in the old agricultural system.

In that system, livestock raising was both ubiquitous and secondary. Herds were numerous, and it was rare that a farmer did not keep livestock. When asked if he could conceive of agriculture without animals, the agronomist Adrien de Gasparin answered yes, but only among "Negroes and the gardeners around Paris."[5] At the same time, if animals were numerous in the country, they were considered competitors for crop cultivation, grain in particular, which took precedence. And it was almost standard practice to expect one's animals to find food where they could. Stabling was rare, except in winter. On good days, animals were turned out in the fields to forage. And it was then, in the heart of summer, that the great epizootic crises struck. Epizootics ripened like grain.

The seasonal nature of diseases did not escape contemporaries. They saw a causal relationship in the coincidence between the extreme temperatures and the outbreak of mortalities. Summer heat, they said, favored "noxious ferments" and "poisoning of the blood by heating of the bile." But none of these learned men lingered over the etiology of diseases beyond their comprehension. Classical medical research put to one side the "first causes," considering them out of reach. "It is very difficult to reform the seasons and to change the temperament of animals." And rural economists, a fortiori, left "the physicians to philosophize over the causes that produced the disease."[6]

Put out to graze, the animals roamed and rambled, barely supervised by young herders, eight or nine years old. Sometimes, these boys and girls were attacked by wolves. This recurring tragedy is not news, but what about the average age of the victims? It was very close to twelve years old, like the little servant girl whom the parish priest in Restigné, Anjou, buried, "devoured by one of the ferocious beasts who are eating the pasture children this year."[7] That pasture supervision was left entirely to an underage workforce hardly led to vigilance with regard to the herds' health. Called by two Burgundy farmers in 1776 to care for their six sick cows, two students from the new royal veterinary school in Lyons, dispatched by the Burgundy state, arrived too late. They could only proceed to open the cows, that is, to perform autopsies. The farmers confessed to having noticed the disease too late, since their cows were tended by children "whose age did not permit them to make observations."[8]

Grazing was collective, in shared pastures. The animals were gathered into herds watched collectively; they shared the same grass on common grazing land and, of course, in the high summer pastures. Cévennes shepherds knew from experience that contagions occurred in summer, particularly at night, in the sheep enclosures. Doctors confirmed this: it was "cohabitation" that favored epidemics. And cohabitation was inevitable in the open countryside where community practices were strong. And when animals entered the stables, the crowding grew worse. The stable was dirty, hot, and like a hospital. Too much like a hospital for the tastes of Doctor Bongiovanni, a good observer of rinderpest in 1784.[9] In times of plague, he recommended banishing beggars and drifters, who wandered from town to town, spending the night in stables, carrying and collecting "in their rags contagious miasmas." He wanted to prohibit evening gatherings of women in the cowsheds and to kill dogs that slept in the stables and then ran around the countryside, since they often licked the foam of infected beasts. In the old economy, the livestock sector was the one most subject to collective practices. There was very great sociability among the animals, opportunities for contact, meeting places. In times of epizootics, these gathering places were strongly denounced as so many sources of contagion. An ordinance from the king listed them, advising that they be avoided: public grazing land, watering places, major pathways, fairs, and markets.[10]

The partial freedom of animals within an extensive system; the young, untrained herders, sometimes transporting disease germs in their wool clothing; the dogs that dug up the carcasses of dead beasts: everything conspired to creating a multitude of opportunities for contagion. And what about the way the stables were kept?[11] The culture of uncleanliness was not shared by all livestock raisers, and Descartes admired the neatness of the Dutch cowsheds. A century later, the abbot Rozier would sing the praises of Bavarian ones. At the same time, French and Spanish breeders could not simply be accused of negligence or inherent uncleanliness. The uncleanliness was, at least partly, deliberate. It had its own logic since, according to farmers, the accumulation of manure in stables promoted warmth, and warmth helped animals get fat. It was also noted that during times of epizootics, the animals struck hardest were those best cared for, and those in poorer condition had more resistance. If the doctors considered the first theory false, they could only confirm the second one, and their prognosis was always less pessimistic for a scrawny animal than a fat one. In short, a fine, well-cared-for animal was even more susceptible to the virulence of disease.[12]

And it was not only how livestock was kept but also how it was sold that increased the risks. Let us open the eighteenth-century reference book, the *Dictionnaire de commerce*: there we will find, in alphabetical order, articles on steers, sheep, cows, but nothing on meat. And for good reason: the trade of meat, of fresh "dead flesh," did not exist. Health safety required that all trade be done on the hoof.

A steer traveled. At a young age, three years old, it left its land of birth to be sold to a plowman or a cart driver. That was the first trade, what Savary called the draft trade, the first journey on foot. Once out of use, that is, too old to draw a plow or cart, it went back to a food-producing region to be fattened. A few months later, having grown fat, it left for its journey to the fair and from there to the city and the slaughterhouse. Little wonder that this walker, this well-traveled steer, was "small in stature, and reasonably fat."[13]

As the urban population grew and the demand for meat increased, the food circuit grew longer. In the first decade of the eighteenth century, cattle destined for the Parisian market, arriving at the markets in Sceaux or Poissy, came from Normandy, Auvergne, or Poitou. For example, we can trace the last journey of Corrèze cattle. Leaving from the mountain of Ussel in herds of about fourteen, they took twelve to fourteen days to travel the hundred leagues that separated them from the capital. They arrived there after having crossed through Orléans. By then, they had lost half their original weight.[14] The Paris consumer preferred a steer fatter than the Limousin one, like the Dutch steer, which, since it was destined for the slaughterhouse, did not work and was immediately fattened. But heavy and never driven, the imported animals could hardly cover more than four leagues a day, with a very big toll in exhausted and dead cattle in the two days following their departure. Getting them to the Paris stalls was a delicate, costly affair.[15]

In the 1750s in Brionne, a farmer had the idea of sending his fattened cattle to Paris in short stages, over three or four weeks. This method immediately proved a success, and cowsheds multiplied in the Brionnais and nearby Charolais regions. That was how the white Charolais breed was established, a walking breed from the start, by necessity.[16] Animals came from Alsace but also Franconia, Brisgau, and Lorraine to supply the Strasbourg markets.[17]

This constant tide of livestock on foot involved all species. A ewe from the Crau who regularly spent summers in the high mountain pastures of Ubaye and who ended up in a Marseilles butcher shop had traveled an average of 20,000 kilometers. The lack of transportation, the fluctuating nature of the market, and the need for reliable sources of fresh meat all helped to determine the status of these itinerant beasts. One of the city authorities' big concerns was avoiding livestock deaths from exhaustion. An ordinance from Louis XVI charged Paris butchers to "guard against too great exhaustion or lack of care that could precipitate the death of cattle." They were supposed to "have them led from the markets to Paris in small herds, and with a sufficient number of herders, to feed them appropriately, to provide them with good bedding in all seasons, to keep them tied, and to shelter them in well-covered and well-maintained cowsheds."[18] This ordinance aimed less at protecting the interests of the butcher than those of the consumer. It was not the loss of the animal that it sought to avoid but the sale of meat from exhausted animals, meat that was bound to be unhealthy. If the animals' long walk and their collective fatigue presented a latent danger in normal times, in times of epidemic, that danger was increased tenfold, and the authorities found themselves facing this dilemma: either prohibit the fairs and thus paralyze supply circuits or permit them and spread the scourge.

When the epizootic arrived, a certain number of risky behaviors also surfaced. Since they were a matter of popular veterinary medicine, as practiced by the farmers themselves or the blacksmiths, or irrational customs, as when the farmer entrusted his animals to a charlatan, they are hardly familiar, except through denunciations of them. The doctors called them popular errors, the enlightened parish priests superstitions. The agronomists preferred to say nothing, for fear of spreading deadly secrets. In abbot Rozier's dictionary, the article "Charlatan" refers to the article "Charm," defined as magical practice. But the search for an article on that subject would be in vain. An encyclopedia promoting new and rational agricultural methods could clearly not divulge such nonsense. A few pages later, in the article "Contagion," Rozier's collaborator, a veterinarian from Lodève named Thorel, gives an example of these superstitious practices. Thorel refers to the stable where epizootic cases had been reported: "Consulted in the same case, going to the premises, we had the ground dug up, and it was at a depth of four, five, or six feet that we found the remains of one or several carcasses buried in the lodgings themselves, on the advice of some so-called sorcerer who thus undertook to preserve the other animals."[19] Thorel had the ground of the stable dug up because he strongly suspected this practice, which the abbot Thiers had already cited in his *Traité des superstitions* and consisted of having buried in the stable or the cowshed the animals who had died there, to keep other animals from dying in the same way.[20] To ward off disease, some sort of secret ceremony was celebrated around the death of the animal. Even today, in Languedoc, certain procedures are performed for healing sick animals, for *desenmasca*, or releasing them from a spell. They involve a ritual walk, over the course of which the ground is struck hard with a staff of wild fig, the cursed tree, and words are repeated that only the initiates know. Elsewhere, people are content with taking the animals from the grounds to a crossroads where they are made to "change tithe territories."[21]

When epizootics struck, the traditional reflex was to do exactly the opposite of what veterinarians recommended, that is, to isolate the sick animals. Sometimes, procedures were permeated with magic, with secret or public ceremonies, gathering all the herds, healthy and unhealthy, and leaving the cowshed. Sometimes, they were connected to popular religion and involved collective benedictions. That was the case in Cavaillon at the end of June 1682, according to the testimony of the canon responsible for organizing the ceremony: "Passing before the Saint-Michel door, our provost, as officiant that day, blessed all the beasts that had been brought from the whole region to protect them from a mortal disease that comes to them by the tongue, that is contagious and pestilential. To prevent this disease, I have ordered this procession and three days of fasting."[22]

In Sologne around 1700, the parish priest of Sennely wrote that each animal disease prompted a pilgrimage to solicit the intercession of a saint. In Picardy, Saint Etton specialized in the healing of sick animals.[23] Elsewhere, the miracle-working saints seem more generalists than specialists, and, depending on the region, whatever the disease, one went to ask for the help of Roch, Antoine, Blaise, or Véran. In 1700 the Sologne parish priest did not take too much offense at the idolatry of his parishioners, but, as the century progressed, priests more and more frequently refused to perform certain rites of protection. On the other hand, they did not officially condemn resorting to the formulas of healers or the charms of charlatans. These were interventions of necessity, the final recourse when all hope was lost, and they did not fall under the jurisdiction of the church.[24]

Thus, by their very nature, traditional livestock raising and early trade practices promoted the spread of epizootics. The herds were certainly smaller than later livestock industry herds, but they had frequent or continual contact with each other. The reactions of their owners, unprotected and powerless against disease in their herds, also contributed to the spread of disease. And disease spread, oblivious to borders and natural barriers. In 1777 Haller wrote from Switzerland to Vicq d'Azyr that the borders of his country "are always tormented by epizootics, yours especially, so mixed with our mountains that it is extremely difficult to keep the contagion away." Microbial unification on the scale of all of Europe was achieved early on. As trade became international, its scope increased. The Auvergne cattle arriving at Minorca in the summer of 1756 brought a pernicious fever to the indigenous livestock and to those who ate it. In 1774 an epizootic left Guadeloupe and entered France by the Bayonne port.[25]

The Dangers of Hungarian Cattle

Of all ambulant bovine, none traveled so long and so far as Hungarian cattle. It was to fulfill the needs of the big cities in northern Italy that this longest circuit came into being. The Hungarian cattle trade stretched over hundreds of kilometers and involved numerous countries, even connecting two empires with borders that were otherwise sealed: the Ottoman and the Germanic.[26] This trade was confirmed early on, since there is solid evidence of bovine traffic along the Danube beginning in the thirteenth century. The circuit linked a supply to a demand, the supply coming from seminomadic livestock-rearing regions in the central plains of Europe that played the same role as the Argentine pampas played in the nineteenth century. The demand came from large urban meat-consuming centers in the Rhine valley and northern Italy: Cologne, Nuremberg, Venice. When the demand for meat grew at the end of the Middle Ages, the circuit expanded, and cattle were drawn from beyond Hungary, from the Carpathian basin, the coasts of the Black Sea, and even the Crimea. Hungary, the favored provider, was also an assembly and transit center for more eastern herds. Actually, what they called Hungarian cattle in Venice was also Bosnian and Ukrainian. No matter where they came from, these horned beasts were all of the same gray breed of the steppes: big, hardy, and, above all, formidable walkers. They were led to western markets following two routes. The first route to Germany followed the course of the Danube almost exactly, with Vienna and Nuremberg as its principal markets. Vienna, the market for sales and transit, saw an average of sixty-six thousand animals pass through each year in the mid-sixteenth century. The other route was determined by Venetian buyers. It passed through Slovene regions below the foothills of the Alps and ended in Venetian territories. From 1600 to 1610, it is estimated that twenty thousand head of cattle were imported from the plains of central Europe to Venice. The problem was that they did not travel alone. They often brought with them a "poison," as it was then called, that is, a virus: the plague virus.

On August 27, 1711, a herd of Hungarian cattle being led to the slaughterhouses in Padua crossed through the village of Semeola. One steer escaped, getting lost in the domain of Count Borromeo. It was taken in by a shepherd, who stabled it in his patron's cowshed before returning it to its owner. Eight days later, all the count's cattle fell sick, and all but one died.[27] All the top experts—Ramazzini; Cogrossi; Vallisneri; Lancisi, the pope's chief doctor—agreed about how the scourge spread into northern Italy. And they all made the same diagnosis: it was a matter of a cattle plague unknown there until that time.

Thus the issue of the epizootic mobilized scientific circles in Italy about two decades earlier than the more widespread European revival of an interest in questions pertaining to livestock rearing and its risks. This renewed interest helped to reawaken veterinary medicine, which had remained dormant until then, repeatedly trotting out Végèce and the Latin authors and leaving the care of sick animals to blacksmiths and other rural practitioners. Rinderpest provided the opportunity for an epidemiological study that did not go by that name, conducted using the most basic methods of investigation. Each researcher studied his own region, but they were linked together by the classic means of a network of exchanges in which the art of letter writing figured importantly. Thanks to one such letter from a relative of Count Borromeo to Lancisi and thanks to scholarly dissertations by Ramazzini and Lancisi, the bovine plague was well documented, every stage of its development analyzed beginning with its outbreak on the Paduan plains. The history of the Borromeo cattle is so well known that we even know which asymptomatic carrier introduced it to the west.

In the summer of 1713 the Frusino livestock fair in the ecclesiastical domain was prohibited. Thus leather hides and parchment were probably secretly rerouted to Rome and sold at very low prices, explaining why, it is assumed, the whole Roman countryside was affected in its turn. From October 1713 to August 1714, according to Ramazzini, this disease carried off 8,466 working cattle, 10,125 white cows, 2,816 red cows, 108 horned bulls, 427 young bulls, 451 nonworking cattle, 2,362 calves, 862 male or female buffalo, and 635 buffalo calves in the Papal State, that is, a total of 26,252 animals. An impressive statistic that Lancisi confirmed when he claimed 30,000 dead. And that was only the beginning.

In 1714 the Piedmont was struck, and then the contagion tore through all of Italy, along the Padua-Milan-Ferrara-Naples axis. The peninsula thus became a hub from which the plague spread to Switzerland, Germany, and France, entering by way of the Dauphiné and then Alsace and Brabant until it reached the two great cattle-breeding countries, Holland and England. The disease took the name of *steppe murrain*, the plague of the steppes.

Actually, the disease was named for the only thing that was known about it: its geographical origin. Like the other plague—the human plague—people knew it came from far away, from the east. "The most formidable cattle plagues are nearly always from Hungary," said Palet, who was hardly mistaken, even if Hungary was often just a relay station for a virus raging endemically in the Caspian basin.[28] It was also known to be a plague, that is, a fatal epidemic, killing nine of out ten animals it struck. But everything known for certain inhered in those two words: "plague" and "steppes." As for the unknown, how many questions there were! And the debates among Italian doctors proved this over and over.

Regarding the etiology, the mode of transmission, and the remedies, we can search in vain for scientific unanimity. Was it the summer heat that provoked the infection of the Pannonian prairies? Or the fatigue from so long a journey? Ramazzini favored the first interpretation. For him, the initial trouble was atmospheric in nature, and the disease was directly linked "to the infection of the pastures caused in Hungary in 1710 by an extremely hot and rainy summer and fall."[29] Supporting the second hypothesis, Bongiovanni claimed that the disease was caused by fatigue from the journey, since the animals were very strong when they left their country. Carlo Francesco Cogrossi of Milan proposed the most original theory of all, applicable, moreover, to rinderpest as well as to all other contagious diseases.[30] The disease, he claimed, was communicated from a sick animal to a healthy one through the medium of "animated atoms" similar to those *animalcula* that could be discerned under a microscope lens. Cogrossi was the spiritual heir of Girolamo Frascator. Frascator, whom the Italians call the father of modern pathology, had studied the 1514 hoof-and-mouth disease epidemic with remarkable intuition about the causes of propagation. Let us not exclaim too quickly over this inspired foresight, because Frascator's *seminaria*, like Cogrossi's atoms, with their ambiguous spiritual/material nature and their gift for "antipathy" that led them to attack one species but not another, harkened back to alchemy more than they heralded microbiology. In the thinking of the time, the invisible was always very close to the occult.

This theoretical construction was ingenious but badly received and useless since it led nowhere.[31] What it described was very difficult to fathom within an intellectual framework dominated by the Galenic paradigm, in which the idea of contagion took a very secondary place in the genesis of disease. It was easier to conceive of an epizootic with primary causes confined to climatic or dietary complications—closer, with the necessary adjustments, to BSE than contagion.

In any case, the debate between the "humorists," who blamed climate or food, and the "contagionists" is of little practical import, however crucial it may be to the history of medical ideas. As Michel Foucault has clearly demonstrated, each doctor bears within him several layers of doctrine, theoretically irreconcilable, that he nevertheless puts to use, collectively or individually, without knowing it. Even a "humorist"

might believe in a live vector, chase away stray dogs in times of epizootics, be convinced of leather's power to infect, and the necessity of
confining the disease inside the cowshed.

Lancisi's Ten Commandments

1711: Pope Clement XI asked his chief doctor, Giovanni Maria Lancisi,
for a report on the plague that infected his states and especially for
proposals for remedies. Lancisi had been chosen from among the best
of the pope's doctors to frequent the most secret antechambers of His
Holiness. Here was a medical luminary who had given up his chair
in anatomy at the University of Sapienza for the prestigious office
of the pope's chamberlain. He had to his credit many publications
that showed his areas of interest to cover the whole field of medicine
and even beyond. He had studied the mechanism of the secretion
of humors, the location of the seat of the soul, heart diseases, the
relationship between medicine and surgery and in addition had produced papers on navigation, archaeology, and botany.[32]

Since the association between Clement XI and Lancisi was based
on a prior model, it is not inappropriate to examine how it came
about. That a pope should appeal to a doctor when a health crisis
struck was not a new thing. Let us recall the formative episode of
1347–1348, when the black death arrived for the first time in Europe
and the pope of Avignon, Clement VI, asked for advice and aid from
his surgeon, Gui de Chauliac. Working together, drawing from their
observations and biblical references, they established a method of
fighting the scourge that authorities for decades afterward adopted
and supplemented. The Italian city-states brought their health protection system to the point of near perfection. It was this model that
the Clement XI–Lancisi duo would reproduce four centuries later.

In his report, Lancisi described the progress of the epizootic
by appealing to the metaphor of fire: rinderpest was born in "the
summer ardor."[33] "The blaze of contagion" gradually engulfed all of
Italy, before provoking a continentwide "conflagration." To analyze
the disease itself, establish a diagnosis, and formulate a prognosis,
Lancisi considered the concept of prediction to be essential. For him,
prediction was twofold. It was, first of all, a prevision, a mental image
that the doctor had to create for himself in order to make his diagnosis.
Lancisi's prevision, based on Hippocratic observation, broke out of
the Galenic framework. He did not reach a verdict on the etiology
of the disease, but he did recognize its contagious nature: "I do not

have the courage to determine the specific nature of this contagious poison [virus] ... that, I suppose, passes from sick cattle to healthy animals, either because of proximity or by means of things they have come into contact with that can penetrate the bodies of healthy cattle especially through the nostrils or the mouth."[34]

His caution matches that of his colleague Vallisneri, who wrote regarding the origins of rinderpest: "Perhaps it is one of those things that God wishes to keep hidden from us, and on which our posterity will work as fruitlessly as we have."[35] Putting the first causes to one side, moreover, is one of the postures of medical research, as we have said. But was prediction also Lancisi's response to the fundamental question posed by the pope: what to do? He answered that there existed no treatment at all. Speaking from this observation of powerlessness and rejecting any Galenic therapy notable only for its failure, he proposed drastic preventive medicine. One did not treat the plague. The remedies that he proposed would not eradicate the epizootic. They only helped to fix its limits. Taking up the fire metaphor again, Lancisi operated like a fireman faced with the blaze of the scourge. To contain it, he advocated firebreak measures.

Lancisi's administrative directives were formulated into ten commandments—plus an eleventh recommendation that generally repeated the first.[36] The first commandment was to prevent all communication with animals that could have been in contact with sick animals. The second was to kill sick animals and those suspected of having been in contact with plague-stricken animals. The articles that followed recommended sequestration, a prohibition against circulating, the establishment of quarantine lines, disinfection, and so on. In eleven practical and effective rules, Lancisi called on old wisdom, disregarded until then. Among his sources of inspiration was the Old Testament, a text that provided many of the basic preventives, like quarantine.[37] The fifth commandment, on complete disinfection of the stables, repeated almost word for word a verse from Leviticus (Leviticus 14) that indicates how to purify the houses of the "leper" by scraping the walls. The tenth commandment repeated a recommendation made by Charles Estienne in La Maison rustique (1565) not to put an animal in a stall previously occupied by a sick animal without cleaning it thoroughly first. It is not necessary to believe that Lancisi had read all the authors who wrote on rural matters. His knowledge did not only come from books. It was the sum of experiences that Lancisi recapitulated and logically organized. In 1599, at the time of an earlier cattle plague, Venice and Padua had prohibited the importation of Hungarian cattle, thus marking the birth of the veterinary health policy. Lancisi completed the plan of defense, inspired largely by measures taken in cases of the human plague. All the health offices had enacted regulations and applied measures in the same spirit to halt the progress of the human plague. Since the 1660s, the Papal States had intervened and the struggle had changed scale, with the demarcation of a boundary between unaffected and contaminated zones, the establishment of a safe area guaranteed by regional quarantine lines, and the closing of borders and ports if it was deemed necessary. Lancisi's preventive program copied the proven model of the human health policy.

But the incontestable novelty in Lancisi's program, unheard of in earlier veterinary regulations, unthinkable for measures against the human plague, was preventive slaughter.

> Article 2: If the disease spreads, immediately place the sick cattle in an isolated cowshed. For cattle visibly stricken with disease, it is necessary to execute them immediately with a blunderbuss, so that not a single drop of contaminated blood be spilled (*statim conficere scopetariae glandis ictu, ne quid tabidi sanguinis effudatur*)....
>
> Conclusion: If so formidable a plague comes to threaten our cattle, I am of the opinion that all animals either sick or suspected of being sick should be executed, rather than letting the contagion spread, in order to have the time and the honor of discovering a remedy that is often sought in vain.

If it was applied, Lancisi's solution—which was a solution by default— meant eliminating contaminated or even simply suspect animals.

The method of elimination "with a blunderbuss" was entirely new. Later, the French term *abattage* would be used, or "stamping out" in English. The verb *abattre* existed in the veterinary vocabulary, but it had a more benign meaning. Traditionally, *abattre* meant to fell, to knock down, as a pig was turned on its back in order to inspect its tongue, or a ewe, stricken with *picote*, to lance more easily the boils on its belly. To speak of *abattage* instead of execution was a euphemism rich with meaning.

This was actually a very specific treatment to be inflicted only on sick or suspect animals, very different from the one practiced at the slaughterhouses. To kill an animal to be butchered, one stunned it first. Inventorying the tools of the perfectly equipped butcher, Savary listed an iron mace to put down steer, called a "merlin" (a wooden one for calves), a ring anchored to the ground, and a harness for attaching to it the animal to be stunned.[38] One knocked out the animal first, "making it dizzy," before slitting its throat. The best butcher was a stunner of beasts, a *massabiau*, as they said in Toulouse, or a *massicot*, the nickname for a Pyrenees butcher. In Spain, another butchering method was used, as well as in Naples and certain Mediterranean parts of southern France. It consisted of curtailing the slow agony of the stunned animal by means of pithing: severing the spinal cord by thrusting a thin, tapered stylet between the occipital bone and the first cervical vertebra. This technique, which seems to have been borrowed from art of bullfighting, struck the animal dead.[39] But, whether animals in the slaughterhouses were put to death according to the French method or the Spanish, that only constituted a small difference in degree, nothing comparable to the qualitative leap that Lancisi's method represented. To kill, to kill from a distance with a shotgun, was to treat domestic animals—healthy or infected—like wild beasts. Human health resided in "the gun barrel."[40] In becoming the business of the hunter and the customs officer, the epizootic assigned domestic animals an entirely new status.

The Lancisi Moment: When Brutes Became Beasts

"The Great Teacher": that was how British historians characterized the human plague of 1348, because of its impact and its lessons. The same expression could be used for the Hungarian plague of 1711, which led to conceiving and experimenting with methods that would become the European model for fighting animal diseases. The Lancisi plan arose within a whole network of favorable environmental contexts—the transition from the human plague to the animal plague—but also political and intellectual ones. We should note that putting such a regulatory system into place, on a regionwide or indeed a nationwide scale, with surveillance at the borders, assumed a state policy. In effect, this disease prevention put absolutism to the test, and it is clear that the spread of the preventive system coincided with the height of development in administrative monarchies, capable of intervening in the area of public health, until then left to local communities and the church. These administrative monarchies were capable of intervening not only with edicts and ordinances but also with the construction of barriers, quarantine lines, surveillance of the comings and goings of people and herds through the inspection of certificates. In other words, they had at their disposal the military means necessary for ensuring the disease prevention system's success. From this perspective, the implementation of the inspection and regulatory system with each epizootic surge, and its degree of effectiveness, was a good test of absolutism. The victories against epizootics were military victories. Félix Vicq d'Azyr, adviser to the king of France during the great rinderpest of 1774 that decimated herds throughout the country, except in western France, also established an ambitious defense program against the disease. Its first commandment was: "It is military power that one has every right to expect given this opportunity for activity, unselfishness, and success."[41] But to study the Lancisi moment in the context of state expansion and military discipline is, in the end, to respond to the question of how and leave suspended the question of why. Why, in 1711–1714, did the shooting of animals become thinkable? Why did people begin to shoot cattle, gentle, domestic animals, as they had previously shot only wild or mad beasts? It is a question here of mental attitudes, of how man conceived his role in nature. In particular, it is a question of man's attitude regarding animals.

These are old questions, part of an old debate, which others have already explored brilliantly.[42] It interests us, however, to the extent that the Lancisi moment coincides with a fundamental shift in Western thinking with regard to animals. Beginning in the second half of the seventeenth century, a certain number of old assumptions were called into question, and thinkers designed a whole new intellectual framework, from which Lancisi and his followers were able to draw justification for their extreme measures.

The foundation of traditional beliefs with regard to animals was the sum of certitudes deeply anchored in popular thinking and theology. It resulted in an anthropology based solely on the Bible for the masses but also drawing on the old sources of ancient philosophy for the educated.

One of the best-known biblical stories after the Creation is the story of the Flood. Thus in 1700 B.C.—because that is how the moderns counted—the flood ended, God blessed Noah and his sons (that is to say, all humanity), and established them as the managers of Creation. Essentially, the story can be read two ways: either God established man as the shepherd responsible for his flocks and entrusted to him the protection of nature in general—that would be a pre-ecological reading of the text—or God sanctioned man's dominion over the animals. It was this second interpretation that the classical exegesis chose. For centuries, Genesis was read according to a complacent, assured anthropocentrism that satisfied the narcissism of the creature of the seventh day: here was man, already consecrated as the most beautiful creature, made in the image of God, established at the peak of a creation that, finally, existed only to serve him. This biblical account was the "the Old Testament charter" that founded the empire of man over nature in general and animals in particular.[43] There was little distinction between the popular image of the animal condition and the learned image. Philosophers who read Aristotle and his *History of the Animals* only found in his work a confirmation of biblical anthropocentrism combined with philosophical finalism. Nothing in nature was gratuitous, nothing was there only to sing the glories of God; no, everything existed to serve the needs of man.

Two other postulates completed this reading that, by classifying animals among themselves and in relation to man, allowed the burgeoning world of creation to be ordered and assigned to mental categories (or procrustean beds) that rendered it widely intelligible. According to the first postulate, three categories of animals were generally distinguished, organized into three sets: wild/domestic, useful/harmful, edible/inedible. Useful to whom? To man, of course! Edible for whom? For man, needless to say. The naturalist categories were ordered according to human uses, not according to the intrinsic nature of the animal.

According to the second postulate, animals had souls. This commonly held belief did not come from the Bible, which hardly addresses the question, but from ancient philosophy, recycled by the church fathers. It came from Aristotle, for whom the soul was the vital force that, once introduced into the body, directed the organism like a pilot did a ship. He claimed that the soul consisted of three elements: the nutritive or vegetative soul, the sensitive soul, and the reasonable soul. The first was shared by all three realms, the second by humans and animals, but only man possessed the third, the reasonable soul. This hierarchy introduced the idea of continuity as well as a certain amount of confusion: was the difference between man and animal only one of degree, not nature? According to the commonly held view, creation formed a ladder that began in the depths of the oceans and climbed toward the heavens and God. At the bottom were the fish, followed by the wild terrestrial animals; at the top were the angels. Between these two extremes, the domestic animals were arranged according to a precise hierarchy, and man was above them, below the angels. This view suggested a continuity among the species and a certain solidarity between man and the useful beasts. Those who read Thomas Aquinas knew that if we humans did not have responsibilities with regard to animals, we at least had to show consideration for them, treat them with compassion. And this was fundamental: if one felt compassion toward animals, it was undoubtedly a sign that one also felt pity toward man. Anthropocentric Christianity rejected that pernicious alternative inherited from the ancients: either pity for humans or pity for the beasts.

That was the tradition, stemming from Judeo-Christian roots—or, more precisely, because its roots intertwined, from a traditional interpretation of the Bible—and Greek theories, revised and slightly edited by Thomas Aquinas. It determined the intellectual landscape in which thinking with regard to animals evolved over the centuries. Within this landscape, pity for animals existed, and also the feeling of a kind of solidarity, especially for certain species, specifically those that served humans and shared their life to some extent. That is really what the word "domesticity" means. But, around the middle of the seventeenth century, this perception of the animal world was challenged by some learned thinkers, thus causing a fracture within the "domestic" circle.

The new view of the man-animal relationship was part of classical European philosophy's long struggle against Aristotle's physics. To consider the animal condition in a whole new light, philosophers called into question the *History of Animals*, full of mythical accounts of animal feats, the very ones that, despite scholarly scoffing, inspired La Fontaine. Except for La Fontaine, the republic of letters agreed that the Aristotelian examples were worthless, like the story of the horse that, having understood it committed incest, killed itself. Absurd nonsense! But refuting Aristotle became more difficult and also more radical when it came to the theory of continuity, which considered the differences among beings in terms of degree and distinguished the three types of souls. That task fell to Descartes, who was not content simply to dismiss Aristotle but also proposed a new physics relying on a mechanist explanation of the life force.

Unlike traditional philosophy, Cartesian thought did not directly address the question of the status of animals. What interested Descartes was man. The *Treatise of Man*, published posthumously in 1633, presented the Cartesian conception of the soul. Conceived clearly and distinctly, the soul had to be immortal and thus capable of salvation. It could not be granted to animals, because if it was granted to one, it had to be granted to all: "if they [the animals] thought as we do, they would have an immortal soul as we do. But that is not probable, since there is no reason to believe this of some animals without believing it of all of them, and there are some too imperfect for us to be able to believe this of them, like the oysters, sponges, etc." Descartes was categorical: "The greatest of the prejudices of which we have been persuaded since childhood is that living brutes think."[44]

"Cogito" was distinctive to man. Single-handedly, Descartes dug the gulf that separated humans from animals. The difference was no longer one of degree; it was a difference of nature, a qualitative leap. A radical separation existed between man, endowed with reason, and animal, only a machine, endowed with instinct and reflexes but nothing else. The wagging of a dog's tail, for instance, signified a reflex but should not be interpreted as any sort of language. Because language was strictly tied to the cogitative faculty. According to proper reasoning, the brute was a dumb beast.

The gap that separated man from animal became greater with Descartes's followers, such as Malebranche. Second-generation Cartesians would take the question of animals further and more seriously. They shifted the debate. Henceforth, it no longer revolved around whether animals were capable of reason, passion, and pleasure, since that was decided, but whether they were capable of feeling. This dialogue between Ariste, the anti-Cartesian, and Théotime, Malebranche's mouthpiece, offers a clear illustration. Ariste says, "If I jab this dog in the paw, it immediately retracts it, and never fails to do this.... I therefore conclude that it has a soul and feels pain." As for Théotime, he asserts that this is only a matter of an action done mechanically, the dog being prompted by its instinct for self-preservation. But, Ariste counters, "it cries, it whines: certain proof that it suffers." "Ah ha!" replies the Cartesian, "certain proof that it has lungs and that air is emitted from them violently through movement of the diaphragm."[45] The cry of the stricken dog is like the sound an organ makes when someone strikes one of its keys. Malebranche concludes: "thus, among animals, there is neither intelligence nor soul as we ordinarily understand it. They eat without pleasure, they cry without pain, they increase without knowing it, they desire nothing, they fear nothing, they know nothing."[46]

Cartesian thinking was a remarkable attempt to widen the distance between humans and animals. Elevating humans, it debased animals. We are not here to assess the intellectual consequences of such a moral schema. Let us simply note that all this doomed animals to the worst.

Two Paradoxes: London and Rome

Everywhere rinderpest struck, Lancisi's recommendations were circulated, discussed, and finally implemented at various times, so much so that one could speak of the gradual establishment of a European health policy between 1714 and 1770. Never did an epizootic prompt such scientific frenzy across the Continent as in 1711–1714. Everywhere, doctors were consulted as experts. Authorities solicited them either individually, because of reputation, or as a medical school faculty, as in Paris or Geneva. Reports flourished: Lancisi's "dissertation," Ramazzini's *De contagio epidemia* (appearing in Padua in 1712), Cogrossi's "new idea," Biumi's *saggio*. In England, the king assigned the task to Thomas Bates, his top surgeon, who submitted to him "A Brief Account of the Contagious Disease," published in London in 1717. From Prussia to England, expertise was channeled by way of royal advisers. France adopted a process that could be characterized as more modern. There, doctors were enlisted into the cumbersome, but finally effective, Colbertian system, a very centralized administrative circuit. But what a striking contrast with Italy! The realm was devoid of "men of quality," capable of carefully observing the epizootic in the field. After a search, the controller general of finances found a few country surgeons and a few inventors of remedies who were "more harmful than useful."[47] Chirac, the court doctor, made a preliminary synthesis based on two reports sent from Lyons and Chalons. Then all the reports were examined by the Paris medical school, after which it published its "opinion on the reports concerning the mortality of livestock."[48] Montigny, a member of the Royal Academy of Sciences, prepared instructions and advice, providing the material for the decisions made by the king's council in April and September 1714. Finally, Louis XIV's instructions were distributed throughout the realm. The king ordered sequestration and pits, but there was still no question of euthanizing animals. It would take further epizootic waves and about half a century for the Lancisi model to become the European prophylactic norm.

But let us return to 1714. At that time, all European countries had taken measures, implemented more or less strictly. From this perspective, we can compare the energetic rigor of the English to the inertia of the Papal States: a fairly paradoxical situation, considering that the country that had asked Lancisi for his solutions applied them badly or not at all, while England, though remaining reticent regarding what might seem like papist inspiration, proved to be the most enthusiastic adherent.

In 1713 Pope Clement XI detonated the *Unigenitus* bull against the Jansenists. But papal authority could not be exercised so rigorously in the temporal domain, and, in the Papal States, Lancisi's recommendations remained what they were: *consília*, plans, optional measures. Lancisi did not succeed in convincing the assembly of cardinals to begin killing all horned beasts "in the least suspect."[49] Appalled by the reluctance of the assembly charged with organizing a health policy, he pointed out that between October 1713 and April 1714, thirty thousand cattle and buffalo had died in the Roman countryside and countered administrative inertia by reproducing the text of unanswered prayers addressed to God, the Virgin Mary, and all the miracle-working saints. But he gives us no indication of the underlying reasons for the Roman administration's attitude. Without knowing the content of the Roman debate, we can only conjecture that he found himself facing objections of a different nature, primarily involving questions about the effectiveness of his preventive measures.

Responding to Count Borromeo, who objected that herds located far from the infectious epicenter had been contaminated long distance and doubted the usefulness of anticontagion barriers, Lancisi said that "the disease can be spread by fabrics, clothes, other animals, or humans."[50] And, in fact, the measures were meant to combat contagion spread from one creature to the next; they could not prevent it long distance, spread by the wind or by birds. That was the first misapprehension, to which other doubts of a different nature were probably added. There were, for example, the moral reservations of Paola Biumi. Biumi was the author of one of those essays on the plague that enjoyed great success. His pamphlet, entitled *Naturalezza del contagio bovino*, was dedicated to the Infant Jesus and was extremely sympathetic to the bovine species, present at the scene of the Nativity. Biumi spoke up against slaughter. He favored trying to confine the disease in the cowsheds through sequestration, burying the decaying carcasses, and fumigation. In addition, he proposed gentle and perfectly inoffensive cures like blessing the stables, which had long figured into the rituals of the church.[51] All that confirmed papal passivity. The pontifical government's attitude was a matter of overcautiousness and habit, but, from another perspective, we can see it as a reflection of a bioethical debate. Various sources fed that debate: distrust of the Cartesian doctrines; the moral question of animal sacrifice, which could seem like an expiatory ritual from another age.

"Holocaust" and "hecatomb" were words with a sinister ring to the ears of religious authorities, like throwbacks to paganism. As difficult as it was to fathom mass slaughter within the orthodox religion of the time, it was just as difficult to comprehend the status of suspect animals, reduced to the level of ferocious and harmful beasts, without even considering how killing with a rifle, long distance, also debased man: it was a crime of cowardice. In 1627 the last wild bovids disappeared in Europe, which is to say, they were exterminated by man. The last wild auroch was killed that year in the heart of the Jaktorow forest in Poland. Three-quarters of a century later, the invention of domestic-but-suspect bovids disrupted orthodox culture.

Thus Lancisi's defense plan met crossfire originating from different sources: doctors still attached to the idea of spontaneous generation, especially with regard to rinderpest; administrators frightened by the cumbersome logistics of implementing such a plan; and, finally, conscientious objectors recruited from the whole social structure. If Cartesian thinking had spread among the elite and had become the mode of thought among the decision makers, the simple man persisted in believing that there was a difference between the village bull and the church clock.[52]

England was hit by the epizootic that came from the Continent in 1713. Again, we witness that effective and proven duo, the prince and his physician, in this case, George I and his surgeon, Thomas Bates (or Batz). Assigned to the task in July 1714, the surgeon left for Issington to determine if the disease was contagious, a conclusion that he reached after having cut open sixteen cows. Thus he recommended that the Lancisi method be strictly applied. He made sure that the importation of livestock and leather from the Continent was prohibited, and, on his orders, six thousand cattle were executed in Middlesex, Essex, and Surrey. Drastic remedies, but in three to five months, the country was purged of its plague, and this rapid halt was credited to these health regulations. Administrative victories against epidemics are always debatable and debated; no one knows if the same results would have been obtained had the disease simply run its course. Bates's measures were thus dismissed in two lines of verse: "A generous bounty that destroy'ed / More cattle than the plague annoy'd."[53]

This success encouraged persistence, and England would remain faithful to the policy of "stamping out" (henceforth, the English name was used for the technique invented in Italy). Actually, English authorities added two modifications to Lancisi's principles, expressed in Bates's first recommendation: "to buy and have burned all the herd stricken with diseases, and to keep the others in separate places."[54] This recommendation took on normative value in England and would later be adopted in all European countries. Bates invented compensation for slaughter, paid out of the pocket of George I. These indemnities were granted less as reparation than as incentive in the face of livestock owners' resistance. The second innovation was the cremation of the carcasses. Whereas Europe dug pits, England lit pyres.

What was the British paradox? The country that most zealously applied Lancisi's directives, in all their harshness, was the one that, at the same time, invented a new relationship to the animal, inaugurated by those who called themselves the friends of animals. This extraordinary emotional experiment originated in England. And, by the early seventeenth century, it resulted in the creation of an incongruous category in the animal order: the pet. It arose first in the cities and among the wealthy classes. To put it another way, the pet was a useless animal: it did not serve man, could not be eaten, did not work for him. It only lived with him, kept him company, went where it wanted about his house. It was necessarily small, a dog or cat or monkey.[55] With the household animal, the gulf between man and animal diminished. That goes without saying. But, at the same time, another barrier was constructed, a division that had not existed between the animals. The companions of man were now isolated from the large livestock, which were useful to man and could be slaughtered if they threatened to become useless or, worse, dangerous to human health.

The cattle plague, it seems, rekindled dire memories in England, a horrible trauma: the London (human) plague of 1665. The English believed that this plague had been caused by unburied animal carcasses. Behind the stringency of English measures loomed this fear of the human plague's return. As an explanation for the policy of "stamping out," England's geopolitical position is often cited. If England's insularity did not protect it from invasion by the plague, it allowed its borders to be closed and supervised more easily. We can nevertheless posit that the English zeal for "stamping out," which has marked their health policy for over two centuries, may owe as much to history as geography. In fighting animal diseases, the real goal is, in fact, to protect human health.

TEN

FROM THE EPIZOOTIC TO THE EPIDEMIC

Rumors travel quickly, but, in the case of the great epizootics, it happened that people were warned too late, and the disease kept pace with the rumor, covering the equivalent of four or five kilometers a day. In 1683 a contagion crossed central Europe, according to "a fixed march, covering about two miles in Germany in twenty-four hours."[1] But whether the disease was outstripped by the rumor or caught the villages off guard, the effect was the same: everywhere it prompted great alarm.

In the summer of 1714, when the cattle plague was ravaging the entire realm, the court doctor, Pierre Chirac, warned Louis XIV:

I believe it is very important to let the villages ravaged by these diseases know that they are not contagious for humans. If a peasant is warned and seized with the fear of catching the disease, he will abandon his animals to their unfortunate destiny. He will not dare to tend them or get near to them, and, as a result, a greater number of them will die. But, besides that, the fear of catching the disease, on the one hand, and the unhappiness of seeing himself ruined by the loss of his herds, on the other, will make him all the more susceptible since he has been exposed, like his animals, to the heat of the summer sun and is thus disposed to fall ill with a similar disease.[2]

Through other sources, coming from the provinces by way of the intendancies, the old king was "informed that, in the places within the realm where herds were attacked by diseases, most of the owners abandoned their dead animals in the countryside and along the roads after having torn off and removed the hides."[3]

If it is legitimate to look again at the way Chirac's analysis breaks down fear, it could be said that rural fears had a dual nature. The first and most immediate was the peasant's anguish over the imminent loss of his livestock. In the case of the cattle plague, he knew that the chances of saving his animals were very slim, on the order of about one out of ten. Once the cattle were dead, he tried to recuperate the skins, but in 1714 the king's council expressly forbade skinning carcasses and leaving them unburied. The economic loss was total, since it struck at the heart of the livestock business as well as at farming. Without draft animals, how could land be cultivated or merchandise transported? Besides the loss of capital, there was the rupture of an emotional tie that must not be over- (or under-) estimated. To lose a steer or a cow is one thing, to see Rousset or Marguerite die is another, and an old song like "I Have Two Big Steers in My Stable" shows how, for the young peasant, the loss of cattle would be just as or even more catastrophic than the loss of Jeannette, his companion. The last straw would be the loss of both his herd and Jeannette to the same disease. And it was very much this obsessive fear that made the epizootic such a curse. It does happen that an animal disease will cross the species barrier and spread to humans. Today, that is called a zoonosis. The fear of zoonoses haunted the countryside.

The Great Fear of Zoonoses

Fear of the cattle plague prompted a certain kind of flight, though not exactly the same in nature as in the case of urban plagues, where Galen's almost Olympic watchword applied: "cito, longe, tard" (flee [early], [run] far, [return] late). But what would lead someone to abandon his herd to its dire fate? The same instincts, the same fear and discouragement, seized the rural livestock keeper in all cases of epidemic outbreak, and experience made no difference; let us remember that, in the average life span of a peasant, even limited as it was to thirty years, the risk of witnessing livestock mortality arose a dozen times. Doctors and, later, veterinarians were also helpless. A Montpellier doctor wrote: "Livestock epidemics are the most formidable challenge in practicing veterinary medicine.... What alarm at the announcement of a rapidly approaching disease! Consternation spreads at the same time as the contagion, and, if the contagion accompanies an epidemic, it's all over. Fear and discouragement take hold of the farmers. They abandon their herds to a band of ignoramuses. They put faith in their unfounded promises. In the end, they have the misery of watching all their animals perish and thus squandering their wealth."[4]

If the contagion accompanied an epidemic, then one was dealing with a general plague. The plague: before Turgot and the Versailles bureaucracy introduced the neologism "epizootic," that was what animal disease was called, understood in the classic sense of an epidemic disease but also as a disease that was particularly serious and fatal. Depending on its effects, actual or alleged, it would then be classified as a "specific disease," that is to say, affecting only one species, ruminants, for example, or as a "general disease," capable in this case of being transmitted to humans, which we call a zoonosis. But, whether it was general or specific, all animal diseases represented a potential danger to human health. One could contract the disease directly, or one could indirectly contract it or another type of "putrid" disease by ingesting infected meat. How was this dual risk, as described in scholarly treatises, perceived in the modern age? In rural areas and among the people, anxiety merged the notion of contagion, on the one hand, and belief in the solidarity between humans and animals, on the other. On these two essential points, there was a certain discrepancy between commonly shared convictions and the opinion of enlightened circles.

In the villages, the fear of contamination dominated. A direct, immediate contagion that occurred through contact, through touching the sick animal, was the first meaning of the word "contagion" (cum-tangere), in its oldest and most widely accepted sense. "They are afraid of everything, a dog, a cat, a marten, even a fly."[5] This remark is not insignificant. It suggests that general opinion went far beyond the strict etymological perspective, that this broad view of contagion led to a distrust of all possible animal carriers. Theoretically, those animals were passive carriers, and disinfecting them was sufficient. In practice, it seems that more radical methods were used (there are some reports of urban massacres of dogs and pigeons). Things were done infinitely more discreetly in the country, but any cow disease also marked a bad period for cats or hedgehogs.[6]

As with human plagues, animal plagues could be deliberately spread by humans. These sowers of plagues, who unleashed bacteriological wars, were quick to be denounced. In the case of animal plagues, one sees an accusing finger pointed at the Jews. In rural Rhineland, Jewish horse dealers were accused of buying and transporting sick livestock, despite the risks of contagion and in contempt of the law. But, in the order of scapegoats, worse than those who transported the disease were those who sowed it, with the help of "powers," spells, and poisons, and who perpetuated the secular tradition of rural witchcraft. The witchcraft that applied to herds was peculiar in that it was predominantly masculine, mostly practiced by shepherds who victimized the livestock of others. The *Grand Calendrier des bergers*, one of the most popular and widely distributed almanacs in rural areas, indicated how to protect oneself against the work of poisoners. In the 1651 edition, there was still a chapter on "the way the shepherd must behave to prevent any sorcerers from killing his herd." If the formulas in the *Grand Calendrier* proved ineffective, one could still pray to Saint Blaise, the great protector of the herds:

> Let no wizard nor poison
> By potion nor wicked spell
> Cause a damage to their fleece.[7]

Robert Mandrou has shown how, even though the great wave of witchcraft ended under Louis XIV, the crime of livestock poisoning was still a statutory offense. The king's law court heard many complaints during epizootics, and it often pronounced sentences.[8] The Brie shepherds' lawsuit was a good example. The affair broke out in 1687, when the shepherd Pierre Hocque was condemned to the galleys and died in chains. But, since he had passed his "secrets" down to his children Nicolas and Etienne, who were also shepherds, they found themselves, with three other shepherds, called before the court in the following years, accused of "evil spells on animals they killed using poisons that they left in the pastures." There were reports of bewitched herds in Bessin and in Burgundy, even though a share of populace began to have doubts and to think "that, independent of any charm, mortality begins in a herd, and a shepherd or some other person believed to have bad intentions is accused who nevertheless has no part in it."[9] In the decades that followed, when an enlightened judge rejected witch hunts, villagers took matters into their own hands. That was the case in Beaucouzé, near Angers, in 1780. Beaucouzé peasants suspected a parish woman they regarded as a witch of casting a spell on their herds. They dragged her into a cowshed to force her secret from her, and, learning nothing, they burned her feet and then drowned her in a pond.[10]

Anxiety arose as well from a deep conviction that, in the chain of creation ascending from earth to heaven, man was located between the angels and the beasts and that, if he resembled the angels, he equally resembled the beasts. Of course, the story of the Flood and the natural inventory done by Moses and then by Noah taught that each creature was well confined within its own species. It was forbidden by religious law to cross the dividing line between species. Any transgenesis was a transgression. The monster or the hybrid were not part of the natural order. Modern man had to guard carefully the sealed borders between himself and animality: in his ways of eating, dressing, even moving. Wearing fur, which could make humans pass for animals, could only be tolerated if the hair was on the inside, as a lining for clothes. Swimming was considered by some to be a sin of disorder: wasn't it the privilege of fish?[11] But if man, obeying the commandments of his god, could not transgress these boundaries, he could only note sadly that diseases could. A disease as horrible as rabies, which had persisted through the centuries entirely immune to human influence, was strong proof of this cunning ability to cross the thresholds between species. Leprosy was another example that was considered proof. All this derives from Descartes or, rather, from the rejection of Cartesianism in popular thinking. The strong solidarity between man and animal, the intimate proximity of living beings, made it easy to imagine that disease could easily steal from one creature to another.

And there was more: the barrier between species seemed even more permeable than, in reality, it was. People believed they could catch rinderpest, even though such transmission was impossible. That was the case in the Upper Rhine in 1798, where official statistics counted 12,000 cattle succumbing to the epizootic then raging and 195 people dead of rinderpest.[12] Whatever the pathological reality, for the people of past centuries, zoonoses flourished, or at least they seemed to. This conviction stemmed from two observations:

• Epidemics and epizootics being frequent, it often happened that they coincided.
• Epidemics and epizootics manifested seemingly comparable characteristics and symptoms.

In other words, even if the zoonosis did not exist, the fear was real.

We are dealing with an epidemiological landscape that was so uncertain that, more frequently than credited, two diseases spread simultaneously and affected humans and animals. If, in their visible manifestations, they presented two symptoms that resembled each other, an eruption of spots, for example, or diarrhea, then the analogy became an amalgam. Two eruptive diseases, one affecting sheep and one affecting humans, were both called variola, and diseases primarily affecting the digestive systems of humans and ruminants were called dysentery.[13] "Be careful!" warned Rabelais. Those who wish for too much risked *tac* and *clavelée*, that is, diseases similar to measles, which affected Panurge's sheep.[14]

This amalgam occurred all the more frequently because people stubbornly believed that plagues, whatever they were, formed a procession, that calamities were sequential or synchronous, and that they were linked together by a diabolical continuity in disease. The deadly association between shortages and epidemics was well-known. In the same way, there was a tendency to link temporally, and also causally, the epizootic and the epidemic. Doctors, when they were consulted, had a hard time convincing people that the coincidence of diseases did not necessarily signify contagion and that establishing a relationship between human and animal pathology was not necessarily relevant. How difficult it was for even the most reasonable human beings to distinguish between chance coincidence and true contamination! Two diseases arising simultaneously always strongly suggested communication. In his *History of Verona*, Moscardi recounts that the 1630 plague first raged among animals, but he prudently adds: "On these occasions, a combination of epidemics and epizootics is very likely to be found." In 1690 Ramazzini gave his opinion on a mysterious animal disease in Padua, coinciding with a fever in humans. He established that they were not related, but he convinced no one.[15]

Let us be content with this handful of examples, because such cases are legion; in any case, they were striking enough to be recorded for posterity. Paulet noted that the ancient authors only mentioned animal epidemics when the disease was shared by man. We can read and reread the testimonies of Homer, Ovid, Lucretius, and Livy, who left prodigious accounts of the great health catastrophes, of which the great plague in Athens was the prototype. And we cannot avoid the morose thought that history repeats itself.[16] In short, epizootics were only traced when there were associated epidemics. And thus the combined phenomenon was terrifying.

Hoof-and-Mouth Disease Domesticated

It is important not to minimize the terror provoked by epizootics but not to exaggerate it, either. Thus the historian must always navigate between Scylla and Charybdis.

Not to minimize it: the fear recounted in medical and administrative documents was authentic. One can dismiss certain reports of crises. That people ate grass in times of shortages is a cliché in the literature of grievances, a topos meant for effect, often aimed at obtaining a reduced fiscal charge for the community suffering from those shortages. But one must trust reports of zoonosis. The terror was real, as in times of human plague or cholera. Observing the reactions of Parisians to the terrible cholera epidemic of 1832—the temptation to flee and the rupture of social ties—Charles de Rémusat wrote this revealing line: "It is in such situations that the absence of religious sentiment is most strongly felt; in this respect, it all has more the air of an epizootic than of an epidemic."[17] The expression of fear could be further complicated by additional symptoms, convulsions or paralysis, for example. A pronounced tendency toward hysterics characterized society during the ancien régime. Reactions in the face of disease took on strong hysterical aspects, whereas today they present as depressive symptoms.[18]

In 1603 a good Avignon gentleman, the descendant of a dynasty of butchers from Auvergne, wrote this minor postscript in his journal:

> Note that, in the current year, a disease like the plague has stricken the livestock and can kill them in twenty-four hours. It appears under the tongue like a little black "floret" and often attacks livestock like cattle, horses, and mules. And those treated promptly hardly ever die of it.
>
> The remedy is that, as soon as one perceives the disease, he must scrape said "floret" with a silver spoon until the abscess bursts and drains and then move the beast's head up and down in order to purge the wound further, afterward washing the tongue thoroughly with vinegar, salt, and burnt alum.[19]

Retrodiagnosis is very complicated. It comes up against the obstacle of vocabulary. We do not know if the black "florets" or "pustules" that Roubert discovered under the tongues of sick animals were aphtae or anthrax, and, without knowing the true nature of the growth, we are thus reduced to guessing. Was this hoof-and-mouth disease? Doubt arises because Roubert lists horses and mules among the animals at risk, and we know that the horse family is not subject to this affliction. Hoof-and-mouth disease can be confused with ten others, including anthrax and glossanthrax, a disease that is now extinct. In any case, Jean Roubert seems informed and calm. The remedy he recommends was well-known; we find it copied down dozens of times in books of "secrets" or family "recipes," and not just among peasants. The silver spoon was borrowed from current medicine. Sixteenth-century surgeons like Ambroise Paré, powerless against the risks of infection, thought that scalpels made of gold or silver, incorruptible metals, improved the chances for postoperative patients. Roubert's calm seems to reflect the severity of the disease, which would have had a much lower mortality rate than rinderpest, for example. He knew that it was curable and that, treated in time, the animal had a good chance of avoiding septicemia. No doubt he also knew that this disease, whether it was hoof-and-mouth or glossanthrax, could be transmitted to humans but could be avoided by taking certain precautions. The principal risk of infection lay precisely in the treatment of the sick animal, whose mouth had to be opened several times a day, thus exposing the caregiver to the infected saliva. Cautionary tales circulated on these very real dangers. Here, a man died because he ate from the spoon he had used to scrape the tongues of sick beasts. There, another succumbed from carrying in his pocket and handling a piece of silver that had also been used to scrape large pustular tongues.[20] One avoided sick animals' saliva but did not reject their meat, much less their milk, all the more precious since sick cows produced less of it.

Advice circulated from village to village or, more precisely, from the magistrates of one village already stricken with the disease to another. Thus the Avignon consuls received from their colleagues in Aix a whole series of recommendations, preventives, and cures for this epidemic, applicable to all epidemics. These included recommendations to feed the livestock "bread, oats, sage, oregano, thyme, rue, garlic, juniper, carrots, mint, lavender, laurel, and rosemary."[21] Therapy for all animal diseases was a process of trial and error. Thanks to biological solidarity, the diet was not fundamentally horse medicine but rather a very human and very regional pharmacopoeia. Classical dietary regimes that doctors prescribed for humans also applied to beasts.

Doctors in the Pastures

On this enormous question of human health risks in times of epizootics, it seems that, for a long time, the learned community remained uninvolved and, as it were, silent. That was very clearly the case in France. French doctors, puffed up with the nobility of their art, did not deign to concern themselves with the health of animals. Jean Héroard, doctor for the young Louis XIII, was the exception that confirmed the rule. This great pediatrician, who monitored—step by step and hour by hour—the young king's health, devoted his leisure time to the veterinary arts and compiled an anatomy of horses. This earned him the sarcasm of his colleagues. Guillemeau, his colleague at the medical school but not his friend, offered this uncomplimentary portrait of him: "I'd have to compare him to the sorcerers of Scythia, called Bythians, to that race of Thibians of whom Plutarch wrote to Pliny that they had two pupils in one eye and the figure of a horse in the other, if a friend of medicine can even speak of a horse doctor, of an arch-ass like Héroard."[22] We see what a doctor concerned with something besides human health exposed himself to! The care of animals was left to the rural empirics and the blacksmiths, who were "their shoemakers, their doctors, their surgeons, and their apothecaries all in one."[23]

All Europeans did not abide by France's strict dichotomy between learned medicine for humans and empiricism for animals. The Spanish supervised the health of their herds with the help of preveterinarians, called *letrados*, who had some experience with medicine. The Italians had a long tradition of medical intervention in cases of animal disease, inaugurated by the great Girolamo Frascator, the doctor who identified both syphilis and hoof-and-mouth disease and recognized how they were spread, sexually in the first case, through rapid contagion in the second. A happy coincidence found the great Padua medical school at the heart of great epizootic centers. In 1711 the Italians were well situated to observe the plague, at the crossroads of the epidemic and medical knowledge.

Half a century later, a spectacular reversal took place. In veterinarian medicine, the French made up for lost time, and so quickly that henceforth they formed the vanguard in the struggle against epizootics. Things changed radically between 1762, when the first French veterinary school opened in Lyons, and 1774, when Turgot assigned Félix Vicq d'Azyr, a young scientist passionate about anatomy, to study the current epizootic. The very powerful Royal Society of Medicine, founded in the years 1774–1778, again at Turgot's instigation, was a novel attempt to institute state medicine to serve public health. Vicq d'Azyr was thus charged with establishing a centralized information network for human and animal diseases and organizing a health-care system.[24]

This reversal in the French attitude toward animal medicine may seem paradoxical: why this renewed interest in veterinary medicine in the second half of the eighteenth century, even as the Enlightenment encouraged an exaggerated anthropocentrism and utilitarianism? We can find the answer in the agrarian ideology of the epoch, marked by the physiocratic movement and mindful of the importance of the agricultural economy. Henceforth, maintaining livestock populations was elevated to the level of a national economic interest. But it would be a bit myopic to view this scientific conversion only through the small end of the physiocratic telescope. More precisely, if the Cartesian intellectual horizon appeared to act as a restraint, at its deepest levels, it actually served as a powerful stimulant. A new use was found for those animals that had become beasts: to serve medical research for the greater benefit of human health. Veterinary medicine became valuable as it became useful to human medicine because of experiments it permitted on animals. Henceforth, all the health professions agreed that sick animals must not be left to empiricists and country blacksmiths. First, maintaining livestock populations was too important a priority to be left in their hands. And, second, certain experiments could be done on animals that could not be done on humans; thus veterinary medicine promoted scientific progress. Comparative medicine flourished in the shadow of mechanistic philosophy.

It is within this context that we must locate Félix Vicq d'Azyr. For him, the animal was a study aid for the human. His research on comparative anatomy convinced him of the profound unity between human and veterinary medicine: "medicine is one."[25] Certainly, for him, medicine, the noble science par excellence, if still not clearly defined, was annexationist, and the veterinary arts, which had not yet evolved into a practice, were subordinate to it. That explains the conflict that arose between him and Claude Bourgelat, the Lyons horseman who served as director and inspector general for the veterinary schools. For Bourgelat, the Ecole d'Alfort could only be a center for training future "veterinary artists," whereas Vicq d'Azyr wanted to make it a research center, a laboratory for the Royal Society of Medicine.[26] At the same time, nascent veterinary medicine was founded on radically different principles from those that governed human medicine. "All out attack," was its motto. It established "the distinction between treatment of an animal, considered as an individual, and treatment that regarded an animal as part of a species." Useful distinctions: "They defined an important difference between human medicine and domestic animal medicine. Here, it was permissible to abandon the individual, even to sacrifice it, for the benefit of either the farmer or science."[27]

"What is the Society?" asks Marphorio, a comic character, referring to the Royal Society of Medicine. And Pasquin answers him, "It is a society established for the beasts, but it meddles with treating humans. It is made up of the most skillful country doctors."[28] Of course, the comedy's definition is perfunctory. But it points to the central role the Royal Society would henceforth play in coordinating efforts in the struggle against all epidemic diseases. Beginning from the moment when associate members and correspondents declared themselves competent in the matter of epizootics, an entire information network was established, and "skillful country doctors" sent memo after memo, report after report, to the society. To their clinical observations they attached comments and hypotheses on the possible effects on human health. This provides good fodder for the historian, who can finally follow them into the cowsheds and stables to evaluate the pathological and especially the psychological effects of the solidarity between man and beast.

The Disease that Spread Terror

"There is no disease that spreads as much terror in the countrysides of Burgundy, the Franche-Comté, Champagne, etc., as malignant pustule; it is a scourge that brings dismay to the farmer in his stubble fields, which he cuts to the ground; it often penetrates the walls of the cities and carries fear and death into the artisan's workshop."[29]

Other regions in France had comparable diseases, *maladie de sang*, *maladie charbonneuse*, *antrac*, or *sang de rate*. Since Pasteur, we have known that this was one and the same disease, anthrax, but, in earlier pathogenesis, the ailment had no single identity: a response by organisms to external influences, it was born and reborn always differently.[30] Under its various names, the disease was omnipresent. It struck Roussillon as it did other regions. That was where the earliest studies of it took place.

Under Louis XVI, the Roussillon region counted 56 doctors in its hundred parishes, 15 of them established in Perpignan, the heavily populated county seat, 174 surgeons, and an unknown number of healers and bonesetters, called *saludadors* in this area. There was not a single veterinarian.[31] In Perpignan, the official correspondent for the society was a Doctor Costa, who in 1777, at the request of the intendant, wrote a report on anthrax addressed to the still nascent group. The report is copious, in keeping with a disease occurring frequently enough to be considered "ordinary." It was also cruel, "carrying off many every year," but Costa does not specify the morbidity or mortality rates. Victims of anthrax did not all die, but those who recovered from it were left with debilitating scars, faces with ravaged lips and eyelids, diminished intellectual faculties.[32]

The fever raged especially in the villages at the foot of the Corbières, stretching along the small Agly river from Tour-de-France to Saint-Laurent-de-la-Salenque. And it was in the village hit hardest, Estagel, that the doctor established his residence to observe and research the disease better. It was in the warm season, at the time the crops and grapes were harvested, that the disease ran wild. The symptoms he described were spectacular: the afflicted ones' heads literally inflated, they had high fevers often accompanied by convulsions, they presented pustules covered with a black crust, called coals or anthrax, that Costa was wise enough not to confuse with the buboes of bubonic plague. Treatments were generally ineffective. Villagers rarely called on a doctor and had no confidence in the classical triple therapy: bloodletting, purging, and administering enemas. They treated their growths by applying a caustic unguent, the specialty of the local priest. The Estagel priest confided the "secret" to Costa, at the risk of undermining its effectiveness: the formula consisted of quicklime, black soap, and leaves from the scabious plant. The disease manifested itself in different forms. At its most acute, it killed its victims in forty-eight hours, before the appearance of anthrax. If the anthrax broke out, or one happened to make them suppurate, the victim recovered, but with dire aftereffects, because the anthrax tumors created irreparable lesions. People recognized the seriousness of the disease by refusing to call it by its name; the Cévenols avoided using its Occitan name of *carbounele*, calling it *la méchante* or *la mauvaise*.[33] For Costa, there was not the shadow of a doubt that the disease was a zoonosis, that it was transmitted from ovines to humans. The uncertainties were of an etiological nature: How did this disease get to the animals? And how could humans in turn be stricken by it?

On the origin of the animal disease, the doctor delivered a fine dissertation in three parts, according to the three environmental factors defined by the father of medicine, Hippocrates, cited respectfully in the epigraphs: air, water, and place. The dossier is perfectly documented, drawing from all sources without distinction, whether the testimonies came from Pliny, the priest, or the shepherd.

The air, Costa said, was healthy, purified by the strong tramontane winds. The waters of the Agly were by nature limpid and light, "they are a remarkably good base for soap and cook vegetables well," and they were enriched upstream by various thermal springs. In short, at the risk of disappointing the gentlemen in Paris, so infatuated with the "epidemic constitution" of each region, it had to be admitted that there were no pernicious miasmas or recognized pestilences, that the environment was healthy and not at all conducive to disease. Nevertheless, the epidemiological map that drew such a positive correlation between the "theaters of anthrax" and the course of the Agly led him to designate the river as responsible for the disease. Air, water, place: of the Hippocratic trio of predisposing causes, it was the second term that was blamed. It would be pointless to reproach Costa for missing what would later be recognized as the real factor in spreading the disease: the soil itself. The pastures were perennially contaminated by anthrax spores, especially when a few carcasses of animals killed by the disease were buried there. Nevertheless, the idea of a telluric origin for the disease already clearly existed, but it was expressed in terms of other epizootics such as sheep pox. The contaminated meadow, the "cursed field" was a danger that many recognized. In Orange in 1488 two butchers complained to the consuls that Jonquière livestock breeders had pastured their sheep, stricken with *picota*, in meadows forbidden to them to discourage the spread of the disease. A Montpellier doctor named Astruc observed how diseases surfaced during the transhumance in Haut-Languedoc. He thought that blaming the season or the atmosphere was too easy. He attached more importance to the ground:

> There is one repeated and familiar observation, made by all those who care for the sheep, which is that, when a sick herd has been in a pasture, the herd that comes there afterward gets the disease. This is observed especially in the Cévennes. There is a mountainous part of this district with excellent pastures that serves as a meeting ground for all the herds in the area. In this migration, the leaders of the herds are aware of what happens. If they learn that an infected herd just passed through, they stop wherever they are and wait until the next day to move on. It is their thinking that they must let at least one night pass, in which the cool air, combined with the morning dew, destroys the pestilent particles that can communicate the disease. Whether or not this opinion is well founded, it is generally held in this country, where experience has proved that such precaution is very wise.[34]

Costa went along with the general opinion and thought that anthrax ran rampant because some ecological balance had been upset and the waters of the Agly transported the anthrax virus. On the other hand, there was debate over how the water originally got poisoned.

The most widespread idea was that the partridge was the source: its saliva was enough to infect the water, and sheep, driven by the summer heat to quench their thirst in the clear waters of the river, thus contracted the disease. For that reason, the poor lambs, thirsty, parched from the dry and sunbaked plants they browsed, their muzzles scratched by thorns and thistles, were kept from drinking along the poisoned river. It was a popularly held opinion but also supported by authorities such as François Boissier de Sauvages, a Montpellier professor. Costa went to great lengths to demonstrate the absurdity of this theory. He set up two laboratory experiments bringing sheep and partridge together to destroy the belief. Then he proposed his own theory: if the Agly waters were pure by nature, humans had polluted them. To take fish from the river easily, fishermen poisoned the water with *coque du Levant* or *titymale* or even quicklime. *Coque du Levant* was a drug sold at a grocery or drugstore; quicklime was more often used in the Pyrenees mountain streams. The Catalans preferred to use *titymale*, a kind of euphorbia with a toxic milky juice that grows abundantly in the Languedoc scrubland.[35] "Giving *titymale*" happened to be a legal and well-known practice, since the right to "*donar la llatresa*" (give *titymale*) for fishing in the Salses pond was leased to the duke of Hixar for three thousand pounds a year. It was also very effective, since it allowed two or three hundred quintals of mullet to be caught during Lent and again in November. For that reason, Costa claimed, "the life of men is entrusted to the punishable greed of fishermen."

The sociology of diseases that he then established is suggestive: "The anthrax virus principally attacks shepherds, those who prepare the skins of large and small livestock, those who render their fat, butchers, and robust men. It spares no gender, no station; it attacks those who enjoy honest good fortune and who live comfortably just as it does the poor. Only nursing infants and those who never eat butcher's meat are exempt from it."[36] Here, Costa informs us in passing that meat consumption was not just the privilege of the rich. The good people of Roussillon were also carnivores, unfortunately for them.

Two means of contamination are suggested here and later developed. Direct contamination was known to all. No one was unaware that anthrax primarily struck those who handled skins, wool, or even raw flesh, so much so that anthrax was, in some respects, almost a disease of the profession. Doctor Costa did not dwell on the recognized dangers of infection. But he laid more stress on transmission by way of digestion, raising the question of butchering in passing. How was it that anthrasic meat from animals that died of the disease, classified as *carn de mori*, could appear on the family dinner table? Through various means of distribution, answered Costa, and then he enumerated them. First of all, there was domestic consumption, heaviest in the summer on farms where seasonal workers were fed meat derived from the herd; then there was fraud, the butchers selling bad meat as good meat after eliminating the most visibly diseased portions.

The "greed of fishermen" and the abuses of butchers find us in familiar territory, that of human malice. Costa's colleague Fournier, who studied the same disease a few years earlier, shared his views. Those "vile mercenaries," butchers and merchants, were completely to blame. They sold infected meat at low prices to poor people who were not aware that in that flesh were "hidden the agents that cause their death." In their writings, the great Lancisi and, later, Fodéré sound the same refrain. In Strasbourg, Fodéré compared the cows of Fribourg, which were never sick, to those of Alsace or Bresse, which were frequently stricken with anthrax. This difference, he explained, stemmed from the cleanliness of the cowsheds. And he randomly blamed the livestock breeders, their credulity in face of the cowherds "calling themselves the possessors of infallible secrets" and the Jewish horse dealers who bought and sold sick animals at the fairs. These remarks can be read in the light of his acknowledged powerlessness, expressed further on: "We still have nothing positive to propose for healing stricken animals."[37] Thus we can consider doctors' continual abuse of livestock breeders and merchants as a way of distancing themselves. It allowed the doctor, and later the veterinarian, to protect himself, to be exonerated from too much responsibility. But, most important, this indictment is in perfect accord with the optimism of Enlightenment medicine. Because, if the fault was human, wasn't it easily remedied through good law and good policy? Each dossier, each inquiry, ends not with a prescription but with a regulatory plan to be submitted to the appropriate legislator. Thus the state law officer was provided the means to combat anthrax contamination. Everything was a matter of political will.

And, on closer analysis, the intentions of the sellers and the consumers appear much more complex. The impoverished consumer was not always an innocent, unknowing victim. In a suggestive annotation, Costa himself alludes to completely public advertising campaigns: "[Anthrasic meat] is sold at a very low price. The abuse has been carried so far that those who want to sell this infected meat will loudly advertise it." Sellers and consumers were not two distinct species, just as the shepherd who sold his anthrasic mutton kept some for his own consumption. It is difficult to accuse him of knowingly poisoning others, when he ate it himself.

Dead Beast, Dead Venom

In the area of epizootics, doctors did not possess any etiological certainty, and they knew it. Nor did they know if it was dangerous to eat the meat of an animal that had died of the disease. Costa, who was convinced of this, acknowledged that he had many opponents. They pointed to the collective experience of the villagers living on the shores of the Leucate pond, who rarely contracted the virus, though, like others, they consumed anthrasic meat. And the practice of the Catalans could be generalized to the entire countryside. They noted, considering all diseases and all time periods together: (1) that diseased meat was eaten there; (2) that this was even one of the rare instances when the peasants ate fresh meat, beef in particular; and (3) that apparently they were not afraid of eating it.

Since this was a lasting phenomenon, we have later, and more detailed, testimony: "As for meat, we know it is not the habit in rural areas to let anything go to waste. So no one hesitates to use the flesh of dead diseased animals as food; this is a health danger that the peasant rarely worries about at all. Moreover, meat inspection being nonexistent in the villages, it is especially in rural areas that nearly all the sick animals are killed and cut up, since their owners, fearing confiscation, are very careful not to take them to the city slaughterhouses."[38]

Let us return to anthrax. The people of Beauce or Burgundy behaved like the Catalans, and, in most of the farms where anthrax periodically raged, it was standard practice to use the meat of anthrasic sheep for one's personal food needs if it was possible to slit their throats before they died of it.

It would be false to believe in a total lack of concern, in an absolute, beatific calm. Other documents reveal that diseased meat was not prepared in the same way as healthy meat. The most common practice was to salt the flesh, a custom hardly ever practiced in modern times, except with healthy or leprous pork, but extended to other meats in times of disease. In Embrun, an epidemic of anthrasic fever struck among the inhabitants "after the use of salted meat from beef cattle and cows that died of anthrax."[39] Slaughtering and salting are the oldest attested practices in the case of epizootics, and ancient authors, such as Columella, recommended them as final measures, when all others had proven to be useless in quelling an epidemic.[40]

Costa teaches us how to prepare the meat of infected sheep and goat Catalan style: "They reject what is most spoiled in this flesh; they then wash with vinegar what they believe to still be edible, they season it heavily with salt and pepper, and finally they cook it, or, more accurately, they let it roast on the grill or in the oven, or perhaps they make it into those kinds of ragouts similar to what we call beef à la mode."[41]

Two precautions are better than one, they say, but here precautions were multiplied, first by eliminating the pieces considered a risk and then by using a whole range of classical antidotes: vinegar, salt, fire. Fire was especially important, grilling or even roasting the meat, or preparing it according to a current method with wine and salt and letting it simmer for four to six hours. Thus Parisian stew, with its supposedly disinfectant qualities, was introduced to the outer reaches of the realm as a recipe with therapeutic virtues.

In the mountains, precautionary preparations seemed to be unknown. Meat from dead diseased animals was eaten "without scruples" and, according to inquiries, without "dire" results. One of the keys to this absolute lack of concern is entirely contained in the Italian proverb: *morta bestia morto il veneno*, dead beast, dead venom. Proverbs traveled, like shepherds, according to the seasonal nomadism that led each year from the pastures of the plains to the high grounds. The practice of the *estive*—later called the transhumance—helped to circulate knowledge. Thus the worship of Saint Véran, the protector of herds in the Crau and the Camargue, moved from the low plains of the Rhône to the heights of the Alpine pastures. Likewise, the Italian proverb was exportable, and it became a commonplace on both sides of the Alps. The stockbreeders of the Dauphiné made it their own. The Arles shepherd who migrated to higher pastures ate the meat of dead animals as long as it was not spoiled.[42]

Among the consumers of infected meat, two groups were easily identified. In the grain-producing plains, where cattle were raised for milking and sheep grazed in the fields after the harvest, it was the farmhands and seasonal workers, in short, the agricultural proletariat, for whom the farm owner provided meat in the summer to give them strength for the heavy fieldwork. Feeding the harvesters was a major concern, just as, later, feeding the men hired to build the railways would be. Their salary converted itself into cash in kind, and their employers were careful to see that rations were sufficient in quantity and quality. In particular, they included an unusually large share of meat products. To satisfy these requirements, a pig was often killed midsummer, or else sick animals were earmarked as high priority, an "avarice" Champier denounced, without saying if the employer participated in this carnivorous feast.[43] But the principal group of dubious meat lovers was the shepherds themselves. All those convinced that eating diseased meat was harmless referred to this everyday shepherding practice. The shepherd was the favorite guinea pig for the advocates of a laissez-faire policy with regard to meat. In fact, nothing was known about the long-term effects on the shepherds who consumed such meat. No protoepidemiologist worked up a pathological portrait of that particular group.

Good or Bad: Precautionary Slaughter

During the Enlightenment, animal diseases drew attention from all sides. Farmers as well as naturalists were interested in them. Michel Darluc, who visited Provence in the 1780s to write a natural history, observed the herds, their diseases, and the shepherds' treatments, sometimes similar to human medicine, sometimes involving empirical methods that were effective but strange, which he compared to the acupuncture of Japanese doctors.[44] The shepherds had treatments, but they did not even try to treat a sheep if, for example, it became *calu*, "mad," an epithet that also applied to humans: "The animal that is stricken with it seems deprived of sight, hence the word *calu*, squinting. It cannot keep to a regular path, runs, jumps, and often hits its head against walls and trees, until it falls to the ground. Shepherds know no remedy for this disease. They kill the ewes who are stricken with it, as much out of superstition as to sell the meat. They are convinced that, as long as the herd is in heat, this disease is passed from one sheep to another. It results from numerous causes well worth knowing. Often a corrosive humor is found in the sheep's brain that brings it about."[45]

It is difficult to say if this disease that affected the brain was coenurosis, an infestation well known to stockbreeders, or if Darluc was describing a case of scrapie, an emerging disease that the English first detected in their herds in 1732. Perhaps, as it often the case, there is a nosographic confusion. But the important thing is the shepherds' behavior in such cases. Once diagnosed, they preferred to slaughter without delay. Access to the legal market was undoubtedly impossible, since a sheep arriving on foot but turning in circles was too easily spotted. The only alternative was domestic consumption and neighborhood distribution, no doubt forgoing the dish that marked a high point in rustic open-air gastronomy: sheep's head split open and grilled over a wood fire.

In 1809 in Cavaillon, the mayor issued a decree regarding a "disease of the bristle" that was ravaging the city's pigs. Let us not attempt to identify that disease. Porcine diseases were of interest to no one and prompted no literature. The prevailing opinion was that all pig diseases were fatal: "sick pig, dead pig," according the popular expression.[46] The sick pig's fate was clear: it would end up sooner than expected in the salting tub. That is what the town councillors denounced: "Out of a sordid avarice, the owners intend to salt this meat, unhealthy for eating or selling, without concern for the accidents that could result.... It is only too true that individuals who have had the temerity to eat this type of meat have been the victims of it."[47] That same meat would be either eaten by the producer or sold.

An alternative solution emerged, which consisted of taking the animals to the nearest slaughterhouse before the disease attained its clinical expression. This was a practice already well-known in Burgundy in the sixteenth century, where young animals were led to slaughter if the disease was not yet proven, as the local stockbreeders said.[48] It became more and more common with the repeated epizootics of the eighteenth century.

To sacrifice young animals in the event of an epizootic made economic sense since, on the one hand, young creatures were known to be more susceptible to diseases and, on the other hand, it was better to sell a young beast than none at all. That was the reasoning of the English stockbreeders, who observed that, after the age of three, a sheep had a good chance of dying from a very widespread disease they called "rot." In the last decades of the eighteenth century, leg of lamb less than three years old became a great hit on English tables, and, concomitantly, a severe enzootic disease affecting wool-producing beasts disappeared.[49] The decline of the animal's age, at first sporadic and then continual between 1740 and 1850, was good news for the quality of meat, understood here in the gustatory sense. It created new tastes among consumers. From the gerontophiles they had been, eaters of castrated males or overage females, they became lovers of younger and younger meat. Preparation methods took on new life. Beef was no longer necessarily boiled for hours. More and more often it appeared on the table roasted, a culinary technique formerly reserved for poultry.

We have certainly not assessed all the repercussions of epizootic crises. They accounted for the sale of an excessive quantity of "green" or salted meat. For a long time—going back to antiquity—these crises increased dried meat production. At some point, probably in the eighteenth century, there was a reconversion from salted to fresh meat, butchered very young.

Let us emphasize this paradox: precautionary slaughter presents itself to the historian in two versions. The first version, which we just mentioned, is poorly illuminated and poorly understood. It involved an almost secret, though very widespread practice. The other version is better known. It is the massive and systematic all-out attack that the states tried to impose increasingly during the course of the eighteenth century. This slaughter was anything but silent because it was official. It was announced by royal decrees, and it so mobilized the troops that even any partial victory against an epizootic resonated like a military victory. Government slaughter created all the more noise because it set off many disputes. If people pointed the finger at and sometimes taunted the learned gentlemen of the Royal Society of Medicine, it was not for the remarkable wealth of epidemiological studies and medical topographies that they were in the process of compiling, as no one dreamed of contesting their usefulness. But they were considered, and justly, moreover, as accomplices in these methods of the state. Indeed it was the society's secretary, Félix Vicq d'Azyr, who convinced first the French and then other European governments to follow the English method of "stamping out" rather than the Dutch method that sought to treat affected herds. He paid personally by directing the preventive operations in the southwest, ravaged by rinderpest in 1774–1775. His marching orders were "kill without relenting." An old word was used to characterize his acts, but it took on new meaning. It was, they said, true "butchery" he committed. A pamphlet targeting Vicq d'Azyr put it succinctly:

> One practices it [slaughter] thus, lacking other resources
> Or when the number of the affected is very small,
> Or when the best care is entirely unsuccessful.
> But to begin there, that is butchery
> To flaunt the horrors with bravado
> Then, when the conquering Doctor has been cut off,
> To finally prove oneself ignorant Apprentice.[50]

The last two verses may be alluding to Vicq d'Azyr's relative failure. Because, despite the massive means deployed and the eight million pounds spent, the plague was not completely eradicated, and it flared up sporadically, in Béarn or in Agenais. In short, the most radical preventive method did not prove to be entirely effective, and Vicq recognized that himself: "Let one be very wary of so severe a law when one does not have the means to implement it everywhere and at the same time, since, instead of a useful project, one may implement a series of vexations so onerous to the state that private individuals may pay for them."[51]

"Vexations" was to put it mildly. In fact, despite financial incentives that theoretically amounted to one-third the value of the slaughtered animal, the almost unanimous attitude was resistance. Selective slaughter may have been understandable, but an all-out attack struck at the heart of the shared sentiment that sacrifice, in every sense of the term, made no sense. The soldiers charged with guarding quarantine lines were accused of all sorts of offenses, for example, of introducing diseases unknown in the healthy, remote countrysides, such as gonorrhea and other venereal diseases.[52] Resistance to government-imposed slaughter sometimes bordered on rebellion. Many soldiers were killed in Béarn.[53] In 1776 the alarm sounded in the Audruicq parish in northern France. The villagers there became alarmed not because of the epizootic but because of the announced arrival of the police force and army troops to carry out preventive slaughter on the village herds. The situation became so tense that news of it reached the inspector general. Had not the first magistrate of Audruicq made downright seditious remarks, going so far as to threaten the intendant's subdelegate that he'd have *him* slaughtered?[54] This was not simply temper, complained the intendant. It verged on sedition, that is to say, the crime of lèse-majesté.[55] It is worth noting that sedition seemed to be limited to questions of bread. Fear of contaminated meat never led to sedition. Administrative precautions against it did, though.

What were the reasons for such resistance? Whatever they were, the years between 1810 and 1880 saw a general relaxing of health policies regarding meat in France.

Of course, the epizootic landscape had changed, in France as throughout Europe. But it had not changed very much. Certainly, rinderpest was less prevalent, its incursions diminishing in frequency and virulence. Western Europe was protected by the medical policy system that the German states had instituted and continued to reinforce, Prussia benefiting from a solid lead with an efficient, respected detection and information system for animal diseases. Viruses continued to collect on the shores of the Caspian Sea, but the pestilent waves crashed up against the health shield of Austria, Hungary included. Not until Europe was engaged in another conflict, in 1870, did the viruses successfully penetrate farther west, for the last time. The geo-epidemic configuration changed, the paths of propagation shifted and adopted other routes. Henceforth, bacterial exchanges followed a west-east or north-south direction. They followed the lines of commerce rather than war. They reached the sea with the exportation of animals, in particular, stallions intended for reproduction.

The nineteenth century witnessed a formidable effort at improving breeds, bovine breeds in particular. Genetic improvement had a counterpart: selection weakened indigenous breeds. The French merinos, crossbred with the Spanish, were more susceptible to scrapie and scabies. The dairy cow, improved by the Durham breed, more easily contracted tuberculosis. Progress in stockbreeding was often double-edged. The more the animals were crossed, the cleaner they were, well cared for and fat, the more subject they were to disease! All in all, the epidemiological balance sheet was mixed; gains against widespread contagious pandemics were offset by increased endemic diseases. An overall decrease in pathology was hardly observed at all. Between 1813 and 1821, Alsacian herds suffered from typhus, gangrenous angina, and gangrenous peripneumonia, that is, three epizootics in the space of eight years.[56] It was not until 1850–1870 that the old epidemic patterns were broken.[57]

But let us not be deceived. The health threats for animals and humans were just as present in the nineteenth century as in the centuries preceding it. What changed was that epizootics were viewed differently and severe methods for containing them were abandoned.

The royal decree of 1784 crowned the preventive work of the Enlightenment by making the declaration of disease mandatory for a certain number of animal ailments and by providing for systematic slaughter in the cases of incurable animal diseases. But it fell through. The postrevolutionary specialists took a dim view of systematic slaughter: "In truth, slaughter cuts the disease short, but only does so by destroying the animals stricken with it as well as those suspected of having been exposed, consequently ruining the owners and thus adding to the sum of ills."[58] Constraints were loosened. Regulatory work came to a halt, and between 1784 and 1881 no legal mechanism existed for the declaration of disease, slaughter, or compensation. Regaining everyone's goodwill was a high priority, under the accommodating authority of the mayor or the prefect, and interfering in the commerce of animals was especially avoided.[59]

Among the public authorities and decision makers, the threshold of tolerance for health risks, which seemed to decline during the

Enlightenment, seemed to rise to new heights, never before attained, rivaling the threshold adopted by most stockbreeders. This alignment in attitudes toward food had great political advantages. The clashes between opposing views subsided, and, henceforth, social tensions no longer surfaced, except on the local level. Sick pigs in Cavaillon provoked the mayor's indignation, and the subsequent appointment of André Serre, the city blacksmith, as health inspection officer. That was not a drastic step.

Such reduced vigilance was due to a combination of factors that are very hard to untangle. Political stakes (the political clout of a peasantry that could now vote) intersected with economic ones (the cost of state-paid compensation). For good measure, let us add the triumph of liberalism in matters of commerce and, finally, in the medical sphere, the increasingly adamant rejection of contagionist theories. To end the list there, it seems, would be to forget one decisive factor: veterinary medicine had perfected health evaluation procedures. In place of an overly rigid dichotomy between healthy and unhealthy meat, it tried to establish a graduated scale of risks. It distinguished between types of ailments and degrees of infection, and it calculated incubation periods. Infected in the first degree, meat was not dangerous, and young animals could be taken to the slaughterhouse. The essential thing was to consume the meat very quickly, freshness being the first guarantee. At the second degree of infection, the meat was questionable, but it was only truly dangerous at the third degree. At that point, it had to be absolutely prohibited. Generally speaking, the veterinary arts considered the flesh of an animal slaughtered on the first or second day of a disease to harbor no danger. Also, they did not think chronic diseases rendered meat harmful. They were more attentive to a risk largely unknown until then: consuming worn-out meat.[60] In short, there were as many risks in eating sick beef as in eating the bull from a bullfight—as many, if not more. The veterinarian tended to make food risks relative and so to minimize them. Most important, the veterinarian paid a different kind of attention to animal diseases than the Enlightenment doctor had, whose primary concern was human health. The veterinarian had other priorities: his job was to care for animals, not slaughter them. Thus the Lancisi system was condemned to a long period of remission.

The attitude of rural populations faced with animal disease, so obsessive between 1740 and 1850, was a matter of both fear and a certain kind of fatalism. That fatalism, a commonplace in the discourse on the peasantry, was demonstrated by two different kinds of behavior. Their reaction facing an epizootic was truly fatalist. "Who's to blame? It's the nature of evil," was a common remark.[61] The epizootic was like a hailstorm or the winter cold, just another natural risk. They accepted it as such. On the other hand, to eat meat during an epizootic, even indulging in fresh meat, was not a danger one ran but a risk one took. It was an acceptable risk, because it was a matter of individual free will.

ELEVEN

THE POLITICS OF PRECAUTION

Between the city and the rural world, there was a permeable boundary. City dwellers could be affected by animal plagues in the same way as villagers, especially if they owned livestock. Indeed, some of them with interests in stockbreeding placed animals in the country. Such contracts were most often signed in the second and last quarters, the lessor and lessee thus splitting the rewards but also the possible losses "in case of pestilence."[1] This practice of leasing livestock was very widespread, and a good number of merchants became "bankers of beasts."[2] This meant that urban areas were implicated, more than it seemed, when epizootics occurred. Nevertheless, the anxieties expressed in the city were often of a different nature. They centered primarily on the quality of meat. If eating meat presented no risk of directly contracting the animal disease, that did not mean "that one could consider infected flesh disposed to putrefaction, like the flesh of animals that died of epizootics, as a healthy food, and there are examples of putrid diseases caused by that bad foodstuff."[3]

June 1714. Even though a pandemic plague had spread throughout the realm, one enclave was still safe "from the evil that runs rampant among the beasts": Avignon and the Papal States. Spared for the time being, Avignon citizens were no less nervous, as this ordinance from the vice-legate who governed the city makes clear: "The widespread rumor about the mortality of service animals, especially those used for food, has caused many people to refrain from eating meat.... For these reasons, [we] would like to prevent the contagion that the meat of animals stricken by said disease could cause among humans and

❊

reassure people about the meat that is cut up in the butcher shops."[4] *To refrain* from eating: there we have the precautions taken by individuals. *To prevent and reassure*: there we have the concern of public authorities, in Avignon as elsewhere. It remains to be seen how these worthy principles were put into practice.

Authorities in the Grip of the Precaution Principle

"In all cases of epizootics, the public is in fear and the magistrates are in suspense regarding which course they must follow with the butchers."[5] These are the words of François-Emmanuel Fodéré, under the empire. They apply to all epochs.

During epizootics, butchers were as threatened as bakers during bread shortages. In 1746 rinderpest struck the Vevarais and the Cévennes, killing nineteen out of twenty horned animals. In Alès, a butcher was providing meat to the soldiers of Royal Bavaria when they found themselves stricken with diarrhea or dysentery. The one responsible for these ills was immediately identified, the soldiers tried to seize him, and only by fleeing did the butcher escape with his life.[6] Latent urban fear, which translated into a decline in meat consumption; active demonstrative fear, which expressed itself in riots against the butchers: either case required that public authority be involved. Its intervention in any health crisis was standard, a part of its classic regulatory role, which dictated taking those measures necessary for the public good. For a long time, meat policy was the exclusive responsibility of the cities. The rinderpest pandemic, superbly oblivious to regional and national boundaries, transformed the givens with regard to health and demonstrated the limits of regulations and inspections confined to the level of the city and its surrounding area. The prince then granted himself the right to interfere. The states intervened throughout, applying to rinderpest prevention formulas proven effective during the human plagues. Henceforth, two regulatory systems, on the local and the national level, complemented or duplicated each other.

The authorities acted in two steps. First, they consulted to evaluate the threat, and then they came to a decision. Two examples will suffice, one coming from a republic (Venice), the other from a dukedom (Milan). The decision-making circuits were different, but the procedure followed was the same, passing by way of a preliminary scientific expert evaluation. In Venice and in Padua, in 1614 and once again in 1699, an unidentified contagious disease ran rampant among the bovid family. The conjunction of a plague affecting horned beasts and human dysentery raised fears of grave health dangers. The populace rose against the butchers, accusing them of secretly selling Hungarian beef stricken with dysentery. While rumors spread, the authorities consulted. The Padua medical school faculty was called in as the leading authority. After some debate, they decided it was possible to "eat such meat without danger, because the contagion was particular and specific to beef cattle, and that, moreover, all the 'malice' had been corrected and dispelled by the exercise these animals had to do before they were killed." But in Venice, the doctors, consulted as a group, did not share the same opinion. They thought that such "contagious and deathly" flesh should be prohibited. A certain Fabius Paulinus, an Udine doctor, presented yet another point of view. He was of the opinion that one could eat it, but with certain precautions. It was necessary to soak the meat first in a brine of salt and vinegar to render it comestible, but, above all, he said, it was advisable to discard the entrails along with the intestines "as being the source and the nest of the disease." As for the muscle and the milk, they were presumed innocent. The dangerous pieces were the viscera.[7]

Prognosis relied on visual observation. Dissection of diseased animals was the principal means of investigation, which doctors practiced with a vengeance, not without risk to themselves but with a will to try to understand the nature of the disease. The autopsy generally revealed flesh with a normal appearance and rotting, engorged viscera. That is what gave the anthrax disease its common names of "anthrax" and "spleen blood," since the blood of the dead animal appeared clotted and black like coal, and the spleen swollen and voluminous. If the examination sometimes allowed the disease to be named, it always allowed it to be detected. That was an additional reason for requiring that animals arrive whole and on their feet at the slaughterhouse, because, skinned and gutted, they deprived the inspector of essential information. "It is impossible to recognize the disease when the skin is removed."[8] Without lungs or liver, the butchery inspector felt like a haruspex unable to read what was in the animal or accomplish his mission. One was sure of getting right to the seat of the disease by opening the entrails. That was where "the evil ferments of a pernicious intestinal war" nested.[9]

The suspicion directed at the viscera had something to do with the nutritive qualities attributed to different pieces of meat. There existed an entire subtle hierarchy, which Champier summarized: barely nourishing or digestible were the tongue, pancreas, testicles, and kidneys. Very nourishing, choice morsels eaten without reservation were the fat and the marrow, at least the marrow of the long bones. The other marrow, from the backbone, which went up to the brain and merged with it, was more phlegmatic, cold, and difficult to digest in nature. Good but difficult to digest were the stomach and the intestines, all the organs that the urban proletariat preferred for breakfast. Those "born with a solid stomach or who did physical labor could eat them without risk." Muscles of any kind were considered noble food, especially if they were loaded with blood and fat.[10] In short, to ban the intestines as the seat of infection and a possible source of digestive contamination was a minimal measure, relatively easy to take, because in the end it only penalized the lower classes who ate tripe.

In Venetia, the expert evaluation was independent, and it was contradictory. It is not clear how the divergence in scientific opinion affected the decision makers, that is, the senate. Because it was the senate that finally had to decide.

At the end of the seventeenth century, the Venice senate was no longer principally composed of representatives of the trades and international commerce. Alongside the shipowners and the galley captains sat landowners, a consequence of the migration of capital toward property investments since maritime transactions had dried up and industrial activities showed no signs of growth. The large landowners from the city transformed their villas into efficient agricultural enterprises and subjected their lands to intensive agricultural practices, without leaving fields to lie fallow. Many fields had been planted in grass, and wheat cultivation gave way to livestock raising.[11] Merchants and landowners sat side by side, but they did not share the same interests. There was a major split between those who wanted to maintain commerce with Dalmatia and, beyond that, Hungary and those who feared for their herds. But, on this point, the senate had already decided. Importing cattle was forbidden, and the borders were closed. On the sale of meat, they adopted the most radical opinion of the city doctors, regardless of the specific economic stakes. In 1699 the senate forbade, under penalty of death, the sale of beef, fresh cheese, milk, and butter in the city. The inhabitants were condemned to eating sheep—at least those inhabitants living in the city, because it seems that this decision did not apply to the rural areas.[12]

Let us move to a different epizootic and a different city. Milan in 1714, the year of all dangers: the city was threatened with rinderpest and fell under Austrian control. The city and the dukedom benefited from a model preventive health system, with ad hoc standards and personnel. At the center of the health network stood the figure of the doctor *condotto*, the doctor of the poor, paid by the city. The *condotti* were assisted by the paramedics, also paid with public funds: surgeons for external operations, barbers who raised leeches for bloodletting, "gossips" for childbirth, and *norcini*. The last of these were incontestably the most original figures among the Milanese health personnel. Generally natives of the Norcia valley, these empirics did their training in the country, and their first vocation was the care of pigs. Their expertise in matters of porcine castration designated them experts in all sorts of ligature operations, and thus they were put in charge of hernia reductions and gall-bladder stone extractions in the Milanese hospitals.

So much for the therapeutic side of municipal health; as for the prevention side, that fell under the jurisdiction of the health tribunal, which appointed two public health commissioners, chosen from among the city's "liberal" doctors. In times of health, the tribunal oversaw livestock traffic. They kept a close eye on the Swiss border, which they considered dangerous territory. They set up inspections for animals passing over the Tresa, Mendrizio, and Bellinzona bridges, and they issued health certificates for herds entering the dukedom.[13] In 1714 one of these two commissioners was Paolo Girolama Biumi, mentioned previously as an observer of rinderpest and enemy of the Lancisi measures. The other commissioner was Ignace Carcano. The two colleagues agreed on what measures to take. These consisted of bolstering the already existing system, confining suspect herds, and quarantining their herdsmen. The most important thing was making very sure that the bodies of dead animals were buried to avoid putrification and its dangers and then disinfecting the cowsheds by fumigating them and finally having them blessed. As for the rest, they were convinced (and justifiably so) that the cattle plague did not affect humans, and they concluded that the meat could be used without danger. Their Paduan colleagues came up with a completely opposite assessment. For the first time, they designated the meat of animals dead of a contagious disease as *carni infette*. In the winter of 1714, there was much talk of the horrible devastation in the lower plains of the Pô, and many attributed it to these *carni infette* that had been secretly eaten.[14]

Thus, confronted with the same threat, two cities of the same culture took fundamentally different measures. The senate's behavior resulted from precautionary thinking. As soon as an expert opinion— especially when, as here, it was contradictory—pointed to a risk that could not be measured or controlled, the senate considered it its duty not to use the pretext of uncertainty as grounds to procrastinate. Would we say, then, that the Milanese magistrates, who made different choices, were not following the same logic of precaution?

Let us concede that the crises were not the same and neither was the nature of the contagions. On the other hand, let us also recognize that the uncertainties were equally great for both diseases and that there was no reliable scientific information to guide the behavior of the politicians one way or another. It remains true that in the second phase, the decision-making phase, a gap opened between the Venetians and the Milanese. The whole standpoint of Biumi and his colleague consisted of weighing and evaluating the risks. On one side of the scale, there was a health risk, the risk of consuming unwholesome meat that was not a contaminant but could very well be unhealthy. But attempting to avoid one risk meant courting another, the risk of completely disrupting the supply circuit and depriving the consumer of necessary foodstuffs. In that case, the remedy would be worse than the problem and would lead to starving the people. Actually, in considering a decision to ban the meat, the health commissioners weighed its negative effects: it might succeed in producing shortages, that is, in obtaining exactly the opposite of the results they wanted.[15]

Biumi and his colleague were not choosing between a risk and the absence of risks but between two risks. Their fears were not in vain; even without forbidding retail sale, the measures to counteract the disease—forbidding livestock traffic, canceling certain fairs—were enough to disrupt and sever the supply circuits. Even simple inspection led to paralysis. That was what happened in French Roussillon a few decades later. In 1774 Turgot congratulated the intendant for the drastic measures he had taken: sequestration of suspect animals, a ban on livestock traffic, closing the provincial border. "One can only applaud all the precautions you have ordered to prevent the invasion of this disease." Of course. But the effects were catastrophic, because the Perpignan butcher shops could not provide beef without the help of the Languedoc. And Perpignan suffered. The price of replacement meat, from sheep or pigs, skyrocketed, and the municipal butchers canceled their leases, leading to a loss of ten thousand pounds for the city. And finally Turgot, despite himself, had to retract his rigorous directives.[16]

In Milan as in Perpignan, the stakes were complex. Essentially, the conflict arose between two health values, one involving the quantity of food supplies and one involving the quality. Compromising food supplies or risking health: between these two evils, it was not clear which to choose, and either choice would evoke food fears.

Solutions varied according to the time period and the state. Confronted with rinderpest, Venice authorized butcher shop sales, except for the riskiest pieces of meat. Milan did the same, but Rome opted for a complete prohibition.

It was once again because of rinderpest that Bernardino Ramazzini issued this warning: "ubi enim de morbo contagioso agitur, numquam satis cavemus, dum cavemus" (when it is a matter of a contagious disease, if one takes any precautions, one can never take enough precautions).[17] And the illustrious professor added that one could safely consume the meat from cattle dead of a contagious disease, but, for one's health, it was better to abstain (sed pro salutis tutela melius est abstinere). In other words, even if there was no risk of contracting the same disease, concern for protecting one's health still ought to lead to abstinence.

Ramazzinian suspicions originated in a completely new method of investigation, micrography. Until that time, doctors based their diagnoses on the general experience of the disease, which was more or less comforting, since there was no zoonosis. The exploration of the infinitely small, on the other hand, opened a mysterious and rather disquieting new expanse. On this point, Vallisneri was to blame for his colleague's doubt, as Vallisneri had been the first to observe a drop of liquid between two transparent slides. That drop was infected bovine blood, and the doctor had seen little worms moving around in it. He drew from it this dietary moral: "I would never trust eating the meat of sick animals as some people advise, not only because it is not nourishing and because of the contaminated, adulterated, and corrupt juices that it can introduce in our bodies but also for fear that those fatal little worms will not be tamed in us and could belong to that starved race that feasts as well on human blood as on the blood of bovine or other animals."[18]

The advice to abstain was addressed to the individual. It was the classic advice of the clinician. At the bedside of the sick and witnessing the struggle of the patient's vital powers against the disease, the doctor's first duty was to do no harm, to do nothing that could interfere with that struggle. The famous maxim primum non nocere was perhaps more a therapy of patience than an invitation to abstain.[19] The great principle of curative medicine was somehow transposed here into the domain of preventive medicine for the individual. This was an appeal to individual responsibility, as the old model of the health contract necessitated.

Ramazzini agreed with his country's policy of letting meat be sold, but he was not enthusiastic about it. He did not know what to think of the "rotgut" measure that banished tripe from the butcher stalls. Was this precaution effective and sufficient? He would let each person be the judge of that, he said: "Qualis cautio num sufficiat, et omnem dubitationeme tollat, liberum cuique esto judicium."[20]

Meat Under Surveillance

As it was formulated by the Italian doctors, precautionary behavior had two facets. For each individual, there was the principle of abstention. No statistic will ever tell us the extent to which this advice was heeded, except the anxious remark of Avignon's vice-legate: people "refrained" from eating meat. The other facet was purely political and thus better known. This involved a principle of action. It was implemented by the cities, with regard to retail commerce, and by the states, with regard to the long-distance commerce in live livestock.

Faced with an epizootic, the cities organized. The ones with municipal regulations enforced them. The ones without any established them.[21] Where there was no permanent health official, as in the Italian cities, the authorities usually charged with supervising the markets and butcher shops were then relieved of their responsibilities, in favor of another authority, an emergency organization that was established on the model of the health department mobilized in times of human epidemics. Or else the health department itself returned to active duty for the occasion. In Lyons, the health department was created in 1577 and confronted all the epidemic outbreaks between 1581 and 1720. Beginning in 1668, with human epidemics subsiding, it intervened in the domain of butcher shops and animal diseases. From 1744 to 1749, the various "diseases of beasts" demanded the whole attention of the Lyonnais health commissioners, and the policy decisions that they issued at the time constituted the full extent of their activity.[22]

In the way it was organized, the health department was just a replica of the city council, which relinquished to it a few of its exclusive powers. Its fundamental mission consisted of developing health regulations and seeing that they were implemented. This public office, like all health offices, was peopled with doctors—doctors of law, that is. That was a constant in all public health offices, a constant that is perfectly understandable. Since medicine had no power to treat or cure epidemics, all efforts were directed toward preventive medicine, and thus policy. The health department was no more and no less than a health dictatorship, solely empowered to suspend basic freedoms: for men with animals, the freedom to circulate and the freedom to trade. Royal administrative and provincial offices organized a system of strict supervision—always on the model proven by the struggle against the human plague—with patrols in the grazing lands, mandatory certificates of health for animals in transit, arrest and seizure of suspect animals. This last measure generally went hand in hand with the old charitable tradition: the seized meat was distributed to the poor. That is what the Swiss did until the early nineteenth century.[23]

The epizootic marked a time of stringent law and consumer advocacy. Sanctions were increased. In Avignon, the butcher who illegally sold uninspected meat was normally liable to a fine. In times of epizootics, if the disease affected sheep, he risked "three cords of rope," that is, torture by strappado. In 1603, when a "mysterious" disease struck cattle, prompting sudden death, butchers were forbidden to sell the meat "under pain of death."[24] Within the empire, the same fate lay in store for those who did not declare the disease; they risked being hanged. This penalty also applied to the butcher who bought a sick beast and to the livestock raiser who sold it. According to the law or local custom, woe to the merchant! Or woe to the butcher!

The health departments faced the daily problem of organizing even more stringently the "visit," that is, the health inspection of herds that entered the city. The animals that arrived *intra muros* could present no sign of the declared disease. If they had it, they could not arrive on foot at the slaughterhouse. Recalling Fodéré's classification, the animals that arrived were never sick "in the third degree," but they could be in the first or second degree, which made detection more difficult.

Finding experts who were capable and experienced was no small matter. In normal times, one called on retired butchers, pastry chefs, and cooks. If the meat was suspect, one took the time to deliver it to the city hall, where the requisite doctor or surgeon performed a more thorough examination. But these laborious procedures were ill suited to urgent cases. In northern Italy, butchers were forbidden to slaughter without the presence of a city deputy or at least a parish priest or some other expert who could carefully examine the animal's intestines.[25] In Liège, during the rinderpest epizootic of 1745, the city's prince-bishop, Jean-Théodore de Bavière, toughened health inspections for animals. New regulations were issued by the city and the suburbs to organize an inspection system on three levels. The *connoisseurs* were responsible for inspecting the livestock on foot; the *rewards* had to examine the slaughtered carcasses; the *contrôleurs généraux* were charged with supervising the two preceding categories, as a kind of superpolice.[26]

The crises of the 1700s prompted two new precautionary procedures. The first consisted of putting newly arrived animals in observation cowsheds outside the city long enough for the disease to announce itself or not. The problem was that no one had any idea of the incubation period. For the human plague, it was known, established as forty days, a number that was derived less from experimental observation than from assiduous reading of the Bible.[27] But for the quarantine of animals, there was doubt: was forty days too long? And how to provide stables at the city gates for such a length of time, when normal operations involved a steady flow? Responses varied. The most commonly established waiting period was twenty or twenty-one days, as if animals developed diseases twice as fast as humans.[28]

Between the slaughterhouse and the butcher stall display, even if the distance was not great, there was still the risk of fraud, against which people tried to protect themselves. When rinderpest struck, the Roman prefect in charge of provisions came up with an intelligent response, rendered public and obligatory by a *bando*, an edict: bovine and buffalo meat was first evaluated by the *periti* at the slaughterhouse. Meat that was declared good and faithful was immediately marked with a bulla, or seal, and was then sent to the butcher shop display. The Roman model circulated along with the contagion in all the Papal States and the certificate of guarantee was made obligatory in Avignon and in the Comtat: "So as to assure those who do not buy the whole quarter but who buy some part of it, let the said mark be at the extremity of each quarter, and let it remain there for the one to whom the last part of the said quarter is delivered, so that those who buy the said meat before him have something to convince themselves with their own eyes that it has been verified and that they can eat it without fear."[29]

The same year, the consuls in Aix copied their Avignon colleagues.[30] The risk there was the peddling of meat clandestinely slaughtered in the surrounding areas. To avoid this, the consumer was informed through a visual communication system, accessible to all those who could not read, that is, about half the population of southern cities around 1700. The city label was legible to all. As the health law was mandatory, the smallest village with a municipal butcher had to enforce it. And in Caderousse, a little town on the Rhône, the consuls had a seal made for the occasion with the town initials on it: K and A! With its seal, the city accepted its responsibility.[31]

It is not known if the invention of the certificate of guarantee, the equivalent of a quality label, dates from 1714. In any case, that was when the practice came into general use. As the century advanced, health certificates for animals in transit also came into general use—becoming obligatory in the realm in 1746—as did certificates of origin, specifying the parish from which the animal came and the state of health in that parish. The royal administration provided for a chain of accountability, with the parish priest or syndic at one end, the butcher at the other.[32]

Managing Fear

Another question tormented the authorities in times of epizootic crises: how to manage the perception of risk, that is to say, fear? It gave rise to another model of precautionary logic, which consisted of managing not the technical dimension of the risk itself but its psychological effects. We must reconsider this important warning from Pierre Chirac to the old king, Louis XIV: "I believe it is very important to let the villages ravaged by these diseases know that they are not contagious for humans.... It is the fear of catching the disease, on the one hand, and the unhappiness of seeing himself ruined by the loss of his herds, on the other, that will make him all the more susceptible since he has been exposed, like his animals, to the heat of the summer sun and is thus disposed to fall ill with a similar disease."[33] A doctor—the chief doctor of the duke of Orléans—was advising the king in a crisis situation. It was a matter of reassuring or pacifying in the name of a well-understood paternalism: wasn't the king the father of his people? If there was uncertainty regarding the risks, which could not be reduced, at least confidence could be restored, especially in that terribly fragile and essential relationship between the sovereign and his subjects. That is one way to read Chirac's message, but we would no doubt be mistaking the meaning of his warning. Chirac stuck to his role—a medical one—and his advice stemmed from what he believed to be absolutely necessary and within the domain of health: to struggle against fear.

From the scientific perspective of 1700, fear was not a direct pathogenic agent but an agent that favored disease. As a Galenist, Chirac rejected the neat dualism of Descartes. Like Montaigne, he believed in that "close stitching of mind to body, each communicating its fortunes to the other," so much so that the affections of the soul also affected the health of the body.[34] Like air or food, emotions and passions were classified among the "unnatural" factors that predisposed one to health or, conversely, to disease. If they were negative, like fear or distress, they could easily engender "ill" humors, in particular, that black humor, so harmful, as everyone knew. If they were positive, they dilated the spleen, diluting the black secretions at the same time and protecting the body from disease. That was why Chirac's case of the villager—a case replicated thousands of times throughout the realm—was to be taken seriously. Doubly affected by the epizootic threat, Chirac's villager felt both distress and anxiety, the two states of the soul most contrary to vital dynamism. Chirac, the court doctor, believed this man accumulated the means to debilitate his vital faculties, even with his robust constitution. He did not contract rinderpest, as he believed, but a disease with a psychosomatic origin. The phenomenon was well-known specifically regarding the oldest animal disease transmissible to humans: rabies. Doctors had long recognized that it was transmitted only through the saliva and that there was no risk in consuming the meat of a rabid cow. But they also knew that it was necessary to forbid absolutely the sale of it, because those who might buy it to eat without being warned risked dying ... of terror.[35] Let us repeat: the court doctor was not stepping outside his function here. He conceived of his bedside presence as a kind of psychotherapy. He was convinced that the psychosomatic factor played an important role in spreading a zoonosis, just as it did with an epidemic, to such a degree that in 1720 his view became the official interpretation of the Provence plague.[36] He considered his social role to be a fervent obligation to allay popular fears.

In this case, both the doctor and the king had to intervene. The doctor could prescribe the only medication without contraindications: joy and serenity. The king could reassure, pacify. Nothing was more favorable to spreading an epidemic than fear. Nothing was better for avoiding it than good humor:

> Whoever wants to maintain bodily health
> And resist the epidemic
> Must have joy and bury sadness.[37]

In the case of the epizootic, Chirac was only invoking the experience common to all doctors in the field: the importance of psychological factors and morale in resisting disease. The king had to reassure, to announce loud and clear, with the blare of trumpets or with notices posted on the church doors, that contagions spread from animals to humans did not exist.

The desire to inform encountered no objections in this case. The fear already existed, and there were good reasons to believe it was unfounded. But was it necessary to inform of epizootic dangers, at all times and in all circumstances? Situations sometimes developed that caused the administration consternation, so much so that they did not know whether to issue warnings or to opt for minimal publicity, even silence: "It is prudent, on such occasions, to avoid alarming the people by magnifying things."[38]

With the accession of Louis XVI, a serious epizootic struck throughout the southwestern part of the realm, affecting the generalities of Auch and Toulouse. It was so severe that it prompted the Toulouse bishop in a pastoral letter—pastoral in both senses of the word—to try and make his diocese accept the necessity of preventive slaughter. The legislative arsenal was ready; by 1771 it had been perfected. But, in addressing the circulars to the intendants, the minister Bertin carefully avoided asking them to publicize the new regulations immediately. On the contrary, he recommended great prudence to each of the king's representatives in the generalities:

> As long as these kinds of diseases do not attack your generality at all, it seems prudent for you to keep to yourself the regulations and to leave them in some way unknown.... Even in the case where some disease is spreading, further study is necessary to discover if it is truly a contagious and pestilential disease. Because, outside of that case, remedies and assistance are only needed within the afflicted cantons, and implementing the regulations could only do harm and raise unnecessary alarm in your generality. Finally, if the disease is known to be contagious and it is necessary to avoid spreading it from one place to another, you will still have to consider if it might not be sufficient to begin by publicizing the 1746 regulations once again, which are much less onerous for commerce, less severe, and less alarming than the ones I am sending you.[39]

To avoid any premature public announcement, not to provoke alarm, as long as it did not exist; if it existed, to verify that there were solid grounds for it: that was the administrative maxim. It was followed, to the letter, by the subdelegate sent to the Sault area, when the bad news of the anxieties of Puyvalador and its environs arrived. Now it appeared as though their fears were not well founded. "I believe," wrote the subdelegate to the intendant, "that the public outcry ordinarily magnifies the calamity into more than it really is."[40]

A policy of prudence was applicable to recognized dangers. A policy of precaution aimed at preventing potential risks. If we can accept these preliminary definitions, then we can say that the prevention of food risks themselves was always and everywhere a matter of a policy of precaution, to the extent that, in the prescientific era, no danger was established with certainty. Ramazzini and the senators in Venice had at their disposal all the available intellectual and deontological means for apprehending risk; they only lacked a rudimentary base of experimental proof. They regretted this, like the vice-legate who worked so quickly "to be informed of the truth of things."[41] But they acted. Precaution is not inaction or endless deliberation. Public men take political risks, the first being the risk of making mistakes. Since the plausible is plural (only the truth is singular), the policies it inspired took various forms. As for the term "prudence," it reappeared frequently under the administrators' pens. They used it to designate appropriate behavior in the face of dangers engendered by epizootics. Perhaps the only identifiable and avoidable danger was public fear.

TWELVE

THE DANGERS OF IMPERFECT METALS

Chemistry and metals invited themselves into human food very early, creeping in through *secrets*. These secrets, or recipes, were set forth in a brief and descriptive fashion: "stick a copper nail into a piece of meat to conserve it better."[1] The secrets conveyed a whole little domestic alchemy, spread through word of mouth and then peddled by the means of printed collections of a heterogeneous nature, mixing home economics with popular medicine.[2] It was through these that nitrate, lime, and copper entered the kitchen or the pantry. *Sel nitre* was often called for, that is, saltpeter. It was put to use in the salting tub, to both conserve and "redden" pig meat; in the cellar and storeroom, to keep ice and water cold and to keep the oil from setting in winter.[3] The recourse to nitrate was attractive because it was not produced by big industry and because in the city and the country, everywhere there were damp vaults or old walls, saltpeter could be recovered by scraping the surfaces. It was called *nitre de murailles* or *nitre de houssage* because it was collected "by dusting it, sweeping it, or raking it." As for common niter, it was drawn from ashes.[4]

These processes were generally described as "ways of correcting" natural food or "means of conserving" it. This miniature protochemistry allowed the cheating of time and nature. But, beginning with the Renaissance, some people also thought it sometimes meant playing with health.

Preserved Foods in the Renaissance

In the Renaissance, when two or three people conversed, if they discussed everything and nothing, it was said that they were exchanging fresh and salted talk. This was a pleasant activity that could be practiced throughout the year, a repeated pleasure that food did not offer. One ate according to the season, which meant that one ate fresh products only during a few months of the year. Climate determined diet. The Italians could eat fruits and vegetables eight months of the year; the Scottish, five months, from August to December; and the Parisian poor, deprived of vitamins during the excessively long winters, found themselves at the Hôtel-Dieu, exhibiting to Gui Patin all the symptoms of what he called "land scurvy." For all alike, capturing the seasons in a canning jar was a matter of physiological need and desire, a desire that grew increasingly stronger as it went unsatisfied.

This dream was perfectly in keeping with the old dietetics, which demonstrated prejudices with regard to fresh fruit that were as strong and they were persistent. The standard prejudice blamed the consumption of raw fruits for most intestinal disorders: "It is certain that the green juice, which in medicine is called leek bile and which is vomited most of the time, is not caused by bread, or meat, or other foods of this type.... We must remember here that, except for one or two, all fruits have bad juices. That is why Galen included among edible foods only those fruits that were perfectly ripe and excluded all others."[5]

Since all men were not as reasonable as the great Galen, that paragon of good health who "had abstained from eating fruits, thus allowing him to live free of disease," doctors did not forbid the consumption of fresh fruit, but they issued an avalanche of recommendations regarding it: to stay away from green fruit at all costs; to choose dry fruits over "hourly" fruits, like plums or melons, fruits so moist that they rotted within an hour after being picked and threatened to disrupt the "animal machine," unleashing terrible floods in the stomach; to eat fruits at the beginning of the meal preferably, since their coction in the stomach took such a long time; to correct them by balancing their cold nature with warm foods. Thus melon had to be eaten as an entrée, with salt or ham to correct its aqueous and corruptible nature and with cooked wine to compensate for its coldness. Moreover, it was not certain that these precautions were sufficient: "At court and among the rich, peaches are eaten peeled and soaked in wine, to remove harm if necessary. This is clearly useless, given that their harmful juices spread more quickly."[6] The only fruits that could be eaten without restraint were dried fruits; among fresh fruits, those that kept were preferable, the late varieties of pears and hard apples that could be kept throughout the winter by packing them in straw or storing them on racks in a cool, dry place.[7] And one could eat preserved fruits and vegetables with no ill effects. Of course, they were not nourishing; these were condiments rather than foods. But they were perfectly healthy, since the cooking and the sugar corrected the flesh of its natural faults, and since vinegar and salt were good disinfectants. Medical casuistry was complex, and it was more or less respected in the city food markets, where sale dates for fruits were strictly controlled, but it was widely ignored elsewhere.[8] The villagers in the outskirts of Rimini "considered it harmless for them to eat raw fruit." The result was that "they did not live long; a great number died in childhood, which came from the fact that they ate an overabundance of fruits and that they did not take care of themselves."[9] For different reasons, doctors and consumers agreed on one point: preserved foods were good. Still they needed methods for keeping them.

What was true of land transport methods was also true of conserving techniques: from Julius Caesar to Napoleon, they hadn't changed. More precisely, there was no definitive transformation before Nicolas Appert and his little bottles sterilized in a double boiler. Preserving processes were described in Greek and Roman works of agronomy. They were passed down to the Middle Ages, and in the Renaissance they were translated and taken up again by authors such as Nostradamus and Olivier de Serres in France. For fruits and vegetables, the only known method was protecting them from air and decay through the intermediary of salt, fat, oil, or sugar. The principle was simple, and the recipes repetitive, but the art difficult.

The Tastes, Colors, and Fears of Olivier de Serres

Does he need an introduction? Olivier de Serres, a Huguenot gentleman, was a companion of Henri de Navarre. When the civil wars subsided and Henri was crowned king of France, Olivier returned home to Vivarais. The return of peace meant the return to the land. On his Ardèche holdings in Pradel, Olivier became the manager of an estate, which he managed according to the best methods. In his own way, he participated in the necessary reconstruction of the realm by publishing his *Théâtre d'agriculture et mesnage des champs* in 1600. We have to thank this Protestant farmer—a rare species in the realm— for the best information we have about the domestic economy of his time. The *Théâtre* traces what we might call the "agro-alimentary" network from one end to the other, on one particular spatial scale (the family-run farm) and on one specific temporal scale (the farming year). In completing the cycle that begins with production and ends with consumption, Olivier quite logically ends his book with a chapter devoted to jams, that is, to preserves.

Let us reread that chapter. There, we learn that any homemade preserve must have two qualities: its goodness, that is to say, its gustatory value, and its beauty. As for taste, the processes of conservation, whatever they involved, inevitably transformed the organic properties of the fresh produce. This transformation was unavoidable, but it was also desired. Thus Olivier de Serres admitted his preference for capers in vinegar: "In vinegar, capers become more delicate than those dried in pure salt.... Thus some pleasant taste is added, which makes them delectable to eat."[10] The added flavor that pleased him was the sourness, a taste widely shared with his contemporaries. All sorts of vegetables were preserved in vinegar, from fennel to truffles and including small cucumbers and green melons, their close relative. Each preserving process added a particular taste for which it was valued: salt for a pungent flavor, vinegar for an acidic flavor, sugar or fat for sweetness or smoothness. Thus any preserved foodstuff, subverting nature, offered a fabricated taste, far from its "primitive nature."[11] From its "primitive nature," nothing was retained, except its color. A preserve must not have the taste of nature, but it should have the color. Good to eat, beautiful to look at, that described Olivier's preserves. Thus, for orange preserves: "The orange peel will be beautiful, white, translucent, thick, and full, according to its quality, and also pleasant tasting, without retaining anything of the bitterness."[12] Preserving changed the sensual relationship of man to food. Artificial beauty made it so that the eye was the judge here and decided the quality of things.

That explains Olivier de Serres's perennial worry: that all fruits should retain "their naive color," that cucumbers should remain "without loss of beauty, wholly conserving their greenness," like peas, artichokes, and also almonds and walnuts, for which he indicated three methods for keeping them green. Fruit jellies had to be "pleasant to the eye and to the taste." Green and red were highly esteemed, as well as the quality of transparency, since the "beauty of a preserve depends on the clarity of its body." This concern for the "naive," primitive color can be interpreted as nostalgia for the natural.[13]

Olivier de Serres collected recipes that were already well-known, except for one process that, it seems, he was the only one to mention.

It was a recipe for pears in syrup, made beginning with autumn pears, like the Good Christian variety (ancestor of our Williams variety). The peeled quarters were put in glazed earthenware pots, with sugar and cinnamon, and the pots were sealed with bread dough, "so well sealed [lutté] that the fruit does not breathe at all," and then placed in the oven for as long as it took to bake a batch of bread, over two hours.[14] The lut technique was borrowed from alchemy, where one activity consisted of preparing a paste, or lut, to cement the cracks that appeared in stoves and experimentation vessels. Before Appert, this may have been the best technique for preserving: isolating the preparation from the air and cooking it a long time. The intuition was a good one; we do not know if the results were likewise and the isolation succeeded. English preserves in the baroque era, involving vegetables or pickles and sealed with paper and leather, resulted in many mishaps.[15] Prudent as he was, Olivier gave an expiration date for consumption. These pots had to be eaten quite quickly, in a period of fifteen days to three weeks.

To improve the presentation of preserves, Olivier indicated no natural coloring, native or American. His whole art lay in two devices. The first was to achieve a "good cooking"; the second, to do this good cooking in adequate receptacles, made of copper. Cooking in copper: that was the great secret. More than that, it was the technological leap that separated Olivier from his predecessors in the art of preserves. Whereas Nostradamus stirred his preserves in earthenware or iron pots back in 1555, Olivier had at his disposal revolutionary new cooking utensils. Copper prevailed in all the equipment used to prepare preserves: the preserving pans, of course, but also the strainer that was used to filter the grape jelly, the slotted spoons (skimmers), the ladles.... Preparing sweetened jams in red copper preserving pans had two advantages. Copper was a good conductor of heat; it allowed for uniform cooking and reached the desired high temperatures. In addition, it had that essential psychological advantage of preserving the color of the fruit. For preserves using salt or vinegar, steeping the foodstuffs in a copper vessel allowed them to retain their good green color, since the metal, attacked by the acid, produced a "green rust" that was an excellent coloring. But, as fervent a fan of copper as Olivier was for sweet preserves, he was equally opposed to its use in the preparation of condiments. This green rust was verdigris, a toxic substance, as we now know. Like his contemporaries, Olivier did not know this, but he was wary of these "copper salts." "You must take care not to put either iron or copper in the brine, for fear of corrupting it;

general advice for all salt preserves." He categorically advised against preparing those preserves in copper, despite his passion for the "naive green color." In this way, he opened a debate that would be argued widely in the centuries to follow: at what cost must the natural color be obtained?[16]

The agronomist's ambivalence with regard to copper is striking. Insofar as he approved of the copper-sugar marriage, he thought like his contemporaries. Insofar as he had deep reservations about the copper-acid marriage, he appeared to be a pioneer, no doubt the first sounder of the alarm in the French language to usher in the era of suspicion. It is not quite clear where his prejudices came from. He could not have found them in the works of the ancients, Columella and the other *scriptores rei rusticae* from whom he drew so eagerly. *Le Mesnagier de Paris* was suspicious of copper containers, but only for storing milk.[17] The question of metallic salts was largely unknown in the Middle Ages, and it would not really be explored until the fifteenth century in pseudoepigraphic texts.[18] Serres's knowledge was, I believe, totally new, shaped by his chance war encounters with German or French Protestants, such as Roch Le Baillif, who had become a passionate believer in the ideas of Paracelsus, who died in 1541. When Henri, who would become the fourth of that name, entered Paris, Olivier was with him, as were the doctor-chemists, headed by the first doctor of the future king, Jean Ribit. Jean Ribit, Joseph Duchesne, Théodore Turquet de Mayerne, destined for high medical careers, were all three Huguenots and all three Paracelsians.[19] The Paracelsians used different treatments. They enriched the pharmacopoeia with mineral substances never before used, such as antimony, sulfur, and mercury. New disease, they said, new remedy. Thus syphilis, that scourge that appeared after the discovery of America, was treated with mercury vapors, a far more drastic remedy that the Galenic mix of herbs but finally more effective. Paracelsians were dissidents with regard to established medicine and religion, roundly condemned by the Paris medical faculty for whom this "metallic" medicine smelled so much of . . . sulfur.

Studies by German alchemists were circulating at the same time as new treatments. In the sixteenth century, the Latin countries boasted botanists who cultivated trial gardens, but it was in Germany, the richest mineral region in Europe at the time of the Fugger family, that metallurgy flourished. Paracelsus (Theophrastus Bombast von Hohenheim) and Agricola (Georg Bauer) both demonstrated the superiority of German protochemistry in its two branches: medical chemistry and metallurgical chemistry. They were closely connected.

Just as they were exploring medicinal uses for metals, Paracelsus and Agricola were also observing the risks of the metallurgy trades and drawing conclusions about the pathogenic effects of extracting and working with certain metals. The gilding trade, for example, was extremely dangerous to one's health because the ambient atmosphere contained poisons, mercury and lead. Thus the first German monograph on work-related health risks was devoted primarily to the gilding trade.[20] Those who extracted copper and lead from mines in Hungary and Germany experienced a daily descent into hell ending in a frenzied colic that they called "mines cat," because it made them spin in circles howling like an enraged cat. They rarely lived more than forty years, and Agricola tells how, in the Carpathians, it was not unusual to encounter widows of miners who had remarried as often as seven times.[21]

Of course, with these professional diseases, health was compromised by what was inhaled, thus by the air. But it was very soon extrapolated that the "salts" could be harmful as well if they were absorbed. The unique characteristic of poison was its extreme subtlety. If underground gases were capable of extinguishing the miners' lamps in mines, couldn't they also work their way into the human body? The alchemists had classified ductile copper with the imperfect metals, because it rusted, oxidized, and had the tendency to combine with many other elements. But, in all their fantastical attempts to transmute an imperfect metal such as copper into silver or gold, they had encountered mineral acids along the way and had suspected them of pernicious effects. The protochemists of the Renaissance denounced metals for their role in profession-related diseases and began to suspect the risks of food contamination.

Copper and Preserved Foods

After Olivier de Serres, the taste for condiments did not diminish; in fact, it became more pronounced. The acidic and the sour were not dominant flavors in modern high cuisine but peripheral ones that accompanied and brought out the flavor of the main dishes. Preserves had their place throughout the meal. Vinegar preserves accompanied entrées and boiled stews; sweet preserves accompanied desserts.

It is difficult, however, to distinguish between taste and necessity, since preserving vegetables in vinegar was the only process available before Appert. All vegetables were preserved using this means: little cucumbers, cabbage, asparagus, lettuce, chicory, green beans, peas, and even fruits such as apples, pears, and plums. Whether or not they were deacidified, whether or not they were sterilized, the expectation remained the same: they had to be green. Those living in Provence relished "grasses," as those living throughout the Continent called for "greenness," as in a vegetable eaten completely fresh. Now, it was not certain that making them beautiful made them good for the stomach. The taste for tartness and green seemed quite democratically shared throughout modern Europe, though perhaps it was more pronounced in England, where not only vegetables but also apples had to maintain their "natural" greenness. That explains the particular treatment of English apples, subjected to a bath of alum and boiling vinegar.[22] Parisians preferred a white, translucent apple jelly, with sugar and deer antler scrapings as its base.[23]

With English green apples, we leave the register of ordinary inoffensive colorations to enter the thornier one of dangerous preparations. We cannot dismiss our suspicions about cucumber pickles, the leading condiment on the Continent. Green and aqueous as they were, fresh cucumbers were considered a real danger. At the very most, their cooling nature recommended them as a "food medicine" for temperaments that were too hot. Thus Champier suggested that textile workers, known for their nymphomania, eat them without reserve.[24] On the other hand, preserved in salt and vinegar, the little cucumber became something altogether different. It lost its harmful humidity, and the vinegar had an "incisive" effect on it, cutting the coarse fibers and juices. Thus transformed, it traded its name of cucumber for the name "cornichon," and all temperaments could digest it. The cornichon did not exist in nature; it was a preserved product.

According to the terminology of Darluc, the Provençal botanist, there were two varieties of cornichons, the true cornichon, fruit of the caper bush, and the false cornichon, the little green cucumber, both of them preserved in vinegar. In the Provençal shops where "true" cornichons were produced, two processes were used that the naturalist described and decried: "The artificial green color is due to the acid of the vinegar that has been kept for some time in a copper vessel or to copper coins tossed into the acid liquid where the capers are kept. Stringent laws must be established against the merchants and rascals who use such tricks, as nothing is more dangerous than copper dissolved by acids or verdigris taken internally."[25] Darluc visited those shops in the 1770s. Forty years later, they were busier than ever, and, according to Bouches-du-Rhône statistics, eight hundred thousand one-pound jars of cornichons were made and sold yearly in that area alone, as well as two or three hundred thousand jars of capers, sold throughout Europe.

And that was only the beginning. The Languedoc made a specialty of the production of verdigris, known as *verdet*. In and around Montpellier, the wives of winegrowers devoted themselves to this domestic protochemistry. Theoretically, their process was simple. The two primary materials they used were, first, strips of red copper that they bought and that came from Sweden, via Hamburg and Sète, and, second, a product coming from the vineyard: grape clusters, dried in the sun and preliminarily steeped in the wine dregs. By layering the grapes and copper strips in earthenware pots, they obtained a verdigris within a few days that, dried and sold, turned a good profit. The copper was imported from the Baltic, the verdigris was sent to northern Europe. For a cottage industry, the quantity produced was "nearly unbelievable," "prodigious."[26]

Holland was an especially important outlet, according to a certain Montet, a Montpellier pharmacist and academician. Montet proposed several explanations for Holland's prodigious demand, noting that the Dutch who lived both in the cities and the rural areas were among the cleanest and most tidy people in Europe (Descartes had said so himself) and that each year they painted all their doors green as well as all the wooden fences around their gardens. In addition, they used Languedoc verdigris as a dye for hats and cloth.[27] Others suspected it was used for foods. In Paris, if we are to believe Demachy and his *Art du vinaigrier*, Dutch cornichons were the most prized, even more than the Provençal semipreserves, because they were greener. Demachy wondered if that color could be completely artificial, but then he reassured himself and the consumer: "I cannot believe that the Flemish use a metal as pernicious as copper to give their fruits this color that, in truth, the cornichons prepared in specialty houses do not have."[28] Greener than nature: that described the English apple and the Dutch cornichon.

Even if "regreening" was not as pronounced in Latin countries, domestic practices included using vinegar and copper in preserves. To prepare condiments, *La Cuisinière de la campagne et de la ville*, reprinted fifty times between 1818 and 1900, advised the use of a nontinned red copper cauldron. All the recipe books for urban or rural cuisine offered this "secret," with or without a warning, as recently as 1966![29]

The Stew of Good Reason

The case against copper, generally speaking, concerned contact with food. It involved the preparation of preserved foods. But increasingly it also touched on cooking itself.

Copper cooking equipment developed during the three centuries of the modern period, giving a great boost to the copperware industry. Technological shifts in the area of cooking are not products of spontaneous generation. They come about through changes in consumer tastes. Here, three tastes came into play. First, the taste for sour became widespread with such condiments as cornichons, relishes, and pickles. Consumers turned to them for the piquant, that hint of acidity that could enliven their bland diets. Second, the taste for sweet accompanied the huge development of the sugar industry, making jams and marmalades basic components of household production. Third, the taste for the natural informed the new Parisian—and soon to be international—cuisine. Paris chefs sought out the best ways of cooking and found that copper and tin-plated copper provided them the tools they needed. With La Varenne and his emulators, the black-bottomed stew pots were relegated to the attics, and the reign of the copper casserole was ushered in. Their royal status proclaimed itself visually. The bright, gleaming panoply of red copper utensils, hung on the walls or the fireplace mantle, proved to be an additional element in culinary distinction. We can still admire the palace kitchens of Montgeoffroy or Raby Castle. Victor Hugo relates that at Sainte-Menehould he saw something beautiful: the kitchen of the Metz hotel, an immense room, one wall of which was covered with copper. "The blazing hearth sent rays into all the corners . . . and made the fantastic edifice of casseroles gleam like a wall of embers. If I were Homer or Rabelais, I would say that this kitchen is a world, for which this fireplace is the sun."[30]

Even without the poet's lyric gift, everyone can understand and share his reaction, can feel as he did how that riot of color seemed to announce the good kitchen. That illusion had to be dispelled. Such ostentation harbored terrible threats. Once again, poison hid behind deceptive beauty. But there were increasing numbers of health experts on guard in the last decades of the eighteenth century to warn against the duplicity of copper.

In February 1749 the medical school of Paris examined a thesis on this question: was the use of copper vessels in the preparation of foods to be rejected completely? The answer was yes and the proof impeccable. The candidate was a young man from Toulouse who defended his thesis for six straight hours and painstakingly articulated his three-point argument. Copper was a poison. It was a slow poison, resulting in "unknown" diseases that would lead slowly and surely to death even if the copper only contaminated a tiny portion of the food. In conclusion, it was the duty of doctors, as ministers of health, carefully to warn citizens of the peril copper casseroles presented them. The candidate was approved by the faculty, and Falconet, presiding over the board of examiners, went a step further: "The vessels are whited sepulchres and truly poisonous. They must be forbidden."[31]

Had copper to be forbidden? Had people to be persuaded to use copper only with great caution? Both strategies were considered and put into action.

Let us hear first from one of the advocates for changing the status quo. He thought the heads of households must be persuaded to stop using copper for cooking and that it was their responsibility in turn to convince their staffs. He imagined the following dialogue between a master and his cook. The master is sensible but strict: he rejects all copper, not only the beautiful pure red kind that has the essential advantage of preserving the color of the fruit but also tin-plated copper; the cook is stubborn:

But the cooks will say that iron vessels burn the stew. The masters have only to answer them: use less coal; that will be less of a bother for you, and it will cost less. But the cooks will say: it is a lot of trouble to regulate the flame with iron vessels, especially when we are in a hurry. The masters can respond: study how to regulate it, pay more attention, and come to work early. But the cooks will insist: the stew will not have a beautiful color, they will say. It doesn't matter, the masters will say, we only want to see the stew through the eyes of good reason. We like safety and health better than a pleasant blonde or white color. But iron vessels blacken, they rust, and soon become useless. The masters will respond: that's an annoyance, it's true; but it can be avoided with a little care. In any event, isn't the visible, healthy rust of iron better than verdigris, which is often invisible and lethal? ... But the stew will have the taste of rust, the cooks will insist. Well, the masters will say, experience nevertheless teaches us that it is easy to make a good stew in an iron vessel, and, if you serve stew at our table that does not taste good, that will be your fault, and we will have to ask you to resign.... And one word more. We want no risk of poisoning at our house. How many people of quality invited here and there eat only the roast, for fear of some mishap? ... Thus obey, or leave."

"That is the line that the masters must take," but did they take it?[32] We can hear in this imaginary dialogue echoes of the old animosity doctors felt toward cooks, those cooks "who have the talent for combining all that nature has separated even by the greatest distances, also have the talent for shortening life, or rather for delivering a true poison."[33]

This was almost a rhetorical process: the doctor, tired of being called a murderer, in turn accused the cook of being a poisoner. In fact, the author of this fictitious dialogue was mistaken on two points. First, he gives the cook too much credit for acting autonomously, as cooks had to conform to the tastes of their masters. After three months, a French cook engaged by an English gentleman found himself "ruined by the tastes of the master and his guests, which gradually reduced him to the principles of English cooking."[34] Second, he forgets or pretends to forget that stew obeys demands other than those of "good reason," that flavor, delight, and pleasure at the table were increasingly important values in French society at the time. The tyranny of taste was manifest in the great houses, where imprudent servants would throw out newly tin-plated vessels because of the bad taste that comes from the materials used to attach the tin to the copper.

Given such resistance, it appears that the cautionary dialogue recorded here probably remained fictitious.

Metallic Colics

The use of copperware was not limited to the family kitchen. Large copper receptacles were used by confectioners for making jams, by brewers for making beer, by dairies for transporting milk, by tripe preparers, by bakers, in short, by most of the professionals in the food network. Now, wherever there was copper, there was the potential for verdigris, as was the case with the common salt sellers who generally weighed salt on copper scales, always covered with verdigris, or with the Parisian water carriers, who saved the Etampes sand to scour their water buckets, which turned entirely green on the inside.[35] A copperware arsenal was not the exclusive prerogative of the great houses, even if it was true for such houses that the kitchen was a specialized room where that gleaming arsenal was deployed. Many copper objects, such as fountains or chocolate makers, found their way into more modest urban homes. The fountain, also called a washing fountain, had two functions. It was used for a washbasin and drinking water reservoir and for food preparation. Set against the wall, the reservoir was a good size, with a capacity equal to six pails of water. Through so much contact, copper could contaminate both liquid and solid foods. And if it had only been copper! Unfortunately, that was not the only metal in question. Other metals and their uses worried the scientists.

Enter Lavoisier. The great chemist demonstrated an underestimated, marked interest in food safety. In 1777 he denounced the tin-plating methods of one Monsieur Bribel, who used zinc and perhaps lead in his preparations and claimed to be covered by the Académie des Sciences. By contrast, he maintained that the tin-plating methods of Monsieur Duhau and the steel-tin alloy of Madame du Mazis were not toxic. On October 20, 1780, Benjamin Franklin had his grandson ask Lavoisier for his opinion on metal for cooking pots. Lavoisier answered that certain Paris coppersmiths used illegal mixtures of tin and lead and advised Franklin to find an honest polisher and pay him well, a big tip being a good guarantee of safety. And he hardly confined himself to the question of cooking pots. He was also preoccupied with the question of women's makeup, wondering about the white base of ceruse—a lead carbonate—and about rouge, which was sometimes made from saffron and cochineal, both harmless, and sometimes from cinnabar and vermilion, both toxic mercuric sulfides. He analyzed samples taken from twelve Parisian perfume makers before confirming their clients' trust in them. In 1785 and 1786 he was one of the reporters designated by the Académie des Sciences to address the issue of cider adulterated with lead monoxide, and he warned against the danger of colic associated with it.[36]

Colics: here we touch on what, in the history of past populations, is most likely to discourage the historian, since they are so present, even omnipresent, and nevertheless impossible to identify, to quantify, even sometimes to understand; how to assess their impact? How fortunate the modern epidemiologist is to have at his disposal the biological tools to identify them and the figures to count them (one or two deaths out of a thousand in our medically advanced cultures are due to food poisoning). A retrospective epidemiology would be doomed to failure; at the very most, the prudent historian, supported by ample demographic studies, might offer a simple but distinct impression: colics were more numerous in the past. Must we discuss colics? Alas, yes, because people from the thirteenth to the nineteenth centuries discussed them at length, and unofficial private sources demonstrate an insistent, indiscreet, and sometime even immodest attention to the body. In the private register, colic occupied a place of honor. It struck with astonishing frequency. That is how Gilles de Gouberville happened to be sick so often between 1550 and 1560. Since infectious diarrhea from dysentery was not raging in his area then, we can assume our Norman gentleman was the victim of his food supply, as questionable as it was abundant. Bad fish left him vomiting and confined to his bed from October 6 to October 27, 1555. Another "poisoning" left him ready to write his will![37] The pains were violent. Moreover it was the intensity of the pains that provided the basic nosology, apart from any etiology: colic, colic passion, iliac passion, when "the ill is ambulatory, the intestines making noise, with torment and great pain."[38] In such cases, the victim hardly waited for the help of canonical medicine, which, ironically, advised an evacuant, and turned instead to proven and nearly as effective remedies such as a plaster on the tortured stomach—the panacea prescribed by Serres—treatments involving bits of string, or prayers to the Trinity, uttered with a finger on the navel of the afflicted one: "Colic or passion that is in my liver and my heart, between my spleen and my lung, stop, in the name of the Father, the Son, and the Holy Spirit."[39]

Colics, stomach upsets, vomiting: these were nonevents. For them to rise to the status of event, for them to take on the importance of an epidemic, they had to affect at least a whole region, and they needed a certain number of victims, many more, in any case, than today, when any disease attacking more than two subjects and caused by the same bacteria or virus is considered an epidemic. According to observers at the time, epidemics of this type had a season, summer, and they were mostly provoked by intemperate consumption of fresh fruits and vegetables. Doctors were unanimous in condemning the mad rush for the first fruits, a reflex exacerbated when emerging from the difficult gap, in February or March, when people were starved for fresh produce. People threw themselves on the first fruits, eating them in too great quantity and too green. The resulting stomach and intestinal upsets were blamed on overconsumption of fresh fruit. Such colics were legion, such as the one suffered by a girl of twelve, whom the doctor watched die after twenty days of futile care. At the autopsy, nearly four hundred cherry pits and a quantity of (green) grape seeds were found in her intestines.[40] All types of dysentery and its ravages fell into the same category, as well as all types of infectious diarrhea like those "malignant fevers" that we now recognize as typhoid fever. But, for those who were victims or witnesses, that etiological distinction had no meaning. For them, all such diseases were poisonings of nutritional origin, and dysentery that struck in spring was attributed to badly ripened fruit, "malignant fevers" to polluted well water. The Enlightenment would illuminate this confused nosography a bit by detecting and isolating the metallic colics.

They were acute and dramatic, as described in the *Encyclopédie*:

> It begins with a heaviness in the stomach and sometimes with severe colic in the intestines; victims experience a sickly sweet taste in the mouth, their pulse is weak, their legs grow weak and numb, and they feel tired throughout their bodies. They lose their appetites and digest food badly. Sometimes diarrhea occurs, which can relieve the victim if it does not last too long. If these early symptoms are not cured, the disease gets worse. There is a steady pain in the stomach and intestines, especially in the lower part of the abdomen. The victim curls up and feels as though his insides are being torn to pieces. His pulse is very fast, his skin burning. Then follows a terrible headache accompanied by delirium that is followed by trembling, convulsions and a kind of frenzy that makes the afflicted tear at themselves and bite their own arms and hands. Their pulse becomes irregular, and they die in a kind of coma or apoplexy.

These crises were epidemics, according to the criteria of the time, and thus one spoke of the Poitou colic, or the Devonshire colic, or the Madrid colic. Doctors discussed them at length; the bibliography on the metallic colics is one of the largest in the medical writing of the second half of the Enlightenment. They did, in fact, represent a medical victory. In calling them metallic colics, the doctors made a good diagnosis. They understood their origin and could even propose an effective treatment, since the antidotes to mineral poisons were known. The dangerous liaisons between copper and drinks had been unraveled, less dangerous, nevertheless, than those between lead and liquids, which led to cases of lead poisoning.

This disease, as we have seen, had been identified since the Renaissance, but it remained limited to those high-risk professions first inventoried by the Paracelsans and then by Ramazzini: miners, painters, plumbers, gilders, casters, and potters; in short, all those who worked with metals and in a noxious atmosphere. But in Poitou and Devonshire, where the colics widely affected the rural populations, it was understood that the contamination was produced by ingesting metallic salts dissolved into food or drink. It remained to be discovered what foods and drinks were contaminated; what metals were to blame: lead itself, or alloys (pewter), or oxides derived from lead, such as ceruse or litharge; and how these metals were implicated, whether they were present as chance pollutants or as an unusual ingredient added to foodstuffs, in other words, an additive.

While studying the Poitou colic (Geneva, 1757), Théophile Tronchin found a link between the symptoms of working-class painters and those of wine drinkers. It was ceruse, another derivative of lead. Ceruse was widely used and easy to make. It was obtained through the contact of lead with horse manure, wine grape residue, or the pulp from apples or vinegar. Used in small doses, ceruse made skin whiter. In large doses, it turned painters' hair green and gave Poitou wine drinkers colic. Drinking wine with ceruse or litharge added was standard practice. Litharge was an oxide derived from lead commonly sold in all good apothecaries and used very frequently in external medicine, for making many plasters, for example. The use of litharge was thus totally standard and legal. It had another totally standard and legal use, in wine. In 1695 in Lausanne, an attempt was made to sweeten wine "by mixing it with the dross of silver and other pernicious things, which caused extraordinary colics in various individuals, some of whom fell sick and others of whom died."[41] Two years later, in Paris, a master tapestry maker and his entire household, including servants and the boys who worked in the shop, fell victim to colics that brought them to the brink of death. The doctor tested wine that they had bought from Jean Nicolle, a winegrower in Argenteuil: it contained litharge.[42] But that should not come as a surprise, not in an era when such additives were standard practice and not against the law, which magisterially ignored them. All the winegrowers in the Paris basin did what Jean Nicolle did, for at least three good reasons.

1. Vegetables had to be green and bread had to be white, but, for good wine, there was debate over the ideal color. For a long time, *clairet* and *gris*—a very light wine with an indecisive color but nevertheless capable of *griser*, intoxicating—were the popular favorites. Between 1650 and 1750, the taste for wine took a different turn. Acidic white wines were abandoned for darker-colored, fuller-bodied wines. The rough red wines that stain began their ascension, and they had to offer "good color" and "fire." We would say a beautiful "robe" and sufficient alcohol content.[43]

2. Wine could not be green, because clearly it must not be made from unripe grapes. To counter this risk, a very old rule existed, called the wine harvest proclamation. In every community, each member was subject to quite strict collective constraints, and this proclamation was one of them. It forbade anyone from harvesting grapes before one or several experts had decided on the degree of maturity for the harvest. The one who had the right to make proclamations—generally, the lord—established the requisite day when everyone could begin harvesting and the timetable for the harvest.

3. This rule could not guarantee maturity. What to do, then, when the grapes were not ripe and the first autumn frosts were approaching? That was often the situation in northern vineyards, around Lausanne as around Paris. Let us keep in mind that, during the reign of Louis XIV, northern vineyards accounted for more than half of all French wine production. In addition, the two years in question here, 1695 and 1697, fell at the heart of the miniature ice age that caused early frosts and hurried harvests. If grapes were collected too early, the basic winemaking process caused the wine to begin to "go" in early summer and then turn sour.[44] Where were the harvests of yesteryear, like the one in 1540, which followed a summer so hot, Champier said, that a Burgundy wine was known to keep six years![45] Premature harvests of either grain or grapes were always full of dangers. The caprices of weather, the poor state of enology: everything led to widespread recourse to lead and copper salts at the end of the seventeenth century. They gave wine "a more brilliant color, more fire, and diminished its greenness."[46] This was more than an additive; this was a coloring, a preservative, a panacea! Who could reproach Jean Nicolle and company not for trying to obtain the impossible, a wine that kept, but for simply trying to make a sour wine almost drinkable?

Wine was not the only drink at risk. All alcoholic beverages were subject to metallic additives. The seventeenth century saw the popularization of alcohol. The ancien régime's average consumer rejected pure water—which was very rare, in any case—but also rejected pure wine. He disinfected his water with wine or vinegar, or he drank cheap, local wine. According to pre–French Revolution estimates, the alcohol ration for the Parisian or Lyonnais worker was close to a liter of wine daily. The gradual rise in alcohol use among Western populations accounted for some health benefits. Abundant water of good quality in cities was the exception (Rome figured among those exceptions). Since water was polluted, it was better to drink wine, or cider, or even beer. And let us remember that, for the mindset of the time, to drink was to nourish oneself. Doctors affirmed this, and people willingly believed it: all alcoholic beverages, as long as they were ingested in reasonable quantities, were balancing, beneficial, and wholesome foods.[47] Theoretically, they were healthy, but, in fact, it often happened that they were contaminated, deliberately or unintentionally.

Throughout the eighteenth century across the English Channel in Devonshire, a colic raged that was initially attributed to the unhealthy air. But was the air quality really to blame? In 1769 Thomas Halwek published a study, the title of which both posed the question and provided the answer: *The Endemical Colic of Devonshire Caused by a Solution of Lead in the Cyder.* The presence of lead in the cider was explained by the fact that casks were hooped to prevent the staves from splitting apart while the cider was fermenting. For several reasons, lead, a malleable and stable metal, was preferred over iron, which was more rigid and posed the risk of rusting. The casks used on the Continent were not much better than those in Devonshire. In the next century, cider-making conditions in western France prompted many doubts.[48] Criticism mounted: too many squalid presses painted with red lead paint and ceruse; too many casks without hatches, impossible to clean at the bottom, lined with sheep intestines to prevent acidity; and, as a result, too much cider that caused colic.

Let us summarize: grape harvests were strictly supervised. In every other way, the producer had total freedom and winemaking remained a private affair. And there was total freedom as well for the wine dealer and for his improbable concoctions.

Deadly Secrets

As the eighteenth century drew to a close, alarm sounders were everywhere in France, at the bakeries, in the oil mills, in the dairies, where butter was made in copper receptacles, in the groceries, at the vinegar maker's, in the taverns.[49] Especially in the taverns: taverns and dance halls multiplied in the cities. In 1790 Paris counted forty-three hundred bars, which had become popular places to socialize. Innkeepers were showered with accusations, forming an early discourse on the tavern as a corrupting influence on the people. Grievances were of a moral and religious nature, but health concerns were never far behind.

Innkeepers normally served wine in pewter pitchers with a high lead content; they sold it on "counters lined with strips of lead."[50] They did not taste the wine; they were content to verify the intensity of the color by the purple stains it left on the tablecloths. "By this means, they distribute to the people a slow poison that gradually entirely destroys their health."[51] The drink they sold was not the juice from the wine press:

> They make a drink that they call wine, for those unfortunates who cannot pay much, with water, juniper berries, and rye bread right from the oven; and they color it with a red beet infusion, using hot water. They make another one with bad cider, which they boil in copper boilers, until thirty-six pots are reduced to eight; they mix this type of syrup with water; they let the mixture ferment, and they color it the same way. They often add dried sage to these drinks to make them pungent; and sometimes crude, ignorant winesellers even substitute narcotic substances for this plant, to give the wine an intoxicating quality, or they throw in pieces of copper to make it stronger.[52]

In Marseilles, they used a similar process; into the vat went quicklime, plaster, sea salt, and pigeon droppings "to give it a pungent taste."[53]

The innkeeper altered or adulterated his wine. *Gargotage*, as Ducreux called it, was not an act of negligence but the result of a dual necessity, both technical and economic: without it, the Vaugirard wine merchant could not support his family.[54] It was not fraud, because, for a very long time, no laws controlled wine.

In 1767 the Royal Society of Agriculture in Limoges, which had lost interest in promoting the potato, proposed a competition on the subject of wine fermentation, wine being defined—or not defined—in the following manner: "Wine is the generic name given to all liqueurs that are subject to fermentation of the spirits," with the understanding that, in Limousin, it was made beginning with grapes or "other fruits."[55] No one seriously considered challenging the freedom to make it. At most, health professionals would have liked to establish a blacklist of dangerous additives, basically copper and lead. Also, in addition to the innkeeper, they denounced two responsible parties.

The first was no more or less than the guild system itself, with its monopolies and its jealously guarded trade secrets. These professional secrets were methods, processes transmitted from master to novice when the latter demonstrated his mastery. Some of them were good, others deadly. For example, the vinegar makers guild possessed good ones (for mustard) and deadly ones (for cornichons). But how to make such distinctions when the whole system "works under the cloak of mystery"?[56]

The health profession's second target was the French farm generally and its sprawling network charged with managing the entire food business. In fact, farmers and shopkeepers were more preoccupied with determining rights over beverages and foodstuffs than with safety. "They consider foodstuffs a financial matter."[57] Here, the state became involved. Regarding agriculture, its vigilance was limited. The officers it appointed to oversee the markets were primarily concerned with market revenues, their assistants had other concerns, and the regular police were more attentive to public disorder than to possible food adulteration.

Despite this lack of personnel, health professionals believed in the state. They demanded more state regulations, without considering how well they would be enforced. Their demands remained a pious vow or were transformed into rigorous intervention, depending on the state. It was in enlightened Germany, where the concept of a medical policy was born, that state intervention was most vigorous. Following a report from the chemist Eller, the Academy of Berlin decided that the use of copper vessels was not as pernicious as believed; according to Eller, foods had to remain in copper receptacles for a long time to risk intoxication. Nevertheless, Prussia went beyond the academy's recommendations in forbidding copper vessels in the preparation of cheese and dairy products. Sweden introduced similar legislation, a courageous move, according to the *Encyclopédie*, since a portion of its trade was in copper.[58] In France, the measures taken involved first the hospitals and armies. This was not a matter of chance. Those two human communities offered health professionals privileged opportunities for observation and oversight, and an army doctor such as Brisseau was one of the first to denounce the pernicious effects of verdigris and to recommend that copper be replaced with tinplate.

Prohibition had its limitations, especially when the use of copper and lead derivatives was essentially a matter of the domestic household. *Quid leges sine moribus?* exclaimed Hallé.[59] It was not the law that had to change but habits. Thus health professionals adopted an alternative strategy for raising consciousness and inculcating prudent behavior. For this one, they used two methods, one that addressed the intellect, another that appealed to the senses.

The first method required a public target such as the guild masters or the owners of small craft industries, because those who sounded the alarm generally agreed that it was useless to address the workers or servants. They were too "pigheaded" and "stubborn" to be open to advice, like the cooks in the great houses, or "the workers employed at the mills, who do not respond docilely when it is a question of a new practice."[60]

The second method was much more modern, since it employed the press as its medium. It was hard to read an end-of-the-century newspaper without finding an article relating in great detail a case of copper or lead poisoning and providing the information necessary to convince readers of its authenticity. The names of the victims did not generally appear, but precise dates and addresses were given. And so: A Beauvais merchant perished while traveling from Paris to Orléans from drinking tea made in a copper coffeepot at the Sellette Rouge, Rue Saint-Denis, where he was staying. He was seized with violent colic a few hours from Paris; no remedy could save him. On July 17, 1759, five people died after eating a veal stew made the day before in a copper casserole, its tinplating worn thin. In Mecklembourg, a Grossenlukner farmer brought sour cheeses, curdled in copper receptacles, to the Gustrow market, where he sold them. All those who ate them immediately experienced bad effects: vomiting, convulsions, and other discomforts.[61]

In Paris, mishaps related to fountains constituted an ever-growing martyrology. On Rue Clopin, above the Saint-Victor ditches, five people died in one day, poisoned by the water from a copper fountain. In the Saint Paul parish, three priests were poisoned and died. On Rue Saint-Paul, a wine merchant, his wife, and one of their relatives were also poisoned by the water from a copper fountain. After trying various remedies, the first two resorted to antidotes for verdigris. Thanks to taking these, they were saved. The more stubborn relative refused antidotes and died. At Place Maubert, a foreign clergyman died suddenly as a result of verdigris. The autopsy showed this very blatant poison in the stomach and intestines, which appeared torn to pieces by it.[62]

With such media coverage, the food risk became a commonplace. It actually seemed as though, in trying to raise awareness and prompt fear, such repetition made consumers complacent instead. Lead in wine, copper in water, lead in butter, they all fell under the rubric of minor news. The avalanche of recommendations prompted something like lassitude and resulted in inertia.

If bread was baked over a wood fire of old fence boards painted with lead and turned out to be lethal, how would one know?[63] If wine was dangerous, and water, and cider, what was there to drink? If pewter tumblers were suspect, since English pewter was never pure and could contain lead, copper, sometimes even arsenic, should you use a clay pot instead? But then didn't doctors warn against glazed pottery? And all common pottery, used by the poor, was glazed with vitrified lead. If the iron staves of barrels rusted, and it was not good to replace them with lead ones, what could you do? If pure copper was dangerous, should you use tin-plated copper? Yes, but the tin-plating had to be done carefully, or it melted in the heat or wore thin too quickly from being scraped by spoons.[64] A constant bombardment of warnings can make one stop listening to any of them.

Nevertheless, the media campaign had undeniable effects, and here and there appeared signs of progress. In cities, innkeepers no longer covered their countertops with lead; henceforth, wine was sold on zinc. Dairies switched utensils; in 1770 Venel expressed indignation at seeing milk "stuffed with water and flour" and transported in copper vessels, dirty ones, at that. Twenty years later, his publisher noted that this accusation was no longer valid and that milk cans were all tin.[65]

In the end, salvation would come unexpectedly from elsewhere, from a movement that was fundamentally technological. That was what estate inventories revealed. During the reign of Louis XIV, in the working-class kitchens of Paris, cooking utensils were iron, copper, and pewter. In the period of Louis XVI, iron and cast iron were still present, beaten iron began its ascension, and copper and pewter both witnessed a decline. Pottery dominated, both for dishes and for cooking.[66] And yet the inventories do not reflect the full extent of this change, as they only record estate property with value. Common pottery, plates or pots, did not get inventoried. Thus we will find evidence of the pottery invasion elsewhere, in production records, in the manufacturing of popular earthenware. Copper could remain on the walls: the new cooking methods, slow simmering or oven cooking, required earthenware pots.[67] This decline in metal use was also witnessed in urban infrastructure. Thus P. Fournier found that in the urban water systems, lead pipes were called into question. Charged with piping water at the Carpentras fountains in 1718, the engineer Jean de Clapiès recommended no longer using the old lead pipes but replacing them with glazed pottery piping. With pottery pipes, he said, the water would remain fresher "and healthy, whereas in the others, it got warm and always drew something from the nature of the mineral."

Jean de Clapiès was considering—and this was important—the taste of the water, but had he foreseen the dangers of lead poisoning? Not a single text gives us a glimpse of any suspicion whatever in this regard. But other reservations were clearly expressed: lead was malleable, easily bendable, and it broke under great pressure. Such pressure could just as easily weaken clay pipes, but they were less expensive to replace. And there, in the end, appeared the real reasons behind the choice. They rested on a cost comparison.[68]

Economic reasons prompted the replacement of lead and copper with pottery. But, as a result, food health and safety benefited as well.

THIRTEEN

HEALTH CONFLICTS

In 1763, at the age of forty-eight, a Parisian retired to the country to write *Le Médecin radoteur; ou, Les Pots pourris*. This *médecin radoteur*, or "driveling doctor," was Robert Ducreux, a lawyer by profession, devout, with an embittered nature and fragile health, a doctor to himself. Apart from that, he was, as he describes himself, a grumpy windbag with a bilious temperament. He trotted out his black humors before the spectacle of ills that afflicted his city, the corruption, the air, morals, and food. All these evils were directly tied to one another, according to him. The degeneracy of society went hand in hand with the degradation of the environment.

His basic text treated "the air quality of different parts of Paris." His investigation began at the foot of the statue of Henri IV, to whom Ducreux announced, "I am going to stroll about in Paris." To which the statue retorted, "Paris is no longer what Paris originally was. The air and the seasons there have changed." And Ducreux, an ambler with decidedly little love for his city, embarked on an olfactory stroll, inhaling the air of different streets, identifying the pollutants, since he believed that the quality of the air one breathed "influenced the mind as well as the body."[1]

Judging by his nose, Robert Ducreux was an aerist, one of those for whom air played the essential role among the contingent factors that impacted human health. And a large city like Paris was very much the kind of place where miasmas converged, those dangerous emanations issuing from the decay of organic matter that generated infections and propagated diseases. Thus Ducreux's stroll was just as much a kind of hunt for the city's pollutants, a systematic mapping of foul or putrid odors. Despite its bizarre aspects and fuzzy thinking, his investigation completely reflected the spirit of the times and was in keeping with a popular trend.[2] Air and air quality were rising concerns in the eighteenth century, as the newspapers demonstrated when they dealt with environmental issues. Between 1701 and 1767, the *Journal de Trévoux* devoted fifty-eight articles to air and air pollution and thirty-five articles to food, health, and diet (62 percent as compared to 48 percent). The *Journal encyclopédique* was published later in the century and spanned the period from 1756 to 1793. There, we find a total of twenty-six articles on air and seven on health and food.[3]

But, despite appearances, Ducreux was not an aerist. To the contrary, he was a fervent "nutritionist." The chapter he devotes to the winds, after the one on the air, leaves no room for doubt about this. In it, he treats the products of intestinal fermentation, released either "from above or below," that are engendered by bad food. He is right to characterize himself as a driveler, because not only does he repeat himself, endlessly venting his hostility toward public poisoners, but he repeats an old diatribe attributing health to dietary vigilance. And overall he devotes many more pages to water, wine, milk, and bread than to air quality. For him, the city's pathogens stemmed from "adulterations" of foodstuffs, that is, all the manipulations, all the shady dealings of the local food and agriculture industry. He assailed what he designated by the general name of *pots pourris*: "I call potpourris (for the body) those foods and drinks that, by being mixed and not retaining their natural qualities, acquire the quality of potpourris." And he proceeded to draw up a long blacklist of potpourris, at the top of which was yeasted bread, that "ferment of ferments, that starver of starvers, that bitter of bitters." He condemned and denounced as public poisoners bakers; dairymen who had "a particular talent for making four pints of milk out of one"; wine merchants who made Burgundy by boiling together sugar, brandy, lemon peel, and water and throwing this elixir in a grinder; cider merchants who sent to Paris the cider they made from fallen, rotten apples; and finally cooks who, "knowing best how to spoil a pullet and a partridge, are the most skillful composers of potpourris."[4] The only foods that escaped his diatribe were chicken and milk-fed veal, no doubt exempted by their immaculate white-meat status.

In fact, the royal maxim, "the seasons have changed," is quite ambiguous. The expression was very popular, used by Ducreux himself as well as by all his contemporaries, but with such a different intention that it is important to clarify it. When Ducreux denounced the changing of the seasons, it was to the well-known tune of the myth of the golden age. He referred back to times past, morals that had been corrupted, happy times when products were natural and men did not dream of tampering with them. "The seasons have changed" was translated from a Latin proverb that he was fond of: *o tempora, o mores!* But from the lips of the Parisian on the street, the expression lost all moral connotations and took on an atmospheric or aerist meaning. Thus interpreted, the expression signified that inclement weather, indeed even certain cosmic transformations, were responsible for bad health. This popular diagnosis was echoed by doctors. Ducreux, who visited doctors often and knew them well, pointed out that, when their treatments failed to work, they blamed it on the weather.[5] And it is true that cosmotelluric fears were in the air, so to speak, at that time. Scientists were worried about the deterioration of the climate, which was increasingly "pituituous" in nature, that is, cold and humid. The first meteorological observations, such as those of Toaldo in Lombardy, tended to prove that cold was increasing. Earthquakes, like those in Lisbon in 1755, added to these disturbances "to which we must attribute the frequency of thunderstorms, the sterility of the soil, and the confusion of the seasons."[6]

Ducreux revolted against these ambient ideas:

> So let us not say that the seasons have changed. Let us not say that it seems the laws of nature are not the same in Paris as in other countries and other provinces, but let us admit that all food and drink containing foreign bodies must produce effects counter to those that are properly theirs. When we minimize interior causes, we will once again be immune to exterior ones. When we have eaten barley bread for a year, made from new or spoiled grain, and when we are dehydrated and the habitual constipation that we have brought on ourselves causes our humors to revolt, we say that the weather is unhealthy today. When we have good food, when farmers and wheat merchants are prevented from making a profit on grain that spoils, to the point that they are required to throw it into the river, when we no longer drink the essence of urine or adulterated wine, we will not say that the seasons have changed.[7]

A fine speech, but it constituted rearguard action. Eating fears dimmed in the face of the greater fear of miasmas and infections.

Air or Food?

An aeris quam cibi et potus major necessitas? Air or food and drink, which is more necessary to health? A good question for a doctoral thesis in medicine, and, over the centuries, doctoral candidates used it to demonstrate their cleverness. Their responses inevitably included three parts: first, the necessity of air was demonstrated, then that of food; in the last part, the candidate chose which, among the unnatural things, seemed to him to be the most important, food often prevailing over air.

Medical schools modernized radically in the nineteenth century and no long required Latin theses or posed questions of this kind. The business was settled, despite Ducreux and a few backward thinkers: it was the air one breathed that mattered the most.[8] The notion of diet thus fell under the concept of public hygiene and, later, the concept of public health. The related idea of an official medical policy emerged. The doctor, the judge, and the lawmaker were all police in their own way, taking part in public health programs that, in France, were launched by François-Emmanuel Fodéré and Jean-Noël Hallé. These doctors trained in Strasbourg, at the German school that pioneered in this area. Hallé defined what he meant by medical policy: "The primary object with regard to foods is to take charge, along with the police courts, of the air the inhabitants breathe; the water they drink; the food products, medicinal and harmful, that the soil spontaneously produces."[9] The definition has an old Hippocratic ring to it but sounds a new note as well. By citing as "foods" all the *ingesta* of the ancients, Hallé located himself within an intellectual framework that had hardly changed since the Greeks. But, in listing air and water first, he clearly set forth the priorities that were effectively those of the triumphant health movement. Within this traditional intellectual framework, a movement developed that completely shifted the focus with regard to health.

We can also observe this shift if we examine those manuals meant to educate the public, much like our present-day versions, in which the tradition continues, under new titles. Diet books and health guides gave way to "lessons in hygiene." It was not only the titles that changed, the contents also shifted significantly. In his *Conservation de la santé*, published in 1559, Jérome de Monteux devoted twenty-five pages to air and forty to solid foods and drink, that is, a ratio of 60 percent to 40 percent. That is exactly the ratio we find in the monumental Latin poem by E. L. Geoffroy (1771), which taught how to conserve one's health, in 4,609 alexandrines. This was no doubt the last in a series of 150 printed works in verse devoted to this subject. Geoffroy devoted 928 verses to air, 741 to food, and 652 to drink.

The year 1802 marked the appearance of the French translation of *Domestic Hygiene; or, The Art of Maintaining Health and Prolonging Life*. The title clearly demonstrates the continuity of the genre. An analysis of the contents reveals that the author, a Doctor Willich, devoted less than a quarter of his attention to air and three-quarters to food, the sign of a different national culture where the reported dangers stemmed from excesses and overeating. Gout threatened the English eater, along with diabetes, a new disease affecting those who ate sugar. On the Continent, it was another story. In the great *Encyclopédie* of the romantic period, air and food appeared in a relationship of 60 percent to 40 percent, a proportion that remained almost constant throughout the century and the symmetrical inverse of centuries before. François-Vincent Raspail, the doctor of the poor who delivered to the working classes the good word of the republic and sage advice about inexpensive home remedies, named the lack or impurity of air as the first pathogenic factor and the lack or impurity of food as the second.[10] The hygienist doctrine was extremely attentive to air quality and thus minimized the value of food, unless this was simply the dividing line between what hygienists considered private hygiene and public health. For aerists, certainly, public intervention was especially necessary in the struggle against airborne miasmas. Food was a matter of individual health; it was the responsibility of the individual and his doctor. But we are still in the theoretical realm here. It is important to see how this division played out in reality and how it became, strictly speaking, political.

Postrevolutionary France formalized the domains sketched out during the Enlightenment. The domain of public health was divided between the central authority and the municipalities. The state was responsible for the air and the environment. The first state laws were aerist laws: in 1807, on the draining of the marshes; in 1810, on unhealthy establishments; in 1812, on epidemics. Food safety— limited to the struggle against fraud—was the responsibility of the municipalities. It fell to them to watch over "the healthiness of foods exhibited for public sale" and to forbid the sale of "spoiled medications" or "adulterated drinks."[11]

The city and the state were two players; air and food were two stakes that competed or even conflicted with each other in matters of public health. This was true in the question of the city slaughterhouses.

It was also true, though the conflict took a different form, in the treatment of a diet deficiency disease, pellagra. These two histories, the case of pellagra and the case of the slaughterhouses, can be reexamined as struggles between health values and crossroads where fears intersected.

Animals in the City

Was it necessary for the slaughter of animals to continue to be done in the city, where eaters could witness it? That question was posed very early in the capital when in 1416 Charles VI ordered the demolition and transfer of the large slaughterhouse *extra muros*. In his preamble, the king justified at great length this major move by presenting two arguments, one of which involved city planning ("for the decoration and embellishment of our beautiful city of Paris"), the other health: "To deal with and take precautions against infections and corruptions harmful to the human body that, because of the filth of the slaughter and skinning of beasts, have been an issue for a long time."[12] The ordinance went unheeded, but the debate had been launched and was all the more lively because since 1348 there had been a series of plaguelike epidemics that made the elite more sensitive to the dangers of infection. Was public health more threatened by poor air quality or poor food quality? Because a choice had to be made. Either the quality of meat, under public supervision, was a higher priority, in which case the slaughterhouse remained within the city walls. Or the slaughterhouses were considered major sources of infection, in which case their removal from the city was imperative.

After Charles VI, the royal administration's concerns tended in the direction of this pre-aerist view. In 1567 Charles IX, who declared himself concerned about "the cleanliness and neatness of cities," ordered that "each butchery do its slaughtering and skinning outside the city, *if possible*," and that new slaughterhouses be established "outside city walls and near water."[13] In 1577 Henri III reaffirmed this dictate. But what the king proposes, the city disposes, and it seems that only a few of them, Dijon, Moulins, Tours, and Nantes among them, moved their slaughterhouses into the suburbs. Elsewhere, the king's law remained what it essentially was, that is, largely ineffective. Southern cities remained strictly faithful to their own laws and to *intra muros* slaughterhouses. The centralization and municipalization of slaughterhouses, which took place at different times between the fifteenth and seventeenth centuries, led to reconfigurations and moves, but always within the city walls. Municipal slaughterhouses were established near rivers or ditches to make getting rid of the wastes easier. Or they were established close to hospitals or charity houses so that the sick could have the fresh blood to restore them. The poor from the Orange hospital "recuperate the blood and make it into a solid that sometimes earns them more than six hundred pounds."[14] The advantages and disadvantages of such proximity had to be weighed. In Toulouse, the magistrates made it clear to the intendant that the *affachoir* for cattle "inconveniences the poor, especially the sick in the Hôtel-Dieu who are the closest to it," and notably during the hottest weather.[15] In 1676 an unauthorized slaughterhouse and butchery sprang up on the island of Barthelasse, in the middle of the Rhône, that is, exactly on the border between royal Languedoc and the Papal States. The Avignon consuls protested and had the clandestine establishment closed in the name of the well-established principle: "Slaughterhouses and butcher shops must be established in inhabited places and not in isolated places where supervision is difficult."[16] Everywhere, the necessity of supervision and vigilance was evoked. But not without some ambiguity: the concern for guaranteeing healthy meat to the public became entangled with the city councillors' fiscal preoccupations. The *rève* and other taxes on livestock constituted one of the most reliable sources of revenue for the cities, and the city gates provided a place to collect it.

The last Western plague, the plague of 1721, presented a strange health paradox to the southern cities ravaged by it. Flushing out the wastes, straightening and cleaning the streets, in short, aerating the city was the new order from the city councillors. But the desire to purge stopped at the slaughterhouse doors. That was because the plague had also left behind an enormous debt to be repaid. An increase in taxes on foodstuffs was considered almost everywhere, as in Avignon in 1722, "the most effective and reasonable means" for paying off loans and interest. The Avignon *rève* on meat thus rose to 8 percent, and supervision over the livestock entering at the city gates was reinforced.

In most cities, the old slaughterhouse regime led to the everyday spectacle of thousands of animals entering the city, causing all kinds of pollution, traffic jams, and noise. Toulouse citizens who lived in the neighborhood of the *affachoirs* on the island of Tounis complained of the "bellowing night and day in the parks, where the beasts smell the approach of death, the odor always spilling from the slaughterhouses that are too close, where they are killed; on top of that, it is the custom to let these beasts go without food for several days before killing them. What appalling cries must be endured!"[17] Animals wandering about was a familiar sight to all the citizens of Europe and beyond, in the American colonies. As a Swiss, Zimmermann was astounded at the filth of southern cities. But he also had to admit that in Bern, "even in the center of so clean and magnificent a city, one still sees a slaughterhouse and cemeteries."[18] In Lausanne, the slaughterhouses were in the city; at Pont, on the shore of the Flon and its canal.[19] In Boston, beginning in 1652, on an order from the selectmen, they were along the river at Mill Creek, and the ebbing tide cleaned the city of butcher wastes.[20]

The slaughterhouse was on the street, and, "for as long as one could remember, the street was a place animals could be seen slaughtered."[21] There, blood flowed out in the open, rushed down the streets.[22] For a long time, everywhere, the belly and the entrails of the city, before becoming a literary metaphor, were warm, pulsating realities.[23]

Through whatever eyes one watched the animal massacre, through whatever nose one breathed it or ears one heard it, that perception was not objective. It evolved, and Alain Corbin has noted how the threshold of tolerance dropped dramatically at the end of the eighteenth century. The spectacle was characterized as hideous and immediately became intolerable, if we are to believe certain accounts. Sébastien Mercier, the author of the *Tableau de Paris*, is often cited: "What is more revolting and more disgusting than slaughtering animals and cutting them up publicly? We walk in curdled blood. There are butcher shops where cattle are made to pass the display of meat. The animal sees it, smells it, recoils. It is pulled, it is dragged, it bellows. The dogs bite its hoofs while those leading it knock it senseless to make it enter that fatal place."[24]

But Ducreux, another Parisian just as attentive to pollutants, offers another impression, and it is no surprise to see that it goes against the grain:

"Let us leave," I say to my friend, directing our way toward the market along the street of butcher shops. In passing down this street, I prepared myself to make use of my sword and my cane at each step to defend myself against the savageness of those blood-soaked hands.

But what was my surprise to find I had traveled this street from one end to the other without suffering any offense to my ears, my eyes, or my mind. My nose suffered some displeasure, but the vapors that caused it were much less strong than those I had smelled in the Place des Victoires and near the Palais Royal. Animal blood being more pure than human blood, the second goes more to the head than the first.[25]

It is impossible to know which of these two reactions is the most representative. As for the blood taboo, it was certainly not a constant. For centuries, people put up with the sight of flowing blood, they made it into a drink for the sick and a market product, they drank it fresh and ate it in *sanguette*, a dish made of coagulated chicken blood. They were content to fertilize the fields with it. The city dweller's expectations were contradictory. He wanted good meat, guaranteed, and good air at the same time. He was ambivalent in his displeasures: sometimes the spectacle of slaughter offended his eyes, sometimes the smell of it offended his nose. The slaughterhouse prompted such a complex of emotions that finally the questions it raised could not be answered.

Toward the end of the century, enlightened city councillors almost everywhere had created regular waste removal services and transferred cemeteries outside the city walls. Thus the city's old familiarity with dirt and waste was disrupted. The city councillors had won an easy victory over the dead, but it was more difficult to win over the living, to convince them to give up their old familiarity with animals. Because the persistence of the old slaughterhouse regime was not explained solely by the concern for verifying the quality of meat. It seems that, over the course of the decades, that original objective became entangled with other stakes. Trying to untangle all the reasons slaughterhouses remained in the cities would be a risky business. But if we set aside political and economic implications to consider only health values, then we get the strong sense that city council decisions to maintain city slaughterhouses did not signal a definitive victory for food fears but rather a defeat for aerism.

The Exile of the Slaughterhouses

Emile Littré, a doctor and lexicographer—the man who in 1840 translated Hippocrates and breathed new life into aerist and infectionist doctrines—defined the slaughterhouse this way in his dictionary: "Slaughterhouse: place meant for the slaughter of animals, such as cattle, calves, sheep... that serve as food for humans; slaughterhouses are located outside the walls that surround the cities."

The contemporary slaughterhouse was thus defined by an occupation and a location, the latter representing a complete break with a tradition many centuries old.

The word and the thing are Napoleonic inventions. Paris led the way. In 1810 intraurban slaughterhouses were abolished, eight years after a model establishment opened at Montmartre. There, butchers each had a place for scalding animals after slaughtering them, part of a large courtyard, and access to running water, sewers, and grounds where they could divide up the livestock. Enclosed and on the city's periphery, slaughter was henceforth completely hidden from public view. Montmartre provided an example to follow; the king of Naples and Sicily visited it in 1836. Two years later, Naples boasted similar amenities.[26]

This separation of the slaughterhouse and the butcher shop had two collateral effects. First, regulations and health inspections moved from the butcher shop to the slaughterhouse; second, it redeemed the butcher's profession. The bad reputation of men with blood-soaked hands was transferred to the men of the slaughterhouse, and undoubtedly the event of seven or eight hundred robust, restless, and ruddy men leaving the city played some part in the decision made by the municipal powers.

Because what had been true for maintaining the slaughterhouse in the city applied equally to its exile. The phenomenon was not attributable to a single health priority, such as ridding the city of a source of air pollution. In fact, the Montmartre slaughterhouses were the result of political will, borne and supported by two strong concerns of the city dweller: to avoid infection and, just as important, to avoid the sight of animal massacre.

The relationship between humans—in this case, city dwellers—and animals was in the process of changing. Moving the slaughterhouses coincided with an emerging concern for animal protection and with an increasing presence of dogs in the city. These were friendly pet dogs, no longer strays, and people began to think of such animals differently from others. The law adapted to this change in urban sensibility. In 1833 animal fights were prohibited in Paris. In 1850 the Grammont law penalized abusive treatment of domestic animals. Of course, it was limited to abusive treatment in public, but its symbolic value outweighed its practical consequences. Another relationship shifted in a parallel way, the relationship between the city dweller and animal flesh. There was now a disjunction between what one saw and what one ate, and meat was no longer linked with the living animal. It became an anonymous substance, harmless and without history. Surreptitiously, slowly, the disembodied culture that characterizes the contemporary epoch fell into place. A distance imposed itself between the eater and the eaten, a distance that was required for the phagic act to be performed.[27] Basically, slaughtering out of sight assured the eater a certain peace of mind and appeased the carnivore's conscience. The contemporary consumer-turned-sarcophage abandoned his inspection responsibilities to the public authorities. He gave up worrying at the very time when food risks involving meat were on the rise.

That slaughterhouses were slow to be exiled from provincial cities clearly shows that old habits and behavior cannot be changed by decrees, even Napoleonic ones. It is true that, as a last resort, the new regime, like the old one, left the initiative and responsibility for building new slaughterhouses to the municipalities. The municipalities resolved the issue more or less quickly, and only after complaints reached city hall regarding both air quality and the spectacle of massacre. In Clamecy in 1834, it was the spectacle that shocked citizens: "For MM. The butchers don't put themselves out anymore. There are some who kill sheep in the middle of the street, others hang bloody calf heads at their doors and offer the dogs tubs full of blood and refuse; our city is just one big slaughterhouse where blood runs from all sides."[28]

In 1843 the administrators of the Carpentras poorhouse expressed their grievances before the municipal council. The municipal slaughter yard adjoining the old almshouse was a "breeding ground for infection from which an unbearable odor rose," to the point that "the service of the almshouse is often compromised because of infections that render the wing of buildings closest to the slaughterhouse uninhabitable." The mixed organic smells of manure, blood, entrails, and excrement had scented the charity since its creation in the early seventeenth century, but, two centuries later, they became unbearable.

In small towns, the aerist debate that had been alive in the capital since before the Revolution hit its stride in the romantic period, and the first transfers of slaughterhouses took place between 1820 and 1840. The fear of miasmas was very much the decisive factor. The attitude toward animals evolved more slowly, and the old intimacy between man and beast persisted. The daily experience of secondary school students provides a single example of this. During the Second Empire, a pigsty could be found at one out of three secondary schools, generally in the back of the courtyard, near the latrines. The pigs were fed the leftovers from the dining hall and other "slops."[29]

Even if it was inspired by aerist ideas, the reorganization of the slaughterhouses did not turn its back completely on the concern for food quality. The imperial decree provided for inspections by a competent service. In fact, the facility the slaughterhouses offered for these inspections was one of the determining arguments for their creation. Lawmakers prided themselves on a single, universal, comprehensive health measure, vigilant with regard to the quality of air as well as the quality of meat. For all that, meat inspection, like the inspection of all other foodstuffs, was left to the municipalities. The laws of the National Assembly abolishing butchers' monopolies had also abolished all earlier legislative mechanisms that regulated supervision of the quality of meat.[30] By midcentury, thirty-seven thousand local ordinances affected the sale of meat in France.[31] They were terse, in general forbidding the sale of "spoiled, corrupt, or harmful" meat. The negative list, case by case, of forbidden meats no longer existed. The local expert, appointed by the mayor and paid by the city budget, was a "man of the art," and, as the law did not explicitly specify "the veterinary art," the cities generally appointed a butcher.

In practice, the municipal slaughterhouses were supervised poorly or not at all. There were many private slaughter yards, with no legal status. Animals were slaughtered in the back courtyard of a horse dealer or a butcher, far from any health inspector. The meatmonger became a familiar figure, providing a link between these illicit slaughters and the fairs and markets, where he delivered meat that was sold "by hand," at low prices and without any guarantee.[32]

In many European countries, the old regime of butchering was not abolished with a stroke of the pen. The old regulations remained. Veterinary supervision was particularly well organized in some of the German states. But, for several decades in France, something like a health-inspection vacuum appeared. Consumer supervision no longer existed, and veterinary inspections were only instituted beginning in 1890.

The contemporary slaughterhouse clearly signaled the victory of aerist values, without regard for food risks.

Pellagra, Corn, and Air

Pellagra was described for the first time by a Spanish doctor, Gaspard Casal (or Cajal). Around 1735 he observed that the farmers of the city of Oviedo were affected by a mysterious disease that he called *mal de la rosa*, after the disease's first symptoms. Pellagra victims' bodies were covered with scaly, peeling patches, especially on the hands and neck, that turned red when exposed to the sun, similar to the effects of sunstroke. The disease only affected the poorest among farmworkers. It was cyclical and seasonal in nature: it was at the end of winter—a period of shortages and single-food diets—that men began "to lose their scales." Their troubles lasted throughout spring and summer, disappearing again in winter. All the victims were chronically underfed and also undernourished. Their diet was based on corn cakes, supplemented with cabbage, turnips, green beans, and apples in season. Animal products were almost absent. Convinced the disease was nutritional in origin, Casal recommended as a corrective a more diversified diet, including cheese and milk products.[33]

The disease first spotted in Spain made its appearance in Lombardy, where it became so widespread that a hospice for those suffering from it was opened in Milan in 1784. The hospital doctor noted with regard to his patients: "They hardly ever eat animal foods. Their food consists at the most of polenta and bread. The polenta is made with corn flour,... and the bread is made with a mixture of corn, rye, and millet, from which are produced, with the addition of a little sour leaven, thick cakes, difficult to cook."[34]

Gaetano Strambio did not know whether to blame the type of grain, or its quality, or the way it was prepared. But he was sure of one thing: the causes of the disease were nutritional. He was not wrong about that, and neither was Casal. Since 1937 we have known that pellagra is a deficiency disease, caused by the lack of niacin, belonging to the vitamin B complex.

In the nineteenth century, pellagra extended its range, particularly dramatically in Lombardy, where this chronic disease took on almost epidemic proportions. In 1830 an estimated twenty thousand out of two million inhabitants suffered from it. That earned Italy the dubious honor of seeing Casal's *mal de la rosa* replaced in international nosological vocabulary by the Italian term, *pelle agra* (rough skin). The opinion of the doctors was thus well established: pellagra did not come from the air or the water; it was linked to the ingestion of corn. "Zeism" (from *zea*: corn) became the classic interpretation, and it appeared in the lexicon of received medical ideas until 1930 and still appears in the historian's lexicon today.

France considered itself immune. But in 1829 a doctor from Landes who practiced in La Teste, in the Arcachon basin, conveyed to the Medical Society of Bordeaux a series of observations on "a skin disease that I believe to be unknown and that is among the most serious, which threatens to attack the entire population of the country where I live."[35] A regional study identified the disease quite rapidly as pellagra and described its various pathological phases:

Pellagra is a complex disease. It is characterized by three orders of symptoms:

1. a squamous erythema on parts most exposed to the action of heat and light
2. a chronic inflammation of the digestive tract, the most common symptom of which is persistent diarrhea
3. a more or less serious lesion of the nervous system resulting in mental derangement and paralysis.

In the last stage, pellagra triggered depression and suicidal tendencies. Also, in the extensive statistics on mortality among pellagra victims, should those officially dead from "drowning and strangulation" be excluded?[36] But then we risk going from underestimating to overestimating the numbers, since most of the suicide cases in Landes or Gironde usually tried to secure a medical certificate affirming pellagra as the cause of death so that religious funeral services would be permitted.

The study also demonstrated that the disease was endemic, from Bordeaux to Bayonne. The problem was that, here, corn could not be held accountable. The Landes region was behind the times, still beyond the reach of the agrarian capitalism that obliged Lombardy farmers to market their wheat and be content with corn as their staple foodstuff. Landes peasants, the poorest of the poor and undoubtedly poorer in the early nineteenth century than they had ever been, had not switched from a grain-based diet. They ate millet. But in the 1820s and 1830s their diet grew considerably worse and dwindled to basically just vegetables.

Thus, since French doctors could not point to corn as the cause of the disease, they sought a combination of reasons for pellagra. They related it to overwork, an unhealthy diet, uncleanliness, the foul air of these flat lands covered with stagnant water. Pellagra was the new leprosy, a disease of "barbarity and ignorance," declared Moreau de La Sarthe.[37] And the hygienists of the romantic period painted a lurid picture of the typical Landes farmhouse, with a ceiling so low one hit one's head on objects hanging from it; an earthen floor on which the family dumped water, spat, and defecated; and without windows, the air, light, and sometimes cold entering only through the door.[38]

The unhealthiness so strongly denounced was not a matter of food but of air, air contaminated by the farms, the stench of the marshes, the shepherd's bad smells. The air seemed to have pellagrogenic powers.

It was through aerism that the fight against pellagra was waged. The study was regional, but the decision was national. The health policy adopted was dictated less by field observations than by the ideology of the decision makers who, like Roussel in the 1840s, did not examine the biological roots of the disease at all but only the natural and agricultural environment. While doctors in the field advocated a diversified diet, Roussel in Paris argued for eliminating the marshlands' poisonous vapors. It was Roussel's position that was heard. Moreover, it was quite generally shared, and even Landes natives such as the novelist Edmond About thought that eradicating the disease required ecological transformations:

Tant que Lande sera lande
La Pellagre te demande.[39]

[So long as Landes is marsh
Pellagra will call for you]

In truth, only environmentally based disease prevention could involve the state, which left food concerns to doctors and individuals and which acted according to the principles of subsidiarity. But great public works fell into its domain, as well as a certain idea—already present under the July monarchy—regarding land development. Beginning in 1849, the marshes were drained and planted in maritime pines; they were crisscrossed by canals and stone-lined roads. Draining and clearing led to an agricultural boom and improved living standards. Landes inhabitants ate more and better. Pellagra, which had exploded between 1830 and 1852, started on a descending statistical curve. When the American Civil War prompted a rise in the price of pine resin, cases of pellagra dropped by two-thirds.

A Chalosse doctor described the beneficial effects of these changes in retrospect:

My father began to practice medicine in 1835, and, at that time, there was no pellagra to be seen. Winegrowing was the area's only industry. Wine sold cheaply, but, because so much was produced, it paid the grower well. About 1840 our vineyards began to decline, and poverty made itself felt. Then cases of pellagra were observed. Poverty grew, and victims of pellagra became more numerous, and their deaths by hanging quite frequent.

That lasted a few years. That was when oidium decimated our vineyards completely. Henceforth, our lands were cultivated as everywhere else, by varying the crops. Corn was grown in considerable quantity. Throughout winter until the month of June, only corn was eaten in the country. It was precisely in that period that pellagra began to be more rare.[40]

Here, the correlation between corn and pellagra was exactly the inverse of what was observed in Lombardy. In fact, whether the basic diet changed hardly mattered: the essential thing was whether it was sufficient and varied enough to provide the necessary B vitamins. In the 1830s the Landes diet slipped below the threshold that offered resistance to pellagra. It regained its footing three decades later.

At the time, a totally different perspective on Landes's progress reigned, an interpretation in which odors played an essential role. The noxious fumes from the marshes had disappeared, replaced by plantations of resinous pines releasing balsamic scents that purified the country and relieved it of endemic diseases. The aerists could pride themselves on having made Landes inhabitants healthy by rehabilitating the whole country. Health's heroes were no longer doctors but engineers who built bridges and roadways. In fact, they had treated a disease of nutritional deficiency for what it was: a disease of poverty.

In the early nineteenth century in France, the concept of aerism, confronted with reality, confirmed by experiences like those involving the slaughterhouses and pellagra, triumphed over other ideas and facts, to the point that authorities neglected and abandoned efforts to prevent food risks.

FOURTEEN

BOURGEOIS SERENITY

July 1818. A strange phenomenon occurred in Venetia and especially in the countryside around Padua. The polenta turned red. For a long time, polenta had been the staple food that nourished countless generations. It was a flour cake made with milk and secondary grains such as millet or barley. Venetian polenta was at first gray, made from millet; by the turn of the century, it was more generally made from corn.[1] Ordinarily yellow in color, it sometimes became covered with little red dots or spots. But, in the summer of 1818, many families' polenta suddenly turned completely red, bright red, even crimson. This *polenta porporina* was a domestic phenomenon of the type that generally attracts little public attention, but in this case it was so widespread that it took on the air of an epidemic outbreak. Any luminescence related to food awakens a sense of wonder. Peasants interpreted the paranormal as supernatural, either for good—as some version of the miracle of the bloody host—or for evil—as an act of witchcraft perpetrated on the level of an entire region or the first sign of dire predictions coming true.[2] Red polenta aroused emotions, emotions spread through rumors, "a rumor that swelled to the point of awakening the suave and always vigilant attention of the police," as the ironic Bartolomeo Bizio wrote.[3]

Bizio was a pharmaceutical student at the University of Padua. He was twenty-eight years old. He did not believe in miracles or in witchcraft. He thought that the crimson matter was vegetable in nature and that it developed on the surface of polenta under certain conditions, which he tried to determine. In the laboratory, he managed to reproduce the metamorphosis. He made red dots appear on the polenta and then red spots that coalesced and gradually covered the whole surface, in a humid atmosphere at a temperature of 21 degrees centigrade. Higher heat halted the process. Bizio was the first to cultivate a bacterium and describe the culture as a colony. In 1823 a memorandum he wrote appeared in the *Gazetta privileggiata de Venezia* in the form of a letter addressed to a canon by the name of Angelo Bellani. Bizio explained the phenomenon of red polenta, maintaining that it was not the result of any change in the corn flour but of a coloring agent, a "vegetable being" belonging to a new genre that he called *serratia*.[4]

And so the microscope and experimental research could explain many mysteries. Bizio and his colleagues were convinced that they were about to realize the dream of the Enlightenment and succeed in penetrating the secrets of Mother Nature. Armed with the vaccine, mercury, electricity, and methods for measuring humidity and temperature, man was capable of dis-covering, that is, of revealing to the light of day, what had until then been hidden. It seemed to these learned gentlemen that the field of possibility, of the "thinkable," that was so open in prescientific times tended to shrink, that it no longer offered vast spaces for deploying irrational fears. The bourgeois century was basically optimistic. It is true that outside the red polenta affair, there were few signs of food fears, at least in the form of serious crises. Between Napoleon and Pasteur, fears diminished, or they never reached the press.

Must we correlate this calm in the face of food fears with the appreciable, undeniable improvement in nutrition that the United States and England experienced first, followed by the rest of Europe? This improvement was measurable and measured by the yardstick, which showed that the average height of the conscripted soldier rose beginning midcentury. In France during the Second Empire, a new food system was put into place, more diversified and integrating the potato and sugar. A generation later, the consumption of meat, fat, and fresh produce reached a per capita figure in the cities that had never before been attained, the daily caloric ration rising from 2,480 calories to 2,875, a sign that the country was no longer in the grip of underdevelopment.[5] But we must take a second look at this transition insofar as it appears to be double-edged, calming fears of food shortages but inciting other fears about food quality. Even before the late 1850s, calming powers were at work on society through the means of industrialization. The West was reassured about its food, not by the actual facts but by ideals. Its images of food and nourishment were profoundly revised by trends in thinking and the sciences. Aerism, which we will not revisit, the image of the human machine, the sciences of nutrition and gastronomy—insofar as the latter claimed to be a "science of the mouth"—helped to alter deeply general perceptions with regard to food.

Optimism and Hypochondria

By exploring what was called "the animal economy"—which included humans—medicine and physiology altered the generally held image of the body. When the gastronome Brillat-Savarin asserted that "digestion is an entirely mechanical operation, and the digestive apparatus can be thought of as a mill fitted out with its sifters,"[6] it seems as though he was relying on an old image. That is true, but with a few qualifications. First, this "mill" was no longer considered the body's essential engine. The mechanist physiology taught by Boerhaave a few decades earlier had taken hold: the body was a hydraulic machine with the heart as its piston. The era of cardiac hegemony had begun. The doctor at the patient's bedside had become more interested in taking his pulse than sniffing his excreta, and it was acknowledged that, if someone died, it was because his heart had stopped. As for digestion, contrary to Brillat-Savarin's views, it was envisioned less as a mechanical operation and more as a chemical one, bringing into play various juices and fermenting agents. Most important, it was no longer the central phenomenon of the new physiology. The lungs played just as major a role in the animal machine, which used respiration not to refresh the blood, as had been believed, but, beginning with foods, to release the energy necessary for human activity and the heat indispensable to life. The implicit idea of energy flow followed, chemical in entering the organism, calorific in leaving it.[7] The body's functioning was much more complicated and much more fluid than ever imagined. The common image remained mechanistic, but henceforth man no longer focused on his stomach: this was the end of stomach supremacy.

The new knowledge about the internal body found its counterpart in the aesthetic conception of the body. Georges Vigarello has drawn attention to the transformation in the topology of masculine beauty in the romantic era. Whereas the silhouette of the late ancien régime was dominated by the stomach, emphasized by suits with flared tails, the new silhouette downplayed the stomach, which was sunken, constricted with a belt. On the other hand, the chest, seat of the heart and lungs, was emphasized, girthed in a waistcoat with flattering shoulder pads. Wide chest, puffed out: this was the image of a man full of strength and good health.[8]

Doctors, physiologists, chemists, and hygienists founded and propagated a new science: nutrition. They analyzed food as Lavoisier had water, isolating the various components, working with the scale and the thermometer. On August 19, 1816, François Magendie explained to the Academy of Sciences the importance of a comparative study of food substances. His own laboratory experiments had convinced him that only nitrogenous foods were indispensable. Thus he provided a rational explanation for Western man's preference for meat and grains, since animal muscle and grains are rich in nitrogen.[9] After 1840, thanks to Justus von Liebig and the German school of chemistry, all the nutritive categories were profoundly revised. Under the researcher's microscope, food decomposed, it split apart. The holistic conception of food gave way to the idea that it was a combination, a synthesis of various nutriments.[10] Food as such disappeared. One learned to recognize proteins—which appeared in the scientific vocabulary in 1839—carbohydrates, and—the master word, the key notion—the calorie. The calorie's dazzling career began in 1864, when physiologists borrowed from Marcellin Berthelot his principle of thermodynamics. One could thus measure the flows of energy that entered and left the human machine by establishing energy balance sheets, the calorie being the universal unit of measure. Each food was assigned a specific caloric value. The notion of quality was entirely absorbed into the quantity of nutriments, evaluated by calories. A good food was a food high in calories.

Ultimately, the theory of energy was easy to understand or at least to represent: food was fuel, and the animal machine needed these "biocarburants" with their varying amounts of caloric power. And it was easy to accept because it proposed a food hierarchy more or less reproducing the old hierarchy of food quality. The dietetic bible of the Second Empire, compiled by Anselme Payen, established a pyramid in which meat—beef especially—and fats were at the top. At the very bottom were fruits and vegetables, low in calories.[11] The theory of energy gave a scientific base to already well-known values. It provided the eater with reasons to persist in his eating habits and his tastes. It exempted the doctor from including the diet in his practice of preventive medicine.[12]

The great novelty lay elsewhere. Since physiology was the same for all humans, that meant they had the same nutritional needs. It was no longer necessary to adapt the diet to each temperament or to differentiate it according to social status. There were no longer certain groups at risk. There were certainly populations that were more vulnerable, but they tended to be those suffering from poverty and malnutrition. In shattering the Hippocratic concept of idiosyncrasy for good, the nutritionists of the nineteenth century proclaimed a new food democracy.

But one cannot dismiss a decade of old images. The myth of the little digestive fire persisted but slowly sank to embers. The bourgeois readily expressed their stomach complaints and digestive difficulties. One could flaunt a ruddy face and a fine chest but experience fear in the belly. Called to the bedside, the doctor found patients concentrating on their stomach pains, nervous and distressed. The phenomenon was so widespread that in 1772 Hugues Maret described it as one of the century's two diseases: "One is peculiar to women, and it is known by the name of hysteria; the other, called hypochondria, is common to both sexes." The following century brought a few alterations. It turned abdominal pains into "gastric ills" and "dyspepsia." It decided that such pathologies were basically masculine, hypochondria being to men what hysteria was to women. Everything happened as if food fears, which public health policy had consigned to the private sphere and which could no longer be expressed overtly, had become internalized.[13]

Health and Pleasure

The century rid itself more easily of the long literary tradition that merged the medical aspect with the hedonist aspect in cooking. Reconciling the two positions of pleasure and health was no longer the order of the day, and the Aristotelian philosophy of the golden mean was definitively dismissed. Of course, kindly doctors always had better success with the general public, and Raspail dispensed dietary advice along with his panacea, camphor: green beans were only a delicacy; they were less nutritional than starchy foods, but starchy foods were less nutritional than beef.[14] And, of course, gastronomes wrote books that sometimes contained, as the *régimes* had, medical advice. In his *Physiology of Taste*, Brillat-Savarin punctuated his discourse with a few medical considerations, noting the "*restaurant*" dishes that restored the eater's strength. He also pointed out aphrodisiac ingredients, such as truffles.[15] Cookbooks were not totally liberated from Galenic precepts, and a culinary artist such as

Carême—which was the name he took—provided a recipe for blanc-mange "because the almond is good ... for sweetening the acridness of the humors." But Galen was consigned to a back burner in this new kitchen devoted to other values. The practical handbooks on cooking squarely rejected dietary moral codes that advised the middle course when it came to deciding between health and pleasure. They adopted an openly optimistic tone and celebrated the pleasures of the table without restraint.

Other arbiters had arrived on the food scene: the gastronomic critics. They gave the new cuisine its tone and style, imposing its discourse and its values on the nineteenth-century middle class. We have already cited Brillat-Savarin's classic text *The Physiology of Taste*. In fact, skimming though all the gastronomic discourse of that century (France's most prolific), among the words recurring most often are "taste," "savor," "pleasure," and this neologism coined by Brillat-Savarin during the Restoration, "conviviality."[16] These four words were called on to form a lasting association, the assumption being that the pleasures of the table must be shared and were inseparable from the art of entertaining. Everything in France, said Grimod, and especially meals, must end in song.[17] To follow Grimod de La Reynière in his *Nutritive Itinerary; or, A Gourmand's Stroll through Various Paris Neighborhoods* is, in fact, to follow a gourmand, or, we would say, a gourmet, and occasionally an advertiser secretly sponsored by the Maille mustard manufacturer, but never a consumer conscious of the wholesomeness of food products. His epicurean itinerary completely broke with those practical guides in which shopping well meant buying fresh and healthy foods. At the very most, Grimod noted the Parisian butchers' "absent-mindedness" while weighing meat, which increased its price; that was the only occasion when he called for police vigilance over provisions.[18] Otherwise, said Grimod, "let the doctors scream."[19]

It could be argued that we should not expect gourmand writing to abound in health or utilitarian considerations. That may be true. But let us consider the 673 pages of the abridged version of Alexandre Dumas's *Dictionnaire de cuisine*. This was a work with a different scope and ambition, claiming to embrace cooking in all its aspects. One is struck by the wealth of details regarding history, tastes, colors, time, and temperatures for cooking. But regarding health? Nothing, or nearly nothing: a note on the choice of pork, which must be free of trichina (Dumas confuses trichinosis and leprosy), another on adulterated vinegar. In the "Oyster" article, he warns against what "could give these innocent mollusks toxicological qualities that the oysters in Venice acquire by attaching themselves to copper vessels."[20] Here we must agree with the opinion of Pascal Ory: although not totally indifferent to health concerns, the founding fathers of bourgeois gastronomy had a tendency to minimize, that is, to scorn, such preoccupations.[21]

The bourgeois century was passionate about good food, but it is hard to define this notion of goodness or of food quality. Bourgeois consumers learned from the nutritionist that nutritional quality was measured completely objectively by an instrument, the calorimeter. They learned from the gastronome that quality was measured completely subjectively by one's own taste buds and palate, a palate refined and educated to bring bourgeois tastes well into alignment with the standards issued by the critics. As taught by Grimod and his cohorts, good taste was universal, and the gourmet could not disdain what Grimod considered delicious. In the nutritionist's case, the healthy qualities of food was devalued; in the gastronome's case, they were ignored.

Beginning in 1800 the food domain was divided among the doctor, who had lost his monopoly over it, the chemist, and the gastronome. All three had a different perspective, but they all tended in the same direction: toward undercutting the food-health partnership. Aristotle's golden mean could have been transformed into the bourgeois compromise. Nothing of the kind happened. For a century, concerns over food quality were put on hold.

The Golden Age of Adulterations

In 1830 an old military doctor named Aulagnier published a *Dictionary of Native and Exotic Food Substances and Their Properties*. In the preface, he justified his enterprise: "To be able to make a discriminating choice, one must know the principal constituents of the substances that serve as food, that is to say, those that contain good or bad juices, those that are easy to digest or are dense, hard, and heavy in the stomach and tire it, and, finally, those that are viscous, acid, oily, mucilaginous, butyrous, gelatinous, starchy." The Galenic vocabulary might give the impression of a traditional work, in the line of the medieval *tacuins* of Pisanelli. In fact, the dictionary is just as much a treatise on alterations and adulterations of natural foodstuffs, a precursor to a genre destined to be a publishing success. The list of warnings is long. In alphabetical order, Aulagnier cites: beer, bonbons, bread, butter, capers, cheese, conserves, cornichons, green beans, ham, lemonade, milk, oil, pepper, vinegar. The poisons he denounces are often contaminants. We find the old fear of copper in the articles on capers, cornichons, and green beans and again in "Frying: . . . One must pay attention to the vessels one uses for frying, because we hear today of an entire family from Henin-sur-Cujeul (Pas-de-Calais) that was poisoned by an omelette prepared in a badly plated frying pan. Four persons (the father, mother, son, and daughter) succumbed last May 24, after the most horrible suffering." And again in "Oil: . . . there is a danger involving green oil . . . in many stores, it is kept in lead or pewter vessels, or sometimes it is measured out in copper. . . . It has a greenish color, a nauseating odor, and emetic properties." Aulagnier was not under any illusions regarding the impact of his warnings. Moreover, he had a few suspicions about the motivations of his readers. Were they leafing through his dictionary to get indignant about these manipulations and avoid the most serious ones or to try out a little domestic chemistry of their own? In the article on vinegar, he declines to speak of adulterations, for fear, he says, of teaching those who do not know about them.[22]

"All our products are adulterated to make it easier to sell them and to shorten their existence. Our era will be called the golden age of adulteration," said Paul Lafargue, who celebrated the pantagruelian feasts that Mother Nature, inevitably abundant, reserved for her children—or, rather, would have reserved for them, if the capitalist division of labor had not been invented.[23] Most historians agree with this judgment, the list of publications on food frauds is so long and so ubiquitous. Almost at the same time as Aulagnier's *Dictionnaire* appeared, a best seller was published in Leipzig entitled *Der Chemiker für's Haus*, translated into French and called *Practical Advice for the Detection of Adulterations as Well as Toxic Substances in Foodstuffs*. The United Kingdom was shaken by a series of lawsuits against Frédéric Accum, accused with others of having sold as fresh tea used tea leaves, dried and recolored with lead blacking, and Gloucester cheese tinted a deeper orange with a bit of red lead paint.[24]

Adulteration was common. Such manipulation was even everyday, standard practice in the sense that many adulterations were not viewed by the public with a reproving eye; far from it. Mixing two products was an unconscious, innocent act, performed daily by the housewife and the cook. Most of these adulterations aimed at color. Making sure that the wine was very red, the butter yellow, the cornichons and the green beans green was generally accepted and desired. To enhance the color was to follow the direction of nature. Anglo-Saxon wine was not always made with grapes. In Germany, one found *Apfelwein* and in England cherry wine. Household coffee was very often made from roasted chickpeas; nevertheless, it was served as coffee.[25] But at home one knew what one ate. The problem arose when it was a matter of craft industry or manufactured products. This resulted in the perfectly consistent double standard that could be observed throughout the century: it was fine to practice a little mixing at home, but foods adulterated by others were to be tracked down and not tolerated.

This is the lesson that we can draw from the books of recipes and home economics so common in middle-class circles, sometimes kept by the mistress of the house, sometimes by the master. Oddly disparate collections blithely mixed culinary, veterinary, and pharmaceutical arts, alternating recipes, home remedies, and an endless number of "tricks," little procedures meant to make life easier or improve what one ate. Let us open the one compiled by Louis Mège of Arles, under the July monarchy. Here, we learn how to keep milk: "this is M. Appert's procedure, generally adopted in England and hardly known in France"; here is how to restore milk that has turned: "deturn" it by means of sodium carbonate; and here is a way to keep wine from turning to vinegar.[26] Thus we catch a glimpse of an unlikely do-it-yourself pantry well stocked with little white powders like sodium bicarbonate, silver oxide, potassium sulfate, saltpeter, and arsenic— to chase the rats from the larder, with the hope that there were no fatal mix-ups. Unfortunately, there were, so one was also advised to color the death-to-rats paste, made of arsenic and old cheese, "with Prussian blue," "so as to avoid mistaken identities."[27] In other words, one fought the damaging effects of domestic chemistry with more chemistry. We can also imagine Mège's table, wisely administered in the style of the Balzacian bourgeois who served stale bread and rotten fruit first, since good economy required that one use up the foodstuffs that were going bad.[28] Nevertheless, his olive oil cuisine was better than that of the poor Parisian household, where the cooking was based on a mixture of butter, bacon fat, and chicken fat, the leftovers from bourgeois kitchens. To purify this mixture, one melted it together and added salt.[29] For all his skill at domestic concoctions and little "corrective" processes, Louis Mège rejected "sophisticated" products bought at stores and collected recipes, methods, and tactics for "recognizing a drugged food" or for "ascertaining if a wine is adulterated."

Aulagnier's *Dictionnaire*, which borrowed much from the *police judiciaire* manual of Remer, did its best to provide the eater with means for detecting the unhealthy and the adulterated. Most of the tests he proposed for detection were empirical, drawn from a store of well-grounded biases. Anecdotally, we might note the role allotted to small animals, charged with detecting what humans could not. If a mushroom was gnawed by a rodent, that was a sign that humans could eat it; to make sure vinegar was not adulterated, it was to be placed on the windowsill, and, if it attracted many fruit flies, that proved it was pure. We may wonder what kind of reasoning ruled in such beliefs. According to this logic, meat covered with bluebottles would be high-quality meat! But old rationales had their inconsistencies, just as ours do.

To test flour and bread for adulterations, Aulagnier describes various procedures. If curling powder was mixed with fine wheaten flour, it was quite easy to flush it out with a pour of vinegar. On contact with the plaster or the chalk that curling powder contained, a bubbling was produced. A whole series of tests had to be done to discover if bread contained copper sulfate: mixing, heating in a crucible, decanting, filtering—a long experiment, Aulagnier remarks, that could only be done in a chemist's laboratory.[30]

It all would have been so simple if one only had to soak a little strip of litmus paper and verify that the color did not change![31] But detecting adulterations using complicated procedures would increasingly become the business of professionals. After 1830 methods of detection would multiply and improve. Before Lavoisier's time, experts had no equipment at their disposal to answer a question as simple as, is this water drinkable? And we witness the abbot Tessier, while researching ergotized rye in Sologne, also expressing concern about the quality of the water and beginning by tasting it to assess its "perceptible qualities." At La Ferté-Imbault, he judged it "limpid, tasteless, and odorless." That first test being positive, he went on to the second, consisting of two experiments, neither of which was too technical: washing and cooking. "I saw that soap dissolves well, and the vegetables cook in it in no time." That was enough for him to declare La Ferté-Imbault water potable. Two generations later, water analysis had become a complex, costly procedure, requiring time, instruments, and solid grounding in chemistry. Needless to say, it was no longer left to just any amateur, even one as brilliant as the agronomist Tessier. Even if the language of chemistry was slower to impose itself with regard to other substances, here, a gap quickly opened between the layperson and the expert.

By the end of the century, methods of investigation had developed considerably with the progress of microbiology. They completely changed the relationship between the authorities and the eater. The eater's abilities to detect the properties of a food had not increased, whereas the state—if it so desired—had access to experts, equipped with incomparable tools. The layman, who felt doubly vulnerable, rarely noted anymore in his private journal domestic methods for testing the reliability of a product. This he left to the state, asking it to take charge of verifying and removing adulterated foods from the market. Manipulation, deception, fraud: these things were very confused under the ancien régime, blocking, as did the "secrets" of the guild monopolies, legislation on supervision. The penal code clarified the legal landscape by distinguishing between nondangerous adulterations, which fell into the category of deception, and dangerous adulterations (art. 318, art. 475).[32] The state thus had at its disposal adequate technical means and legal tools to intervene. But the means are one thing, the political will another.

The End of Serenity

The romantic period witnessed the flourishing of domestic adulterations and craft industry manipulations. Wine was more than ever the food at risk, especially since it was becoming the custom to drink it with meals, in France, at least. Coarse red wine was established as a basic beverage for the people and a required accompaniment to a good meal for the bourgeois, who turned the wine cellar into a mark of social distinction. Chemists and nutritionists did not condemn this new behavior. On the contrary, they confirmed wine's status as a food-beverage by establishing that a liter of wine at 10 degrees provided 850 calories, as much as a pound of bread, a pound of meat, or a kilo of potatoes.

On the other hand, some doubted its healthiness: "Calculate the effect that must be produced on Sunday on the stomach of the poor worker, a drinker of water six days of the week, by this potato alcohol that the merchant diluted the day before with well water and that he hastily colored with blueberries. You can see again why the worker in southern France is almost never drunk, and why the worker in Paris is almost always drunk when he leaves the wine merchant's. In the south of France, the wine is excellent and it is cheap; no one lacks it, and therefore no one adulterates it."[33]

This was 1843, and what Raspail was denouncing here was a small-business practice, in short, an old custom in cheap restaurants. Everything changed in the next decades, when, following—or even preceding—the general economic movement, adulterations entered a new industrial phase. To obtain the color consumers preferred, winegrowers in southern France experimented with growing different varieties such as carignan and grenache. The Spanish experimented with the aptly named teinturier, or dyer, variety, which allowed them to blend and dilute. Elsewhere, winemakers resorted to other potentially more dangerous processes, like artificially coloring wine. This process became almost obligatory because the practice of diluting was so widespread. One manipulation led to another, and diluting, sweetening, and coloring became three common practices in the wine industry, which found it easy to claim consumer tastes as its inspiration.[34] Between 1870 and 1875, fuchsin, a derivative of coal tar, experienced unprecedented popularity, thanks to its tinctorial powers and its low price. It was sold freely under such innocuous names as *colorine, cramoisine, scarlatine, purpurine*, and especially *caramel*. Thanks to the additions of water and fuchsin, it is estimated that France's total viticultural production went from 65 million hectoliters produced to 90 million actually sold and consumed.[35] Paul Brouardel opened an 1889 health conference with these words: "Some years ago in all countries, these adulterations took on an increasingly general character. All their populations realized at the same time that the laws protecting them were insufficient. It is no longer a matter of the little shopkeeper who deceives and poisons a few of his neighbors." In a certain way, the great hygienist's declaration sounds like the announcement of the end of a long period of public serenity.[36]

The politician could not be counted on to sound the alarm regarding additives and their dangers. That role belonged to the chemist. Even so, the researcher was suspect. In most cases, he worked in the laboratories of the manufacturers. His occupation was rife with ambiguities. He was well versed in methods of imitating nature, and, by discovering artificial colorings derived from coal tar, he opened unforeseen horizons to traffickers, beginning in the 1870s. At the same time, he was the one who explained how adulterations could be detected. He was the one who, in analyzing substances, warned against toxic additives and drew up the double list of toxic and nontoxic colorants. In fact, it was the chemists who spoke of chemical risks, in all countries but first in Germany, benefiting from the clear lead provided by Liebig's work.[37]

The other sounders of the alarm were the health professionals. They posed the question of adulterations in all the pubic offices where they were represented: the health commissions in German cities, the health bureaus in English districts, the health committees established in French counties, the conferences everywhere that represented the intersection of scientific advances and health studies. Beginning in England in 1875, and almost everywhere in the decade that followed, monitoring foodstuffs constituted a major innovation for public health, because these offices had generally been established after epidemics to fight infectious diseases and the pernicious miasmas believed to provoke them. Thus all their efforts were directed toward tracking down bad smells, and they dealt primarily with sewers and squalid housing.[38] Such a conversion was possible because of new medical ideas that were just emerging, the offspring of the science of bacteriology that dealt a blow to anticontagionist theories and reestablished something like a balance between sensitivity to the air and sensitivity to food. Brouardel's discovery that "all that dies does not reek and all that reeks does not die" announced the beginning of a new age; he took the lesson to heart in inaugurating the 1889 health conference in Paris and making adulterations the central question there.

But, eleven years earlier, a previous international health conference had already seized on the issue, driven by the urgency of it and by the public shock following revelations concerning "fuchsinated" wine. In 1878 the question of colorings was approached from every angle. The congress especially debated the colors of red and green.

Could fuchsin be tolerated or not? It was proven that, if it was pure, free of any arsenic residue, fuchsin was inherently inoffensive. Nevertheless, according to the general opinion of conference participants, "one cannot tolerate the coloration of wines with foreign materials, even inoffensive ones."[39] This led to a clear and firm definition: "Wine is the product of the fermentation of grape juice." This definition, of course, disregarded French regulations that authorized, under certain conditions, chaptalization, or the addition of sugar to the must.

For preserved foods, the question of greening processes arose, which the conference also examined. The technique most widely used in the canning industry consisted of plunging the vegetables as they were cooking into a very diluted bath of copper sulfate. This was done to 95 percent of the canned goods sold in France. It was a practice that the chemists did not condemn. Advances in research had shown that copper existed in the animal economy: its presence was demonstrated in the human liver, in a great number of vegetables, and in the blood. The question shifted: if copper was no longer poisonous in the absolute sense, but a necessary substance, at what level did it become toxic? The French chemists proposed an acceptable threshold of 18 milligrams of copper per kilo of strained vegetables.

On all these points, the public health authorities generally followed the chemists' recommendations in their labeling policies. In fact, their consensus hides a great deal of confusion about what meaning to give to the notion of "undesirable substances." The meaning varied depending on the case. For wine, no additives were acceptable, even if they were part of the product's natural composition. Diluting and sweetening were forbidden, even though nature used only water and sugar to make wine. The French decree of 1907 defined wine as a drink produced "exclusively from the alcoholic fermentation of fresh grapes or the juice of fresh grapes." At the same time, chaptalization was completely legal. For butter, unlike wine, inoffensive colorings were tolerated. Adulterated butter was not butter that was colored, but a butter slab loaded with other substances, fat or suet, for example. For preserving vegetables, greening processes were allowed—using products that were not harmless—within certain limits. Thus the question of additives' harmlessness received a varying response, case by case.

In fact, in trying to define standards for production, one touched on the very definition of the natural, "authentic" product itself. The idea of nature that thus emerged was radically different from nature as perceived by the medievalists and moderns, who made no essential distinction between natural and artificial bodies. But the opposition between nature and artifice is not always operative, and the hygienists were confronted with a malleable, unstable concept. Their discussions clearly demonstrated their hesitations and second thoughts with regard to human actions that might or might not be considered natural. A whole makeshift epistemology seemed necessary to arrive at definitions for effective standards. They did not succeed in their enterprise, caught as they were between the opinion that any and all additions were to be condemned (if performed by the industry) and the chemists who distinguished between good and bad additives. By their standards, for example, wine was a kind of hybrid, a product of nature (grape juice) and of the supernatural (chaptalization).

In 1865, celebrating progress, Edmond About wrote:

All the good things you enjoy today you owe to the heroic efforts of men who preceded you in this world. There is no fruit, no vegetable, no condiment, no wine on earth that has not been the object of a patent, a certificate of importation, and 100,000 improvement patents. You thank nature when you stroll through a magnificent garden: it is man who must be thanked.... The grains in the fields, the trees in the orchard, all that seems to come from the earth itself is imported, developed, perfected, improved, and transformed by the hand of man.[40]

At the same time that Edmond About was celebrating progress and human acts, which were also natural acts, a monk in Brno, Gregor Johann Mendel, turned the idea of nature upside down with his research into genetic biology. Before Mendel, field experiments by horticulturists had multiplied the number of hybrids. By crossing green beans in his garden-laboratory and by formulating the mathematical model for the laws of selection, Mendel clarified a posteriori the effectiveness of horticulture. Thus arose the problem of hybrids in nature, which was organized into species. The hybridizer was in something of the same Promethean position as the chemist, capable of inventing and improving, indeed, of altering the work of the Creator. This was also the era when scientists learned how to domesticate microbes, to *cultivate* them, and diluted poisons became vaccines. All this strangely complicated the perception one could have of the healthy and the unhealthy, the natural and the artificial. Under these conditions, was it any wonder that the best European health professionals failed to arrive at a coherent definition for a "natural product"?

FIFTEEN

ENGLISH CATTLE DISEASE

In a May 1839 edition, under the title of "A Slaughterhouse Anecdote," the *Journal de commerce* published the edifying story of Babet.

A young woman of fifteen or sixteen, Toinette, appeared at the Montmartre slaughterhouse, leading by a rope a "Paris milk cow, suffering a lung infection, exhausted, no longer able to give milk, and so about to be slaughtered to be offered for public consumption if the meat was judged healthy enough and, if not, to be fed to the fierce beasts in the king's royal gardens." This cow was named Babet, and Toinette, poor and illiterate, believed that she had led her there to be cured. When Babet was slaughtered, Toinette fainted. It was then learned that Toinette was an orphan, taken in by a stockbreeder who treated her harshly, making her sleep in the cowshed, and that Babet had been her only friend, almost a mother to her. Moved by her distress, the butcher boys of Montmartre got together and offered Toinette a new Babet, proving in this instance, as in others, which the journalist cited, that they had generous dispositions.[1]

The article ended by specifying exactly how to read this story and what lesson to draw from it: the reader had to rid himself of "his prejudices toward a useful, industrious, and really quite humane class," that is, the boys of the slaughterhouse. That Babet was "pulmonic" in the final degree, that is to say, suffering from tuberculosis, and that her milk and her meat could infect children and adults—that was a fact the newspaper did not note. To discover what aroused readers' fears, to find the journalistic sensations of this era, we would have to search for canards in other news briefs: natural plagues, train catastrophes, cholera, or crimes. If the canard clearly reflects the dreams—and the nightmares—of the people, then reading the popular papers printed between 1810 and 1860 would convince us that the people did not fear food risks.[2] But, two generations later, the Babets and her tubercular sisters prompted great obsessive fear.

The Ambiguous Cow

In 1830 selling Babet was perfectly legal. All ancien régime prohibitions regarding the meat of animals stricken with what was then called *fy* or the *pommelière* had been abolished. Likewise, leprous pork was sold freely, and the *langueyeurs* were mostly out of work. They were no longer consulted and paid by stockbreeders at the fairs, anxious about maintaining the quality of their herds. If Babet's meat revealed too serious tubercular lesions on examination by expert butchers, the pieces at risk were thrown to the lions in the zoo. In cases where the tuberculosis was not so far advanced, the meat was declared good for selling.

At any rate, Babets at the slaughterhouse were rare. They usually took another route to end up in the family stewpot:

> The owners of sick animals are very wary of taking them to the slaughterhouse, where they know the meat will be confiscated. They sell them; they butcher them in the villages where there is no surveillance. That explains why one encounters no more than 500 consumptive cows per year in Paris, the great majority of which are made available for human consumption, while everyone knows that most of the cows filling the cowsheds and producing most of the milk Parisians consume are fatally doomed to consumption. But, as soon as their diminished milk production, rapid weight loss, and general condition indicate the consumption is getting worse, their owners hurry to sell the sick animals to butchers in the suburbs, where particular slaughter yards are under no supervision and where their meat is sold at the same price as healthy meat.[3]

If Babet's story moved readers, their relationship to neither the food nor the animal was at issue. In hindsight, readers felt no fear about consuming a tubercular cow simply because they made no connection between the cow disease (*la pulmonie*) and human tuberculosis (*la phtisie*). Making a simple comparison, an analogy between the two diseases as Laennec had done, was considered a mistake, imagining that they were transmittable an aberration. Until midcentury, European scientists were convinced of this, even if general opinion was shaped by latent prejudices, no doubt the result of long memory. Louis Bizet, inspector of the Montmartre butchers and an intelligent, well-informed observer of Paris meat consumption, noted that "cows are poorly rated in the public mind." They were known to arrive at the slaughterhouse old and exhausted, and too often "they would succumb to one form of tuberculosis or another if they were not promptly delivered to the butcher." He added, "We are less prudent than the Jews.... We offer for human consumption cows with tubercular lungs that have necessarily altered the health of the meat."[4] The absence of rigorous health standards was, in his eyes, such an aberration that twice in his report he recommended "imitating the Jews." Bizet, an enlightened, nonreligious veterinarian, for want of good health standards, looked longingly to religious prohibitions for the "hygienic" role they played!

The problem was that this man, so clear-sighted about the dangers of tubercular meat, was very much alone. This was 1847, and hardly any scientists believed there was a risk. The problem, too, was that the proportion of French livestock stricken with tuberculosis was undoubtedly growing, but there was no way to measure this upsurge, since it was not obligatory to declare the disease or record it. Bovine tuberculosis raged especially in the cowsheds around the cities, precisely those responsible for providing the cities with fresh milk for their children, elderly, convalescents, and, remarkably, their consumptives. It is easy for us to understand how such a contagious disease can be spread through stabling. The veterinarians of that century had other explanations. The most common was the aerist hypothesis, illusive but accompanied with an effective recommendation to stockbreeders: Clean up your stables! Air out your cowsheds! The French aerists proposed two models in matters of cleanliness, Switzerland and Bavaria. By the turn of the century, the Swiss remained the only example to follow.[5] The other hypothesis was that this was a hereditary disease, which Bizet no doubt had in mind when he claimed those suburban cows were "fatally doomed" to consumption. This was a view widely adopted among those who, refusing to believe in contagion, looked to environmental and genetic factors. It was also believed to be spread by certain species, which allowed responsible parties to be named. Since the progress of bovine tuberculosis in France coincided with the first efforts at selection, notably the crossing of native livestock with a breed imported from northern England—the short-horned breed from Durham—bovine tuberculosis was called English Cattle Disease. And thus the Durham cow became the scapegoat.

Many other observers, Bizet among them, called into question the diet of the livestock in suburban cowsheds: "In the place of that mature, fully developed animal with thick, heavy meat, sallow flesh, and the delicate fat produced by fattening it up in the pasture, we now have only an animal fattened through artificial means. Cooked rye, potatoes, and beets, stretched over a skeleton, are only capable of producing soft, hollow, inflated meat, flabby, without weight, or body, or soul."[6]

Here, the gustatory quality of the meat is at issue. But others went further, establishing a positive (or negative) correlation between the new artificial feeding methods and animal diseases: "Our stockbreeders no longer know how to account for the very high mortality rate in their stables. Nevertheless, it is very easy to see that this calamity dates from the time when our economists advised them to use distillery residues, beets, and potato peels as a substitute for hay.... That explains all these putrid fevers, in other words, these verminous fevers that break out and carry off a good milk cow in no time at all."[7]

The fear of "unnatural" foods confused etiological trails and led clear thinkers like Raspail astray. It also, however, clearly demonstrated how the natural tended to become a moral standard. What was not "natural" was contrary to morality, for instance, the phenomenon of feeding cows with something other than grass.

In twenty years, everything changed. The great alert began in 1865–1866 when Jean-Antoine Villemin demonstrated that the disease was both unique and transmissible: "Eating meat from consumptive animals presents an ongoing danger to public health."[8] The publication of his works aroused "extreme fear" among the public. Tuberculosis was so common that, in Paris, it accounted for thirty out of one hundred deaths. Could it come from eating the meat of consumptive animals?[9] Anxiety increased when Chaveau demonstrated that tuberculosis could be transmitted through the digestive system. These were just the experiments done by the French. Others were done elsewhere. Gerlack, Leisering, and Klebs in Germany, Fleming in England, Perroncito in Italy produced a fine network of intersecting experiments and simultaneous discoveries with few quarrels over first rights. But the scientific community still had doubts. It did not contest the repeated experiments that all reached the same conclusions. But it simply did not understand why, if the disease was transmitted, it was not more widespread, why some people were susceptible and others were not. That was the sticking point. Accepting tuberculosis as a contagion was difficult because its incubation was so slow and its contagiousness neither consistent nor general.

Not all the French veterinarians were convinced by Villemin. In 1873 Reynal's very serious and very official *Traité de la police sanitaire des animaux domestiques* (Treatise on health policy for domestic animals) appeared. It is worth the trouble of rereading, as the most complete summary of aerist prejudices and the most meticulous attempt to negate the threat of tuberculosis. For example, bovine tuberculosis was only triggered by two conditions: excessive lactation and abrupt shifts from hot to cold. Thus to avoid the disease, eliminating these two predisposing causes was enough. There was nothing to fear about consuming tubercular meat; avoiding the pieces at risk, like the lungs, was sufficient.[10]

In 1882 Robert Koch discovered the bacillus that bears his name and definitively established the viral and contagious nature of tuberculosis. The problem was that there were so many mechanisms of contagion that it was hard to know which was the most threatening: air? meat? milk?[11] The ways of transmission were indeed inscrutable. They pushed the politician toward prudence, understood here as abstention. The man on the street, however, focused on just one of them and concentrated his fears on milk.

A New Image of Milk

It was difficult to call the cow into question. The cow was the milk giver, maternal, peaceful in the meadow. Stabled like Babet in urban cowsheds, she was hardly a menace to the neighborhood; on the contrary, she served it, supplying it with warm milk and milk products, considered such useful protection against consumption.[12] The cow was man's foster mother, and just recently she had bestowed on him a kindness for which he would never be able to thank her: the vaccine. Lending her name to the most decisive advance in disease prevention was the least of it, when one considered the ravages of smallpox, especially on children, before Jenner had the idea of using cowpox to immunize humans.

But couldn't the cow pass her disease to humans? That was the hackneyed argument of the enemies of the smallpox vaccine, whom Doctor Sacco, initiator of the vaccine in Italy, denounced in these terms: "One might as well say that, through the milk and meat we use each day, we ought to contract the germs of all bovine diseases.... If there has never been such transmission, why should we fear it today, and why, because of the fear of an impossible disease, should we abandon a real and certain advantage?"[13]

In short, at the turn of the century, those who might have had some fears regarding tubercular milk were as much obscurantists as those who rejected the vaccine. The image of the cow thus remained intact, like the image of green pastures.

The image of milk was complex and oscillating; for a long time, animal milk was suspect, considered a poor food and a food for the poor.[14] Anselme Payen, the pioneer in food science during the Second Empire, hesitated to include it in his dietetic pyramid. He listed it under the rubric of "Leftovers and Various Edible Animal Products" as a by-product of stockbreeding, not yet a noble product meant for everyone. He limited himself to listing the twenty-three elements of which it was composed, without offering an opinion on its nutritive value.[15] On the other hand, milk was a good food, a "superfood," in Anglo-Saxon countries; in Latin countries, it was willingly included among medicinals. In the first case as in the second, immaculate virtues were attributed to it. It was the ideal food for infants, the sickly were regularly put on milk diets, as well as those with lung ailments who had to devote all their vital energy to breathing and for whom milk was recommended because it did not overtax the stomach. They were also advised to spend time in the cowsheds where the atmosphere was considered beneficial to the lungs.[16]

For milk to cease being reassuring, a great psychological break with inherited patterns had to occur. For milk to provoke fear, these patterns had to disappear completely, and humans had to stop believing that nothing provided better protection than the maternal breast. That was going too far: only animal milk was called into question.

Adulterations prompted the first doubts, not about milk in general but about milk from the suburban cowsheds distributed to the cities' children:

First of all, the milk! Ah, the milk! It is already adulterated in the body of the cow before she is milked! Because the animal is fed with a heap of things that increase her milk production but diminish its richness and quality. And then the farmer proceeds to skim his milk first, before selling it. That's the first thing! Thus the wholesale merchant is already sure of no longer getting cream. If only the wrongs ended there! But naturally he waters the milk down, and on top of that, to keep it from turning, he boils it and adds what is called a preservative, that is, sodium carbonate. Then it is off to the city. It goes without saying that the city creamery (!) adds more water in its turn to stretch out the sauce. But since the milk no longer has any quality or taste, a bit of starch or horse brain is added to thicken it. This is not poisonous, as they say, but it is hardly appetizing.[17]

That last line indicates the limits of suspicion: it was not appetizing, but neither was it dangerous to one's health. Moreover, small industry practices resembled domestic practices. Diluting? Watering down? That was what one did at home, on the advice of more or less well-informed hygienists: "Since the milk of animals is richer in cream than that of women, it must be cut with water when it is given to children."[18] Boiling? On advice from the same sources, that was also something one had learned to do. Because the taste for the natural in romantic Europe would have led instead to drinking milk raw. It was not in milk's nature to boil, and its tendency to escape the pot when it reached the boiling point was good proof of that. It was also thought that boiled milk turned acrid and developed the odor of urine and that the best and most nutritious of its restorative particles evaporated.[19] As for the additives, the Paris Board of Health "proved" that these substances were not harmful. "It was thought that the public authorities did not have to intervene and that merchants acting in bad faith were punished by buyers losing confidence in them."[20] That was in 1829. But, half a century later, it was a completely different story. Adulterated milk prompted reservations. Tuberculous milk engendered the worst of apprehensions.

By the end of the century, the popular imagination thrived on this bacterial swarm that no one had seen but everyone knew about: nine thousand bacteria in a single drop of milk from a sick cow two hours after milking, which became twenty-one thousand three hours later. In the century's last decades, everything conspired to create a true fear, a real terror, with two explosive ingredients: a basic food and a very widespread disease.

Milk had become a basic food since animal milk had replaced mother's milk. Putting children in the care of a wet nurse, which had been standard childrearing practice among city dwellers of all classes, had begun a decline, increasingly pronounced after the turn of the century. Only the bourgeois could afford a nurse in the home, but the fear of syphilis, which could be transmitted through breast milk, led the upper classes to resort increasingly to bottle-feeding with cow's milk as well. In rural areas, cow's milk replaced goat's milk. In short, the question of milk affected all the social strata of the country, which was not the case with meat, eaten less among the lower classes.

At the same time that they provided the primary grounds for the fear, the chemists indicated the antidotes. Prevention was available in three different forms: boiling, pasteurization, and sterilization. Two pacifying powers were put to work, one involving individual hygienic practices, the other involving manufacturing processes. It was recognized that microbes were more effectively destroyed in food-processing plants than at home, and manufacturing processes were more reliable than domestic boiling. That undoubtedly explains the success of artificial milks for feeding infants, on which corporations such as Nestlé built their industrial fortunes. Even though, as we have seen, the conversion to industrial products was long and difficult, paradoxically, it was with the product considered the most essential and most natural that substitution took place earliest and most completely. Powerful emotional engines must have been behind the paradoxical victory of powdered and condensed milk.

By 1890 pasteurization was made obligatory in Copenhagen. On the eve of World War I, the Anglo-Saxon countries provided themselves a regulatory arsenal to confront bovine tuberculosis. At the turn of the century, the vigilance of the bacteriologists coincided with the concern of doctors and politicians to battle the demographical and biological demise of their populations. All countries were obsessed with the idea of biological decline. Not all of them, however, took the same measures.[21] Milk regained its virgin status with pasteurization. France proved the exception to the rule. As no one is a prophet in his own country, so Pasteur was better heard outside France, and his lessons wholly assimilated. Pasteurized cheeses were demanded by the public almost everywhere, except in Latin countries where the attachment to raw milk remained strong. Milk became the white line that tended to separate national food cultures then in the process of being established.

The State and the Consumer

"If the knowledge of food had been as thorough in all times as it is at present, many ills would have been averted, but it has been reserved for our century to take on this particular responsibility."[22] Parmentier was not mistaken. The nineteenth century—a long nineteenth century that stretched until the dawn of World War I—was the time of great discoveries in the area of nutrition. It discovered calories and vitamins, the first so-called indeterminate foods. With calories, it introduced quantitative science, and, with vitamins, it provided the basis for the twentieth century's qualitative science. But the scholar's sound premonitions were accompanied with sweet illusions: knowledge did not necessarily lead to prevention.

The century was also the one of great official serenity regarding food. We must wonder about the causes for this, and will we ever know its effects? Did state intervention in the area of food risks reassure the eater? Or was the opposite true? Was it the state's lack of intervention that calmed fears? It really seems as though the liberalism that set the century's political tone opted for the second theory.

"We must learn to view all things from the perspective of the consumer," the economist Frédéric Bastiat was supposed to have said on his deathbed, as a last testament for the benefit of his liberal emulators. Of course, preserving the rights of the citizen, including his physical integrity and his health, was inscribed in the liberal agenda. It was the principle that justified the intervention of public authority in cases of fraud. But should the state go further? In the minds of ultraliberals like Bastiat, there was absolutely no need to assure the consumer's safety by adopting other measures for his benefit: free competition would take care of that.[23] In the ideal market system they envisioned, the producer naturally strove to satisfy the client's expectations. Thus the consumer, like a king, only had to let himself be served.

Charles Gide, professor of law in Montpellier and founding father of the consumer movement in France, was one of those rare individuals who questioned the official creed.[24] The facts, he said, contradicted the theory: the short-term objective of producers was profit. And that accounted, in particular, for the increase in food adulterations so harmful to the consumer. "The consumer will do well not to trust laissez-faire economics to guarantee his rights or to slack off in the role of lazy king. He must defend his interests."[25] Such premises would lead one to expect an appeal to the protector state. But this reflex—to turn to the state—was not in the least contemporary, and neither was it Gide's. "We are no longer in that time when the state freely distributed bread, and there is no desire for those times to return."[26]

Apostle of social economics, Gide saw salvation in partnerships between consumers and the cooperative movement. End-of-the-century consumerism went hand in hand with some of the oldest frameworks for supervision over the food professions, such as the bakery trade. All the institutions cited by the economist as examples to follow were cooperative or municipal enterprises: the municipal butcher shop in Lisbon; school cafeterias in French cities, "economy cookstoves" in Berlin, and especially purchasing exchanges and workers' cooperatives. For him, tuberculosis was a social disease, and to eliminate it, its causes—unhealthy and overcrowded housing, alcoholism—had to be eliminated. In the end-of-the-century hygienist discourse, "consumption" was used in a restrictive and pejorative sense; the word designated an alcoholic drink that was ordered or offered at a bistro and posed a health risk if abused. "Consumption is served at the bar" was a common invective, since there was thought to be a direct relationship between tuberculosis and alcoholism. Charles Gide cited food quality as another factor in the contagion. On this subject, however, he did not expand very much. Not only did this means of contamination seem very secondary to him, but it did not depend on public intervention. He expanded even less on the notion of protection, which targeted the producer and which, under the name of protectionism, had become a firmly established state policy by the dawn of the twentieth century. Consumption, consumer, protection: these end-of-the-century words had connotations that were nothing like our own today.

Were questions of food risk issues strictly political? The political elite answered no, except ... except if those risks fell into the domain recognized by and reserved to the state.

The principle of nonintervention could only be shaken by one consideration, an endogenous argument that caught liberalism in the trap of its own logic. According to the theory, the consumers are the best judges of their own interests. There was the rub. Were infants poisoned by adulterated milk or infected by milk contaminated with tuberculosis really the best judges of their interests? And in 1900 did the layman really have the means for being his own expert?

Each to his place. The state was no substitute for the producer, or the consumer, or the doctor. Only higher necessities allowed it to exert pressure, for instance, in the name of the principle of subsidiarity. Its intervention was limited to two areas: adulterations and the protection of children.

Bonbons offer a minuscule but illustrative example of this. Minuscule? Well, maybe not. The confectionery posed many problems that were already issues for the ancien régime. For example, could the confectioners sell sweets with curative or preventive properties, or was that the exclusive right of the pharmacists, as in the case of a M. Guichon who, at the 1867 World Fair, introduced a nutritious sweetened fruit paste with beef, particularly recommended for the convalescent? Despite the end of guilds, manufacturing secrets were still well protected, and mystery hung over the factories, where the right to remain silent was recognized among the makers of sweets.[27]

What is striking is the prolonged nature of the dispute. But that was a matter for the courts. The state, especially the Third Republic in the 1890s, had other motives for getting deeply involved here, concentrating almost all its vigilance on a single object: the bonbon. What seemed to children doubly good (bon/bon) appeared to the higher powers highly suspect. The protection of the child, which had become a government directive, embraced the public opinion that had always been sensitive to what children ate. Early on, the meat pies sold to small boys on the street aroused the suspicions of adults and the vigilance of the police. Almost everywhere, strict regulations over confectioneries were put into place. It seems that there were some abuses and some mishaps. In Epinal, France, five children were poisoned eating bonbons colored with arsenical green, that is, as the *Journal de pharmacie* strongly emphasized, green coloring from Scheele or from Schweinfurt, German colorings. Similar poisonings were reported in Béziers in 1840.[28]

Each country took measures and drew up a list of prohibited substances and colorings, sometimes longer than the list of substances declared harmful by the chemists. The chemists, for example, saw no need to prohibit "false gold" wrappers, as France did beginning in 1862, giving silver wrappers a monopoly. They thought that the Swiss went too far in prohibiting fuchsin, a red coloring that was used in a tiny number of bonbons. The public authorities were not concerned with consumer protection in this case; they were acting in the two domains recognized as theirs: the health of children and the suppression of fraud.

Useless Knowledge

Bovine tuberculosis clearly illustrated how the political machinery seized up as soon as it was a matter of intervening in a domain—consumer protection—where the state had not allowed itself any involvement. It is true that before 1882 and Koch's discovery of the bacillus, nothing had been certain. Even scientists had been opposed to a policy of precaution. In 1878, when suspicions concerning transmission of the disease from animal to man grew stronger, health professionals in every country became nervous, but they did not push the state to take measures.

Their arguments are worth hearing:

Is this to say that we must, from now on, absolutely prohibit the use of meat coming from consumptive animals? That is far from being what we think. It is very important to remember, first of all, that all the experiments have been done with the raw tuberculous element, that no one has proven that muscle tissue uninfiltrated with tuberculosis shares the same properties, whereas even if it would present some danger, which seems unlikely, the cooking to which it is subjected before being eaten will, as a necessary consequence, extinguish in it any virulent activity. Second, we must not forget that meat is a food of prime necessity and that current meat production already cannot fulfill the demand for it. The destruction of very considerable quantities of butchered meat would have the effect of greatly inflating meat prices and making it unaffordable to the working class, which has the most vital need for it. When in the presence of a possible but definitely minor danger, it is appropriate to consider carefully if, by avoiding it, one does not replace it with a worse one, if, in the end, the measure meant to safeguard public health would achieve exactly the opposite result.[29]

The stakes were very carefully defined here. We might note, however, that the economic stakes, so important in a largely rural France, were not mentioned. In this instance, it was a matter of working out a scientific—and purely scientific—compromise. That is why we see meat considered a food of the highest necessity. Good health was given as the rationale for this. But though meat was desirable, the need for it is not an objective fact. In the calculations of risks and benefits figured a plea for meat on the worker's plate. This was at a time when, in the garrisons, the good effects on the irregular recruits of a 300-gram meat ration per day were being measured. The contented soldiers sang, "Each day, meat and soup, no work, no work."[30] Medical doctors recorded gains in height among the recruits, and the officers found them finally able to endure the stresses of training after a few months of this diet. Health professionals thus began to wonder if the republic's call for obligatory education should be accompanied by a second slogan: obligatory meat. In terms of this debate, though, it is not clear that they remained true to their role: not only did they name the risk, but they said clearly that it was a risk worth taking.

In 1882 the risk of tuberculosis contagion was recognized and verified under the microscope of Robert Koch, and the method for detection was perfected a little later with tuberculin. Once the risk had become a danger, the givens completely shifted. The choice was no longer between an argument for precaution and an argument for familiarity, the latter justifying adopting no measures as long as a product's harmfulness had not been demonstrated. In truth, it was no longer just a matter of a simple policy of prudence. Now the choice was between what was called "obligatory prevention," handled by the state, which would do the screening, and dismissing the need for consuming unhealthy meat, and "voluntary prevention," combining the efforts of stockbreeders and the dairy industry.[31] The response varied according to the state.

The response of Bismarck's Germany was quite comprehensive. It was able to draw on political authority and an already long tradition of inspection and supervision over meat and beer in all the German states before they were united.[32] The most liberal countries, like the United Kingdom, took measures in the name of public health, putting into place a warning and inspection system. In France, regulatory work with regard to animal diseases had come to a halt between the Revolution and 1881.[33] The law of July 21, 1881, required the stockbreeder to declare contagious diseases that his animals might have contracted: rinderpest, glanders, sheep pox, hoof-and-mouth disease. The declared animals were isolated, inspected, and treated or slaughtered, depending on the case. Lawmakers took this opportunity to forbid the importation of American and German pigs suspected of trichinosis. As for bovine tuberculosis, the authorities were clearly reluctant to write it into the law. Thus the major health law of 1881 made no mention of it. A decree would rectify the oversight in 1888. Ten years later, slaughter was made obligatory. But the parliament, voting on the decision unanimously, had no idea how many animals were involved and, moreover, provided for no systematic screening. In the final analysis, it furnished French legislation with one of the finest examples of a dead letter law.[34] The tuberculin test would not be made obligatory in France until ... 1935, at which time the French ran two times the risk of dying from tuberculosis than any other Europeans.[35]

Elsewhere in Europe where obligatory or state-reimbursed warning and screening systems were put into place by the end of the century, the high rate of contamination was discovered. In Belgium, a pioneer in the matter of obligatory testing, 60 percent of the cattle were infected. In Germany, Holland, and the United States, the rate oscillated between 10 and 75 percent. In France, where the test was not required, they boasted of having a lower contamination rate. A map and statistics were drawn up based on numbers from the slaughterhouses, which had only very relative value. Since the most serious upsurge in tuberculosis occurred between 1850 and 1900, the authorities' estimates around 1900 were reassuring: one horned animal in one hundred was supposedly tubercular.[36] As for the veterinarians, they said it was present throughout the territory and that it affected perhaps 25 percent of the bovine livestock in Brittany, 40 percent in the Vosges, 50 percent in the Pyrenees and in the Beauce, which is to say one cowshed out of two.[37] Nevertheless, tuberculosis was assumed to be a foreign plague, a British disease, the price paid for the importation of those Durham cattle bought for a small fortune. It was also assumed that French herds escaped its ravages more easily if farmers remained faithful to traditional extensive methods and open-air cattle rearing. The observations seemed plausible enough. We cannot measure the degree of underestimation in these statistics or know the extent to which underestimating was part of a deliberate policy to reassure the consumer.

Tuberculosis—the two forms of tuberculosis, animal and human—was the privileged place where two fears crossed and became inextricably bound: the public's fear, which put pressure on the authorities, and the authorities' fear of inciting public panic. Analyzing the inertia and procrastination that characterized the struggle against tuberculosis in France, Lion Murard and Patrick Zylberman observed that fear more often seized the public authorities than the public. They discerned in the policy of the Third Republic "a hopeless knot of fear and unconcern."[38]

Whereas the nervousness of the experts, as publicly expressed at the big health conferences, prompted awareness and moral responsibility, the ruling elite seemed to adopt Stendhal's stance. Consul to Civita-Vecchia when the cholera pandemic struck in 1832, Stendhal wrote: "Here, we never did believe the newspapers.... Here, a little hole with 7,500 inhabitants, the flu killed seven people a day. But no one took it into his head to become afraid. The press had not incited imaginations. I saw for the first time that the freedom of the press can be harmful; Napoleon might have forbidden the word cholera."[39] The delay in inscribing the word "tuberculosis" in the law can be interpreted as an attempt to avoid panic over its official declaration. It was a taboo word, and not until World War I would it appear in official texts.

We have already encountered the heuristic aspects of fear under the ancien régime among the ruling classes. Medical theory agreed: one had to do everything possible to avoid those emotions that produced the black humors, one of the predisposing causes of disease. But the Galenic paradigm collapsed with Pasteur's discoveries, and the scientific justification for such an attitude no longer existed. Exhausted as a theory, the doctrine of fear only continued to survive in individual preventive medicine ... and as a political ploy. Dieticians taught that it was not possible to have good digestion without a good attitude: "Avoid worries and, above all, do not read the political newspapers!"[40] The Republic's elite clung to, and even promoted, a certain vision of the citizen-eater: the adult male, capable of exercising rational free choice in the marketplace, was supposedly incapable of making good use of information regarding food risks. By fostering uncertainty, scientific controversies increased the perception of such risks, creating a kind of psychosis. The role of the state was not to alarm and, if there was alarm, to pacify, to say what would reassure: that transmission occurred essentially through the respiratory tract—which was true— and that a contaminated cow rarely gave contaminated milk—which was also true. The rest was a matter of individual protection. Do not spit, boil milk: these were the watchwords to be spread throughout the country. State vigilance essentially came down to this: seeing to it that the population was not stricken with terror. "Fear is the daughter of ignorance," said Lucien Febvre. The Republic's ruling elite were very close to thinking the opposite, that it was the daughter of knowledge.

The men in power seemed more preoccupied with public relations than with public health, fearing, above all, the effect of public announcements. The public policy that France adopted might be characterized as a struggle not against the risk but against the psychological effects of the risk. Perhaps that is an oversimplification. In the case of milk, it is important to note that Pasteur was never a prophet in his own country. In the case of meat, there were good reasons for abstaining, especially the fact that it was not a commonly consumed foodstuff, that it was only dangerous in the exceptional case, and that scientific experts were not in favor of prohibiting it. The ascending curve of tuberculosis victims, since that was the issue here, did not really give the profile of a disease originating in food. A posteriori, it justified the great tolerance allowed the muscle tissue of tubercular animals.

In the end, progress in matters of health safety, which really did occur, did not follow any uniform, state-controlled path, in France or in other free countries, where the law largely left the initiative to municipalities or state-appointed representatives. Nowhere was there a national policy, only isolated or ad hoc governmental actions. We can cite, for example, the role of men like Camille Leblanc, official veterinarian for the Paris police headquarters, who pushed for the organization of a real health service. The new police chief after 1870, Léon Renault, was the son of the director of the veterinary school in Alfort. He provided Paris and the Seine department with a health service, in perfect accord with the veterinarians' desire to the take the public service role. It was the veterinarians who took charge of supervision over animal diseases and the slaughterhouses beginning in 1890, thus supplanting the butchers in their privileged role as slaughterhouse experts.[41] In areas like Vaucluse, it was not until 1892 that inspection of public slaughterhouses became a routine requirement and not until 1913 that it became the exclusive occupation of appointed veterinarians.[42] Cities like Nice and Arcachon attempted to ensure the quality of the milk distributed there by requiring dairies to put guarantee labels on their milk bottles.[43] In New York, all dairy cows were given the tuberculin test. In England, the Milk and Dairies Act prohibited the sale of tubercular milk and gave local authorities complete supervisory powers.

The historian and doctor Giorgio Cosmacini noted with regard to the 1888 health reforms in Italy how the law lagged behind medical knowledge.[44] At the time of the 1348 plague, with no etiological certainty, the pope and Gui de Chauliac had improvised therapeutic measures based solidly enough on medical intuitions to be effective. The delay between knowledge and regulation was slight. Under the reign of the Galenic paradigm, the policy of prevention followed fairly consistently—and fairly well—the injunctions of the scholars. With the new Pasteurian paradigm, the lag between academic knowledge and public policy was pronounced, even though that knowledge was more definite and even though doctors were one of the best-represented professions in the bodies of democratic deliberation, such as the French senate.[45]

The political men of the Third Republic shared with the scientists—and the historians—an optimistic and positive vision of history: propelled by science, progress would bestow its blessings, inexorably and successively. They were wrong. Their political practices in response to food risks clearly demonstrated the complex relationships that exist between power and knowledge. In their epoch, the distance between them was at its greatest.

SIXTEEN

THE POISONERS OF CHICAGO

The Consumer at the End of the Century

The health contract defined in the medieval cities had suffered a few blows, but it retained all its significance. It was understood that, if consumers could count on the city or the state to protect them against adulterations, they must also protect themselves. The health culture at the end of the century taught how to shop at the markets and how to prepare food properly. The informed consumer had a very precise identity: she was a woman, the housewife, whose share of domestic roles had come to include the care and responsibility for family health. Cooking was not the housewife's only duty, though she had to be a good cook, using good products, since her children's health was at stake. On this point, the health manuals and the women's journals were in perfect agreement.

The choice of fresh and healthy products remained a major preoccupation, insofar as food expenditures still represented more than half the family budget.[1] How could one tell good flour from bad? Should one buy white bread or dark bread? How did one select a meat pâté? How did one distinguish cat from rabbit in a rabbit stew? These questions were repeated, along with the answers, in the manuals and practical guides that were published at the beginning of the last century and intended to educate and reeducate each generation of innocent laypeople.[2]

Consumers brought to the market their own sensory antennae, principally their noses and eyes. Did you want to know if the pâté was fresh? First examine the crust, which had to be very dry, with no fat leakage or crazing; then smell it to detect possible hints of staleness or mold; finally touch it. Always touch it, to confirm or deny what the eye or nose had spotted. Pass your finger over the gills of the fish to make sure they were not dyed red with eosin or cochineal. Take it in your hand to test its stiffness; detach a scale with the nail of your forefinger. The best guarantee was always to buy things as close to alive as possible. This was the case with snails, which received much attention. Buy them live to be sure that you were eating the mollusk. Otherwise, you ran the risk of buying shells stuffed with other substances: strips of lung, salt, flour, pieces of liver coated in butter and heavily seasoned.[3]

The informed buyer was always that paradoxical human who regressed to the animal state, sniffing, smelling, and feeling. So had the consumer's behavior changed at all over the last several centuries? A short comparative assessment indicates a few subtle shifts.

The consumers of 1900 remained zoophagous but only with regard to the smallest, least bloody animals: poultry, fish, snails. They knew the comparative anatomy of the cat and the rabbit—at least, they could distinguish them by the scapula. They could bear the sight of an unprepared calf's head. They identified fish whole and could still understand the power and the impact of certain fishmonger insults. In the Provençal markets, to be called a monkfish head, the ultimate insult, still had meaning and could unleash great female brawls. Since the buyer always wanted to be able to look a monkfish in the eye to judge its freshness, the honest fishmonger would never try to sell a headless monkfish, skinned and anonymously euphemized "monkfish tail."

If behavior at the fishmonger's stall remained the same, everything had changed at the butcher's. Rid of the stigmas attached to the status of knacker, the butcher had been a grocer like any other in France since 1863, a purveyor in whom one could have confidence. Confidence in one's supplier: that was a new phenomenon, a kind of relationship unknown (or unrecognized) in earlier centuries, when urban statutes conveyed a general distrust toward professionals in the business of supplying food. For the food trades, the era of official suspicion was over. The supplier was not anonymous. He was around the corner, and that proximity as well as his name, which he willingly displayed in his shop window, adding "house of confidence," reassured the buyer. It would not be wrong to consider this interpersonal relationship as a way of placating the consumer regarding the source of food products. It was an alternative to the direct control the zoophagous consumer once exercised over meat, no longer possible because the slaughterhouses were exiled far from the butcher shops and because, having become a sarcophage, the consumer wanted to know but not see. The shopkeeper in 1900 took on a very new function: adviser to his clientele.

The sarcophagy that characterized the end-of-the-century consumer was no doubt a factor in the acceptance of horse meat. The aversion to it in France had a long history. Eating horses was forbidden until 1815, and then it was done surreptitiously, as in the greasy spoons where students ate and rumor had it that the appearance of steaks on the menu was linked to an equine epizootic.[4]

In France, Isidore Geoffroy Saint-Hilaire made himself the promoter of horse meat. In Paris, the first horse meat butcheries were opened in 1867. That year, 2,152 horses, donkeys, and mules were slaughtered at the gates of the capital, and the number would grow before reaching its well-known and fitting peak in 1870: during the siege, Parisians consumed more than 65,000 horses. In 1878 "horse meat found its market in the working-class population, which began to seek it out and to understand that it was better to eat healthy and nourishing horse meat twice than to eat inferior-quality beef once. Indeed, the price of horse meat was never over half the price of beef."[5]

Repugnance gradually faded, and the appearance of the automobile had something to do with severing the old companionship between man and horse. It was true, nonetheless, that horse meat was never marbled or veined. Horses were not fattened for the slaughterhouse, and the quality of this lean meat, all by itself, was enough to lower the price. The provinces followed but not the rest of Europe. In Germany, Austria, Belgium, Spain, and Switzerland, the practice of the small butcher shops continued. From these free stalls (*Freibanke*), butchers sold third-grade meat or meat known to be diseased. Commerce was done completely legally and following health inspections. Slaughterhouse employees, under supervision by both the veterinary service and the city police, prepared the meat, sold raw or cooked in huge autoclaves. The free stalls did a good business and at a good price. Their clientele was the working class. The French, who had abolished the small butcher shops, established a kind of equivalent to these free stalls with the horse meat butcheries. The final taboos disappeared: one consumed horse meat voluntarily and cat meat involuntarily. Cat/rabbit fricassee and tomcat stew were the stuff of urban legend, but, in becoming a commonplace, they lost their power; no one was afraid of being poisoned anymore.[6] The liberated consumer was, at least theoretically, more calm.

Consumers also benefited from technological advances that allowed them to protect themselves against certain kinds of fraud, the pepper mill, for example: a practical little innovation with great beneficial effects. The last surviving ingredient from the great medieval passion for spices was pepper. For a long time, pepper was sold ground, but with no guarantee of purity. Analysis revealed a variety of additives, which were classified. First were the materials with no taste, like sand, potato starch, various kinds of flour, sweepings from the warehouse, powdered olive pits, nutshells, hazel nuts, almonds, various kinds of wood, dried-out oil cakes, various oil-producing grains, pulverized remains of bread or biscuits. But, with so many tasteless substances added, pepper no longer had any flavor. Thus it was "restored" with other substances to give it color and taste, like garden-variety peppers, malaguetta, laurel, black mustard....[7] The reassuring thing about this catalog of end-of-the-century additives is that it contains fairly edible or neutral substances, compared to those used in earlier centuries, when soot held a place of honor. There also existed an artificial pepper, made of basically natural ingredients: rye flour, Provençal pimento, and mustard flour.[8] The little invention made popular by the Peugeot Company would henceforth allow pepper to be bought whole, as peppercorns. The pepper mill was the first household device of its kind to become rapidly and widely adopted in all kitchens and among all classes.

It must be noted that, as the consumer's identity slowly transformed, he no longer used his sense organs in the same way. Henceforth, sight became the essential thing, more important than smell. That was because, to be informed, the consumer had to be able to read, as labeling became more and more prominent on both fresh and preserved products. With canned goods, the market was sterilized and deodorized, and henceforth one "ate with one's eyes," rather than one's nose. In the free stalls of German butcheries, labeling was required. It was also required on bottled wine and canned goods. But there was so little regulation regarding the information to be provided, labeling more often became an aesthetic issue. The label was a lovely image, a chromolithograph that served as advertisement for the brand. On the canned product was the trademark, and, for French products, the guarantee of a "natural" process using no green coloring—or no guarantee. Neither a manufacturing date nor an expiration date appeared. Wine bottle labels were supposed to protect the producer, not the consumer, and before 1919 it was not required that the wine actually originate in the region specified on its label.

It was in the United States that advertising techniques were most commonly used. Like Europeans, American consumers were hampered by the loss of direct contact with the product, which had allowed them to exercise their rights and responsibilities fully informed. Moreover, manufacturers understood this very well and used advertising on a grand scale to create an artificial bond between product and consumer. We may think of advertising as the instrument of choice for creating new consumer needs. But, in fact, the growing gap between producers and consumers made recourse to this new means of communication necessary.[9] In 1900 brand names such as Joseph Campbell, H. J. Heinz, P. D. Armour—note how they are private names and not anonymous—made themselves familiar through bright advertising displays and little labels where the name was often accompanied by epithets such as "better" and "superfine," as laudatory as they were void of guarantees.

Thus, far from regressing to their animal state, consumers underwent this slow ascension to the most intellectual plane, the one that would make them experts in consumer literacy. As compensation for the loss of direct contact with their food, meat in particular, they were offered two things: first, a new means of knowledge, through reading; and, second, a new kind of relationship with their supplier, who, knowing what they bought, served as guarantor of this mediatized information.

The North and the South

The Consumer, with a capital C, does not exist. When the food supply networks were extended, when production became industrialized, a whole array of differentiated behaviors appeared, different ways of ensuring the safety of one's daily food sources. Let us consider one example: fresh milk.

The Germans and Danish were undoubtedly the first to organize an industrialized network, running from the farm to the dairy, from the dairy to the milk wagon, and then to the urban market. In the city, milk was distributed through the shops but also, increasingly, through a service provided by the dairies: they delivered sterilized bottled milk to consumers early in the morning. In English urban culture, the milkman making his rounds earned an almost mythic place. Anglo-Saxon consumers regarded the milk chain as a convenient if unreliable system. They demanded sterilized, no longer just pasteurized, milk. They traded in their milk jugs for glass bottles, which were more hygienic.[10]

In southern Europe, the intervention of various intermediaries in the milk chain was considered a calamity more formidable that all the bacteria combined. Consumers remained faithful to the old guarantee that consisted of reducing the distance between the cow and the milk drinker. Naples in 1900 woke each morning to pleasant scenes of animal life. First, one heard and saw the cows with their bells circulating throughout the city, making their morning rounds distributing fresh milk. Then came the city goats. At each apartment building, the herd stopped and settled down to rest while the goatherd caught a goat and led it under a porch to milk it. "Sometimes the mistress of the house is suspicious, she does not believe in the goatherd's honesty nor the servant's; then the goatherd and the goat climb to the third floor, and a family council gathers on the landing to supervise the milking."[11] In other European cities, milk was bought in "very clean shops, white as marble," but the Neapolitans preferred this home delivery, alike in some way but also very different from English households.

Another solution was to go fetch the milk from the urban cow-sheds still present almost everywhere. That is what Lyons residents did under the Second Empire, stocking up on milk crammed into the city's thirty-eight cowsheds. The Health Board found no fault with their presence, and, if their closest neighbors complained about pollution, others demanded the cowsheds be retained "because the milk they find there seems to them more pure and better than milk coming from outside." In Montpellier at the beginning of the century, the cowherds were attentive to their cows. They rubbed the cow's teats and udders with manure. This facilitated milking, they said (and also facilitated infection, health workers responded). Then, they mixed the different milks: this homogenized the product delivered to consumers (but only one tubercular milk could render the whole mix dangerous, observed the health workers, who seethed: is it any wonder that out of ten samples tested, the municipal laboratory regularly found three or four of them infected!)[12]

As the milk market expanded, gaining new customers among healthy adults who consumed fresh milk in their morning coffee, the direct supply route became notoriously inadequate. But it survived, and Carpentras residents at the end of the century went at vespers to fetch milk from a stable at the edge of the city holding thirty Savoyard cows: "In a room called the dairy, one found jars full of milk and flies. I have never seen so many in my life [jars or flies? the author does not say]. The dairy workers had a young baby in a cradle, Savoy-style; interlaced straps kept it from moving, and it was covered with flies."[13] This mention of flies demonstrated a new sensitivity to them, in evidence almost everywhere.[14] But there, again, the concern for health varied widely.

The Raw and the Cooked

Protecting the eater always occurred by way of the kitchen, after the market. Boiling was always the first precautionary measure. Nevertheless, the century opened with this categorical gastronomic denouncement of boiled meat by Brillat-Savarin, the great professor of taste: "Boiled meat is healthy food, which promptly appeases hunger and is easily digested, but which, by itself, is not very nourishing, because, in the boiling, the meat has lost a portion of its animal juices." And he mocks the boiled meat eaters, in particular the "creatures of habit who eat it because their parents ate it and who submit to this practice unquestioningly and with the fervent hope that their children will imitate them."[15]

Boiled meat was attacked on a second front; by 1850 it was denounced for health reasons. It was the productivist health authorities who led the offensive, after having conducted the first inquiries into the food habits of specific groups. They had observed, for example, that the English workers hired to build the railroad from Paris to Rouen and fed on roasted meat completed a third more work than the French workers fed on a diet of boiled meat, soup, and dried vegetables. The Ivry foundries were forced to bring in English workers for the hardest work until that time when French workers, put on the same diet, were capable of accomplishing the same tasks.[16] From this, and armed with their new ideas about nutrition and convinced of meat's superiority, they concluded that the carnivorous English diet was better. In addition, preparation methods other than boiling, which deprived workers of nourishing juices, were superior. Dietetic and gastronomic fashions concurred: boiled meat was condemned, braised meat was recommended, and it was best to eat roasted meat rare, if possible, as Doctor Willich advised, "approaching raw."

And were Willich's contemporaries creatures of habit or innovators, ready to convert and to cook "green," or "blue," as it was later called? Certain upscale restaurants in Paris or Lyons served raw beef filet, chopped fine and seasoned with shallots. They called this dish *filet à la Hottentote*. This English fashion irritated more than one Frenchman, such as Charles Fourier, who criticized the new style of eating "meat half-raw, with forks curved backwards and impossible to use."[17]

The vast majority of French consumed dishes very different from those concocted by Parisian gastronomy. Country cuisine remained faithful to its traditional cooking method, to its national *pot-au-feu* as it was celebrated in 1847: "The national *pot-au-feu* is the foundation of domestic health in France, around which the family gathers, which supports it from within, which strengthens the ties, and which is a source not only of the vigor and energy essential to work but also of the order, the economy, the legitimate affections, and the morality of the working classes."[18]

Bizet was a veterinarian. Raspail was a doctor, and he elaborated on the moral and dietary usefulness of the *pot-au-feu* for workers in the big cities who, leaving the prisons of their workshops, had to be saved from falling into the "abyss of the taverns." "Let the worker know that he is never so well fed as within his own family; what will he find at the bars on Sunday and Monday except quarrels and vile indigestion?" This much was understood: only a harmonious home and good cooking could divert the worker from the evil temptations of the cabaret.[19] French health discourse was quick to moralize, and the *pot-au-feu* found itself invested with extra-alimentary values. It became a symbol of the model of the middle-class home and domestic roles that republican ideology tried to transmit to the working classes. Coincidentally, it guaranteed healthy meals that centered around the *pot-au-feu* made with beef in the north and mutton in the south, boiled slowly for three to four hours, ample time to destroy all the germs with which the meat could be infected. In the French countryside, salted pork was preferred to beef or mutton, the Revolution's great achievement being the end of the salt tax. In the Scottish countryside, ham was smoked over coal, which was more risky.[20] But a salted ham was rarely eaten raw; it passed from the salting tub to the smokehouse to the cooking pot before appearing on the dinner plate.

National food cultures engendered different fears. Germany feared trichinosis and botulism, two evils—and two words—for a long time unknown among the French.

Trichinosis in pigs, a parasitosis transmissible to humans, is fatal. When inspections using the microscope were begun in the slaughterhouses, it was discovered that, in Gotha, 1 pig out of 800 was trichinous, in Halle, 1 out of 300, in Rostock, 1 out of 340, and, in Stockholm, 1 out of 266. No statistics of this kind existed in France, where the importation of pigs from across the Rhine was prohibited. It was especially during the 1865–1866 epidemic that trichinosis was carefully studied and described. Its relative frequency in northern Germany and its rarity in France raised questions. Experts concluded that, in France, pork was eaten very well cooked, which killed the parasites, whereas, in Germany, the opposite was the rule. German peasants had pinker, fatter, and better-tended pigs. They ate the meat pink at the center or in the form of sausages prepared with the intestines, highly subject to spreading infection.[21]

It seems very likely that the dietary backwardness of rural France protected it from serious parasitoses. Of course, French pigs, especially those in the Massif central, continued to be infected with cysticercus, but tapeworms were not fatal. And also the larva of single worms could survive neither salting nor prolonged cooking. It was the city dwellers who became increasingly plagued with parasites. Thus it was discovered that beef cattle were also carriers of tapeworm and that the new practice of eating beef rare favored parasitosis. In Montpellier, all or nearly all cattle imported from the Upper Pyrenees were suspected of carrying tapeworm; if only they were subject to the *langueyage*, like the pigs! But, no, the slaughterhouse inspector, a retired mason or farmer, was incapable of detecting leprous animals, and they entered the food circuit.[22]

The French also seemed to escape botulism. The first cases (or, rather, the first attested cases) were detected in southern Germany in 1720. In the early nineteenth century, this paralyzing toxicosis was linked to the consumption of sausages and salt meat. In 1895 the toxin was isolated; a most virulent poison in a raw ham killed ten people.[23] *Botulus* is the Latin name for sausage, and so this poison was called botulism. Botulism made its entry into France later. The word can be found in health publications from the early 1900s.[24] One study shows that botulism hit Wurtemberg the hardest: 920 cases, with 366 deaths, between 1735 and 1874; 65 in Prussia, 688 in the rest of Germany. In France, where records of the disease date from 1875, we find 21 cases, only 3 of them mortal, between 1875 and 1924.[25]

Faced with the danger of trichinosis, the reaction of public authorities in France was swift and decisive. In 1878 the only known epidemic in the national territory struck, in Crépy-en-Valois. That same year, the United States made public some alarming statistics: 8 percent of the pigs slaughtered in Chicago were trichinous. Without hesitating, France prohibited all importation of pigs from America or across the Rhine. Was this measure taken strictly for health protection reasons? As far as American pigs were concerned, health authorities could easily demonstrate that the Crépy epidemic originated at home and that American meats had never threatened health in the least on the

Continent. At the end of their transatlantic voyage, any possible trichina were dead or nearly so and hardly capable of causing the slightest infection.

For the specialists, vigilance regarding suspect meat did not involve government measures but rather precaution on the part of the family or individual. It was more effective to alert the housewife than the customs officer. Their repeated warnings led to an about-face in public opinion in the last third of the century. A curse on meats eaten rare and bloody!

Pasteur and the discovery of microbes accelerated the return to boiled meat. This was not a huge leap backward to the Middle Ages. Henceforth, one cooked meat thoroughly for good reasons and used otherwise more sophisticated methods. Cook! Eliminate the parasites and microbes! Those were the new marching orders.[26] Above all, boil, because all methods of cooking were not equal, and only boiling assured the complete destruction of germs. One no longer used the copper cooking pot suspended over the hearth but materials such as tinplate and fuels that offered servants and housewives incomparable opportunities for controlling the cooking process. Charged with protecting herself and her family, the housewife hunted down the little beasts and killed the microbes wielding the weapon of heat, 75 degrees Celsius for tuberculosis or anthrax, 50 degrees for trichinosis or tapeworm, 101 degrees for milk, according to the advice of health authorities, who were confident and reassuring.[27]

There were a few excesses—which the discovery of vitamins after 1912 would expose—and a few illusions. Lamentably, very widespread public opinion held that cooking acted to purify anything unhealthy, no matter what the cause: putrefaction, animal disease, chemical poisoning.[28] What is more, the lessons of Pasteur (who died in 1895) were far from being thoroughly assimilated: kitchen hygiene left much to be desired, even though a new chapter on domestic cleanliness was added to the health manuals. If the necessity of cooking took hold quickly in popular thinking and practices—as another version of the myth of lustral water and purifying fire—the microbe was difficult to understand and the salmonella bacterium unknown. Stories of mishaps abounded, involving individuals or families. There was talk of poisoning, but much more evidence was needed to warrant an epidemiological inquiry. The Cholet wedding feast was one example among hundreds. In 1913 a wedding feast was served in Cholet, with all the safeguards that a family-prepared meal represented. For dessert, the guests enjoyed *crème anglaise*, which, despite its name, was a classic dish throughout the French countryside and a good example of autoconsumption. The dish required only products from the farm: milk and eggs. But the cook was a carrier of salmonella: a total of forty people were poisoned, and ten of them died.[29]

Poisonings and domestics accidents were high in number. No doubt, they even constituted the majority of food pathologies. But, to prove that, we must have figures. First of all, such incidents were hard to count. Second, they were hardly publicized. Serious mishaps hidden behind the veil of family cooking did not become affairs of state. When French newspapers discovered botulism in 1900, the cases they denounced loudest were those involving greenish sausages rotting in the sun at open-air fairs and markets.[30] Here, the press served as a mirror for the general attitude. The perception of risk was relative: there was less fear about risks that were actually more likely (the logic of probability running counter to intuition) than those less likely but easier to imagine. Thus one overlooked the risks represented by asparagus canned at home and, correlatively, exaggerated those linked to a store-bought can of peas or, worse, corned beef made in the USA. These cognitive illusions were characteristic of the food fears at the end of the century.

Industrialization Anxieties

If the end-of-the-century consumer had found himself only facing the problems of making choices at his local market and taking precautions in his kitchen, his behavior would not have changed drastically. But industry had created an impersonal market where one no longer came face-to-face with one's food. The consumer lost his bearings, and his growing freedom of choice resulted primarily in perplexity. One popular image shows a woman consulting her family doctor: "But honestly, Doctor, in our cities today, one no longer knows what one is eating!"[31] That idea was common at the end of the century and popularized by Epinal prints. But there were other questions that raised a kind of unspoken anxiety, if not fear.

In analyzing the industrial food revolution, the anthropologist Jack Goody distinguished four components: the rise of canned food; mechanization; shipping; and innovations in retail sales. Let us put aside for the moment the changes in retail commerce, which appeared only after 1914, and mechanization, which was neutral from the perspective of consumer expectations. That leaves two anxiety-producing factors: canned food and shipping.

The shipping revolution expressed itself through a lengthening of the supply routes at the global level. Pasteur declared to Napoleon III what a shame it was "to see meat sold in Europe at an exorbitant price, while, in Buenos Aires, people had more than they knew what to do with." Ten years later, in 1876, the first refrigerated freighter returned to Rouen with its cargo of 21,000 kilos of Argentine beef. That imbalance was being corrected, thanks to new cooling techniques. Consumers were torn between their admiration for the miracle of cold that allowed food reserves to be kept and used for a much longer time and their nervousness about products that had traveled such a long distance.[32] The refrigeration networks, like the canning factories, extended the supply circuits beyond measure and organized food exchanges at the global level. At the same time that the food network expanded, it became fragmented, and the circuit leading from producer to consumer no longer included just one intermediary—the grocer—but many, production itself dividing into an agricultural phase and a phase of industrial transformation. This hypercomplex global market was an impersonal market in which the consumer participated, but without mastery, or even comprehension, of it.

By the end of the century, domestic manuals had a whole new chapter added to them: how to choose canned foods. The array of food products available to the shopping housewife had expanded considerably with the success of the canning industry. The heroes of nineteenth-century food history in France were not Parmentier or Geoffroy Saint-Hilaire but Appert, his nephew Chevallier-Appert, and Pasteur. Under the Empire, at his home in Massy, Nicolas Appert had perfected the canning process, empirically at least: "M. Appert discovered the art of fixing the seasons. For him, the spring, the summer, and the fall come in bottles, like those delicate plants the gardener protects under a glass dome against the seasons' bad weather."[33]

Appert's method was still very much a cottage industry. Quasi-alchemical in its use of the double boiler, it was perfected with two innovations. The soldered tin can was invented in England in 1847. The first ones were made by hand, but a machine was then devised that could mass-produce them, and another to seal them hermetically. The metal can replaced Nicolas's little bottles and jars. In 1852 Chevallier-Appert used the autoclave, raising the temperature and especially succeeding in controlling it by means of a pressure gauge. In the second half of the century, when cottage industry methods evolved into industrial techniques, canned food entered the industrial age.

That canning eliminated dangers was well known, but not why, until Pasteur established the scientific grounds that allowed Appert's method to be interpreted correctly. Pasteur made it clear that the role of heat was not to eliminate oxygen from the small metal cans but to destroy bacterial germs. The vocabulary then changed, and one no longer spoke of *appertisation* but of *stérilisation*, that marvelous process that stabilized food without altering it.

Canned food had technically been invented to feed Napoleon's armies. Its success was assured by the California gold rush, and Californians were the first to use it on a regular basis. By the time of the American Civil War, it had been completely perfected, feeding, in particular, the victorious Northern troops. This flip-flopping from one continent to the other is not insignificant. It shows how canned foods fared, facing different food cultures, and how they were integrated more or less completely.

In France, food sealed in little tin cans prompted many prejudices. The word itself, *conserve*, had a hard time penetrating French thinking and language. Emile Littré's 1877 dictionary gave three meanings for the word:

1. A kind of jam made of plant substances and sugar.
2. A pharmaceutical term.
3. A food substance preserved in tin cans or bottles without air.

In defining *conserve*, Littré remained closer to Olivier de Serres than to Appert. His reservations were completely quantifiable.

The French canning industry was Europe's first, beginning in 1870, and it exported 85 percent of its production. And French canning still mainly produced sardines packed in oil, that is, an already very familiar product and canning method. Alexandre Dumas recognized that a good broth could be made from Baron von Liebig's extract of beef, but that was one of the rare concessions high French cooking made to the food industry, restaurants discovering a new gastronomic legitimacy in officially turning their backs on canned goods.[34] In the United States, Germany, and Switzerland, the cans that sold best contained a new product, condensed milk. Within France, the market was flat. "The same cans that allow legionnaires to advance in the desert and arctic explorers to surmount the glaciers cannot guarantee victory on the domestic front among consumers," said Capatti.[35]

Aside from travelers, the first groups to try canned foods were soldiers and high school students, captive consumers of collective cooking. French high schools matched pedagogical uniformity with dietary monotony. Friday was fish and canned vegetables. Saturday, for a special treat, was roast beef and canned vegetables.[36] The noncaptive consumer seemed torn between an attraction for these long-lasting products that allowed one to disregard the seasons and a repulsion based on not knowing what was in there. There were some health concerns, because even though scientists praised their remarkably hygienic packaging, a commission was created in 1899 to study the frequent cases of "dry colic" in the army, the principal user of these canned goods, leading to the assumption that perhaps health quality was not the strong suit of such products. In practical handbooks in France, under the heading "how to chose canned goods," the answer was immediate: above all, reject cans that have swollen; the ones with bulging tops indicate possible fermentation. For domestic canning, on the other hand, preparation methods were given, but no precautions regarding consuming the canned products.[37] It is remarkable how distrust for canned goods abated and even disappeared completely as soon as it was a matter of domestic preparation.[38] This paradoxical attitude reflects the psychological themes that we have already examined: home canning was transparent, doubly transparent since the canning jar hid nothing of the contents, the source of which, furthermore, was known. Industrial canning was not to be trusted, since one did not know when or where or with what the cans had been filled. Basically, the ideal canned food was the one that allowed the seasons to be fixed, but with products from one's orchard or vegetable garden. We can recognize here another version of the autoconsumption myth, totally reassuring to the consumer. After the war, the gastronomic critic Curnonsky analyzed this ambivalence in terms of political labels. The Right favored a traditional wood-cooked cuisine, slow cooking, and products from the garden or the market. The Left preferred a quick and simple cuisine, an omelette and a slice of ham. The Left had nothing against canned foods and happily maintained that canned green beans were as good as fresh ones.[39]

The Return to Health Food

Canned goods caused mixed feelings. Eating out of season was a great dream. But, as soon as this dream became a reality, it led to a backlash. One must eat in season, return to nature, respect the food calendar: that was the new leitmotif at the end of the century. Industrialized eating unleashed the first waves of nostalgia for a rural, homemade world, then in decline. Nothing showed this better than the failure of margarine. Margarine was a new product launched according to the old French methods for introducing new products like the potato or *appertisation*. First, the enlightened authority (here, Napoleon III) announced a competition on the old theme: how to provide the working classes with a less expensive, substitute food; this time, it was a matter of replacing butter. Second, the chemist discovered the formula. In 1869 his name was Hippolyte Mège-Mouriès. Mège christened his product *beurre économique*. Butter, ha! The name was rejected and changed to *margarine*, "like a pearl," from the Greek *margaritas*. Like pearls before swine, rather, because, third, the public resisted, roundly rejecting these "pearls" they considered little better than pig feed.

These prejudices were echoed in the United States through the "butterine" affair. In 1886 the United States Congress discussed the status of butterine. The shortening industry, around Chicago, made butterine, which was not butter, though it looked like it, or margarine, since the margarine patent was French. Two lobbies opposed each other in the debate, one for milk producers anxious to defend dairy products and one for the industry, which, relying on scientific research and mobilizing a certain number of chemists on its behalf, intended to demonstrate not only that butterine was as reliable as butter but that it was clearly of higher quality, because of its consistent composition and the many inspections it underwent. Within Congress, the friends of butter were more numerous than those of margarine, and they defended butter with a battery of arguments, every one of them referring back to the consumer, to the consumer's tastes and preferences, as well as his incapacities. The consumer, they said, could no longer judge on appearances and distinguish real butter from butterine, especially if butterine was colored yellow, imitating butter, as the manufacturers wanted. "The four senses that God gave man are totally misled," and "the family dinner table is not equipped with microscopes or reagents for chemical analysis." This argument, one of the few we have seen that challenges the noninterventionist line, was enthusiastically received, but the one that persuaded the legislators sounded the theme of the superiority of natural things.[40]

"The consumer hears the products of a French patent praised within these walls, but what he wants are the products of God's patents, spring water, quality fats, herds roaming free."[41] The defense conjured two utopias, one of farm products and one of rural America, the farm democracy that Jefferson wanted, which was a bankrupt myth in 1886, when American industry dominated, alone producing goods more than English and German manufacturers combined. A moderate tax was imposed on the sale of margarine. As in France, butter sellers obtained a prohibition on the use of the word "butter" for margarine.

You can forbid the use of a name, but you cannot prevent consumption. Less neophobic than European eaters, Anglo-Saxons readily accepted products coming from the agricultural food industry, including butterine. The working classes were won over by its low price, and, according to Jack London, bread with margarine and a cup of tea was the basic meal of the London poor. Whereas the French saw it as a bad substitute for butter, Americans considered it a substitute for animal fat, the advantage being that the housewife did not have to melt the grease, a time-consuming chore. Like this synthetic product, other chemical products entered American kitchens: baking powder, vanilla sugar, powdered gelatin, all things greatly appreciated by the American housewife in the name of a new value: saving time. She no longer had to boil calves' hooves to obtain gelatin. Making pastries took her less time. She no longer turned up her nose at canned or ready-to-eat foods: pickles, tomato soup, ketchup.[42] This domestic modernism helped to construct what was called "the new woman."

The new woman of 1900 was American and belonged to the upper middle class, and she tended to limit her household tasks. Henceforth she gave up making soap, pickles, cheese, and homebrewed beer. At the same time in the Nivernais countryside, the family oven gave way to the bakery oven, and women were relieved of the task of making bread at home. Saving time, however, was not the highest priority for the model woman as conceived and conveyed by the press and advertising. The woman's highest priority was the domestic sphere. To be a good mother, the housewife had to be an informed dietician. Health was very much the rising value, particularly in America at the end of the century.

What developed there was a kind of food counterculture, based on values completely different from the hedonistic and gastronomic perspectives of the Old World. The trend was toward temperance, even vegetarianism. The new consumer models were expressed in the form of slogans: pure food, natural products, health food. Characteristically, this health trend did not involve doctors in any important way, but health "authorities" of all stripes, an informal group made up first of all of moralists, supported by nutritionists and specialists in home economics. The pervading ideas about diet fell within programs of moral reform, based on a puritan revival. One spoke of reforms, but these reforms began in the kitchen. One spoke of crusades against alcohol or altered products, led by men who were both charismatic opinion makers and well-informed businessmen. At the turn of the century, the movement in vogue was called the "new nutrition."

The word "nutrition" can be deceptive. In fact, this nutrition was supposed to be something closer to the Greek *diaíata* of Hippocrates; behind a way of eating, it concealed a whole style of life. The new nutrition crusade aimed in particular at the working class, immigrants who were to be freed from their poverty and protected from alcoholism by being inculcated with a few simple ideas: spending less money on food, for example, by learning the chemical equivalences between beans and meat. This knowledge was easy to attain through a comparative chart of calories or, even more simply, through a two-part food list, a positive list of foods that were good for you, a blacklist of foods that were forbidden. It was as though the graphically eloquent figure of the food pyramid had not yet been invented. Among the foods emblematic of good health were natural products like grains, milk, and spinach. Among those to avoid were meat, alcohol, and sugar. "Unfortunately, having come to America in hopes of eating not beans but beef, most members of the working class did not rise to the bait."[43]

On the other hand, the new nutrition had a considerable impact on the middle classes. Let us consider in particular the crusade promoting grains. This was the most successful of them, since it would radically change American breakfast habits, before changing the morning routines of Europeans as well. In 1863 one Doctor Jackson created granola, based on whole wheat. But the greatest success belonged to "Doctor" John Harvey Kellogg, an Adventist preacher and dietician who counted among his clients the future U.S. president, Theodore Roosevelt. Kellogg advocated pure foods, from a very impure ideological perspective, since he freely mixed religious considerations and health concerns. One should eat what was healthy but also what was closest to the divine creation, what most respected the work of the Creator. The act of eating was not to be considered "a pastime, a diversion, or a pleasure."[44]

In 1895 Doctor Kellogg introduced to the market ready-to-eat "corn flakes." He recommended abandoning the invigorating breakfast based on pork products, eggs, and beer for cereal and milk. In 1911, when the role of vitamin C was discovered, a glass of canned Florida orange juice was added to this repast, perfecting the model of the ideal breakfast. Corn flakes could be replaced with other cereals, such as the German doctor Bircher-Brenner's *muesli*. On the other side of the Atlantic, it was, in fact, in Germany that nutrition was given the same amount of attention. There, vigilance regarding food followed different, already proven paths. Doctors and nutritionists led the movement, following in the steps of the great Justus von Liebig. Books were rediscovered, like the one by Doctor Hufeland, the first doctor to the king of Prussia, published in Berlin in 1800, *Macrobiotics; or, The Art of Prolonging Human Life*. With macrobiotics, new health habits were grafted to the old. At the end of the century, the health dimension of eating was stressed on both sides of the Atlantic by the two countries that led all others in economic development, where the horn of plenty seemed to pour out its edible riches. This was no simple coincidence.

Is it to push the paradox too far to say that attention to health was one result of the food revolution? The food revolution had recognized beneficial effects. Workers were better nourished. Their canned vegetables and milk and their fresh meat sometimes came from far away, from Chicago, which, beginning in the 1870s and 1880s, was able to supply all the states, thanks to trains or boats equipped with refrigerated compartments. American historians stress the role of increased meat rations in the general improvement in health and well-being. Their English counterparts emphasize increased consumption of sugar, evident in all levels of society. Sugar, drunk in tea or eaten in jam, provided the least expensive source of energy for workers.[45] Refined sugar from the English West Indies became an essential part of the British working-class diet. Sugar or meat, sugar and meat, whatever the case, the good effects were recognized, measurable in increased human height or the body's more vigorous and successful struggles against infectious diseases. At the same time that vaccines became increasingly numerous and effective, omnipotent, victorious epidemiological medicine permitted a return to nutritionism. Now that one knew how to defeat the plague or cholera, now that microbes were being exterminated and most diseases were classified as infectious and therefore avoidable, the health stakes shifted, and interest in food as an essential risk factor mounted.[46]

Beyond the threshold of satiation, the well-nourished can invest either in anxieties about health or in gastronomic refinement. A French cook, Mademoiselle Léotine, noted in 1856 that people were very hesitant about changing their food habits and that they were satisfied simply with having full stomachs. Most people have only a very vague idea about the healthy and the unhealthy, she said, and that was why "half the population was sick."[47] The behavior of a well-fed middle class was not the same in Lyons, Bremen, and Buffalo, a sign that economic conditions were not the determining factor. What mattered was the cultural climate. Who will we invite to dinner this evening? This was the most frequently asked question in the discourse of fashionable French society. What will we eat for dinner this evening? That was the question increasingly posed among the middle classes in Buffalo or Hamburg. Two ways of thinking became clear, establishing what in France was called the law of the twos's: *sécurité et santé*, safety and health, in Anglo-Saxon countries; *saveur et sociabilité*, taste and sociability, elsewhere. Of course, we must not understand this law to be rigid or believe that cultural logic dictated actual behavior. All eating is universal, torn as all eaters are between contradictory values. Seated at the dining table, the French middle class awaited pleasures and delicacies, but the tablecloth was cluttered with Bland, Blancard, and Vallet pill bottles, containing the iron indispensable to the anemic daughter, the mother's remedy for stomach cramps, and the father's heart murmur medicine.[48]

The only society to adopt the slogan "good for your health" and to enter en masse into the era of "delibidinized" food, as an American psychoanalyst called it, was American society. Better fed, at a better price, the American middle classes in 1900 seemed free of an old worry: tomorrow's bread was no longer an obsession; the gleaming stacks of canned goods in the pantries were reassuring. Satiated, sure about the quantity and consistency of their food supply, these consumers, the children of plenty, directed their attention and their vigilance henceforth toward quality. The United States had become the dominant agroindustrial power. In 1906 that was where the first modern food crisis struck.

The Poisoners of Chicago

Chicago 1900: a mushroom town of more than a million inhabitants, the city of butchers and the city of trusts, in particular, the beef trust, built by Philip Armour around beef by-products and canning—the famous "corned beef."

It was there that Upton Sinclair conceived *The Jungle*. A young journalist, Sinclair was twenty-six years old when the editor-in-chief of *McLure's* sent him to investigate working conditions in the Chicago slaughterhouses. Sinclair was a muckraker, as Theodore Roosevelt called those investigative journalists who made it their duty and profession to denounce American big business scandals and corruption, sometimes in socialist, sometimes in puritan tones. In October 1904 Sinclair settled into Chicago and began his investigation. Seven weeks later, his work was complete, and it had taken the form of a novel. It was an apprenticeship novel, in which the reader follows the destiny of an exemplary hero, Jurgis. Jurgis is a Lithuanian immigrant. He discovers America, the world of work "scientifically organized" according to the principles of Taylor, and his "jungle." He is physically afflicted by becoming disabled, he experiences unemployment and alcoholism, he watches his wife become a prostitute and then die. From this descent into hell, redemption follows with Jurgis discovering proletarian solidarity. This novel with a theme was first of all a report. By denouncing the working conditions in the Chicago slaughterhouses and the big agroindustrial factories connected to them, Sinclair also denounced the unhealthy production conditions. He first gives the reader a guided tour of the production lines for stripping cattle and pig carcasses. It is a cold description, without concession, meant to move the heart of the sarcophage, spiced with contemporary scientific considerations on ptomaine (which did not exist) and Koch's bacillus, the extreme danger of which had just been discovered. Along the way, Sinclair notes the flawed screening process for cattle diseases, since only animals to be exported were subject to inspections, responding to the protectionist standards of Europe:

The people of Chicago saw the government inspectors in Packingtown, and they all took that to mean that they were protected from diseased meat; they did not understand that these hundred and sixty-three inspectors had been appointed at the request of the packers, and that they were paid by the United States government to certify that all the diseased meat was kept in the State. They had no authority beyond that; for the inspection of meat to be sold in the city and State the whole force in Packingtown consisted of three henchmen of the local political machine! And shortly afterward one of these, a physician, made the discovery that the carcasses of steers which had been condemned as tubercular by the government inspectors, and which therefore contained ptomaines, which are deadly poisons, were left upon an open platform and carted away to be sold in the city; and so he insisted that these carcasses be treated with an injection of kerosene—and was ordered to resign the same week!"[49]

The text continues:

> It seemed that they must have agencies all over the country, to
> hunt out old and crippled and diseased cattle to be canned. There
> were cattle which had been fed on "whisky-malt," the refuse of
> the breweries, and had become what the men called "steerly"—
> which means covered with boils. It was a nasty job killing these,
> for when you plunged your knife into them they would burst
> and splash foul-smelling stuff into your face; and when a man's
> sleeves were smeared with blood, and his hands steeped in it, how
> was he ever to wipe his face, or to clear his eyes so that he could
> see? It was stuff such as this that made the "embalmed beef" that
> had killed several times as many United States soldiers as all the
> bullets of the Spaniards.[50]

The description of work accidents is the highlight of the report:

> Worst of any, however, were the fertilizer-men, and those who
> served in the cooking rooms. These people could not be shown
> to the visitor, for the odour of a fertilizer-man would scare any
> ordinary visitor at a hundred yards; and as for the other men, who
> worked in tank rooms full of steam, and in some of which there
> were open vats near the level of the floor, their peculiar trouble
> was that they fell into the vats; and when they were fished out,
> there was never enough of them left to be worth exhibiting—
> sometimes they'd be overlooked for days, till all but the bones of
> them had gone to the world as Durham's Pure Leaf Lard![51]

The denunciation began with Taylorism and ended with cannibalism. Sinclair's method of sounding the alarm veered radically from
scientific methods. He went far beyond the objective account—what
he had really seen—to report on what was said ("Jurgis heard of these
things little by little, in the gossip of those who were obliged to perpe-
trate them.");[52] he validated oral traditions and gave them more credibility and dignity than mere rumors by committing them to print.
Far from quelling the rumors, the sensational press (or novel) offered
them unprecedented publicity and unexpected circulation. Published
in February 1906, The Jungle became the year's best seller. The United
States experienced this whole affair as a national crisis and not as
a simple news item. Later, Sinclair would claim to be delighted by
the reaction of readers, delighted but astonished. He had meant to
denounce dangerous working conditions; the outraged reader had

read and perceived something else: the dangers of eating industrial products, with the danger of involuntary cannibalism as an added bonus! "I had aimed at the heart, and I touched the stomach of the nation."

Since it was immediately translated into seventeen languages, the novel's impact extended beyond American boundaries. The food crisis spread through the media in an unprecedented fashion, calling into play all channels of communication, from newspapers to the silent film. The Chicago scandals nauseated the entire world, even if the entire world did not eat corned beef.[53] Germany demanded a prohibition on importing American canned goods. In the United States, meat sales were cut in half under the combined effect of the consumer's disgust and boycott. Sinclair was received at the White House by Theodore Roosevelt. An inquiry was ordered, and the accuracy of Sinclair's criticisms acknowledged. The following year, a seminal law, the Pure Food and Drug Act, was passed.

The Jungle marked the entrance on the food fears stage of three new actors: the press, the consumer, and the state—or, rather, three old actors, called on to play new roles.

Toward a New Food Order

1900: Japanese law against new substances present in foods; August 1905: French law regarding fraud;[54] December 1905: federal Swiss law; 1906: federal American law, Pure Food and Drug Act; 1906: French ministerial circular rendering health inspections in all slaughterhouses mandatory. There they were, not the first laws enacted on the national level—there were precedents—but a wave of legislative texts that still form the basis of consumer law in the countries concerned. They testified to a new role for the state, more deeply involved in safety. The United States led the way. To respond to the food crisis unleashed by Sinclair's revelations, the law of 1906 provided for veterinarian inspections of meat at the federal level. But, even more significantly, it addressed labeling. Labeling was accepted as the necessary remedy, requiring legislative intervention. It hardly went beyond that. No subsequent quality control was provided. If the consumer noticed that a product did not conform to its label, it was up to him to bring the case to justice.

Theoretically, two approaches were conceivable: a minimalist approach that stressed the individual's responsibility and considered the government's primary role to be one of collecting, verifying, and directing the proper information to the consumer, and an interventionist approach that proposed to control not only information but also the quality of food products, by intervening in the market both before and after production. In fact, it was the minimalist option that inspired the majority of this legislative activity, and that was true, depending on the particular state, for scientific, philosophical, or political reasons. Scientifically, in the absence of absolute proof, a state balked at intervention that prohibited certain substances. Philosophically, liberalism and faith in the goodness of free market laws argued for maintaining the consumer's free choice, even while admitting that, for this choice to be rational, it was still necessary that he be informed. Thus inspection took place a priori, not a posteriori; health remained an individual affair.

The political reasons were those of the interests represented in every parliamentary body. In general, they were those of the producers. The context in which the French parliament voted on the 1905 law is significant. France was in the midst of an acute viticultural crisis. Ravaged by phylloxera, the vineyards of southern France had left the winegrowers without resources, even as the market was flooded with adulterated and even totally artificial wines, which the state could not prevent, lacking adequate legislative tools. It was the revolt of the Languedoc winegrowers that pushed the French parliament to act. Article 3 of the law henceforth permitted the state to intervene and to penalize adulterations, for wine as for all other foodstuffs. Within this context, the consumer's status was marginal. Only article 4 of the French law cited it, evoking the necessity of protecting public health. By forbidding alterations and adulterations, the law primarily protected the producers of sound, pure products. These were only the first legislative steps, the first hesitant steps toward the welfare state.

The consumer made his entrance on stage through a little back door. To tell the truth, little is known about his expectations at the beginning of the century. Was he one of the faithful, someone who trusted blindly in his supplier, because the product was beyond him? Was he a welfare proponent, expecting everything from the state? Only one thing was certain: the dream of the direct food route was definitively dead. The twentieth-century eater entered into the reign of a different kind of short circuit. He left everything to intermediaries who, in his name and for his good, would inform him, inspect his food for him, and let him know without seeing.

CONCLUSION

Food fear is a silent fear. Nevertheless, it is not mute. If people in the past were unable to explain their feelings of insecurity, they knew how to express them. Still, it is very difficult to uncover those fears before the turning point in 1870–1900 when the press began to serve as both relay station and echo chamber, circulating and amplifying them. Then, they appeared in the contemporary form of crises or of scandals. The historian is sorely tempted to agree with Balzac in *Les Illusions perdues* that "if the press did not exist, it would be necessary to invent it." Because before newspapers took over the affairs of food, it is incredibly difficult to find recorded evidence aside from isolated, scattered, indirect examples on the scale of fears that were sporadic and local, that is, limited in time and space. To grasp them, one must probe many a corpus, be attuned to the slightest sound, pinpoint in the records those little facts that past historians neglected or considered insignificant, like that ordinance from the secretary of the State of Avignon, dated July 7, 1768. It is not insignificant, this ordinance, because it tells us that each spring most of the inhabitants fed their dead silkworms to their pigs, ducks, and chickens and the fish in their fishponds and that the vice-legate was worried because "that could cause grave illnesses in those who ate the flesh of said animals." And as the political authority here echoes the rising concerns of the consulates in many rural communities, we can be sure that this nervousness over the feeding of animals was widespread. On the other hand, we may wonder if the express inhibitions decreed on this occasion against recycling the wastes of silkworm breeding into animal feed

❋

had the slightest effect. People tend to act against the risk and, at the same time, live with the fear.

From a disorganized collection, one can obtain a spasmodic history, the fruit of a provisional inventory representative of who-knows-what in relation to the whole ungraspable reality. That is the first frustration. But it is not the only one. The other frustration comes from struggling hard to see the rise and fall of a fear, in other words, to grasp fully its historicity. When, how, out of what is a fear born? These remain largely unresolved questions. Strictly speaking, a fear is not born; it emerges, it develops within what we call official forums: the Academy, the University, the Medical Society, the Health Conference. We may imagine that these official forums take over for other official forums where public opinion is expressed more directly. But perhaps we are wrong, as in the case of yeasted bread, in which the fear constantly oscillated between these two theaters, where the various means of communication seemed to function almost simultaneously. At the other end of the process, the outcome is just as difficult to grasp. It is unusual for a fear to subside suddenly and perceptibly following an inquiry or an authoritative report. Fears are not put to death by decrees, even decrees issued by the university. For a long time, the fear of potatoes survived the decree issued by the University of Paris declaring them good to eat. In the queen's bread affair, the authority of the final judgment silenced some of the debate, but it did not exactly close it. Between their explicit ends and their implicit ends, fears live a hushed, stifled life. Their implicit end arrives with the disappearance of the food practice in question. But since food practices are differentiated socially and geographically, the same fear can die out here and survive there. For example, we may reasonably assume that the fear of rye bread and of yeasted bread disappeared in the cities in the nineteenth century—for conflicting reasons—but that it survived, vague and sporadic, in rural areas devoted to dark bread and to sourdough. Every fear has its own movement, sometimes a very complex one, which it has been interesting to follow.

The fears reported on here harbor among themselves secret affinities. Beyond individual fears, there is fear itself, that is, that feeling of food insecurity that is expressed and understood in ways sometimes very close to ours, often very different. Each historical constellation being unique, it is never completely the same and never completely different. It is neither eternal nor universal. It varies in time according to three parameters.

The first one is hunger, the fear of shortages, far more strong and more obsessive. The two anxieties, over quality and quantity, coexist in a configuration that is symmetrical to today's. At present, all potential food fears revolve around the question of health quality. But when a crisis threatens, when a war looms (Suez, the Gulf War), we see the resurgence of lines, consumers stocking up, places where rumors grow loud and fears spread. The empty shelf syndrome observed in these cases is the most current expression of the old food stress. Fear of unhealthy foods expresses itself in periods of calm, in good food times, when the daily food ration seems guaranteed by the coming seasons. During the long reign of Louis XIV, marked by repeated periods of scarcity and famine, the fears of the governing and the governed with regard to white bread surfaced in times of good grain harvests. When shortages arose, bringing along their squalid foods, those fears faded. Thus base foods were deplored but described as the foods of necessity. Fear regarding quantity and fear regarding quality vary roughly in inverse correlation, but the fear of scarcity is primary. Parmentier can easily be presented as an innovator, a pioneer in the introduction of the potato, but he placed himself in the line of quid pro quo researchers, those inventors of substitutes for times of famine. Augustin Escoffier, "the king of cooks and the cook of kings," can easily be presented as a great chef, spreading the reputation of French gastronomy throughout Europe, but it must not be forgotten that his early glory was based on his creative cuisine faced with shortages, as a serviceman responsible for feeding French officers under siege in Metz in 1870. For both Parmentier and Escoffier, the concern about quantity was paramount.

If the first parameter concerns time, the second brings space into play. It is a matter of the food circuit, that pathway of eating that leads from the fields to the mouth. The most basic given, so constant that it can undoubtedly be called a law, is that the shorter that circuit, the happier the consumer. Autoconsumption is reassuring. A good pre–French Revolution middle-class citizen preferred buying a farm over investing in a shop or weapons. How can this common practice not be seen as answering a need for security on several levels? The security of a small (hardly more than 4 or 5 percent on the investment) but certain income, of a house in the country that could be a safe refuge in times of epidemic, of food production that guaranteed an independent, quality food supply. Then one "knew" what one was eating. But we are still in the realm of images, not of certainties proven by the realities of country life. Knowing the origin and the route taken by this or that product was not a guarantee of quality: how many food mishaps were hidden under the veil of autoconsumption, escaping any retrospective investigation? And nevertheless, between the sausage from the pig slaughtered on the farm and the industrial sausage coming from the Chicago slaughterhouses, what a difference in the quality of the image!

The last key in attempting to interpret these fears is the status of the food. This is not a given that goes without saying, and the idea of quality is one of the most illusive in the history of food. What do we expect of a food? That it should be healthy and thus keep us healthy? That it should taste good and contribute to the pleasures of sharing a meal around a well-laid table? Or should it offer all three benefits at the same time: gustatory pleasure, conviviality, and health? Each era and each culture stress one or another of these values. When hedonism prevails, as was the case when nineteenth-century France was discovering the pleasures of gastronomy, the health benefit was given little attention, became parenthetical. When concern for health rules, as in Latin countries after the great plague of 1348 or in Theodore Roosevelt's America, the ground is prepared for receiving the revelations of a food crisis and for taking measures to avoid the risks.

In the West, food fears are not negative or paralyzing. They inspire action. The history of food fears is the history of human efforts to evaluate and, if possible, to reduce or master the risks. It is woven through with compromise. Compromise between the principle of reality and the ideal of security. Compromise among the actors, the government, the public, and, later, the press. Compromise among different food values, though this compromise is of an entirely different nature and very difficult, even impossible to arbitrate.

In 1897 the great chemist and visionary Marcellin Berthelot wrote a book of fiction, *The Year 2000*, in which he prophesied a luminous future for food, made up of pills and synthetic substances, controlled and perfectly healthy. His utopia is far from being a generally shared vision, the new dream of the land of plenty. It is not food habits that make for resistance but the contradictory values that underlie the act of eating. Because these values are not all located along the health-safety axis. If that were the case, if the need to be sure about the health quality of foods prevailed, then the "transfer from heaven to earth" of feelings of security that Lucien Febvre speaks of would have taken place a long time ago.[1] But food is precisely one of those domains where this transfer of the need for security takes place much later and much less convincingly. In the years before the First World

War, what reigned was a fragile compromise, widely questioned, and opening onto very uncertain perspectives. Analyses of it vary widely, but it was a compromise between those for whom the horror was noninspected food that caused death by tuberculosis or botulism and those who foresaw a new food horror made up of entirely identified and thus identical homogenized and sterilized foodstuffs. Between a society where overprotectiveness would lead to the loss of the sense of taste and a society exposed to every risk, was there really a choice to be made? A battle of food values was taking shape, which would be the battle of our own time and our well-fed culture.

NOTES

Introduction

1. P. Volle, "Le Concept de risque perçu en psychologie du consommateur; antécédents et statut théorique," *Recherche et Applications en marketing* 10, no. 1 (1995).
2. Febvre 1956, 244–46.
3. J.-C. Schmitt, "An mil—an 2000: Quelle actualité du Moyen Age," *Magazine littéraire*, no. 382 (December 1999): 27.
4. The question of knowing who, in the year 1000, knew the date of the year in progress has been raised many times, first by Marc Bloch. See Pierre Riché, "Le Pape de l'an mille," *L'Histoire*, no. 41 (1982): 52.
5. Delumeau 1978.
6. Aron 1965, 5–6.

1. Forbidden Meats

1. Le Roy Ladurie 1975, 33.
2. These words are found in the cross-examinations of the inquisitor Fournier at Paumiers. See Fossat 1971, 98.
3. Pasquier 1921. The Mirepoix Charter is reproduced in vol. 2, 43–46.
4. Wolff 1953, 383.
5. See Matthew 15:10–11.
6. Bonnassie, Poulle-Drieux, and Dureau-Lapyssonie 2001, 146.
7. R. Fossier, *Le Travail au Moyen Age* (Paris: Hachette littératures, 2000), 169.
8. Beaujouan, Poulle-Drieux, and Dureau-Lapyssonie 1966.
9. We do, however, find the slaughter of horses forbidden in the regulations for butcher shops farther north: Amiens (1317), Troyes (1374). See Monner 1941, 27.
10. Aymard 1997, 100.
11. Le Roy Ladurie 1975, 380.
12. Estienne, *L'Agriculture*, quoted in Vialles 1987, 118.
13. Champier 1560, 412.
14. Rozier 1783, s.v. "Bouc," 2:388–93.
15. Malta fever or brucellosis can be transmitted to humans; however, meat from an animal suffering from brucellosis presents no risk to the consumer.
16. J. André, *L'Alimentation et la cuisine à Rome* (Paris: Klincksieck, 1980), 142.

17. Convincing examples from Carpentras and Pont-Saint-Esprit. See Stouff 1996, 130; D. Le Blévec, *La Part du pauvre* (Rome: Ecole française de Rome, 2000), 2:790–91.
18. Bodson 1991.
19. F. Brunot, *Histoire de langue française des origines à 1900* (1912; reprint, Paris: Armand Colin, 1966), 6:296.
20. Leclainche 1936, 123.
21. Pastoureau, Verroust, and Buren 1987, 52.
22. Wolff 1953, 399.
23. J. Caille, *Hôpitaux et charités publics au Moyen Age à Narbonne, de la fin du IXe à celle du XIVe siècle* (Toulouse: Privat, 1978), 33.
24. Nicoud 1998, 2:533.
25. Penso 1981, 91.
26. Champier 1560, 322.
27. Quoted in Wickersheimer 1905, 138.
28. Arnaud de Villeneuve, *Compendium médicinae*, quoted in Bériac 1988, 22.
29. "Quod si permissum esset porcos comedere, plateae et domus omnes longe sordidiores forent, quam sterlionia et latrine, sicut in Galiis hodie videre licet" (quoted in Delamare 1729, 2:103, who deplored "the dreadful portrait that this Jewish doctor paints of cities in France").
30. Barthélemi l'Anglais, 1999, 157–58.
31. Aristotle, I, VIII, 21.
32. Guillaume de Salicet, *Chirurgie*, 1275, quoted in Bériac 1988, 32.
33. G. de Chauliac, *Grande Chirurgie*, 1383, quoted in Cougoul 1943, 57.
34. Paré, quoted in Brabant 1966, 54.
35. Bériac 1990, 247. Was the disease imaginary? According to certain doctors, cases of human leprosy could exist in which humans harbor cysticerci as pigs do, in the muscles, under the skin, and in the eye.
36. H. de Mondeville, *La Chirurgie de maître H. de Mondeville* (Paris: Didot, 1897), 2:357.
37. Saint-Sever, 1480: "Que la carne sie dade aus gefats"; in Condom in 1312, the meat seized at market was to be distributed to lepers.
38. Bériac 1990, 84.
39. Vialles 1987, 97.
40. Léonard 1986, 170.
41. Stouff 1970, 133.
42. Castellazi 1995, 884.
43. Ordinance of Charles V. See Deramaix 1932, 3.
44. Carpentras policy regulation, 1561. See Pleindoux 1925, 34.
45. Beaujouan, Poulle-Drieux, and Dureau-Lapyssonie 1966. See Bodson 1991, 235.
46. Beaujouan, Poulle-Drieux, and Dureau-Lapyssonie 1966, appendix 2.
47. Ibid.

2. Political Meat

1. Wolff 1953, 383.
2. Stouff 1970, 126.
3. Gouron 1958, 59; Rigaudière 1993, 133.
4. F.-O. Martin, *Histoire du droit français des origines à la Révolution* (Paris: Domat-Montchrestien, 1948), 171.

5. Lespinasse 1879, 299; Delamare 1729, 2:215, 252.

6. F. Hildesheimer, *La Terreur et la pitié: L'Ancien Régime à l'épreuve de la peste* (Aix-en-Provence: Publisud, 1990), 11.

7. Leguay 1999, 24.

8. Wolff 1953, 389.

9. Vialles 1987, 14.

10. Statutes of Grasse, 1262; Mirepoix, 1303; Carpentras, 1455, art. 1: "Eorum propiis pedibus ad ipsum macellum venerint"; Toulouse, 1394.

11. Statutes of the butchers of Mans, 1317. Quoted in J. Roussy, "Hygiène de la bourgeoisie au Moyen Age" (doctoral thesis in medicine, Paris, 1939).

12. Stouff 1996, 94.

13. Castellazi 1995, 882.

14. Françoise Desportes, "Les Métiers de l'alimentation," in Flandrin and Montanari 1996, 444.

15. Bonnassie 2001, 149.

16. Gouron 1958, 120.

17. Stouff 1970, 133.

18. A. C. Bédarrides, AA1, statutes of 1543.

19. Delamare 1729, 2:506.

20. Delsalle 2001, 14.

21. Delamare 1729, 1:223.

22. The statutes of Avignon, 1246, mention animals dead of *morie*, a general term that designates all infected meat, according to Pleindoux 1924.

23. One can compare *morie* to the English "murrain": plague, epidemic disease. See Fossat 1971, 102.

24. Stouff 1996, 133.

25. Monner 1941, 18.

26. Ibid., 40.

27. Toulouse, *Statuts*, 1394, art. 7. In Paris, *Statuts des chaircuitiers*, 1475, it was forbidden to "put into sausage flesh from grainy pigs, flesh from pigs fed in the leper house."

28. Monner 1941, 61.

29. Mandate of Henri II, art. 17.

30. Desportes 1987, 186.

31. Champier 1560, 402. Champier considered the fat of pigs raised in the city to be of an inferior quality and easily liquefied.

32. Monner 1941, 36–37.

33. Fodéré 1813. See Hallé 1835, 87.

34. 1462 Paris ordinance. See Monner 1941, 37.

35. Lespinasse 1879, 299.

36. Delsalle 2001, 14.

37. Michel de L'Hôpital, quoted in H. Baudrillart, *Histoire du luxe public et privé depuis l'Antiquité jusqu'à nos jours* (Paris: Hachette, 1880–1881), 4:680.

38. Delsalle 2001, 14.

39. Leguay 1999, 56.

40. Monner 1941, 54.

41. *The Legacy*, in Villon 1960, 11. "The crowned ox" is an allusion to the crowns of leaves with which butchers garnished fresh meat.

42. Stouff 1996, 106.
43. Statute of Montpellier butchers, May 6, 1368, *Petit Thalamus*, 316.
44. R. Moulinas, *Les Juifs du pape en France* (Toulouse: Privat, 1981), 141–42.
45. Toulouse, articles 21 and 22 of the 1394 statutes for *mazelliers*. See Wolff 1953, 308.
46. Statutes of King Robert, 1306, translated by Stouff, 107.
47. Stouff 1996, 109.
48. Coulet 1978, 215.
49. A.C. Pernes, FF 1, *Statuts et règlements de police*, 1470.
50. J. Shatzmiller, "Soins de beauté, image et image de soi: Le Cas des juifs de Moyen Age," in D. Menjot, ed., *Les Soins de beauté au Moyen Age* (Nice: Université de Nice, 1987), 51–52.
51. Monner 1941, 21.
52. Kriegel 1976, 340.
53. Verdier 1979, 20–21.
54. Stouff 1996, 108–10. See J. Rossiaud, *La Prostitution médiévale* (Paris: Flammarion, 1988), 75.

3. The Birth of the Consumer

1. *De vita Christi*, quoted in Richelet, *Dictionnaire françois* (1680), s.v. "Consummeur."
2. We find the same myth in the pagan tradition. See Lucretius, *De natura rerum*.
3. Genesis 6:3–4. See Paravicini 1997, 223.
4. Joubert 1579, 76.
5. Jacquart 1998, 399.
6. Stouff 1970, 172.
7. R. Chanaud, "La Foire aux ovins de Briançon: Deux siècles d'échanges avec le Piémont (XIV–XV siècle)," *Cahiers d'Histoire*, nos. 3–4 (1980).
8. Duby 1973, 10–14.
9. *Bulletin de l'Académie royal de médecine* (Paris: Baillière, 1865), 625.
10. Fossat 1971, 94. It is a Béarn and Landes custom to share misfortune.
11. Chevalier 1982, 197; Stouff 1996, 125.
12. Montanari 1995, 105.
13. Boissier de Sauvages, *Dictionnaire languedocian-françois* (Nîmes, 1756), s.v. "Frescun."
14. In Avignon, the "*grand mazel*" on the central square sold the same quality meats as the other small ones. (Information kindly provided by M. Hayez.)
15. Stouff 1996, 95.
16. Fossat 1971, 87.
17. Monner 1941, 28.
18. Fossat 1971, 89.
19. Wolff 1953, 383. See A.C. Barroux, AA1; statutes of Barroux, 1543.
20. Delamare 1729, 2:137–38.
21. Monner 1941, 56.
22. In Court Saint-Gemme, 1275; in Angeville, 1270. See Monner 1941, 273. In Toulouse, 1394. See Gouron 1958, 399–400.
23. Fossat 1971, 94.
24. Paravicini 1997.
25. Vigarello 1993, 83–85.
26. Alexandre de La Tourette, quoted in Bachelard 1996, 173.

27. According to D. Jacquart, this representation differs from the conceptions of scholarly medicine, which is not strictly speaking a humoral medicine. See D. Jacquart, in Grmek 1997b, 186.
28. Dr. Fabre, Montpellier, quoted in Bachelard 1996, 172.
29. Ziegler 1999, 220.
30. Bachelard 1996, 170–81.
31. Lalande 1896, 105.
32. Joubert, quoted in Céard 1982, 21.
33. Jacquart 1998, 744; Nicoud 1995 and 1998; Gil-Sotres 1995, 203; Oldoni 1995.
34. Nicoud 1998, 2:404, 564.
35. Nicoud 1995, 1:203.
36. Dupèbe 1982, 46; among the writers continuing the dietetic tradition were Ambroise Paré and Gui Patin.
37. Deroux 1991, 41.
38. Quoted in Céard 1982, 32.
39. Delamare 1729, 2:979.
40. Monteux 1559.
41. Montanari 1995, 117–18.
42. Ficin 1541, fol. 19.
43. Jen de Mirfeld, *Brevarium*, quoted in Nicoud 1998, 2:514.
44. Monteux 1559, 46–47.
45. Dupèbe 1982, 52–53.
46. J. Liébault, *Le Trésor de la santé*, quoted in Flandrin 1982, 90.
47. Ambroise Paré, *Le Régime de vivre*, quoted in Céard 1982, 31.
48. Vigarello 1993, 74–75.
49. Montanari 1995, 120.

4. The Vigilant Consumer

1. Lesage 1999.
2. Camporesi 1995, 75–76.
3. Flandrin 1996, 507–8.
4. Nicoud 1998, 2:533.
5. Maragi 1982, 81. In practice, this nevertheless resulted in "a system of consumer protection." See La Roncière 1983, 45.
6. Pleindoux 1925, 171.
7. Wolff 1953, 387.
8. Gouron 1958, 121.
9. Delamare 1729, 1:137.
10. Monner 1941, 17.
11. Ibid., 22.
12. Gouron 1958, 165.
13. Fourgoux and Jumel 1968, 65.
14. Statutes of Bédarrides, 1412, A.C. Bédarrides, AA 1; statutes of Pernes, 1470, A.C. Pernes, FF 1.
15. Françoise Desportes, "Les Métiers de l'alimentation," in Flandrin and Montanari 1996, 449.
16. Delamare 1729, 1:78.

17. Agulhon 1981, 85.

18. Vialles 1987, 28.

19. Anonymous 1994, 599.

20. Champier 1560, 398, 392–93. See also Monteux 1559, 43–44.

21. Champier 1560, 391.

22. Ducreux 1999, 72.

23. Mandrou 1974, 82; Corbin 1986, v.

24. Garnot 1996, 220.

25. Fossat 1971, 103.

26. Stouff 1996, 92.

27. Delamare 1729, 1:338.

28. Anonymous 1994, 685–89.

29. Delsalle 2001, 14.

30. Aymard 1983, 183.

31. Mandrou 1974, 14.

32. Ordinance of the Paris Provost, June 1570. See Delamare 1729, 2:86.

33. A. C. Le Barroux, FF 1, statutes of 1543.

34. Laurioux 1996, 470–72; Redon and Sabban 1995, 42–43.

35. Anonymous 1994, 733, 789.

36. Brears 1993, 240.

37. Anonymous 1994, 651, 614.

38. Ibid., 594.

39. Delamare 1729, 1:505.

40. Ibid., 1:512.

41. Fourgoux and Jumel 1968, 66.

42. Pastoureau 1992, 29.

43. Lalande 1896, 89.

44. Ficin 1541, fol. 29.

45. Champier 1560, 370, 374.

46. Bouchon 1952, 64.

47. Aron 1973, 157–58.

48. Rebora 1998, 39.

49. Champier 1560, 433.

50. Brears 1993, 240.

51. Anonymous 1994, 693–95; Laurioux 1997, 153.

52. Chevalier 1982, 197.

53. A. Capatti and M. Montanari, *La cucina italiana: Storia di una cultura* (Rome: Laterza, 1999), 80.

54. Méchin 1992, 194.

55. Monteux 1559, 27.

56. Laurioux 1993, 143.

57. Baillet 1982, 48–49.

58. Sabban 1984.

59. Anonymous 1994, 601, 682. This method is also recommended by the *Thrésor de santé*; see Flandrin and Montanari 1996, 498.

60. Rabelais, *Gargantua*, chap. 39.

61. Anonymous 1994, 688.

62. Anonymous n.d., 10.

63. R. Collier, *La Vie en Haute-Provence de 1600 à 1850* (Gap: Scientific and Literary Society of the Alps of Haute-Provence, 1973), 164.

64. Joubert 1579, 2:270.

65. Estienne, *La Maison rustique*, quoted in Vialles 1987, 118.

66. Hecquet, *Traité des dispenses de carême*, quoted by Méchin 1992, 195.

67. "Boiled capon for those who have not a tooth in their mouth," according to a little book for learning the alphabet, *Rôti cochon*, by S. Girault (1658).

68. Rabelais, *Tiers Livre*, chap. 15.

5. The Phobia of New Plants

1. Champier 1560, 101. See A. Crosby, *The Columbian Exchange* (Westport, Conn.: Greenwood, 1972).

2. J. Cartier, *Relations* (Montreal: Presses de l'Université, 1986), 155.

3. Chaunu 1976, 108. The first mention of manioc dates from 1494.

4. Lévi-Strauss 1966, 14.

5. Champier 1560, 102–3.

6. Fischler 1993, 113–15.

7. Joubert 1579, 280.

8. Rabelais 1955/1985, 86.

9. Monteux 1559, 45, 53–54.

10. *Le Régime de vivre*, 1561, quoted in Céard 1982, 26–27.

11. Champier 1560, 69.

12. Liébault 1572, 72. See Monteux 1559, 52.

13. Montaigne 1991, 134.

14. Jean Bodin, *Les Paradoxes du seigneur de Malestroit* (Paris, 1568).

15. O. de Serres, with regard to the pumpkin. See Serres 1600, 801.

16. Quoted in Roze 1898, 6.

17. Rozier 1787, 3:19.

18. Maleissye 1991, 219. See B. Garnot, *Justice et Société en France aux XVIe–XVIIe–XVIIIe siècles* (Gap: Ophrys, 2000), 41.

19. Quoted by Brabant 1966, 104.

20. Montaigne 1991, 883.

21. Ficin 1541, fol. 24v.

22. All the quotations from L'Ecluse are from Clusius 1605.

23. Smith 1976, 176.

24. Delamare 1729, 525–27.

25. W. Shakespeare, *The Merry Wives of Windsor*, act 5, scene 5.

26. Gerard 1633/1975, p. 928.

27. F. Bacon, *Historia vitae et mortis*, quoted in Roze 1898, 75.

28. Morineau 1985, 127.

29. Garnot 1996, 52. See Moriceau 1999, 135.

30. Rozier 1787, 3:141.

31. Moriceau 1999, 92.

32. G. Bauhin, *Podromos theatri obtanici*, 1620, quoted in Roze 1898, 98.

33. Roze 1898, 122.

34. In Anvers, the health tribunal examined 1,250 individuals suspected of leprosy between 1730 and 1782. Only 17 were declared leprous. Nevertheless, the fact remains that the others were suspected and denounced as lepers by their neighbors and their kin before the tribunal.

35. Bériac 1990, 427.

36. Ibid., 147.

37. Zimmermann 1774, 3:29.

38. Regulations of the noble consistorial Hostel, 1946, XIII, 269. Reference provided by Paul Delsalle.

39. Champier 1560, 76.

40. Léonard 1986, 168.

41. V. Forot, *Monographie de la commune de Naves* (1911), 183.

42. J. Léonard, *La Vie quotidienne du médicin de province au XIXe siècle* (Paris: Hachette, 1977), 98.

43. Quoted in Roze 1898, 82.

44. Lebrun 2001, 215.

45. Poussou 1999, 402; Thomas 1985, 124.

46. Bonnassie 2001, 152.

47. N. Elias, *La Civilisation des moeurs* (Paris: Calmann-Lévy, 1973).

48. Morineau 1985, 127.

49. Jehan Macer, 1555, quoted in J.-P. Duviols, *L'Amérique espagnole vue et rêvée: Les Livres de voyage, de Christophe Columb à Bougainville (1492–1768)* (Paris: Promodis, 1985), 168.

50. Bigot de Morogues, *Essai sur la topographie de la Sologne* (Orléans, 1811), 18, quoted in Poitou 1976, 368.

51. Boissier de Sauvages, *Dictionnaire languedocien-françois* (Nîmes, 1756).

52. Smith 1976, 177.

53. Bourguinat 2002, 150.

54. J.-M. Boehler, *Une Société rurale en milieu rhénan: La Paysannerie de la plaine d'Alsace (1648–1789)* (Strasbourg: Presses universitaires de Strasbourg, 1994), 1693.

55. Ibid., 1734.

56. Muratori-Philip 1994, 132.

57. *Journal de physique*, August 1817, quoted in Aulagnier 1830, 2:168–69.

58. Aron 1973, 134.

59. Aulagnier 1830, 2:172.

60. F. Baldini, *De pomi di terra* (Naples, 1783), quoted in Roze 1898, 109.

61. Quoted in Kiener and Peyronnet 1979, 128.

62. Kiener and Peyronnet 1979, 136.

63. J.-R. Pitte, *Terres de castanide: Hommes et paysages du châtaignier, de l'Antiquité à nos jours* (Paris: Fayard, 1986), 224, 240.

64. Kiener and Peyronnet 1979, 172.

65. Ibid., 230.

66. Seince 1935, 42.

67. G. B. Occhioline, *Memoria sopra il meraviglioso frutto americano chiamato volgarmente patata* (Rome, 1784), 18, quoted in Camporesi 1993, 107–8 n. 3. Cooking potatoes unpeeled keeps the ascorbic acid from being destroyed.

68. Muratori-Philip 1994, 131.

69. The words of the Arles consuls in 1788.

6. Bread on Trial

1. Cited in Montanari 1995, 143.
2. Ibid., 261.
3. Braudel 1967, 1:142. See Montanari 1995, 143–44.
4. Patin 1846, 1:407, March 21, 1662.
5. Kaplan 1996, 47.
6. Ibid., 31.
7. Furetière 1690, s.v. "Pain."
8. Lachiver 1991, 41.
9. Considered the appropriate caloric intake for someone performing physical labor.
10. Lespinasse 1886, 210.
11. Cahen n.d., 2.
12. *Journal des sçavans*, March 2, 1671, cited in Ducreux 1999, 120.
13. Revel 1979, 129.
14. Menon, *La Cuisinière bourgeoise* (Lyon, 1783), 142.
15. Delamare 1729, 2:499.
16. On this whole affair, see Delamare 1729, vol. 2, book 4, chap. 4, "De la police du pain par rapport à la santé," 498. This is a firsthand work, which benefited from information from the parliament registers.
17. Kaplan 1996, 91.
18. Delamare 1729, 2:498.
19. Declaration of the controller general Desmarets in 1708, quoted in Lebrun 1971, 358.
20. Charles de La Condamine, *Almanach des Muses* (Paris, 1770), quoted in Adrian 1994, 58–60.
21. Delamare 1729, 2:499.
22. Abad 1999, 25ff.
23. Ibid., 56.
24. Kaplan 1998, 25.
25. Delamare 1729, preface.
26. Savary des Bruslons 1741, s.v. "Pain." According to Furetière's article "Pain" (1690), "spoiled" meant damaged by mice; "badly turned," too small.
27. O. Ranum, *Les Parisiens du XVIIe siècle* (Paris: Colin, 1973), 328.
28. Raynaud 1863, 96–97.
29. Zimmermann 1774, 43.
30. Devaux 1683, 179–80.
31. Joubert 1579, 149, 152–54.
32. Dandrey 1993, 169.
33. Lémery 1702, v.
34. Delamare 1729, 3:515.
35. Rozier 1783, s.v. "Bière," 265. To save money, brewers replaced hops with absinthe, and "beer with absinthe got very hot."
36. Delamare 1729, 3:515.
37. *Thrésor de santé*, 1607, quoted in Flandrin 1998, 119.
38. Delamare 1729, 3:515.
39. Ducreux 1999, 202.
40. G. Talarigo, *La Vie des aliments* (Paris: Denoël, 1947).

41. Kaplan 1998, 46.
42. Wickersheimer 1905, 56.
43. That is the tone conveyed by La Condamine in his satiric poem (see n. 16, above).
44. The first yeast works for the bakery trade were established in France beginning in 1865. See Adrian 1994, 182–83; Bourguinat 2002, 224.
45. According to S. L. Kaplan, the first president of the parliament was a faithful and practicing queen's bread devotee. See Kaplan 1996, 162.
46. *Journal des sçavans*, March 2, 1671, cited in Ducreux 1999, 120.
47. Ibid., 121. In the Ducreux potpourri, we find a compendium of prejudices against yeast; see 202–3, 217–18, 225, 232, 239, 253.
48. Savary des Bruslons 1741, s.v. "Levure," 80.
49. Buchan 1783, 191.
50. Rozier 1783, s.v. "Pain," 373; Savary des Bruslons 1741, s.v. "Levure."
51. Delamare 1729, 2:498.
52. Patin 1846, 2:733, letter to Falconet, March 13, 1670.

7. Silent Fears

1. Brabant 1966, 91.
2. Extract from Dom Martène and Dom Durand, *Voyage littéraire en France* (Paris, 1717), quoted in Chaumartin 1946, 93.
3. Bishop Fléchier evoked "those tempests of hunger" in a pastoral letter written on May 18, 1709.
4. Fodéré 1813, 192–93. We must note, however, that, at the height of the Saint Anthony's fire epidemic, between the eleventh and twelfth century, it was the lowest classes that were the most affected. See P. Sigal, *L'Homme et le miracle dans la France médiévale (XIe–XIIe siècle)* (Paris: Cerf, 1985), 250.
5. Extract from the manuscript of C. Sauvageon, prior of Sennely, in Sologne, quoted in R. Muchembled, *Société et mentalités dans la France moderne, XVIe–XVIIIe siècle* (Paris: Colin 1990), 106.
6. Read 1774, 18.
7. Ibid., 63.
8. Report from the *Journal des sçavans*, quoted in Chaumartin 1946, 164.
9. Ibid.
10. Read 1774, 85.
11. Brabant 1966, 96. The abbot Rozier also questioned the harmfulness of ergot. See Rozier 1783, s.v. "Seigle"; see also Read 1774, 85–87.
12. Abbot Tessier's report to the Royal Academy of Medicine, May 12, 1778. See Chaumartin 1946, 174.
13. Bigot de Morgues, Essai sur la topographie de la Sologne (Orléans, 1881), cited in Poitou 1976, 368.
14. Abbot Tessier's report to the Royal Academy of Medicine, May 12, 1778.
15. Experiment of the Royal Academy of Sciences, 1710. See Read 1774, 47.
16. Chaumartin 1946, 167–68.
17. Duhamel du Monceau, Eléments d'agriculture, 1:336, quoted in Poitou 1976, 361.
18. Poitou 1976, 361–62.
19. Zimmermann 1774, 3:9.
20. Poitou 1976, 361.

21. Michel Chevreul's paper "Le Seigle ergoté comme moyen d'hâter les accouchements" appeared in 1828. On hospital use, see Thuillier 1977, 83.

22. Champier 1560, 273.

23. Read 1774, 8.

24. These hallucinations are inferred from the visions painted by Matthias Gruünewald on the Issenheim reredos, depicting a sick person covered with pustules. See J.-N. Biraben, in Bulst and Delort 1989, 369.

25. Mandrou 1974, 303.

26. Rozier 1787, 3:1.

27. Lémery 1702, introduction.

28. Quoted in Wickersheimer 1905, 229.

29. Champier 1560, 273.

30. Ibid., 169.

31. Mattioli 1744, quoted in Camporesi 1981, 154.

32. Camporesi 1995, 105.

33. Zimmermann 1774, 3:4.

34. H. Taine, *Les Origines de la France contemporaine* (Paris: Hachette, 1894), 254.

35. Lebrun 2001, 215.

36. Académie de médecine, S.R.M. collection, 142, dossier 19, no. 20, *Mémoire sur une maladie des animaux ruminants*, 1779.

37. Vicq d'Azyr 1787, s.v. "Disette." See Kaplan 1997, 382; Seince 1935, 48–49.

38. Apfelbaum 1998, 89.

39. Camporesi 1995, 266.

40. Goubert 1982, 3. Dr. Ramel's position, as intermediary and mediator between Parisian culture and the rural world, can be compared to that of most of the correspondents for the Royal Society of Medicine, for example, Dr. Lavergne of Lamballe. See J.-P. Goubert, *Médecins d'hier, médecins d'aujourd'hui: Le Cas de Docteur Lavergne (1756–1831)* (Aix-en-Provence: Publisud, 1992).

41. Académie de médecine, S.R.M., 180, dossier 3, *Lettres du dr Ramel à Vicq d'Azyr, 1783–1792.*

42. Raspail 1845, 14.

43. Académie de médecine, S.R.M., 180, dossier 3.

44. F. Raymond, *De la topographie médicale de Marseille et de son territoire*, 1779, article 8: "Du tempérament et de la constitution des habitants et de leur naturel." Raymond was a friend and colleague of Ramel who, at Ramel's death, took over his title of "associé régnicole."

45. Zimmermann 1774, 3:3.

46. Royal Society of Medicine, 180, dossier 3, no. 5.

47. Tissot 1785, 38.

48. Goubert, in Desaive and Goubert 1972, 234.

49. Peter 1967, 168.

50. Académie de médecine, S.R.M., Villars report, 142, dossier 19.

51. Goubert 1989, 398.

52. Cosmacini 1992, 280.

53. Bellinazzi 1982, 382.

54. Cosmacini 1992, 130.

55. Gusdorf 1972, 444–45.

56. Académie de médecine, S.R.M., 180, dossier 3.

57. Ibid
58. Darluc 1782, 1:34.
59. Wickersheimer 1905, 494.
60. Champier 1560, 54–55; Ducreux 1999, 67.
61. Académie de médicine, S.R.M., 180, dossier 3.
62. Anonymous 1774.
63. Rey 1992, 270.

8. The Pâté and the Garden

1. Bicais 1669, 98–99.
2. Assertion of Father Athanase Kircher. See Darmon 1999, 68.
3. L. Febvre, *Le Problème de l'incroyance au XVIe siècle: La Religion de Rabelais* (Paris: Albin Michel, 1968), 406; and preface to Koyré 1955, vi.
4. Paré 1953, 144. See Brabant 1966, 76; Hildesheimer 1980, 40.
5. Kaplan 1997, 380–81.
6. G. M. Lancisi, *De subitaneis mortibus* (Rome 1707). See Hamraoui 2000, 103.
7. Cosmacini 1992, 134.
8. Le Gendre 1733, 388. See Brabant 1966, 23–35.
9. Rozier 1783, s.v. "Seigle," 9:65. During the 1569 plague, London authorities prohibited the sale of fruit; see Brears 1993, 140.
10. Flandrin and Montanari 1996, 508.
11. *Avis aux bourgeois de Paris*, 1649, quoted in Hubert Carrier, *Les Muses guerrières: Les Mazarinades et la vie littéraire au milieu du XVIIe siècle* (Paris: Klincksieck, 1996), 594.
12. R. Baehrel, "La Haine de classe en temps d'épidémie," *Annales ECS*, 1952, 359–60.
13. Campion-Vincent 1994, 85–86.
14. Savary des Bruslons 1741, 943.
15. Furetière 1690, s.v. "Pasté.
16. Bobis 1993, 75.
17. Montaigne 1991, 111–12, 117.
18. Thomas 1985, 151.
19. "Les Pâtissiers," in Sébillot 1895; Radeff 1996, 22.
20. "To escape paralysis of the head or back, one must abstain from eating head or flesh of cat" (*Evangiles des quenouilles*, III, 2). The penitentials also listed the cat among the unclean foods, and eating it was punishable by forty days of penance (Bonnassie 2001, 146).
21. Bobis 1993, 75–76.
22. Champier 1560, 424.
23. Anonymous 1994, 684.
24. Lespinasse 1879, 367.
25. Wickersheimer 1905, 232.
26. *Actes du cabildo de Lima* (1552), quoted in B. Vavallée, *L'Amerique espagnole, de Colomb à Bolívar* (Paris: Belin, 1993), 200.
27. Champier 1560, 392.
28. Aulagnier 1830, s.v. "Menthe," 24.
29. Savary des Bruslons 1741, s.v. "Chat," 253.
30. Delamare 1729, 2:212.
31. Quoted in Revel 1979, 150–51.

32. Delamare 1729, 2:385.
33. Furetière 1690, s.v. "Pasté."
34. Engravings by A. Bosse, around 1635, reproduced in "Les Patissiers," in Sébillot 1895.
35. Bobis 1993, 76.
36. Bizet 1847, 416.
37. "Les Patissiers," in Sébillot 1895.
38. Dumas 1998, 482.
39. A.C. L'Isle-sur-Sorge, AA 2, 1617.
40. Serres 1600, 1188.
41. Foisil 1986, 142–43.
42. Rebora 1998, 50.
43. Figeac 2001, 160–64.
44. Méchin 1992, 60.
45. Figeac 2001, 160.
46. Castellazi 1995, 882.
47. Mercier, 1:1367–68.
48. Rétif de La Bretonne, *Vie de mon père*, quoted in J.-P. Moreau, *Alimentation et régions* (Nancy: Presses universitaires de Nancy, 1988), 104.
49. Champier 1560, 432.
50. Liébault 1572.
51. Sauzet, *Le Notaire et son roi: Etienne Borrelly, un Nîmois sous Louis XIV* (Paris: Plon, 1998), 133.
52. Liébault 1572, 42.
53. Fossat 1971, 95.
54. Serres 1600, 1180.
55. L. Rose, *La Bonne Fermière; ou, Eléments oeconomiques utilles aux jeunes personnes destinées à cet état* (Lille: Henry, 1765), 90. Serres recommends this two-step process for conserving bacon; see Serres 1600, 1180.
56. Léonard 1986, 157, 166, 184.

9. Hungarian Cattle Disease

1. The word is French in origin. With the aid of Turgot, it entered administrative language during the great animal contagion of 1774–1775. See Brunot, *Histoire de la langue française* (1912; reprint, Paris: Armand Colin, 1966), 6:287.
2. Blancou 2000, 189.
3. Leclainche 1936, 52.
4. This is, for example, the interpretation favored in ibid.
5. A. de Gasparin, *Cours d'agriculture* (Paris, 1851), 1:16.
6. Rozier 1783, s.v. "Contagion."
7. Lebrun 1971, 290–91.
8. S.R.M. 1776, 187, dossier 3, statement of Joseph Barré and Pierre Magdelanat.
9. S.R.M. 1784, 195, dossier 18, Z. Bongiovanni, doctor from Verona, *Trattato storico-critico in torno al male epidemico contagioso di buoi delle anno 1784*.
10. Ordinance of Louis XV, July 1746, article 7, reproduced in Isambert n.d., *Recueil général des anciennes lois françaises* 24:188.
11. Fodéré 1813, 366.

12. This is a recognized fact for hoof-and-mouth disease and rinderpest; see Vallet 2001, 76 and 81.
13. Savary 1741, vol. I, s.v. "Boeufs."
14. N. Lemaître, *Un Horizon bloqué: Ussel et la Montagne limousine aux XVIIe et XVIIIe siècles* (Ussel: Musée du Pays d'Ussel, 1978), III.
15. Abad 2002, 359.
16. S. Dontenwill, *Une Seigneurie sous l'ancien régime: L'Etiole-en-Brionnais du XVIe au XVIIe siècle* (Roanne: Horvath, 1973), 224–25.
17. Radeff 1996, 230
18. Official documents involving the statutes for butchers, Versailles, June 1, 1782.
19. Rozier 1783, 467–69.
20. J.-B. Thiers, *Traité des superstitions*, I;329, quoted in Lebrun 2001, 135. In 1745 a ruling by Parliament made this practice official by prohibiting it.
21. Lebrun 2001, 135.
22. Grasse 2002, 93.
23. Muchembled 1978, 39.
24. Beaujouan, Poulle-Drieux, and Dureau-Lapyssonie 1966, 71.
25. Paulet 1775, I:291.
26. The dossier on the Hungarian cattle trade has been compiled by Hungarian, Austrian, Yugoslavian, and German historians. For a good synthesis, see Vilfan 1983.
27. Paulet 1775, I:120.
28. Ibid., I:64. In the nineteenth century, Gasparin uses the expression "Hungarian typhus."
29. Boissier de Sauvages, in *Journal des sçavans* (1746), 340.
30. C. F. Cogrossi, *Nuova idea del mal contagioso de buoi* (Milan, 1713). See Darmon 1999, 90; Penso 1981, 222.
31. Penso 1981, 22.
32. Hamraoui 2000.
33. Lancisi 1748, I.
34. Quoted in Penso 1981, 222.
35. Paulet 1775, I:124.
36. Chap. II (appendix and summary of measures by which the contagion could be repelled most quickly), of Lancisi 1748, 167–69.
37. Grmek 1997a, 42.
38. Savary 1741, I, "Boucher" article, 1050.
39. Bizet 1847, 215.
40. An expression used by Raspail regarding harmful animals. See Raspail 1845, 34.
41. Quoted by Vallat 2001, 77.
42. See, e.g., Fontenay 1998; Baratay 1996.
43. Thomas 1985, 20.
44. Descartes 2000, 277, 296.
45. Malebranche, *Entretiens sur la mort*, quoted in Fontenay 1998, 294.
46. Idem, *De la recherche de la vérité*, quoted in ibid., 295.
47. Gerbaud 1993, 220–21.
48. S.R.M., 180, dossier 22, fol. 5, report by Chirac, August 1714.
49. Vicq d'Azyr 1787, s.v. "Epizootie," 4:267.
50. Cited in Paulet 1775, 120.
51. Cosmacini 1996, 3–4.

52. Thomas 1985, 42.
53. J. Morphew, quoted in Blancou 2000, 184.
54. Vicq d'Azyr 1787, s.v. "Epizootie," 4:269.
55. Thomas 1985, 148ff.

10. From the Epizootic to the Epidemic

1. Paulet 1775, 1:102.
2. S.R.M., 180, dossier 22, August 12, 1714.
3. Decree of the king's council regarding livestock, April 10, 1714.
4. Letter by a Montpellier doctor on veterinary medicine, 1771, quoted in Gerbaud 1993, 220.
5. Dupuy 1833, 371.
6. Thomas 1985, 166.
7. Ronsard 1979, 191.
8. Mandrou 1980, 499–511.
9. Saint-André 1725, 285, 289.
10. Lebrun 1971, 405; Saint André 1725, 299.
11. Thomas 1985, 46–47.
12. Blancou 2000, 187 n. b.
13. Fodéré 1813, 3:116.
14. F. Rabelais, *Pantagruel*, book 4, new prologue.
15. S.R.M. 1784, 195, dossier 18, Z. Bongiovanni, doctor from Verona, *Trattato storico-critico in torno al male epidemico contagioso di buoi delle anno 1784*.
16. Foreword to Paulet 1775.
17. A. Barante, *Souvenirs* (Paris, 1890–1901), 4:509–10, quoted in René Baehrel, "La Haine de classe en temps d'épidémie," *Annales E.S.C.*, no. 3 (July–September 1952): 355.
18. Peter 1967, 165.
19. B.M. Avignon, ms. 1628, *La Chronique de Jehan de Redolphe Roubert*, 1582–1606.
20. Paulet 1775, 1:102, quoting the 1682 *Journal des sçavans* on hoof-and-mouth disease in the Lyons and Dauphiné regions.
21. A.C. Avignon, BB43, fol. 252, *Registre de délibérations*, 1714.
22. Leclainche 1936, 199.
23. Garsault, preface to *Nouveau Parfait Maréchal* (1759), quoted in ibid.
24. Foucault 1963, 26–27.
25. Meyer 1966, 14.
26. Hannaway 1977, 431.
27. Dupuy 1833, 365.
28. Anonymous 1774.
29. Thomassin 1782, 1.
30. Vallat 2001, 71; Baudrimont and Béclard 1878, 29–31.
31. Marcet-Juncosa 1993, 177, 180.
32. S.R.M., 145, dossier 8, no. 3, *Mémoire sur le charbon qui règne dans quelques contrées du Roussillon*. Another—anonymous—copy of this report is found in the collections of the Catalan intendant. It is studied in Marcet-Juncosa 1993.
33. Boissier de Sauvages, *Dictionnaire occitan-françois* (Nîmes, 1756), s.v. "Carbounele."
34. V. Astruc, *Dissertation sur la contagion de la peste* (Toulouse, 1724), chap. 6, quoted in Paulet 1775, 1:154.

35. It is "one of the most typical plantes of the Languedoc scrubland" (H. Harant and D. Jarry, *Guide du naturaliste dans le Midi de la France* [Neuchâtel: Delachaux-Niestlé, 1973], 2:24–25).
36. *Mémoire sur le charbon*, fol. 4.
37. Dupuy 1833, 364–67.
38. A. Layet, *Hygiène et maladie des paysans* (1882), quoted in Léonard 1986, 170.
39. Montdauphin, 1784, S.R.M., 146, quoted in Meyer 1966.
40. Bodson 1991, 237.
41. *Mémoire sur le charbon*, fol. 20.
42. S.R.M., 142, dossier 19, no. 20, Villars, Grenoble doctor, *Mémoire sur une maladie des animaux ruminants*, fol. 5.
43. Champier 1560, 408.
44. Darluc 1782, 1:310.
45. Ibid., 1:311.
46. Vallat 2001, 68.
47. Pleindoux 1925, 100.
48. Champier 1560, 408.
49. Gilbert, *Traité des bêtes à laine*, quoted in Dupuy 1833, 373–74.
50. Anonymous 1774, fol. 27.
51. Quoted by Vallat 2001, 79. The cost of eight million appears in the *Mémoires* of Dupont de Nemours on the life of Turgot. See Dupuy 1833, 369.
52. S.R.M., 168, dossier 3, no. 92, *Mémoire de Dufrechou, maître chirurgien à Simorre près de Toulouse*.
53. J. Caput, "La Grande Epizootie de 1774–1775 en Béarn," *Bulletin de la Société des lettres et arts de Pau* 5 (1966): 86–89.
54. S.R.M., 163, dossier 20, no. 8, *Copie de la lettre de M. le contrôleur général à M. de Caumartin*, March 1776.
55. In the affair of the Lyons butchers, handled first with armed force and then through the courts, the king's prosecutor pointed out in his closing speech to the troublemakers: "There is an essential difference between public sedition, which is a matter concerning the sovereign and the state, and the feeling of a certain number of individuals regarding a particular subject. Sedition is a crime characterized as lèse-majesté. Simple temper is violence limited to one or a certain number of individuals, and, although it may be very criminal because of the effects that it nearly always causes, the punishment must not be the same as for the crime of lèse-majesté" (Guéneau 1922, 264).
56. Dupuy 1833, 360.
57. Vallat 2001, 96–97.
58. Hurtrel d'Arboval, *Dictionnaire de médecine* (1838), quoted in Blancou 2000, 96.
59. Vallat 2001, 96; Monner 1941, 110–13.
60. Decree of the council of June 1782, art. 27. See Dupuy 1833, 117.
61. Letter by a Montpellier doctor, 1771.

11. *The Politics of Precaution*

1. Febvre 1970, 166.
2. Moriceau 1999, 25.
3. S.R.M. 1784, 195, dossier 18, Z. Bongiovanni, *Trattato storico-critico in torno al male epidemico contagioso di buoi delle anno 1784*.

4. B.M. Avignon, atlas 213, no. 173, mandate of Mgr. Salviati, June 18, 1714.

5. Fodéré 1813, 113.

6. Boissier de Sauvages 1746.

7. Fodéré 1813, 113.

8. Tour ordinance, 1462, article 18. See Monner 1941, 37.

9. Cogrossi 1714, quoted in Blancou 2000, 174.

10. Champier 1560, 388–99. See Monteux 1559, 43.

11. J. Georgelin, *Venise au siècle des Lumières* (Paris: Mouton, 1978), 232.

12. Fodéré 1813, 113–15.

13. Di Munno Malavasi 1995, 562.

14. Penso 1981, 224.

15. Cosmacini 1996, 3–7.

16. Lunel 1974.

17. Cogrossi, *Journal de Venise*, 10:141, quoted by Paulet 1775, 1:125.

18. Penso 1981, 223.

19. Cosmacini 1992, 92.

20. Fodéré 1813, 114.

21. In Ussel, for example. N. Lemaître, *Un Horizon bloqué:. Ussel et la Montagne limousine aux XVIIe et XVIIIe siècles* (Ussel: Musée du Pays d'Ussel, 1978), 125.

22. Deramaix 1932, 145.

23. Blancou 2000, 148.

24. Pleindoux 1924, 141.

25. Castellazi 1995, 892.

26. Mammerickx 1994, 494.

27. Grmek 1997a.

28. Blancou 2000, 171.

29. B.M. Avignon, atlas 312, no. 173, mandate of Mgr. Salviati, June 18, 1714.

30. A.C. Avignon, BB 43, fol. 252, June 16, 1714, copy of a letter from the Aix consuls.

31. Pleindoux 1925, 103.

32. Paulet 1775, 1:214, ruling of the king's council 1746, art. 11.

33. S.R.M., 180, dossier 22, fol. 5, report by Chirac, August 1714.

34. Montaigne 1991, 118.

35. Baudrimont and Béclard 1878, 28.

36. Aron 1965, 6; Biraben 1976, 2:37.

37. C. Nourry, *Régime contre la pestilence, faict et composé par Messieurs les médicins de la cité de Basle* (Lyons, 1520), quoted in Brabant 1966, 79.

38. A.C. Avignon, BB 43, fol. 252, letter from the Aix consuls, 1714. This behavior is inscribed in a culture of state secrecy, best known for its wheat policy. The ruling powers in France thought that the masses could misuse information on state estimates for the harvests and on the wheat prices if they had access to it. Hence the state maxim: always think, but never speak of it.

39. Lunel 1974, 357. See Bach-Lijour 1993, 235–36.

40. Lunel 1974, 358.

41. B.M. Avignon, atlas 213, no. 173, mandate of Mgr. Salviati, June 18, 1714.

12. *The Dangers of Imperfect Metals*

1. Chomel 1740, s.v. "Chair," 719.

2. J.-L. Flandrin, "Soins de beauté et recueils de secrets," in D. Menjot, ed., *Les Soins de beauté au Moyen Age* (Nice: Université de Nice, 1987), 13–15.

3. Monteux 1559, 70; Chomel 1740, s.v. "Huile," "Glace."

4. *Encyclopédie*, s.v. "Nitre." See Pomet 1694, 72.

5. Champier 1560, 276, 348.

6. Ibid., 356.

7. Ibid., 363.

8. Delamare 1729, 1:510.

9. Quoted in Camporesi 1995, 159–161.

10. Serres 1600, 1192.

11. Ferrières 2002, 362.

12. Serres 1600, 1192.

13. Ibid., 1233.

14. Ibid.

15. Brears 1993, 241.

16. Ferrières 2002, 368.

17. Anonymous 1994, 669.

18. Berthelot 1893, 165.

19. Debus 1991.

20. Ulrich Ellenborg, printed in 1524. Arnaud de Villeneuve, in the chapter "De artibus" in his *Speculum introductionum medicinalium*, written in Montpellier at the end of the thirteenth century, also mentions the work-related pathology of the gilder.

21. Camporesi 1995, 154.

22. Brears 1993, 240.

23. Ducreux 1999, 249.

24. Champier 1560, 310.

25. Darluc 1782, 2:10.

26. Pomet 1694, 30. See *Encyclopédie*, s.v. "Verdet."

27. Montet's *Mémoires* on verdigris are cited and summarized in the "Verdet" article in the *Encyclopédie*.

28. Demachy, *Art du vinaigrier* (Paris, 1780), quoted in Godard 1991, 200.

29. Godard 1991, 200. The author cites the 1836 *Dictionnaire de cuisine et d'économie ménagère*: "Many people are in the habit of boiling the vinegar drawn from under the cornichons and, when it has boiled, pouring it back over the same cornichons: most of the time they boil it in copper, which it gradually dissolves and which can make the cornichons poisonous."

30. V. Hugo, *Choses vues*, quoted in Dumas 1998, 42.

31. Anonymous 1750, 1, 35.

32. Ibid., 52–55.

33. Zimmermann 1774, 76.

34. Hallé 1835, 842.

35. Anonymous 1750, 37; Ducreux 1999, 249.

36. Valentin 1995, 148–49.

37. Foisil 1986, 210–11.

38. Serres 1600, 1300.

39. Lebrun 1971, 407. See Serres 1600, 1303. Diarrhea in children was "treated" with a string worn close against the child's stomach.

40. Waton and Guérin 1800, 77–78.

41. A. Radeff, *Lausanne et ses campagnes au XVIIe siècle* (Lausanne, 1980), 103.

42. Delamare 1729, 5:514.
43. Garrier 1996, 77.
44. Paulet 1775, 1:xv.
45. Champier 1560, 533.
46. Delamare 1729, 5:514.
47. Champier 1560, 537.
48. Léonard 1986, 173.
49. Rozier 1783, 252.
50. Darluc 1782, 2:58.
51. Hallé 1835, 841.
52. Fodéré 1813, 106–9.
53. Darluc 1782, 1:35.
54. Ducreux 1999, 154–55.
55. Rozier 1770, 6.
56. Hallé 1787, 841. See Godard 1999, 121.
57. Hallé 1835, 844.
58. Zimmermann 1774, 58. See *Encyclopédie*, s.v. "Cuivre."
59. Hallé 1835, 17.
60. Darluc 1782, 1:33, for workers in the oil mills. On the making of butter, see Chomel 1740, 326.
61. Zimmermann 1774, 56–58.
62. Anonymous 1750, 6–7.
63. Aulagnier 1830, 2:106.
64. Fodéré 1813, 142.
65. Venel 1803, 193.
66. Roche 1983, 11.
67. Ferrières 2004, 133ff.
68. Fournier 1999, 328.

13. Health Conflicts

1. Ducreux 1999, 71, 74.
2. Corbin 1986, 11–25.
3. Statistics according to Dante Lenardon, index of the *Journal de Trévoux*, 1701–67; index of the *Journal encyclopédique*, 1756–93.
4. Ducreux 1999, 252–53, 171, 154–55, 193, 254.
5. Ibid. 1999, 199.
6. Tourtelle 1837, preface.
7. Ducreux 1999, 190–91.
8. This triumph of aerist and infectionist ideas must undoubtedly be qualified, according to the country and the school. The French were more aerist than the English. The Montpellier medical school continued to stress individual health habits and food: the lesson of Ribes, inaugurating the chair for hygiene at the Montpellier medical school in 1837, hardly echoes the discourse of health professionals from the east. See Hallé 1837; F. Ribes, *Première Leçon d'hygiène* (Montpellier: Castel, 1837).
9. Hallé 1837.
10. Raspail 1845, 13.

11. Decree of August 16–24, 1790, title II, article 3; decree of July 19–22, 1791.
12. Lespinasse and Bonnardot 1886, 274.
13. Ibid., 276.
14. A.M. Orange, B. B. 392, fol. 223. Deliberation of the city council of Orange, to oppose the transfer of the slaughterhouse outside the city, 1738.
15. A.D. Haute-Garonne, c 319, fol. 9.
16. A.C. Avignon, DD no. 28/29.
17. A.M. Toulouse, B B 169, fol. 11, April 16, 1781. I thank J.-L. Laffont for providing me this information concerning Toulouse.
18. Zimmermann 1774, 332.
19. Radeff 1996, 228.
20. Blake 1959, 15.
21. Agulhon 1981, 85.
22. Corbin 1986, 35.
23. Buchan 1783, 210; Camporesi 1995, 138.
24. Quoted in Vialles 1987, 16.
25. Ducreux 1999, 80.
26. Bizet 1847, 151.
27. Fischler 1993, 125.
28. L'Echo de la Nièvre, December 25, 1834, quoted in Thuillier 1977, 42.
29. According to Etat hygiénique des lycées de l'Empire en 1867: Extrait du rapport présenté à S. Exc. le Ministre de l'Instruction publique par le Docteur Maxime Vernois (Paris: B. Baillière et fils, 1868), in 1867 slops from the secondary schools were given to the poor (4 cases), sold (48 cases), given to the pigs (20 cases), given to the chickens (2 cases). The pigpen was generally located in the rear of the school's garden. Twenty schools had pigpens, holding six, eight, or ten of these animals.
30. Monner 1941, 110.
31. Draft of the butchers' organization, reported by H. Boulay de La Meurthe. See Bizet 1847, appendix.
32. Léonard 1986, 170.
33. D. A. Roe, A Plague of Corn (Ithaca, 1973).
34. Gaetano Strambio, Observationes de pellagra (Milan, 1786–1788), quoted in Cosmacini 1996, 292.
35. Peyresblanques 1985, 270.
36. Ibid., 273.
37. Vicq d'Azyr 1787, s.v. "Pellagre."
38. Peyresblanques 1985, 273.
39. About 1887, 107.
40. Letter from Doctor Degros, 1870, quoted in Peyresblanques 1987, 274.

14. Bourgeois Serenity

1. Camporesi 1993, 105–6.
2. Cosmacini 1996, 4.
3. Penso 1981, 276.
4. Lettera di Bizio Bartolomeo al chiarissimo canonico Angelo Bellani sopra il fenomena della polenta porporina, quoted in Penso 1981.
5. Weber 1983, 203; Aymard 1997, 88.

6. Brillat-Savarin 1996, 186.

7. Randoin 1927, 100.

8. Vigarello 1993, 215–16.

9. Randoin 1927, 51–53.

10. Spiekermann 2000, 39–40.

11. Payen 1865, 279.

12. Randoin 1927, 33.

13. H. Maret, *Mémoire dans lequel on cherche à déterminer quelles influences les moeurs des Français ont sur leur santé* (Amiens, 1772), 90.

14. Raspail 1843, 126.

15. Revel 1979, 133.

16. "A general spirit of conviviality was widespread in all the classes of society" (Brillat-Savarin 1996, 275).

17. Grimod de La Reynière 1997, 265.

18. Ibid., 183.

19. Ibid., 90.

20. Dumas 1998, 256, 394, 630.

21. P. Ory, *Le Discours gastronomique français, des origines à nos jours* (Paris: Gallimard, Archives, 1998), 19.

22. Aulagnier 1830, 2:350.

23. P. Lafargue, *Le Droit à la paresse* (1880), quoted in Léonard 1986, 187.

24. Vincent 1996, 20.

25. Aulagnier 1830, s.v. "Pois chiche."

26. B.M. Arles, Heritage Collection, ms. 435, *Livre de remèdes et de recettes de Louis Mège*, 253 fol.

27. *Encyclopédie des sciences médicales; ou, Traité général, méthodique et complet des diverses branches de l'art de guérir Encyclopédie médicale*, vol. 2 (1835), s. v. "Arsenic."

28. P. Berthier, *La Vie quotidienne dans "La Comédie humaine" de Balzac* (Paris: Hachette, 1998), 181.

29. Aron 1973, 288.

30. Aulagnier 1830, 2:104.

31. Ibid., 1:306, 325.

32. Vincent 1996, 27.

33. Raspail 1843, 132–33.

34. Adrian 1994, 108.

35. Bouchardat and Gautier 1878, 52.

36. Léonard 1986, 188.

37. Spiekermann 2000, 40.

38. Hudemann-Simon 2000, 156–57; Blake 1959, 206.

39. Bouchardat and Gautier 1878, 60.

40. E. About, *Le Progrès* (Paris: Hachette, 1865), 24–25.

15. English Cattle Disease

1. Bizet 1847, 199–203.

2. Séguin 1959, 123.

3. Baudrimont and Béclard 1878, 41.

4. Bizet 1847, 61.

5. Fodéré 1813, 366.
6. Bizet 1847, 325.
7. Raspail 1845, 444.
8. Blancou 2000, 237; Nocard and Leclainche 1903, 2:4.
9. Baudrimont 1878, 26.
10. Reynal 1873, 722, 727.
11. Guillaume 1986. Today, we know that transmission through the respiratory system is responsible for 90 percent of all cases.
12. Faure 1997, 560.
13. Cosmacini 1992, 283.
14. Laurioux 1994.
15. Payen 1865, 270.
16. Théodoridès 1991; Ducreux 1999, 170.
17. Popular engraving, *Les Principales Falsifications*, 1883, reproduced in Lebigre 1986, 124. An 1850 study in the journal *The Lancet* demonstrated that milk was diluted with 10 to 50 percent water.
18. Willich 1802, 240–41.
19. Aulagnier 1830, 1:305; Willich 1802, 241.
20. Aulagnier 1830, 1:306.
21. Vernon, *Milk and Dairy Products*, in Kiple and Ornelas 2000, 692.
22. Parmentier, quoted in preface to Aulagnier 1830.
23. Gide 1911, 635.
24. He was also the uncle of André Gide.
25. Gide 1911, 635.
26. Gide 1905, 165.
27. Branlard 1999, 179, 19.
28. Bouchardat and Gautier 1878, 85–86.
29. Baudrimont and Béclard 1878, 26–27.
30. Aron 1973, 259–60.
31. Nocard and Leclainche 1903, 2:29–33.
32. Spiekermann 2000, 40.
33. Vallat 2001, 96.
34. Nocard and Leclainche 1903, 2:13.
35. Darmon 1999, 480; Zeldin 1979, 5:322.
36. Darmon 1999, 480.
37. Nocard and Leclainche 1903, 2:26; Bertin-Sans 1901, 12–13.
38. Murard and Zylberman 1996, 418.
39. Letter from Stendhal to Di Fiore, quoted in Palou 1958, 104.
40. Roques 1837.
41. Hubsher 1999, 193–95.
42. Pleindoux 1925, 83.
43. Léonard 1986, 158.
44. Cosmacini 1992, 354.
45. Zeldin 1979, 1:35.

16. *The Poisoners of Chicago*

1. In Europe, a working-class household of five devoted an average of 64 percent of its income to food expenses. In the United States, 43 percent. See Gide 1905. The significance of these averages is discussed in Léonard 1986, 185.

2. Marre 1911.

3. Laumonier 1911, 146; Marre 1911, 202.

4. Balzac, *Les Illusions perdues*, quoted in P. Berthier, *La Vie quotidienne dans "La Comédie humaine" de Balzac* (Paris: Hachette, 1998), 218.

5. Baudrimont and Béclard 1878, 39–40.

6. For tomcat stew, see Bizet 1847, 416; for cat meat in rabbit fricassee, see Marre 1911, 113. See also *Larousse gastronomique* (1938), 320.

7. Laumonier 1911, 160.

8. Aulagnier 1830, 1:160.

9. Potter 1966, 230.

10. Vernon, quoted in Kiple and Ornelas 2000, 699–700.

11. Serao 1898, 187.

12. Faure, 1997, 560; Bertin-Sans 1901, 6.

13. M.-T. Chalon, *Une vie comme un jour* (Paris: Stock, 1974), 26–27.

14. Faure 1997, 563.

15. Brillat-Savarin 1996, 82.

16. Baudrimont and Béclard 1878, 2.

17. C. Fourier, *Le Nouveau Monde amoureux*, 235, quoted in M. Onfray, *Le Ventre des philosophes: Critique de la raison diététique* (Paris: Grasset, 1989), 88. See Masse 1876, 4.

18. Bizet 1847, 338.

19. Raspail 1845, 22–23.

20. Brears 1993, 241.

21. Baudrimont and Béclard 1878, 34; Lederer 1986, 297.

22. Masse 1876, 19–20.

23. Théodoridès 1991, 153.

24. Léonard 1986, 168.

25. Dack 1943, 38; Pointeau-Pouliquen 1958.

26. Laumonier 1911, 113, 116.

27. Marre 1911, 75.

28. Ibid., 80.

29. Lassablière 1950, 296.

30. Léonard 1986, 168–69.

31. Epinal image, *Les Principales Falsifications*, 1883, reproduced in Lebigre 1986, 124.

32. Lassablière 1950, s.v. "Conservation des aliments."

33. *Le Courrier de l'Europe*, February 10, 1809.

34. Dumas 1998, 269.

35. Capatti, in Flandrin and Montanari 1996, 803.

36. Aron 1973, 265.

37. Marre 1911, 321.

38. Jacquet and Trémolières 1956.

39. Zeldin 1979, 5:452.

40. Gaudillière 2001, 15–16.

41. Ibid.

42. Comer, in Kiple and Ornelas 2000, 1311–15.

43. Levenstein, in Flandrin and Montanari 1996, 847.

44. J. H. Kellogg, *Life, Its Mysteries and Miracles: A Manual of Health Principles* (1910), quoted in Skrabanek 1994, 170.

45. Nintz, quoted in Kiple and Ornelas 2000, 1485.

46. Vigarello 1993, 256.

47. Mademoiselle Léontine, *La Cuisine hygiénique, confortable et économique, à l'usage de toutes les classes de la société* (1856), quoted in Zeldin 1979, 3:430.

48. Zeldin 1979, 5:325.

49. Sinclair 1986, 115–16, 117, 120.

50. Ibid., 117.

51. Ibid., 120.

52. Ibid., 117.

53. Gide 1911, 655.

54. Article 11 of the 1905 law was the matrix until 1993 of 275 laws, 17 ordinances, 1,150 decrees, and 2,220 arrests. See Vincent 1996, 52–53.

Conclusion

1. Febvre 1956, 246. See Gutton 1994, 19–21.

BIBLIOGRAPHY

Manuscript Sources

References for these sources are indicated in the text in notes. The abbreviations used for the principal collections consulted are:

A.C.: Archives communales
A.D.: Archives départmentales
A.M.: Archives municipales
B.M.: Bibliothèque municipale
S.R.M.: Archives of the Société royale de médicine, Library of the Académie nationale de médicine

Primary Sources

About, Edmond. 1887. "Maître Pierre." In *Nouvelles et Souvenirs*. Paris: Hachette.

Accum, F. C. 1820. *A Treatise of Food Adulteration*. London.

Anonymous. 1750. *Nouvelles Fountaines domestiques approuvées par l'Académie royale des sciences.* Paris.

Anonymous. 1774. *Lassone; ou, La Séance de la Société royale de médicine.*

Anonymous. 1994. *Le Mesnagier de Paris*. Ed. G. Brereton and J. Ferrier. Paris: Le livre de poche.

Anonymous. 1999. *Livres de receptes, ce 15 Juine 1698 pour Madame Catherine Mey, baronne de Montricher*. Ed. V. Barras and M. Tavera. Geneva: Slatkine.

Anonymous. N.d. *Le Secret des secrets de la nature*. Avignon: Chaillot.

Aulagnier, F. 1830. *Dictionnaire de substances alimentaires indigènes et exotiques et de leurs propriétés.* 2 vols. Paris: Pillet aîné.

Barthélemi l'Anglais. 1999. *Le Livre des propriétés des choses, une encyclopédie au XIVe siècle.* Ed. B. Ribémont. Paris: Stock, Moyen Age.

Baudrimont, Alexandre Édouard and Jules Béclard. 1878. *Rapports sur l'hygiène alimentaire*. Paris: Congrès international d'hygiène de Paris.

Berthelot, Marcellin. 1893. "La Chimie au Moyen Age." In *Histoire des sciences*. Vol. 1. Paris: Imprimerie nationale.

Bertin-Sans, Henri. 1901. *Mesures hygiéniques pour empêcher la transmission de la tuberculose par le lait de vache.* Report to the Comité départmental d'hygiène publique et de salubrité de l'Hérault. Montpellier: Ricard.

Bicais, Michel. 1669. *La Manière de régler la santé par ce qui nous environne, par ce que nour recevons, et par les exercices ou la gymnastique moderne. Le tout appliqué au peuple de France, et pour servir d'exemple quelquefois aux habitants de la ville d'Aix.* Aix: David.

Bienville, J. D. T. de. 1775. *Traité des erreurs populaires sur la santé.* The Hague: Gosse.

Bizet, Louis Charles. 1847. *Du commerce de la boucherie et de la charcuterie de Paris et des commerces qui en dépendent.* Paris: P. Dupont.

Boissier de Sauvages, François. 1746. *Mémoire sur la maladie des boeufs du Vivarais* Montpellier: Rochard.

Bouchardat, Apollinaire and Gautier. 1878. *De la coloration artificielle des aliments et des boissons, et des dangers qui peuvent en résulter pour la santé publique.* Paris: Congrès international d'hygiène de Paris.

Bouley and Edmond Nocard. 1878. "Des produits alimentaires avariés ou falsifiés." Paris: Congrès international d'hygiène de Paris.

Brillat-Savarin, Jean Anthelme. 1996. *Physiologie du goût.* Paris: Flammarion.

Buchan, William. 1783. *Médecine domestique; ou, Traité complet des moyens de se conserver en santé, de guérir et de prévenir les Maladies par le régime et les remèdes simples; ouvrage utile aux personnes de tout état, et mis à la portée de tout le monde.* Trans. J.-D. Duplanil. Vol. I. 3d ed. Paris: Froullé.

Champier, Jean-Bruyérin. 1560. *De re cibaria. Libri XXII Omnium ciborum genera, omnium gentium moribus, et usu probata complectentes.* Lyons: Honoré. Translated into French as *L'Alimentation de tous les peuples et de tous les temps jusqu'au XVI siècle.* Paris: ICC, 1998.

Cheyne, George. 1724. *An Essay of Health and Long Life.* London.

Chomel, Noël. 1740. *Dictionnaire économique contenant divers moyens d'augmenter son bien et de conserver sa santé.* 2 vols. Paris: V Estienne.

Clusius, Carolus. 1605. *Exoticorum libri decem quibus animalium, plantatum, aromatum aliorumque peregrinorum fructuum historiae describuntur.* n.p.: Plantin.

Conseil d'hygiène publique et de salubrité du département du Vaucluse. 1859. In *Travaux, 1849–1858.* Avignon: Bonnet fils.

Darluc, Michel. 1782. *Histoire naturelle de la Provence, contenant ce qu'il y a de plus remarquable dans les règnes Végétal, Minéral, Animal et la partie géoponique.* 3 vols. Avignon: Niel.

Delamare, Nicolas. 1729. *Traité de police avec un recueil de tous les Statuts et Règlements des six corps de marchands et de toutes les communautés des Arts et Métiers.* 4 vols. 1705–1722. Reprint, Amsterdam.

Descartes, René. 2000. *Philosophical Essays and Correspondence.* Ed. Roger Ariew. Indianapolis: Hackett.

Devaux, Jean. 1683. *Le Médecin de soi-même; ou, L'Art de se conserver la santé par l'instinct.* Leiden: De Grael.

Dictionnaire des sciences médicales. 1813. Compiled by a society of doctors and surgeons. 60 vols. Paris: Panckoucke.

Ducreux, Robert. 1999. *Le Médecin radoteur; ou, Les Pots pourris et autres textes.* 1763. Ed. Rodolphe Trouilleux and Jean-Michel Roy. Reprint, Paris: H. Champion.

Dumas, Alexandre. 1998. *Mon dictionnaire de cuisine.* Paris: UGE.

Dupuy. 1833. "Rapport de M. Dupuy sur une épizootie observée par M. Fodéré." *Mémoire de l'Académie de médecine* 3: 359–76.

Ficin, Marsile. 1541. *Le Premier Livre de Marsille Ficin: De la vie saine, traduict de latin en françois par maistre Jehan Beaufilz advocat au chastelet de Paris, suivi du second livre La Vie longue.* Fols. 51 and 52. Paris.

Fodéré, François-Emmanuel. 1813. *Traité de médecine légale et d'hygiène publique; ou, De police de santé, adapté aux codes de l'Empire français, et aux connaissances actuelles, à l'usage des gens de l'Art, de ceux du Barreau, des jurés et des administrateurs de la santé publique, civile, militaire and de marine.* 3 vols. 2d ed. Paris: Mame.

Franck, Joseph. 1835. *Pathologie médicale.* 6 vols. In *Encyclopédie.* Paris.

Furetière, Antoine. 1690. *Dictionnaire universel.* Amsterdam.

Galtier, P.-V. 1897. *Traité des maladies contagieuses et de la police sanitaire des animaux domestiques.* Paris: Asselain et Houzeau.

———. N.d. *Manuel de police sanitaire.* Lyons.

Gerard, John. 1633/1975. *The Herbal or General History of Plants.* New York: Dover.

Gide, Charles. 1905. *Les Institutions du progrès social au début du XX siècle.* Paris: Sirey.

———. 1911. *Principes d'économie politique.* Paris: Sirey.

Grasse, Jean-Gaspard de. 2002. *Un Chanoine de Cavaillon au Grand Siècle: Le Livre de raison de Jean-Gaspard de Grasse (1664–1684).* Ed. F. Meyer. Paris: Editions du CTHS.

Grimaud, Jean-Charles. 1687. *Mémoire sur la nutrition.* Paris.

Grimod de La Reynière. 1997. *Ecrits gastronomiques.* Paris: UGE.

Hallé, Jean-Noël. 1787. "Aliment." In Félix Vicq d'Azyr, ed., *Encyclopédie méthodique.* Paris: Panckoucke.

———. 1835. "Histoire de l'hygiène." In *Encyclopédie des sciences médicales; ou, Traité général, méthodique et complet des diverses branches de l'art de guérir.* Vol. 1. Paris.

Joubert, Laurent. 1579. *La Médicine et le Régime de santé: Des erreurs populaires et propos vulgaires.* 2 vols. Bordeaux. Reprint, Paris: L'Harmattan, 1997.

Lancisi, Joseph Marie. 1748. *Opera omnia in duos tomos distributa.* Vol. 1, *Dissertatio historica de bovilla peste.* Geneva: Frères de Tournes.

Laumonier, J. 1911. *Hygiène de l'alimentation dans l'état de santé et de maladie.* Paris: Alcan.

Le Gendre, Gilbert-Charles. 1733. *Traité de l'opinion; ou, Mémoires pour servir à l'histoire de l'esprit humain.* 3 vols. Paris: Briasson.

Lémery, Louis. 1702. *Traité des aliments; ou, L'On trouve par ordre et séparément la différence et le choix qu'on doit faire de chacun d'eux en particulier.* Paris: Cusson et Witte.

Leroux des Tillets, Jean-Jacques. 1779. "Dialogue entre Pasquin et Marphoris." Unpublished.

Lespinasse, René de. 1879. *Les Métiers et corporations de la ville de Paris, XIII siècle: Le "Livre des métiers" d'Etienne Boileau.* Paris: Imprimerie nationale.

Lespinasse, René de and François Bonnardot. 1886. *Les Métiers et corporations de la ville de Paris.* Vol. 1, *Ordonnances générales: Métiers de l'alimentation.* Paris: Imprimerie nationale.

Liébault, Jean. 1572. *L'Agriculture et la maison rustique.* Paris.

Lieutaud, Joseph. 1768. *Précis de la matière médicale, contenant les connaissances les plus utiles sur l'histoire, la nature, les vertus et les doses des médicaments.* 2 vols. Paris: Vincent.

Marre, Francis. 1911. *Défendez votre estomac contre les fraudes alimentaires.* Paris: Henri Malet.

Masse, E. 1876. *Dangers du traitement par la viande crue et de l'alimentation par la viande de boeuf saignante.* Montpellier.

Mercier, Louis Sébastien. 1782–88. *Tableau de Paris.* 12 vols. Paris.

Montaigne, Michel de. 1991. *The Complete Essays.* Trans. M. A. Screech. Harmondsworth: Penguin.

Monteux, Jérôme de. 1559. *Commentaire de la conservation de la santé et prolongation de la vie.* Lyons: Jean de Tournes.

Nocard, Edouard and Emmanuel Leclainche. 1903. *Les Maladies microbiennes des animaux.* 2 vols. Paris: Masson.

Paré, Ambroise. 1953. *Textes choisis d'Ambroise Paré.* Ed. L. Delaruelle and M. Sendrail. Paris: Les Belles-Lettres.

Pasquier, Etienne. 1665/1996. *Les Recherches de la France.* 3 vols. Paris: Honoré Champion.

Pasquier, Félix. 1921. *Cartulaire de Mirepoix.* 2 vols. Toulouse: Privat.

Patin, Guy. 1846. *Lettres de Gui Patin.* Ed. J.-H. Reveillé-Parise. 3 vols. Paris: Baillière.

Paulet, Jean-Jacques. 1775. *Recherches historiques et physiques sur les maladies épizootiques avec les moyens d'y remédier dans tous les cas.* 2 vols. Paris: Rualt.

Payen, Anselme. 1865. *Précis théorique et pratique des substances alimentaires et des moyens de les améliorer, de les conserver et d'en reconnaître les altérations.* Paris: Hachette.

Pisanelli, Balthasar. 1584/1614. *Trattato della natura del cibi e de bere nel quale le virtu e i vizi di quelli si plesano.* Translated into Latin by Arnould Freitag, as *De esculentuorum potulentorum fecultatibus.* Geneva.

Pomet, Pierre. 1694. *Histoire générale des drogues, traitant des plantes, des animaux et des minéraux.* 2 vols. Paris: Loyson et Pillon.

Rabelais, François. 1955/1985. *Gargantua and Pantagruel.* Trans. J. M. Cohen. Harmondsworth: Penguin.

Raspail, François-Vincent. 1843. *Histoire naturelle de la santé et de la maladie, chez les végétaux, chez les animaux en général et en particulier chez l'homme.* 2 vols. Paris: Levavasseur.

———. 1845. *Manuel annuaire de la santé; ou, Médecine et pharmacie domestique, contenant tous les renseignements théoriques et pratiques nécessaires pour savoir préparer et employer soi-même les médicaments, se préserver ou se guérir ainsi promptement et à peu de frais.* Paris.

———. 1854. *Le Fermier-vétérinaire; ou, Méthode aussi économique que facile de préserver et de guérir les animaux domestiques et même les végétaux cultivés, du plus grand nombre de leurs maladies.* Paris.

Read. 1774. *Traité du seigle ergoté.* Metz: Collignon.

Reynal, Jean. 1873. *Traité de la police sanitaire des animaux domestiques.* Paris: Asselin.

Ronsard, Pierre de. 1979. *Poems of Pierre de Ronsard.* Trans. and ed. Nicholas Kilmer. Berkeley: University of California Press.

Roques, Joseph. 1837. *Nouveau Traité des plantes usuelles spécialement appliqué à la médicine domestique.* Paris: Dufart.

Rozier, François. 1770. *De la fermentation des vins et de la meilleure manière de faire l'eau-de-vie.* Lyons.

———. 1783. *Cours complet d'agriculture, théorique, pratique, économique, et de médecine rurale et vétérinaire.* 10 vols. Paris: Librairies associés.

———. 1787. *Démonstrations élémentaires de botaniques.* 3 vols. Lyons.

Saint-André, de. 1725. *Lettres de M. de Saint-André à quelques-uns de ses amis au sujet de la magie, des maléfices et des sorciers.* Paris: Mauduit.

Savary des Bruslons, Jacques. 1741. *Dictionnaire universel de commerce.* New ed. 2 vols. Paris: V Estienne.

Serao, Mario. 1898. *Le Ventre de Naples.* Paris: Plon.

Serres, Olivier de. 1600. *Le Théâtre d'agriculture et mesnage des champs.* Paris. Reprint, Aix-en-Provence: Actes Sud, 1997.

Sinclair, Upton. 1986. *The Jungle.* New York: Penguin.

Smith, Adam. 1976. *An Inquiry into the Nature and Causes of the Wealth of Nations.* Vol. 1. Ed. R. H. Campbell, A. S. Skinner, and W. B. Todd. Oxford: Oxford University Press.

Thomassin, Jean-François. 1782. *Dissertation sur le charbon malin de la Bourgogne ou pustule maligne.* Basel.

Tissot, Samuel. 1768. *De la santé des gens de lettres.* Lausanne: Grasset.

———. 1785. *Avis au peuple sur sa santé.* Lausanne: Grasset.

Tourtelle, E. 1837. "Eléments d'hygiène." In *Encyclopédie des sciences médicales; ou, Traité général, méthodique et complet des diverses branches de l'art de guérir.* Paris.

Venel, Gabriel. 1803. *Précis de matière médicale.* 2 vols. Paris: Caille et Gravier.

Vicq d'Azyr, Félix, ed. 1787. *Encyclopédie méthodique.* Paris-Liège: Panckoucke, 1787.

Villon, François. 1960. *The Complete Works of François Villon.* Trans. Anthony Bonner. Intro. William Carlos Williams. New York: McKay.

Waton, François-Maximilien-Lubin and J. Guérin. 1800. *Essais de médecine et d'histoire naturelle.* Carpentras: V. Raphel.

Willich, Anthony Florian Madinger. 1802. *Hygiène domestique; ou, L'Art de conserver la santé et de prolonger la vie, mis à la portée des gens du monde.* Trans. E. M. Itard. 2 vols. Paris: Ducauroy-Deterville.

Zimmermann, Johann. 1774. *Traité de l'expérience en général, et en particulier dans l'art de guérir.* Trans. Le Fevre. 3 vols. Paris: Vincent.

Secondary Sources

The date given for each work is the date of the edition consulted.

Abad, Reynald. 2002. *Le Grand Marché: L'Approvisionnement alimentaire de Paris sous l'ancien régime.* Paris: Fayard.

Adrian, Jean. 1994. *Les Pionniers français de la science alimentaire: Leur vie, leurs découvertes.* Paris: Lavoisier Tec/Doc.

Agulhon, Maurice. 1981. "Le sang des bêtes: Le probème de la protection des animaux en France au XIX siècle." *Romantisme,* no. 31:81–109.

Allendy, René. 1987. *Paracelse, le médecin maudit.* Paris: Deruy.

Antonioli, Roland. 1976. *Rabelais et la médecine.* Geneva: Droz.

Apfelbaum, Marian, ed. 1998. *Risques et peurs alimentaires.* Paris: Odile Jacob.

Aron, Jean-Paul. 1965. "Histoire et biologie: Alimentation et épidémies au XIX siècle." *Bulletin de la Société d'histoire moderne* 13, no. 1: 3–9.

———. 1973. *Le Mangeur du XIX siècle.* Paris: Robert Laffont.

Aymard, Maurice. 1983. "L'approvisionnement des villes de la Méditerranée occidentale (XVIe–XVIIIe siècle)." In *L'Approvisionnement des villes de l'Europe occidentale du Moyen Age aux Temps modernes,* 165–88. Colloque de Flaran 5, Auch.

———. 1997. "Les pratiques de l'alimentation carnée en France." *Le Mangeur et l'animal: Mutations de l'élevage et de la consommation,* special issue of *Autrement,* no. 172: 87–102.

Bach-Lijour, Béatrice. 1993. "Vicq d'Azyr et l'épizootie de 1774 dans le Sud-Ouest de la France." In Robert Durand, ed., *L'Homme, l'animal domestique et l'environnement du Moyen Age au XVIIIe siècle.* Proceedings of the Colloque de Nantes, 1992. Nantes: Ouest-Editions.

Bachelard, Gaston. 1996. *La Formation de l'esprit scientifique.* Paris: Vrin.

Baillet, Lina. 1982. "Au XVI siècle à Colmar: Cuisine et santé, le recueil d'Anna Wecker." *Annuaire d'histoire et d'archéologie,* 41–53.

Baratay, Eric. 1996. *L'Eglise et l'animal: France, XVIIe–XXe siècle*. Paris: Cerf.

Bardet, J.-Pierre, Patrice Bourdelais, Pierre Guillaume, François Lebrun, and Claude Quétel. 1988. *Peurs et terreurs face à la contagion: Choléra, tuberculose, syphilis, XIXe–XXe siècle*. Paris: Fayard.

Barrau, Jacques. 1983. *Les Hommes et leurs aliments*. Paris: Messidor–Temps Actuels.

Beaujouan, Guy, Yvonne Poulle-Drieux, and Jeanne-Marie Dureau-Lapyssonie. 1966. *Médecine humaine et vétéinaire à la fin du Moyen Age*. Geneva: Droz.

Bellinazzi, Anna. 1982. "Malnutrizione cerebrale et ipoalimentazione da povertà: Dati e ipotesi (secoli XVII–XVIII)." *Timore e carità: I poveri nell' Italia moderna*, pp. 375–391. Proceedings of the conference "Pauperismo e assistenza negli antichi stati italiani." Cremona.

Bercé, Yves-Marie. 1984. *Le Chaudron et la lancette: Croyances populaires et médecine préventive, 1798–1830*. Paris: Presses de la Renaissance.

Bériac, Françoise. 1984. "Le vocabulaire de la lèpre dans l'Ouest des pays de langue d'oc." *Annales du Midi*, no. 168 (October–December): 331–53.

———. 1988. *Histoire des lépreux au Moyen Age: Une Société d'exclus*. Paris: Imago.

———. 1989. "Connaissances médicales sur la lèpre et protection contre cette maladie au Moyen Age." In Neithard Bulst and Robert Delort, eds., *Maladies et Société: XIIe–XVIII siècle*. Proceedings of the Colloque de Bielefeld, 1986. Paris: Editions du CNRS.

———. 1990. *Des lépreux aux cagots: Recherches sur les sociétés marginales en Aquitaine médiévale*. Bordeaux: Féderation historique du Sud-Ouest, 1990.

Bianchi-Bensimon, Nella. 1999. "Alimentation et mélancolie dans le *De vita libri tres* de Marsile Ficin." In *La Table et ses dessous: Culture, alimentation et convivialité en Italie (XVIe–XVIesiècle)*. Cahiers de la Renaissance italienne. Paris: Presses de la Sorbonne Nouvelle.

Bigwood, Edouard Jean and Alain Gérard. 1967–71. *Objectifs et principes fondamentaux d'un droit comparé de l'alimentation*. Basel: S. Karger.

Biraben, Jean-Noël. 1976. *Les Hommes et la peste en France et dans les pays européens et méditerranéens*. Paris: Mouton.

Blake, John Ballard. 1959. *Public Health in the Town of Boston, 1630–1822*. Cambridge: Harvard University Press.

Blancou, Jean. 2000. *Histoire de la surveillance et du contrôle des maladies animales transmissible*. Paris: Office international des épizooties.

Bobis, Laurence. 1993. "L'Evolution de la place du chat dans l'espace social et l'imaginaire occidental du Moyen Age au XVIIIe siècle." In Robert Durand, ed., *L'Homme, l'animal domestique et l'environnement, du Moyen Age au XVIII siècle*. Proceedings of the Colloque de Nantes, 1992. Nantes: Ouest-Editions.

Bodson, Liliane. 1991. "Le Vocabulaire latin des maladies pestilentielles et épizootiques." In Guy Sabbah, ed., *Le Latin médical: La Constitution d'un langage scientifique. Réalités et langage de la médecine dans le monde romain*. Proceedings of the third Colloque international sur les textes médicaux latins antiques, 1989. Saint-Etienne: Presses de l'Université.

Bonnassie, Pierre. 2001. "Consommation d'aliments immondes et cannibalisme de survie dans l'Occident du haut Moyen Age." In *Les Sociétés de l'an mil: Un Monde entre deux âges*. Brussels: De Boeck Université.

Bouchon, Marianne. 1952. "Latin de cuisine." *Archivium latinatis Medii Aevi* 22:63–76.

Bourde, André. 1967. *Agronomie et agronomes en France au XVIIIe siècle*. Vol. 1. Paris: SEVPEN.

Bourges, Michel. 1968. "Essai sur l'histoire de la lèpre: Du concept lépreux à la microscopie électronique." Medical thesis, Clermont-Ferrand.

Bourguinat, Nicolas. 2002. *Les Grains du désordre: L'Etat face aux violences frumentaires dans la première moitié du XIXe siècle.* Paris: Editions du l'EHESS.

Brabant, Henri. 1966. *Médecins, malades, et maladies de la Renaissance.* N.p.: La Renaissance du livre.

Branlard, Jean-Paul. 1999. *Droit et gastronomie: Aspect juridique de l'alimentation et des produits gourmands.* Paris: Gualino.

Braudel, Fernand. 1967. *Civilisation matérielle et capitalisme.* Paris: Armand Colin.

Brears, Peter. 1993. *A Taste of History: 10,000 Years of Food in Britain.* London: British Museum Press.

Brockliss, Laurence and Colin Jones. 1997. *The Medical World of Early Modern France.* Oxford: Clarendon.

Bulst, Neithard and Robert Delort, eds. 1989. *Maladies et Sociétés: XIIe–XVIIIe siècle.* Proceedings of the Colloque de Bielefeld, 1986. Paris: Editions du CNRS.

Cahen, Léon. N.d. "L'Approvisionnement en pain de Paris au XVIIIe siècle et la question de la boulangerie." Paris: Rivière.

Campion-Vincent, Véronique. 1994. "La Véritable Histoire de l'os de rat." *Manger magique: Aliments sorciers, croyances comestibles,* special issue of *Autrement,* no. 149: 85–91.

Camporesi, Piero. 1981. *Le Pain sauvage: L'imagination de la faim, de la Renaissance au XVIIIe siècle.* Paris: Chemin vert.

——. 1993. *La Terre et la lune: Aliment, folklore, société.* Paris: Aubier.

——. 1995. *Les Effluves du temps jadis.* Paris: Plon.

Candolle, Alphonse de. 1886. *Origine des plantes cultivées.* Paris: Alcan.

Castellazi, Laura. 1995. "Legislazione sanitaria per l'alimentazione a Verona in epoca veneta." In *Archiva per la storia dell'alimentazione,* 2:879–93. Rome.

Cazes-Valette, Geneviève. 1997. "La Vache folle." In *Cultures, nourritures: Internationales de l'imaginaire,* no. 7: 205–33.

Céard, Jean. 1982. "La Diététique dans la médecine de la Renaissance." In Jean-Claude Margolin and Robert Sauzet, eds., *Pratiques et discours alimentaires à la Renaissance.* Proceedings of the Colloque de Tours, 1979. Paris: Maisonneuve et Larose.

Chateauraynaud, Francis and Didier Torny. 1994. *Les Sombres Précurseurs: Une Sociologie pragmatique de l'alerte et du risque.* Paris: Editions de l'EHESS.

Chaumartin, Henry. 1946. *Le Mal des ardents et le feu saint Antoine: Etude historique, médicale, hagiographique and légendaire.* Vienna: self-published.

Chaunu, Pierre. 1976. *Les Amériques, XVIe, XVIIe, XVIIIe siècles.* Paris: Armand Colin.

Chevalier, Bernard. 1982. "L'Alimentation carnée à la fin de XVe siècle: réalité et symbole." In Jean-Claude Margolin and Robert Sauzet, eds., *Practiques et discours alimentaires à la Renaissance.* Proceedings of the Colloque de Tours, 1979. Paris: Maisonneuve et Larose.

Coleman, William. 1974. "Health and Hygiene in the *Encyclopédie*: A Medical Doctrine for the Bourgeoisie." *Journal of the History of Medicine* 29: 399–421.

——. 1977. "The People's Health: Medical Themes in Eighteen-Century Popular Medicine." *Bulletin for the History of Medicine,* no. 51:55–74.

Comet, Georges. 1995. "L'Iconographie des "plantes nouvelles"; ou, Une Approche des débuts de la botanique moderne." In *Campagnes médiévales: L'Homme et son espace. Etudes offertes à Robert Fossier.* Paris: Publications de la Sorbonne.

Corbin, Alain. 1986. *Le Miasme et la jonquille: L'Odorat et l'imaginaire social. XVIIIe–XIXe siècle.* Paris: Flammerion, Champs.

Cosmacini, Giorgio. 1992. *Soigner et réformer: Médecine et santé en Italie, de la Grande Peste à la Première Guerre mondiale.* Paris: Payot.

———. 1996. *Medici nella storia d'Italia: Per una tipologia della professione.* Rome: Laterza.

Cougoul, Jacques. 1943. *La Lèpre dans l'ancienne France.* Medical thesis, Bordeaux.

Coulet, Noël. 1978. "'Juif intouchable' et interdits alimentaires." *Sénéfiance* 5:209–21.

Dack, G. M. 1943. *Food Poisoning.* Chicago: University of Chicago Press.

Dandrey, Patrick. 1993. *Le "Cal" argan: Molière et la maladie imaginaire.* Paris: Klincksieck.

Darmon, Pierre. 1999. *L'Homme et les microbes: XVIIIe–XXe siècle.* Paris: Fayard.

Daston, Lorraine. 1988. *Classical Probability in the Enlightenment.* Princeton: Princeton University Press.

Debouzy, Marianne. 1972. *Le Capitalisme "sauvage" aux Etats-Unis, 1860–1900.* Paris: Seuil.

Debus, A. G. 1991. *The French Paracelsians: The Chemical Challenge to Medical and Scientific Tradition in Early Modern France.* Cambridge: University Press of Cambridge.

Delaunay, Paul. 1935. *La Vie médicale aux XVIe, XVIIe, XVIIIe siècles.* Paris. Reprint, Geneva: Slatkine Reprints, 2001.

Delort, Robert. 1984. *Les animaux ont une histoire.* Paris: Seuil.

Delsalle, Paul. 2001. "Façons de vendre, façons d'acheter, sur les marchés au coeur de l'Europe (XVIe siècle et première moitié du XVIIe siècle)." In *Fiere e mercati nella integrazione delle economie euroopee secc. XIII–XVIII.* Florence: Le Monnier.

Delumeau, Jean. 1978. *La Peur en Occident (XIVe–XVIIIe siècle): Une Cité assiégée.* Paris: Fayard.

Deramaix, Robert. 1932. *L'Hygiène et les consuls lyonnais: Le Bureau de santé.* Lyons: Audin.

Deroux, Carl. 1991. "La Digestion dans la *Diététique* d'Anthimus: Langage, mythe et réalités." In Guy Sabbah, ed., *Le Latin médical: La Constitution d'un langage scientifique. Réalités et langage de la médecine dans le monde romain.* Proceedings of the third Colloque international sur les textes médicaux latins antiques, 1989. Saint-Etienne: Presses de l'Université.

Desaive, Jean-Paul and Jean-Pierre Goubert. 1972. *Médecins, climat et épidémies à la fin du XVIIIe siècle.* Paris: Mouton.

Desportes, Françoise. 1987. *Le Pain au Moyen Age.* Paris: Olivier Orban.

Di Munno Malavasi, Carla. 1995. "L'Azione del Magistrato ordinario, del Magistrato della sanità et des Consiglio di governo in materia di alimentazione nello stato di Milano nei secoli XVI–XVIII." In *Acchivi per la storia dell'alimentazione,* 1:551–67. Rome.

Douglas, Mary. 1981. *De la souillure: Essai sur les notions de pollution et de tabou.* Paris: Maspero, Bibliothèque d'anthropologie.

Douglas, Mary and Aaron Wildavsky. 1982. *Risk and Culture: An Essay on the Selection of Technical and Environmental Dangers.* Berkeley: University of California Press.

Duby, Georges. 1973. "L'Urbanisation dans l'histoire." *Etudes rurales,* no. 49–50:10–14.

Dupèbe, Jean. 1982. "La Diététique et l'alimentation des pauvres selon Sylvius." In Jean-Claude Margolin and Robert Sauzet, eds., *Pratiques et discours alimentaires à la Renaissance.* Proceedings of the Colloque de Tours, 1979. Paris: Maisonneuve et Larose.

Durand, Robert, ed. 1993. *L'Homme, l'animal domestique et l'environnement du Moyen Age au XVIIIe siècle.* Proceedings of the Colloque de Nantes, 1992. Nantes: Ouest-Editions.

Elias, Norbert. 1973. *La Civilisation des moeurs*. Paris: Calmann-Lévy.

Fabre-Vassas, Claudine. 1994. *La Bête singulière: Les Juifs, les chrétiens et le cochon*. Paris: Gallimard.

Farb, Peter and George Armelagos. 1980. *Anthropologie des coutumes alimentaires*. Paris: Denoël.

Faure, Olivier. 1997. "Le Bétail dans la ville au XIXe siècle: Exclusion ou enfermement?" *Cahiers d'histoire* 42, nos. 3–4: 555–74.

Febvre, Lucien. 1956. "Pour l'histoire d'un sentiment: Le Besoin de sécurité." *Annales ESC*, no. 2 (April–June): 244–46.

———. 1970. *Philippe II et la Franche-Comté: Etude d'histoire politique, religiuese et sociale*. Paris: Flammarion.

Feillet, Alphonse. 1886. *La Misère au temps de la Fronde et saint Vincent de Paul; ou, Un Chapitre de l'histoire du paupérisme en France*. Paris: Perrin.

Ferrières, Madeleine. 2002. "Les Confitures et l'économie domestique d'Olivier de Serres." In *Autour d'Olivier de Serres*, 359–70. Proceedings of the 2000 Pradel conference. Caen: Belmont.

———. 2004. *Le Bien des pauvres: La Consommation populaire en Avignon (1600–1800)*. Seyssel: Champ Vallon.

Figeac, Michel. 2001. *La Douceur des lumières: Noblesse et art de vivre en Guyenne au XVIIe siècle*. Bordeaux: Mollat.

Fischler, Claude. 1993. *L'Homnivore: Le Goût, la cuisine et le corps*. Paris: Odile Jacob.

———, ed. 1994. *Manger magique: Aliments sorciers, croyances comestibles*. Special issue of *Autrement*, no. 149.

Flandrin, Jean-Louis. 1982. "Médecine et habitudes alimentaires anciennes." In *Pratiques et discours alimentaires à la Renaissance*. Paris: Maisonneuve et Larose.

———. 1998. "Risques et angoisses alimentaires avant le XIXe siècles." In M. Apfelbaum, ed., *Risques et peurs alimentaires*. Paris: Odile Jacob.

Flandrin, Jean-Louis and Massimo Montanari, eds. 1996. *Histoire de l'alimentation*. Paris: Fayard.

Foisil, Madeleine. 1986. *Le Sire de Gouberville: Un Gentilhomme normand au XVIe siècle*. Paris: Flammarion.

Fontenay, Elizabeth de. 1998. *Le Silence des bêtes: La philosophie à l'épreuve de l'animalité*. Paris: Fayard.

Fossat, Jean-Louis. 1971. *La Formation du vocabulaire gascon de la boucherie et de la charcuterie: Etude de lexicologie historique et descriptive*. Toulouse-I: Ménard.

Foucault, Michel. 1963. *Surveiller et punir: Naissance de la clinique*. Paris: PUF.

Fourgoux, Jean-Claude and Georges Jumel. 1968. *Traité de droit alimentaire*. Paris: FRANTEL.

Fournier, Patrick. 1999. *Eaux claires eaux troubles dans le Comtat venaissin (XVIIe–XVIIIe siècle)*. Perpignan: Presses universitaires de Perpignan/CHEC.

Garnot, Benoît. 1996. *Vivre en Bourgogne au XVIIIe siècle*. Dijon: PUB.

Garrier, Gilbert. 1996. *Histoire sociale et culturelle du vin*. Paris: Bordas.

Gaudillière, Jean-Paul. 2001. "Echos d'une crise centenaire." *La Recherche*, no. 339 (February): 14–18.

Gerbaud, Olivier. 1993. "Le Besoin de vétérinaires et la création d'écoles vétérinaires secondaires dans la France rurale à la fin du XVIIesiècle." In Robert Durand, ed., *L'Homme, l'animale domestique et l'environnement du Moyen Age au XVIIIe siècle*. Proceedings of the Colloque de Nantes, 1992. Nantes: Ouest-Editions.

Giamcomo, Mathée. 1999. "L'Or des épices, la chair de l'autre, le langage du même." In *La Table et ses dessous: Culture, alimentation et convivialité en Italie (XIVe–XVIe siècle)*. Cahiers de la Renaissance italienne. Paris: Presses de la Sorbonne Nouvelle.

Gil-Sotres, Pedro. 1995. "Les Régimes de santé." In *Histoire de la pensée médicale en Occident*. Vol. 1, *Antiquité et Moyen Age*. Paris: Seuil.

Godard, Misette. 1991. *Le Goût de l'aigre: Essai de gastronomie historique*. Paris: Quai Voltaire, Histoire.

Goubert, Jean-Pierre. 1989. "Epidémie, médecine et état en France à la fin de l'ancien régime." In Neithard Bulst and Robert Delort, eds., *Maladies et Sociétés: XVIIe–XVIIe siècle*. Proceedings of the Colloque de Bielefeld, 1986. Paris: Editions. du CNRS.

——, ed. 1982. *La Médicalisation de la société française, 1770–1830*. Waterloo, Canada: University of Waterloo.

Gourevitch, Danielle, ed. 1992. *Malades et maladies, histoire et conceptualisation: Mélanges en l'honneur de M. D. Grmek*. Geneva: Droz.

Gouron, André. 1958. *La Réglementation des métiers en Languedoc au Moyen Age*. Paris: Minard.

Grmek, Mirko. 1983. *Les Maladies à l'aube de la civilisation occidentale*. Paris: Payot.

——. 1997a. "Les Débuts de la quarantaine maritime." In Christian Buchet, ed., *L'Homme, la santé et la mer*. Paris: Honoré Champion.

——, ed. 1997b. *Histoire de la pensée médicale en Occident*. Paris: Seuil.

Guéneau, Lucien. 1922. "La Cabale des bouchers de Lyon en 1714." In *Mémoires et documents pour servir à l'histoire du commerce et de l'industrie en France*. Paris: Hachette.

Guillaume, Pierre. 1986. *Du désespoir au salut: Les Tuberculeux aux XIXe et XXe siècles*. Paris: Aubier.

——. 1996. *Le Rôle social du médecin depuis deux siècles (1800–1945)*. Paris: Comité d'histoire de la sécurité sociale.

Gusdorf, Georges. 1972. *Les Sciences humaines et la pensée occidentale*. Vol. 5, *Dieu, la nature, l'homme au siècle des Lumières*. Paris: Payot.

Gutton, Jean-Pierre. 1994. *Guide du chercheur en histoire de la protection sociale*. Vol. 1, *Fin du Moyen Age–1789*. Paris: Association pour l'étude de l'histoire de la sécurité sociale.

Hamraoui, Eric. 2000. "L'Oeuvre d'Hippocrate revisitée par la pensée médicale des Lumières: L'Exemple des traités médicaux de G. M. Lancisi (1654–1720)." In Henri Michel, ed., *Hellénisme et Hippocratisme dans l'Europe méditerranéenne: Autour de D. Coray*. Proceedings of the conference of 1998. Montpellier: Université Paul-Valéry.

Hannaway, Caroline. 1977. "Veterinary Medicine and Rural Health Care in Pre-Revolutionary France." *Bulletin of the History of Medicine* 51:431–47.

Herzlich, Claudine. 1984. *Santé et maladie: Analyse d'une représentation sociale*. Paris: Editions de l'EHESS.

Hildesheimer, Françoise. 1980. *Le Bureau de santé de Marseille sous l'ancien régime: Le Renfermement de la contagion*. Marseille: Fédération historique de Provence.

Hubsher, Ronald. 1999. *Les Maîtres des bêtes: Les Vétérinaires dans la société française (XVIIIe–XXe siècle)*. Paris: Odile Jacob.

Hudemann-Simon, Calixte. 2000. *La Conquête de la santé en Europe. 1750–1900*. Paris: Belin-De Boeck.

Huriet, Claude. 1997. *Les Conditions du renforcement du la veille sanitaire et du contrôle de la sécurité sanitaire des produits destinés à l'homme en France*. Rapport d'information no. 196. Paris: Commission des affaires sociales du Sénat.

Ingrand, H. 1934. "Le Comité du salubrité de l'Assemblée nationale constituante (1790–1791)." Medical thesis, Paris.

Jacquart, Danielle. 1981. *Le Milieu médical en France du XIIe au XVe siècle.* Geneva: Droz.

———. 1998. *La Médecine médiévale dans le cadre parisien, XIVe–XVe siècle.* Paris: Fayard.

Jacquart, Danielle and Marylin Nicoud. 1995. "Les Régimes de santé au XIIIe siècle." In P. Guichard and D. Alexandre-Bidon, eds., *Comprendre le XIIIe siècle: Etudes offertes à Marie-Thérèse Lorcin.* Lyon: Presses universitaires de Lyon.

Jacquet, R., J. Claudian, and J. Trémolières. 1956. "Les Conserves dans l'alimentation de l'homme: Leur rôle en diététique et thérapeutique." *Revue de pathologie générale et comparée,* 80–87.

Kaplan, Steven Laurence. 1996. *Le Meilleur Pain du monde: Les Boulangers de Paris au XVIIe siècle.* Paris: Fayard.

———. 1997. Between Habit and Necessity: The "Ersatz" Question in Eighteenth-Century France." In *L'Histoire grande ouverte. Hommages à Emmanuel Le Roy Ladurie.* Paris: Fayard.

———. 1998. *Les Ventres de Paris: Pouvoir et approvisionnement dans la France d'ancien régime.* Paris: Fayard.

Kiener, Michel Christophe and Jean-Claude Peyronnet. 1979. *Quand Turgot régnait en Limousin: Un Tremplin vers le pouvoir.* Paris: Fayard.

Kiple, F. Kenneth and Kriemhild Coneè Ornelas, eds. 2000. *The Cambridge World History of Food.* 2 vols. Cambridge: Cambridge University Press.

Koninckx, Christian. 1983. "L'Alimentation et la pathologie des déficiencies alimentaires dans la navigation au long cours au XVIIe siècle." *Revue d'histoire moderne et contemporaine* 1:109–38.

Kourilsky, Philippe and Geneviève Viney. 2000. *Le Principe de précaution: Rapport au premier ministre.* Paris: Odile Jacob/La Documentation française.

Koyré, Alexandre. 1955. *Mystiques, Spirituels et Alchimistes du XVIe siècle allemand.* Cahiers des Annales, no. 10. Paris: Armand Colin.

Kriegel, Maurice. 1976. "Un Trait de psychologie sociale dans les pays méditerranéens du bas Moyen Age: Le Juif comme intouchable." *Annales ESC,* no. 2:326–30.

Lachiver, Marcel. 1991. *Les Années de misère: La famine au temps du grand roi, 1680–1720.* Paris: Fayard.

Lalande, Emmanuel. 1896. *La Vie et les oeuvres de maître Arnaud de Villeneuve.* Paris: Chamuel.

Larguier, Gilbert. 1994. "Viandes et espaces urbains à l'époque moderne: Le Cas de Narbonne." In A. Blanchard, H. Michel, and E. Pélaquier, eds., *De l'herbe à la table: La Viande dans la France méridionale à l'époque moderne.* Montpellier: Presses universitaires de Montpellier.

La Roncière, Charles de. 1983. "L'Approvisionnement des villes italiennes au Moyen Age (XIVe–XVe siècle). In *L'Approvisionnement des villes de l'Europe occidentale du Moyen Age aux Temps modernes.* Colloque de Flaran 5. Auch.

Lassablière, Pierre, ed. 1950. *Encyclopédie de l'alimentation: Scientifique- médicale-hygiénique-gastronomique.* 2 vols. Paris: Maloine.

Latour, Bruno. 1991. *Nous n'avons jamais été modernes.* Paris: La Découverte.

Launay, Henry de. 1906. *L'Hygiène publique à travers les âges.* Paris: Vigot.

Laurioux, Bruno. 1993. "La Cuisine des médecins à la fin du Moyen Age." In *Maladie, médecines et sociétés: Approches historiques pour le présent. Actes du VIe colloque d'Histoire au présent,* 2:136–48. Paris: L'Harmattan, 1993.

————. 1996. "Cuisines médiévales." In Jean-Louis Flandrin and Massimo Montanari, eds., *Histoire de l'alimentation*. Paris: Fayard.

————. 1997. *Le Règne de Taillevent: Livres et pratiques culinaires à la fin du Moyen Age*. Paris: Publications de la Sorbonne.

Lazard, Sylviane. 1999. "L'Institution alimentaire dans le Reggimento e costumi de donna de Francesco da Barberino." In *La Table et ses dessous: Culture, alimentation et convivialité en Italie (XIVe–XVIe siècle)*. Cahiers de la Renaissance italienne. Paris: Presses de la Sorbonne Nouvelle.

Lebigre, Arlette. 1986. "Haro sur les 'aliments indignes'!" *L'Histoire*, no. 85:124–27.

Le Breton, David. 2000. *Passions du risque*. Paris: Métailié.

Lebrun, François. 1971. *Les Hommes et la mort en Anjou aux XVIIIe et XVIIIe siècles: Essai de démographie et de psychologie historique*. Paris: Mouton.

————. 1982. "L'Intervention des autorités en matière de santé publique en France aux XVIIe et XVIIIe siècles." *Histoire des sciences médicales* 17.

————. 1983. *Se soigner autrefois: Médecins, saints et sorciers aux XVIIe et XVIIIe siècles*. Paris: Temps actuels.

————. 2001. *Croyances et cultures dans la France d'ancien régime*. Paris: Seuil.

Leclainche, Emmanuel. 1936. *Histoire de la médecine vétérinaire*. Toulouse: Office de livre.

Lecuyer, B. P. 1977. "Démographie, statistique et hygiène publique sous la monarchie censitaire." *Annales de démographie historique*, 215–49.

Lederer, Jean. 1986. *Encyclopédie moderne de l'hygiène alimentaire*. Paris: Maloine.

Leguay, Jean-Pierre. 1999. *La Pollution au Moyen Age dans le royaume de France et dans les grand fiefs*. Vol. 2. Paris: J.-P. Gisserot.

Lenardon, Dante. 1986. *Index du Journal de Trévoux, 1701–1767*. Geneva: Slatkine.

Léonard, Jacques. 1986. *Archives du corps: La Santé au XIXe siècle*. Rennes: Ouest-France.

Le Roy Ladurie, Emmanuel. 1975. *Montaillou, village occitan, de 1294 à 1324*. Paris: Gallimard.

Lesage, Claire. 1999. "Le Savoir alimentaire féminin dans *Il merito delle donne* de Moderata Fonte." In *La Table et ses dessous: Culture, alimentation et convivialité en Italie (XIVe–XVIe siècle)*. Cahiers de la Renaissance italienne. Paris: Presses de la Sorbonne Nouvelle.

Levenstein, Harvey A. 1996. "Diététique contre gastronomie: Traditions culinaires, sainteté et santé dans les modèles de vie américains." In Jean-Louis Flandrin and Massimo Montanari, eds., *Histoire de l'alimentation*. Paris: Fayard.

Lévi-Strauss, Claude. 1966. *The Savage Mind*. Trans. John Weightman and Doreen Weightman. Chicago: University of Chicago Press.

Leyral, Guy and Elisabeth Vierling. 1996. *Microbiologie et toxicologie des aliments: Hygiène et sécurité alimentaire*. Vélizy: Doin.

Linden, David E. J. 1999. "Gabriele Zerbi's *De cautelis medicorum* and the Tradition of Medical Prudence." *Bulletin of the History of Medicine*, no. 1:19–29.

Loux, Françoise and Philippe Richard. 1978. *Sagesse du corps: La santé et la maladie dans les proverbes français*. Paris: Maisonneuve et Larose.

Lunel, Pierre. 1974. "Pouvoir royal et santé publique à la veille de la Révolution: L'Exemple du Roussillon." *Annales du Midi* 86, no. 116 (October–December): 345–80.

McNeill, William H. 1978. *Le Temps de la peste: Essai sur les épidémies dans l'histoire*. Paris: Hachette Littérature.

Malassis, Louis. 1997. *Les Trois Ages de l'alimentaire: Essai sur une histoire sociale de l'alimentation et de l'agriculture.* Vol. 1, *L'Age pré-agricole at l'Age industriel;* vol. 2, *L'Age agro-industriel.* Paris: Cujas.

Maleissye, Jean de. 1991. *Histoire du poison.* Paris: F. Bourin.

Mammerickx, Henri. 1994. "Les Anciennes Méthodes de prophylaxie des maladies animales en Belgique." *Revue scientifique et technique de l'Office international des épizooties,* no. 13:487–98.

Mandrou, Robert. 1974. *Introduction à la France moderne, 1500–1640: Essai de psychologie historique.* Paris: Albin Michel.

———. 1980. *Magistrats et sorciers en France au XVIIe siècle: Une Analyse de psychologie historique.* Paris: Seuil.

Maragi, Mario. 1982. "La Santé publique dans les anciens statuts de la ville de Bologne, 1245–1288." *Histoire des sciences médicales* 17.

Marcet-Juncosa, Alice. 1993. "Malades et maladies en Roussillon à l'époque moderne." In *Du Roussillon et d'ailleurs: Images des Temps modernes.* Perpigan: PUP-CREPF.

Maurizio, A. 1932. *Histoire de l'alimentation végétale depuis la Préhistoire jusqu'à nos jours.* Paris: Payot.

Méchin, Colette. 1992. *Bêtes à manger: Usages alimentaires des Français.* Nancy: Presses universitaires de Nancy.

Metzger, Henri. 1930. *La Chimie: Histoire du monde.* Vol. 13. Paris: De Boccard.

Meyer, Jean. 1966. "Un Enquête de l'Académie de médecine sur les épidémies, 1774–1794." *Annales ESC,* 729–49.

———. 1989. *Histoire du sucre.* Paris: Desjonquères.

Michel, Henri, ed. 2000. *Hellénisme et Hippocratisme dans l'Europe moderne: Autour de D. Coray.* Actes du colloque de Montpellier, 1998. Montpellier: Presses universitaires de Montpellier.

Miller, A. R. 1962. "Slaughterhouse or Abattoir." In *Encyclopedia britannica,* 20:771–73. Chicago: W. Benton.

Monner, Raoul. 1941. *Le Commerce et l'inspection des viandes sous l'ancien régime.* Lyons: Bosc et Riou.

Montanari, Massimo. 1995. *La Faim et l'abondance: Histoire de l'alimentation en Europe.* Paris: Seuil.

Moriceau, Jean-Marc. 1999. *L'Elevage sous l'ancien régime (XVIe–XVIIIe siècle).* Paris: SEDES.

Morineau, Michel. 1985. "Cendrillon devenue fée: La Pomme de terre au XVIIe siècle." In *Pour une histoire économique vraie.* Lille: Presses universitaires de Lille.

Muchembled, Robert. 1978. *Culture populaire et culture des élites dans la France moderne (Xve–XVIIIe siècle).* Paris: Flammarion.

Murard, Lion and Patrick Zylberman. 1996. *L'Hygiène de la République: La Santé publique en France; ou, L'Utopie contrariée (1870–1918).* Paris: Fayard.

Muratori-Philip, Anne. 1994. *Parmentier.* Paris: Plon.

Nada Patrone, Anna Maria. 1995. "Gli statuti comunali come fonte per la storia dell'alimetazione." In *Gli achiva per la storia dell'alimentazione.* Rome.

Nicoud, Marylin. 1995. "L'Adaptation du discours diététique aux pratiques alimentaires: L'Exemple de Barnabas de Reggio." *Mélanges de l'Ecole française de Rome* 107:207–31.

———. 1998. *Aux origines d'une médecine préventive: Les Traités de diététique en Italie et en France (XII–XV siècle).* 2 vols. Paris: EPHE.

Nicoud, Marylin and Danielle Jacquart. 1995. "Les Régimes de santé au XIIIe siècle." In *Comprende le XIIIe siècle: Etudes offertes à Marie-Thérèse Lorcin*. Lyon: Presses universitaires de Lyon.

Oldoni, Massimo. 1995. "I Regimina sanitatas." In *Archivi per la storia dell'alimentazione*, 2:1790–1800. Rome.

O.M.S. 1974. *Maladies d'origine alimentaires: Méthodes d'echantillonage et d'examen dans les programmes de surveillance.* Technical report, no. 543. Geneva.

Palou, Jean. 1958. *La Peur dans l'histoire.* Paris: Editions ouvrières.

Paravicini, Bagliani Agostino. 1997. *Le Corps du pape.* Paris: Seuil.

Pastoureau, Michel. 1992. *Dictionnaire des couleurs de notre temps: Symbolique et société.* Paris: Bonneton.

Pastoureau, Michel, Jacque Verroust, and Raymond Buren. 1987. *Le Cochon: Histoire, symbolique, cuisine.* Paris: Sang de la terre.

Paupert, Anne. 1990. *Les Fileuses et le clerc: Un Etude des Evangiles des quenouilles.* Paris: Honoré Champion.

Peeters, Alice. 1980. "Tuer le cochon à Brantes dans le Vaucluse." *Ethnologie française,* no. 10:247–56.

Pelosse, Valentin. 1981, 1982. "Imaginaire social et protection de l'animal: Des amis des bêtes de l'an X au législateur de 1850." *L'Homme* 21, no. 4: 5–33; 22, no. 1: 33–51.

Penso, Giuseppe. 1981. *La Conquête du monde invisible: Parasites et microbes à travers les siècles.* Paris: Dacosta.

Peter, Jean-Pierre. 1967. "Malades et maladies à la fin du XVIIIe siècle." *Annales ESC,* 711–51.

———. 1971. "Les Mots et les objets de la maladie: Remarques sur les épidémies et la médecine dans la société française de la fin du XVIIIe siècle." *Revue historique* 449:13–38.

Peyresblanques, Jean. 1985. "La Pellagre et les Landes." *Revue d'histoire des sciences médicales,* no. 1:77–90.

———. 1987. "Mal de la rosa espagnol, mal d'arrouzes landais et pellagre landaise." *Revue de Pau et de Béarn,* 269–78.

Pleindoux, Auguste. 1924. *Les Maîtres de victuailles et le commerce de la boucherie en Avignon sous la domination des Papes.* Avignon: Rullière.

———. 1925. *Le Commerce de la boucherie et l'inspection des viandes dans le département de Vaucluse, autrefois et aujourd'hui.* Avignon.

Ploux, François. 2000. "L'Imaginaire social et politique de la rumeur dans la France du XIXe siècle (1815–1870)." *Revue historique* 614 (April–June): 395–433.

Pointeau-Pouliquen, Marie-Antionette. 1958. *Les Causes des intoxications alimentaires en France depuis 1920.* Paris: Arnette.

Poitou, Christian. 1976. "Ergotisme, ergot de seigle et épidémies en Sologne au XVIIIe siècle." *Revue d'histoire moderne et contemporaine* 23:354–68.

Porter, Roy. 1995. *Disease, Medicine and Society in England, 1550–1860.* Cambridge: Cambridge University Press.

Potter, David Morris. 1966. *Les Fils de l'abondance; ou, Le Caractère national américain.* Paris: Seghers, Vents d'ouest.

Pouchelle, Marie-Christine. 1982. "Une Parole médicale prise dans l'imaginaire: Alimentation et digestion chex un maître-chirurgien du XIVe siècle." In *Practiques et discours alimentaires à la Renaissance.* Proceedings of the Colloque de Tours. Paris: Maisonneuve et Larose.

Poussou, Jean-Pierre. 1999. *La Terre et les paysans en France et en Grande-Bretagne aux XVIIe et XVIIIe siècles*. Paris: SEDES.

Prost, Michel. 1994. "Données trophiques en Haut-Dauphiné (XVIe–XVIIe siècle): Panorama de l'alimentation carnée en Briançonnais et Embrunais." In A. Blanchard, H. Michel, and E. Pélaquier, eds., *De l'herbe à la table: La Viande dans la France méridionale à l'époque moderne*. Montpellier: Presses universitaires de Montpellier.

Radeff, Anne. 1996. *Du café dans le chaudron: Economie globale d'ancien régime. Suisse occidentale, Franche-Comté et Savoie*. Lausanne: Société d'histoire de la Suisse romande.

Raimondi, Guilio. 1995. "Commercio e consumo dei generi alimentari nel regno di Napoli: Provvedimenti amministrativi e consuetudini locali nelle università di Monterano, Piedimonte e Novi." In *Archivi per la storia dell'alimentazione*, 1:680–90. Rome.

Randoin, Lucie and Henri Simonnet. 1927. *Les Données et les inconnues des problèmes alimentaires*. Vol 1., *Le Problème de l'alimentation*. Paris: PUF.

Raymond, Jean-François de. 1982. *La Querelle de l'inoculation; ou, La Préhistoire de la vaccination*. Paris: Vrin.

Raynaud, Maurice. 1863. *Les Médecins au temps de Molière: Moeurs, institutions, doctrines*. Paris: Didier.

Rebora, Giovanni. 1998. *La civiltà della forchetta: Storie di cibi e di cucina*. Rome: Laterza.

Redon, Odile and Françoise Sabban. 1995. *La Gastronomie au Moyen Age: 150 recettes de France et d'Italie*. Paris: Stock.

Revel, Jean-François. 1979. *Un Festin en paroles: Histoire littéraire de la sensibilité gastronomique de l'Antiquité à nos jours*. Paris: Pluriel.

Rey, Roselyne. 1991. "La Vulgarisation médicale au XVIIIe siècle: Le Cas des dictionnaires portatifs de santé." *Revue d'histoire des sciences* 44:413–33.

———. 1992. "Anamorphoses d'Hippocrate au XVIIIe siècle." In D. Gourévitch, ed., *Malades et maladies: Histoire et conceptualisation. Mélanges en l'honneur de Mirko Grmek*. Geneva: Droz.

Rigaudière, Albert. 1993. *Gouverner la ville au Moyen Age*. Paris: Anthropos.

Roche, Daniel. 1983. "Cuisine et alimentation populaire à Paris." *Aliments et Cuisine*. Special issue of *Dix-huitième siècle* 15: 7–18.

———. 1997. *Histoire des choses banales: Naissance de la consommation, XVIIe–XVIIIe*. Paris: Fayard.

Roe, Daphne A. 2000. "Pellagra." In *The Cambridge World History of Food*, 1:960–67. Cambridge: Cambridge University Press.

Roze, Ernest. 1898. *Histoire de la pomme de terre, traitée aux points de vue historique, biologique, pathologique, culturel et utilitaire*. Paris: J. Rothschild.

Sabbah, Guy, ed. 1991. *Le Latin médical: La Constitution d'un langage scientifique. Réalités et langage de la médecine dans le monde romain*. Proceedings of the third Colloque international sur les textes médicaux latins antiques, 1989. Saint-Etienne: Presses de l'Université.

Sabban, Françoise. 1984. "Le Savoir-cuire; ou, L'Art des potages dans *Le Ménagier de Paris* et *Le Viandier de Taillevent*." In D. Menjot, ed., *Manger et boire au Moyen Age*, 2:161–72. Proceedings of the Colloque de Nice, 1982. Paris: Les Belles-Lettres.

Schwartz, Jean. 2003. *Réflexions sur l'histoire de la médecine*. Strasbourg: Presses universitaires de Strasbourg.

Sébillot, Paul. 1895. *Légendes et curiosités des métiers*. Paris: Flammarion.

Séguin, J.-P. 1959. *Nouvelles à sensation: Canards du XIXe siècle*. Paris: Armand Colin.

Seince, Franck. 1935. *Parmentier et l'hygiène alimentaire*. Bordeaux: Delman.

Sendrail, Marcel, ed. 1980. *Histoire culturelle de la maladie*. Toulouse: Privat.

Skrabanek, Petr. 1994. "L'Alimentation entre enfer et salut." In C. Fischler, ed., *Aliments sorciers, Croyances comestibles*, special issue of *Autrement*, no. 149:169–79.

Sournia, Jean-Charles. 1989. "Discipline du diagnostic rétrospectif." In Neithard Bulst and Robert Delort, eds., *Maladies et Sociétés: XIIe–XVIIIe siècle*. Proceedings of the Colloque de Bielefeld, 1986. Paris: Editions du CNRS.

Spiekermann, Uwe. 2000. "Food Quality in a Changing Social Environment: A Historical Perspective." In L. H. Grimme and S. Dumontet, eds., *Food Quality, Nutrition and Health*. Berlin: Springer.

Stankiewicz, Georges de. 1933. "Contribution à l'étude de la levure de bière dans l'alimentation humaine." Medical thesis, Paris.

Stouff, Louis. 1970. *Ravitaillement et alimentation en Provence aux XIVe et XVe siècles*. Paris: Mouton.

——. 1996. *La Table provençale: Boire et manger en Provence à la fin du Moyen Age*. Avignon: Barthélemy.

Théodoridès, Jean. 1991. *Des miasmes aux virus: Histoire des maladies infectieuses*. Paris: Louis Pariente.

Thomas, Keith. 1985. *Dans le jardin de la nature: La Mutation des sensibilités en Angleterre à l'époque moderne (1500–1800)*. Paris: Gallimard.

Thuillier, Guy. 1977. *Pour une histoire du quotidien au XIXe siècle en Nivernais*. Paris: Mouton.

Touati, François-Olivier. 1998. *Maladie et société au Moyen Age: La Lèpre, les lépreux et les léproseries dans la province ecclésiastique de Sens jusqu'au milieu du XIVe siècle*. Paris: De Boeck Université.

Valentin, Michel. 1995. "Lavoisier urbaniste, hygiéniste, précurseur de l'ergonomie." In Christiane Demeulenaere-Douyère, ed., *Il y a 200 ans Lavoisier*. Proceedings of the Colloque du bicentenaire de Lavoisier. Paris: Lavoisier Tec-Doc.

Vallat, François. 2001. "Les Epizooties en France de 1700 à 1850: Inventaire clinique chez les bovins et les ovins." *Histoire et Sociétés rurales*, no. 15:67–104.

Verdier, Yvonne. 1979. *Façons de dire, façons de faire: La Laveuse, la couturière, la cuisinière*. Paris: NRF Gallimard.

Vialles, Noélie. 1987. *Le Sang et la chair: Les Abattoirs des pays de l'Adour*. Paris: Maison des sciences de l'homme.

Vigarello, Georges. 1985. *Le Propre et le sale: L'Hygiène du corps depuis le Moyen Age*. Paris: Seuil.

——. 1993. *Le Sain et le malsain: Santé et mieux-être depuis le Moyen Age*. Paris: Seuil.

Vilfan, Sergij. 1983. "L'Approvisionnement des villes dans les confins germano-talo-slaves du XIVe au XVIIe siècle. In *L'Approvisionnement des villes de l'Europe occidentale du Moyen Age aux Temps modernes*, 53–74. Proceedings of the Colloque de Flaran 5. Auch.

Vincent, Jean-Christophe. 1997. "La Mise à mort des animaux de boucherie: Un Révélateur des sensibilités à l'égard des bêtes à l'époque contemporaine." *Cahiers d'histoire* 42, nos. 3–4: 613–38.

Vincent, Pierre-Marie. 1996. *Le Droit de l'alimentation*. Paris: PUF.

Weber, Eugen. 1983. *La Fin des terroirs: La Modernisation de la France rurale, 1870–1914*. Paris: Fayard.

BIBLIOGRAPHY

Weiss-Amer, Melitta. 1992. "The Role of the Medieval Physicians in the Diffusion of Culinary Recipes and Cooking Practices." In C. Lambert, ed., *Du manuscrit à la table: Essais sur la cuisine au Moyen Age et répertoire des manuscrits médiévaux contenant des recettes culinaires.* Paris: Champion-Slatkine, Presses universitaires de Montréal.

Wickersheimer, Charles. 1905. *La Médecine et les médecins en France à l'époque de la Renaissance.* 2 vols. Paris: Maloine.

Wickersheimer, Emile. 1931. *Dictionnaire biographique des médecins en France au Moyen Age.* Paris.

Wolff, Philippe. 1953. "Les Bouchers de Toulouse du XIIe au XVe siècle." *Annales du Midi* 65, no. 23 (July): 375–93.

Yvorel, Jean-Yves. 1992. *Les Poisons de l'esprit: Drogues et drogués au XIXe siècle.* Paris: Quai Voltaire, Histoire.

Zeldin, Théodore. 1979. *Histoire des passions françaises, 1848–1945.* Paris: Encres.

Zeller, Olivier. 1997. "L'Animal dans la ville d'ancien régime: Quelques réflexions." *Cahiers d'histoire* 42, nos. 3–4: 543–54.

Ziegler, Joseph. 1999. "Ut Dicunt Medici: Medical Knowledge and Theological Debates in the Second Half of the Thirteen Century." *Bulletin of the History of Medicine* 73, no. 2: 208–37.

INDEX